Designing Web Services with the J2EE™ 1.4 Platform

JAX-RPC, SOAP, and XML Technologies

Inderjeet Singh, Sean Brydon, Greg Murray, Vijay Ramachandran, Thierry Violleau, Beth Stearns

Addison-Wesley

Boston • San Francisco • New York • Toronto • Montreal
London • Munich • Paris • Madrid
Capetown • Sydney • Tokyo • Singapore • Mexico City

The publisher offers discounts on this book when ordered in quantity for bulk purchases and special sales. For more information, please contact

U.S. Corporate and Government Sales
(800) 382-3419
corpsales@pearsontechgroup.com

For sales outside of the United States, please contact

International Sales
(317) 581-3793
international@pearsontechgroup.com

Visit Addison-Wesley on the Web at www.awl.com/cseng/

Library of Congress Control Number: 2004105588

ISBN 0-321-20521-9
Text printed on recycled paper.
1 2 3 4 5 6 7 8 9 10–CRS–08 07 06 05 04
First printing, May 2004

X

Designing Web Services with the J2EE™ 1.4 Platform

Contents

Foreword

$\mathbf{F}$ROM its inception, the Java™ platform has been focused on the Web. Now a new generation of Web applications—Web services—will play an important role in the way enterprises implement their next generation of services. The Java™ 2, Enterprise Edition (J2EE) platform will be the platform of choice for those enterprises that realize the key to Web services success is to combine the interoperability of Web standards with the portability of the Java platform. Today's J2EE applications are proof that the J2EE platform is the benchmark for both interoperability and portability of enterprise applications.

The world of the Web is bigger than any single operating system. Whether using the J2EE platform, a PHP hypertext preprocessor, the Perl scripting language, or any other open approach, developers are demanding technologies that give them freedom to apply their knowledge broadly across computing environments. J2EE developers routinely apply their development skills across operating systems, machine architectures, and application servers. For developers, portability means more than the ability to run the same service on multiple operating systems; it means using the tools they prefer and having the freedom to apply their skills across Solaris, Linux, Windows, AIX, and HP-UX.

The WS-I Basic Profile 1.0 is a proof point that the J2EE vendor community takes Web services interoperability very seriously. By default, J2EE 1.4 Web service clients and Web service endpoints will conform to the WS-I Basic Profile 1.0, taking the guess work out of getting Web services to talk to each other. With its full support of the WS-I Basic Profile, the J2EE platform is the most interoperable Web services platform ever.

J2EE applications use a mix of relational databases, JMS, and enterprise connectors to deliver sophisticated composite functionality. Web services joins the J2EE platform's already rich arsenal of integration strategies. Each integration technology has its strong points. Broadly, Web services should be used when maximum interoperability is desired. J2EE Connectors should be used when closely-coupled integration with an external system is needed. RMI-IIOP should be used when a rich, object-oriented distributed object model is needed. JMS should be used when a reliable, store-and-forward, publish/unsubscribe messaging system is needed to integrate asynchronous services. Many applications will use combinations of these integration technologies. For instance, many Web services will be implemented as J2EE applications, where these application are business logic tiers that use Connectors to access existing Enterprise Resource Planning (ERP) or Customer Relationship Management (CRM) systems.

J2EE developers are deploying Web services right now. For over a year now, J2EE vendors have been providing production support. Developers have been gaining experience with Java Web services through the Java Web Services Developer Pack. The JAX-RPC technology has been a Java standard since June of 2002; the J2EE 1.4 platform is the first release that makes JAX-RPC a required part of the platform. On November 12, 2003, the J2EE 1.4 platform was unanimously approved by the Java Community Process. Vendors will soon be competing vigorously to deliver the first 1.4-level products.

J2EE developers who are new to Web services can quickly pick up these Web service technologies by leveraging their existing knowledge. The J2EE 1.4 platform not only delivers comprehensive support for Simple Object Access Protocol (SOAP) 1.1 and Web Services Description Language (WSDL) 1.1, it tightly integrates these technologies with the existing servlet and Enterprise JavaBeans (EJB) component models. Both EJB components and servlets now support the full capabilities of JAX-RPC for building Web services. Developers can select between enterprise beans and servlets based on their component approach. Those developers that desire a more formal business component with declarative transaction support and method-level authorization can select enterprise beans, while those that like a less formal, HTTP request-handler style can choose servlets.

With each version of the J2EE platform, Sun Microsystems, Inc. has released the Java BluePrints, Sun's recommended practices for using the latest features of the J2EE technology. Java BluePrints includes a published book, a Web site (http://java.sun.com/blueprints), and a reference application. For the J2EE 1.4 platform, BluePrints focuses on Web services, providing detailed design considerations for taking advantage of the interoperability, portability, security, and maintainability features of the latest platform. Java BluePrints presents this essential information in the practical context of building an application—in this case, the Java™ Adventure Builder Reference application, which has been specifically architected to illustrate the practical use of Web services in the enterprise. This reference application highlights features of the J2EE 1.4 platform's Web services, such as service endpoint design, client design, and XML processing, just as Java™ Pet Store showcased features of the J2EE 1.3 platform, such as container-managed persistence, message-driven beans, and servlet filters.

Since Web services is a major extension of the Web computing model, developers need to understand the Web computing model technology itself as well as how to effectively implement a Web service with the J2EE technologies. Java BluePrints provides an effective way to combine both into one easy-to-follow, step-by-step examination of the architecture and implementation of the Java Adventure Builder Reference application. The application has been written to shed light on implementation details of the Java BluePrints guidelines and J2EE design patterns.

Java BluePrints offers guidelines that will empower developers with a new dimension of flexibility—the ability to develop Web services without the walls imposed by operating systems and application server vendors. Once again, this version of the Java Blueprints is an essential source of implementation and architectural information for J2EE developers who will be using the J2EE 1.4 platform as their Web services platform.

Mark Hapner, Distinguished Engineer
Lead Architect, J2EE platform
Sun Microsystems
January, 2004

About the Authors

Authors listed in alphabetical order:

SEAN BRYDON is a member of the Java BluePrints team at Sun Microsystems. Sean contributed to the design of the Java Pet Store and the Java Adventure Builder Reference applications. He focuses on Web services, design patterns, and security. In the past, Sean has worked on the JavaLoad team and has spent a summer as an intern at Sun Labs. Sean holds an M.S in computer science from the University of California at Santa Barbara and also a B.S. in computer science from the University of California at Santa Barbara.

GREG MURRAY is a member of the Java BluePrints team at Sun Microsystems. He is a contributing author to the first and second editions of *Designing Enterprise Applications with the J2EE Platform*. Greg contributed to the design of the Java Pet Store sample application and the Java Adventure Builder Reference application with an emphasis on the Web tier. Prior to working on the Java BluePrints team, Greg was a member of the Global Products Engineering group of Sun Microsystems, where he developed internationalization tools.

VIJAY RAMACHANDRAN is a member of the Java BluePrints team at Sun Microsystems where he works as the Technical Lead of the Java BluePrints team. Before joining the BluePrints team, Vijay was a member of the Enterprise Server Products Group of Sun Microsystems working on Sun's enterprise server product line. Vijay holds an M.S. in computer science from Santa Clara University, California, and a B.E. in electrical engineering from University of Madras, India.

INDERJEET SINGH is the lead architect of the Java BluePrints team at Sun Microsystems, where he investigates the best uses of J2EE technologies for the design of enterprise applications and Web services. Inderjeet has been involved with the Java BluePrints program since its inception. He is a regular speaker on enterprise application design and is the primary author for the Java series book, *Designing Enterprise Applications with the J2EE^{TM} Platform, Second Edition*. In the past, Inderjeet has also designed fault-tolerance software for large-scale distributed telecommunications switching systems. Inderjeet holds an M.S. in computer science from Washington University in St. Louis, and a B. Tech. in computer science and engineering from Indian Institute of Technology, Delhi.

BETH STEARNS is the principal partner of ComputerEase Publishing, a computer consulting firm she founded in 1982. Her client list includes Sun Microsystems, Inc., Silicon Graphics, Inc., Oracle Corporation, and Borland. She has published numerous articles for developers on the Java programming language and J2EE platform technologies. She is a coauthor of several Addison-Wesley Java Series books, including *Applying Enterprise JavaBeans: Component-Based Development for the J2EE Platform* (both editions), *J2EE Connector Architecture and Enterprise Application Integration*, and *Designing Enterprise Applications with the J2EE Platform* (both editions).

THIERRY VIOLLEAU, software staff engineer at Sun Microsystems, is a member of the J2ME and Java BluePrints teams. He is currently technical lead on a platform for end-to-end mobile enterprise applications project. With the Java BluePrints team, he contributed to the best practices architecture design guidelines for business solutions that use J2EE and J2ME technologies. Prior to this, Thierry was with Market Development Engineering at Sun, where he helped ISVs integrate the J2ME, J2EE, and XML technologies. Thierry has over seventeen years of professional experience in software development. He holds a Maîtrise degree in computer science from Paris VIII University and a university degree in technology, electrical, and automatic engineering from Poitiers University Institute of Technology, France.

Preface

THIS book describes designing Web services using the current technologies available with the Java™ 2 Platform, Enterprise Edition. This book and the accompanying Java™ Adventure Builder Reference application (hereafter referred to as adventure builder) are part of the successful Java BluePrints program created by Sun Microsystems with the introduction of the J2EE platform. Application architects, developers, and students everywhere have used this program to better understand the programming model inherent in the J2EE platform.

Rather than providing information on how to use individual Java technologies to write applications, which falls within the realm of the companion Java Tutorial program, the Java BluePrints focuses on guidelines for application architecture and design, such as distributing J2EE application functionality across tiers and choosing among design options for Web services endpoints. This book describes the Web services and related technologies of the J2EE platform. Its focus is how to best apply these J2EE platform technologies to writing Web service applications. This book assumes that you have a basic knowledge of the J2EE platform, which you can get from *The J2EE™ Tutorial*, and is meant to be read in conjunction with *Designing Enterprise Applications with the J2EE Platform, Second Edition*, since that book covers the J2EE platform technologies for writing traditional enterprise applications.

This book is intended primarily for enterprise architects and application developers engaged in or considering writing Web services and Web service applications with the J2EE platform. It is also useful for product vendors interested in developing Web service applications consistent with the J2EE platform standard.

Obtaining the Reference Application

The adventure builder reference application, which is described in this book, is available on the compact disk included with this book. You can also download it from:

```
http://java.sun.com/blueprints/code/
```

The application requires a J2EE version 1.4-compliant platform on which to run. The accompanying compact disk includes an implementation of this platform and an application server. You can download the J2EE SDK™, which is a freely available implementation of that platform, from:

```
http://java.sun.com/j2ee/download.html
```

The Java BluePrints Web site includes additional content, available only online, that describes in detail the architecture of the Java adventure builder sample application.

References and Resources

Pointers to J2EE documentation can be found at:

```
http://java.sun.com/j2ee/1.4/docs
```

For information on how to use the J2EE SDK to construct multi-tier enterprise applications, refer to the *J2EE Tutorial*, available at:

```
http://java.sun.com/j2ee/1.4/docs/tutorial/docs
```

We relied on many of the following references for technical details and background. These references are good sources for those interested in exploring Web services in greater detail.

1. *Designing Enterprise Applications with the J2EE Platform, Second Edition.* I. Singh, B. Stearns, M. Johnson, Enterprise Team. Copyright 2002, Addison-Wesley.

2. The Java BluePrints Web site, `<http://java.sun.com/blueprints>`.

3. *Core J2EE Patterns: Best Practices and Design Strategies, Second Edition.* D. Alur, D. Malks, J. Crupi. Copyright 2003, Prentice Hall PTR.

4. *Enterprise Integration Patterns: Designing, Building, and Deploying Messaging Solutions.* G. Hohpe, B. Woolf. Copyright 2003, Addison-Wesley.

The Web services standards cited in this book are:

1. *WS-I Basic Profile, Version 1.0.* Available at <http://www.ws-i.org>.

2. *Simple Object Access Protocol, Version 1.1.* Available at <http://www.w3.org>.

3. *Extensible Markup Language (XML), Version 1.0.* Available at <http://www.w3.org>.

4. *Web Services Description Language, Version 1.1.* Available at <http://www.w3.org>.

5. *XML Schema, Part 1 and 2.* Available at <http://www.w3.org>.

6. *Universal Description, Discovery and Integration (UDDI), Version 2.* Available at <http://www.w3.org>.

The J2EE technologies cited in this book are described in their specifications:

1. *Java™ 2 Platform, Enterprise Edition Specification, Version 1.4* (J2EE specification). Available at <http://java.sun.com/j2ee/>.

2. *Java™ API for XML-Based RPC Specification, Version 1.1* (JAXP specification). Available at <http://java.sun.com/xml/jaxrpc/>.

3. *Java™ API for XML Processing Specification, Version 1.2* (JAXP specification). Available at <http://java.sun.com/xml/jaxp/>.

4. *SOAP with Attachments API for Java Specification, Version 1.2* (SAAJ specification). Available at <http://java.sun.com/xml/saaj/>.

5. *Java API for XML Registries Specification, Version 1.0* (JAXR specification). Available at <http://java.sun.com/xml/jaxr/>.

6. *Web Services for J2EE Specification, Version 1.1.* Available at <ftp://www.ibm.com/pub/jsr109/spec1.1/>.

7. *Java API for XML Binding Specification* (JAXB specification). Available at <http://java.sun.com/xml/jaxb/>.

8. *Java™ Servlet Specification, Version 2.4* (Servlet specification). Available at <http://java.sun.com/products/servlet/>.

9. *JavaServer Pages™ Specification, Version 2.0* (JSP specification). Available at <http://java.sun.com/products/jsp/>.

10. *Enterprise JavaBeans™ Specification, Version 2.1* (EJB specification). Available at <http://java.sun.com/products/ejb/>.

11. *J2EE™ Connector Architecture Specification, Version 1.5* (Connector specification). Available at `<http://java.sun.com/j2ee/connector/>`

12. *Java™ Message Service Specification, Version 1.0.2* (JMS specification). Available at `<http://java.sun.com/products/jms/>`

Typographic Conventions

The following table describes the typographic conventions used in this book.

Typeface or Symbol	Meaning	Example
AaBbCc123	The names of commands, files, and directories; interface, class, method, and deployment descriptor element names; programming language keywords	Edit the file `Main.jsp`. How to retrieve a `UserTransaction` object. Specify the `resource-ref` element.
AaBbCc123	Variable name	The files are named *XYZ*`file`.
AaBbCc123	Book titles, new words or terms, or words to be emphasized	Read Chapter 6 in *Users Guide*. These are called *class* options. You *must* be root to do this.

Recommendations, guidelines, and key points are highlighted throughout the book. They are marked with check boxes, as follows:

❒ This is a recommendation, guideline, or key point.

How This Book Is Organized

This book is divided into the following chapters:

- **Chapter 1, "Introduction,"** describes Web services and explains the support provided by the J2EE 1.4 platform for Web services.

- **Chapter 2, "Standards and Technologies,"** enumerates and describes in detail the Web services-specific component, service, and communication technologies supported by the J2EE 1.4 platform.

- **Chapter 3, "Service Endpoint Design,"** describes how best to design and implement a Web service endpoint.

- **Chapter 4, "XML Processing,"** addresses in detail the issues for designing and developing XML-based applications and handling XML documents. In particular, it focuses on those issues that are of most concern to Web service endpoints and clients.

- **Chapter 5, "Client Design,"** describes the different communication modes that J2EE and non-J2EE clients alike use to access Web services. It includes guidelines and techniques for writing efficient Web service client applications.

- **Chapter 6, "Enterprise Application Integration,"** describes the capabilities provided by the J2EE platform for using Web services to integrate applications and data, and shows how to best use these capabilities in an enterprise application.

- **Chapter 7, "Security,"** describes the J2EE security model and how it applies to Web service endpoints and clients.

- **Chapter 8, "Application Architecture and Design,"** pulls the topics in the preceding chapters together into a coherent programming model that illustrates how best to design and develop Web service endpoints and clients.

- **"Glossary"** is a list of words and phrases found in this book and their definitions.

Acknowledgments

This book is the result of many people's efforts. In particular, we want to thank the following people for taking the time to extensively review the contents of this book, often more than once: Smitha Kangath, Roberto Chinnici, Randy Thomas, and Matthias Weidmann. Other reviewers include Yutaka Yoshida, Mark Roth, Phil Goodwin, Arun Gupta, Jon Ellis, Bill Shannon, Sang Shin, Leslie McNeill, and Debra Scott.

Smitha Kangath, while not listed as an author, contributed content throughout the book. She was also instrumental in implementing many of the concepts presented here and verifying their accuracy.

Mark Hapner contributed many of the ideas that are presented in the book. He also reviewed a number of chapters.

Arun Gupta, in addition to reviewing a good part of the book, also guided us on SOAP interoperability issues. Joe Fialli extensively reviewed the XML chapter and provided clarifications for a number of issues. In a similar manner, Ram Jeyaraman provided an insightful review of the integration chapter, and Manveen Kaur did likewise with the security chapter. Rajiv Mordani provided helpful comments on several of the chapters, including the XML chapter. Ron Monzillo did an extensive review of the security chapter and also contributed some key ideas.

We would also like to thank John Crupi, Deepak Alur, and Dan Malks for reviewing many chapters and providing insightful comments.

Other reviewers whose comments helped us bring a much better book to market are Peter den Haan, Kevin P. Davis, Vijay S. Phagura, Rich Wardwell, Bob Withers, and Vartan Piroumian.

We would also like to thank the J2EE group at Sun Microsystems. Some of the key resources for us were Ken Saks, Tony Ng, Harpreet Singh, Vivek Nagar, Bill Shannon, Eduardo Pelegri-Llopart, Craig McClanahan, Doug Kohlert, and Linda DeMichiel. Hans Muller reviewed the client chapter and Eve Maler reviewed the security chapter.

Our special thanks go to our management, Larry Freeman, Jim Driscoll, Vivek Nagar, Karen Tegan, and Jeff Jackson, for their whole-hearted support and commitment to the BluePrints program and to this book in particular. Larry was always very supportive, encouraging, and resourceful whenever we hit a road block. This book would not have been possible without his support and commitment. We also want to especially thank our program manager, Jennifer Douglas. She kept us on track during this project while at the same time encouraging us to have fun with it, too.

CHAPTER 1

Introduction

THE realm of Web services—software components that are programmatically accessible over standard Internet protocols—is expanding rapidly due to the growing need for application-to-application communication and interoperability. Web services expose a standard interface that is platform and technology independent. By conforming to accepted industry-wide standards, Web services provide a means of communication among software applications running on different platforms and written in different application development languages and that present dynamic context-driven information to the user.

Since its successful introduction in 1999, the J2EE platform has become an integrated standard for implementing and deploying portable and distributed enterprise applications. One significant factor contributing to this success is that the J2EE platform has been designed through an open process, the Java Community Process (JCP). This open process has engaged a range of enterprise computing vendors to ensure that the platform meets the widest possible spectrum of enterprise application requirements. As a result, the J2EE platform addresses the core issues that impede organizations' efforts to maintain a competitive pace in the information economy. Organizations have recognized this and quickly adopted the J2EE platform standard.

The J2EE platform has evolved further to accommodate the growing popularity and use of Web services. The platform has added support for Web service-specific components and technologies. The Web services standards ensure interoperability across platforms and programming languages. Also portability—the ability to migrate applications from one platform to another—is just as important. Significantly, the J2EE platform adds portability to Web services. By combining portability and interoperability, the J2EE platform is a compelling platform for developing distributed systems. These new J2EE components and technologies meet the requirements of most enterprises: These technologies allow enterprises to expose their existing applications as Web services and to develop and implement new Web services. This Web-service evolution of the J2EE platform has been achieved with the same open process as before involving leading enterprise computing vendors. It has ensured that the J2EE platform is the platform of choice for developing and deploying portable and interoperable Web services and enterprise applications.

Let's look at some of the reasons why this is so. The J2EE platform has added its Web services features to a platform that has already standardized development and deployment of portable enterprise applications. With these new features, the J2EE platform offers enterprises the following benefits:

- Enables existing enterprise applications to be extended as Web services in a manner that is standard, easy, portable, and interoperable

- Helps extend the reach of existing and new enterprise applications to a new set of clients beyond the already wide variety of clients supported by the earlier J2EE platforms

- Enables using commercially proven, robust technologies (such as enterprise bean components, servlets, and so forth) as the backbone for developing new services

- Helps existing enterprise information systems (EISs) to be integrated to end users in a portable way

This book is about developing robust, effective Web services on the Java™ 2 Platform, Enterprise Edition (J2EE™), version 1.4 or later. The book not only describes the technologies used for Web services, but also presents guidelines for using these technologies to design and develop Web services. Many of these guidelines have been formulated from our own Web service development experience, and, as such, we have illustrated the guidelines with real examples when possible.

This first chapter sets the groundwork for the book—it gives you a look at some of the key concepts underlying the architectural details of Web services and it provides motivations for developing Web services-based applications. It highlights the benefits of Web services and explains why it makes sense for distributed applications to use Web services as their underlying architecture.

1.1   What Are Web Services?

At this point, you might be wondering exactly what Web services are and, more importantly, why your enterprise should consider making some of its own functionality available as a Web service. There are numerous definitions given for Web services, ranging from the highly technical ones to simplistic. For example, the World Wide Web Consortium (W3C) organization, which establishes the standards for Web services, defines them as follows: "A Web service is a software system identified by a URI whose public interfaces and bindings are defined and described using XML. Its definition can be discovered by other software systems. These systems may then interact with the Web service in a manner prescribed by its definition, using XML-based messages conveyed by Internet protocols." A simpler definition, and perhaps more useful, might be: "a Web service is a software application, accessible on the Web (or an enterprise's intranet) through a URL, that is accessed by clients using XML-based protocols, such as Simple Object Access Protocol (SOAP) sent over accepted Internet protocols, such as HTTP. Clients access a Web service application through its interfaces and bindings, which are defined using XML artifacts, such as a Web Services Definition Language (WSDL) file."

Web services are a result of the natural evolution of the Web. Initially, the Web consisted of sites that were plain HTML pages. Later, Web applications dynamically generated these same HTML pages. For example, a map Web site initially provided only static links to maps of various cities and locales. Later, this same map Web site became a map Web application that provided driving directions, customized maps, and so forth. Despite their expanded capabilities, Web applications are still limited to the restricted GUI capabilities of their HTML pages—a Web application is usable only through the limited GUI bound to the HTML pages. Web services go beyond this limitation, since they separate the Web site or application (the service) from its HTML GUI. Instead, the service is represented in XML and available via the Web as XML. As a result, the same map Web site can extend its functionality to provide a Web service that other enterprises can use to provide directions to their own office locations, integrate with global position systems, and so forth.

Web services, or simply services, build on knowledge gained from more mature distributed computing environments (such as CORBA and Java Remote Method Invocation) to enable application-to-application communication and interoperability. Web services provide a standardized way for applications to expose their functionality over the Web or communicate with other applications over a network, regardless of the application's implementation, programming language, or computer platform.

Why should an enterprise consider implementing Web services-based applications? Web services can provide a means for an enterprise to expand its business offerings, increase the efficiency of its business processing, and to improve its customer experience. By including with its own services the offerings of multiple partners, both the enterprise and the partners expand their capabilities and their business base. Not only can Web services help automate business processing, it can streamline interactions with outside services, such as credit card and shipping services. As a result, customers are offered an enriched experience: more options and greater choices, along with more flexibility.

Like any application, Web services-based applications can perform a range of functions. Some may handle only simple requests for information, while others may implement complex business processes and interactions. Whereas browser-based applications are concerned with the representation of data to end users, Web services let clients programmatically not only use the Web to obtain information but also to access these service components and their functionality. Furthermore, applications can incorporate Web service functionality for their own use.

❐ Perhaps the most important reason for the increased use of Web services—the main force for their widespread adoption—is that Web services promote interoperability across different platforms, systems, and languages.

❐ Use of Web services is also increasing because it reduces operational costs by enabling organizations to extend and reuse their existing system functionality.

A Web service enables a *service-oriented architecture*, which is an architectural style that promotes software reusability by creating reusable services. Traditional object-oriented architectures promote reusability by reusing classes or objects. However, objects are often too fine grained for effective reuse. Hence, component-oriented architectures emerged that use software components as reusable entities. These components consist of a set of related classes, their resources, and configuration information. Component-oriented architectures remain a powerful way to design software systems; however, they do not address the additional issues arising from current day enterprise environments. Today, enterprise environments are quite complex due to the use of a variety of software and hardware platforms, Internet-based distributed communication, enterprise application integration, and so on. The service-oriented architectures address these issues by using a service as a reusable entity. The services are typically coarser grained than components, and they focus on the functionality provided by their interfaces. These services communicate with each other and with end-user clients through well-defined and well-known interfaces. The communication can range from a simple passing of messages between the services to a complex scenario where a set of services together coordinate with each other to achieve a common goal. These architectures allow clients, over the network, to invoke a Web service's functionality through the service's exposed interfaces.

In a service-oriented architecture, you have the following:

- A service that implements the business logic and exposes this business logic through well-defined interfaces.

- A registry where the service publishes its interfaces to enable clients to discover the service.

- Clients (including clients that may be services themselves) who discover the service using the registries and access the service directly through the exposed interfaces.

An important advantage of a service-oriented architecture is that it enables development of loosely-coupled applications that can be distributed and are accessible across a network. To enable this architecture, you need the following:

- A mechanism that enables clients to access a service and registry.

- A mechanism to enable different services to register their existence with a registry and a way for clients to look up the registry of available services. Web services are based on an architecture in which the service can be located over the network and its location is transparent, which means that clients may dynamically discover a particular service they wish to use.

- A mechanism for services to expose well-defined interfaces and a way for clients to access those interfaces.

An important point to note is that Web services are strongly backed by virtually all key players in the Web arena. This backing virtually ensures that Web services technology is here to stay, and its acceptance will become more widespread.

Unlike traditional distributed environments, Web services emphasize interoperability. Web services are independent of a particular programming language, whereas traditional environments tend to be bound to one language or another. Similarly, since they can be easily bound to different transport mechanisms, Web services offer more flexibility in the choice of these mechanisms. Furthermore, unlike traditional environments, Web services are often not bound to particular client or server frameworks. Overall, Web services are better suited to a loosely coupled, coarse-grained set of relationships. Relying on XML gives Web services an additional advantage, since XML makes it possible to use documents across heterogeneous environments.

Web services, by building on existing Web standards, can be used without requiring changes to the Web infrastructure. However, while they may be more firewall friendly than traditional computing environments, Web services tend not to be as efficient in terms of space and time processing.

1.2   Benefits of Web Services

Web services are gaining in popularity because of the benefits they provide. Listed here are some of the key benefits:

- **Interoperability in a heterogeneous environment**—Probably the key benefit of the Web service model is that it permits different distributed services to run on a variety of software platforms and architectures, and allows them to be written in different programming languages. As enterprises develop over time, they add systems and solutions that often require different platforms and frequently don't communicate with each other. Later, perhaps due to a consolidation or the addition of another application, it becomes necessary to tie together this disparate functionality. The greatest strength of Web services is their ability to enable interoperability in a heterogeneous environment. As long as the various systems are enabled for Web services, they can use the services to easily interoperate with each other.

- **Business services through the Web**—An enterprise can use Web services to leverage the advantages of the World Wide Web for its operations. For example, an enterprise might make its product catalog and inventory available to its vendors through a Web service to achieve better supply chain management.

- **Integration with existing systems**—Most enterprises have an enormous amount of data stored in existing enterprise information systems, and the cost to replace these systems is such that discarding these legacy systems may not be an option. Web services let enterprise application developers reuse and even commoditize these existing information assets. Web services provide developers with standard ways to access middle-tier and back-end services, such as database management systems and transaction monitors, and integrate them with other applications. In addition, because these services are provided consistently, developers do not need to learn new programming models or styles as integration needs expand.

- **Freedom of choice**—Web service standards have opened a large marketplace for tools, products, and technologies. This gives organizations a wide variety of choices, and they can select configurations that best meet their application requirements. Developers can enhance their productivity because, rather than having to develop their own solutions, they can choose from a ready market of off-the-shelf application components. Tools, furthermore, provide the ability to move quickly and easily from one configuration to another as required. Web services also ensure the standardization of tools, so that development tools can adopt new tools, whether from server vendors or third-party tool developers, as needs arise.

- **Support more client types**—Since a main objective of Web services is improving interoperability, exposing existing applications or services as Web services increases their reach to different client types. This occurs regardless of the platform on which the client is based: it doesn't matter if the client is based on the Java or Microsoft platforms or even if it is based on a wireless platform. In short, a Web service can help you extend your applications and services to a rich set of client types.

- **Programming productivity**—To be productive in the information economy requires the ability to develop and deploy applications in a timely fashion. Applications must go quickly from prototype to production and must continue to evolve even after they are placed into production. Productivity is enhanced when application development teams have a standard means to access the services required by multitier applications and standard ways to support a variety of clients. Web services, by creating a common programming standard, help to enhance programming productivity. Prior to the advent of Web services, developers programming in the distributed computing environment have relied on a diverse set of not-always-compatible technologies. Developers have attempted to tie together various diverse back-end systems, such as both custom and standard database management systems and transaction processors, with traditional Web technologies, but have had to deal with a multitude of programming models. Because Web services introduce a common standard across the Web, vendors, in the interest of staying competitive, are more likely to develop better tools and technologies. These tools and technologies will attract developers because they emphasize increased programming productivity. As a result, the entire industry benefits.

Application development has also been complicated by the requirement that a particular application support a specific type of client or several types simultaneously. Web services, because they promote interoperability, simplify this facet of the application development process.

1.3   Challenges of Web Service Development

There are numerous challenges faced by Web service developers. Web services are a new paradigm, and, as such, they are far from mature. Because they are in their initial stages, Web services technologies are evolving rapidly and sometimes in unexpected directions. No matter what platform a developer chooses to use, there are some specific challenges to developing Web services. For one, technologies and standards are evolving. As a result, developers can expect that these technologies may change as they are extended to provide enhanced Web services support. While such changes may cause some difficulties early on, as time goes on developers should find that using technologies such as those offered with the J2EE 1.4 platform will actually lessen the challenges to Web services development.

It is important to keep these factors in mind when developing Web services.

1.3.1   Evolving Technologies and Products

A key challenge in creating Web services-based solutions today is that Web services are still in their infancy. Web services, because of their emphasis on interoperability across platforms, operating systems, and programming languages, rely on a collection of technologies and various standards and specifications, many of which are still being defined and refined. Additional new standards are currently being defined to enable Web services to realize their full potential.

The emerging Web services technologies and products have a lot of promise and, as standards become formalized and additional vendors sign on, their promise is being fulfilled. More and more products and technologies implementing the Web service specifications have begun to appear, and they are meeting with more success.

Enterprises often use Web services as a means to distribute data or information. In addition, many businesses use services to conduct business transactions. Such business transactions may require a service to access other services; in a sense, to perform a global transaction. Although in the process of being defined, currently there are no universally accepted standards for such global transactions.

Interoperability is a continuous challenge. Web services have already achieved a significant degree of interoperability, but further standards are needed for the sort of widespread interoperability that fulfills the vision of Web services.

An additional challenge with Web services is the coordination of multiple services for processing business logic. Often, what appears to the end user as a single business process is really implemented as a series of stages in a workflow, and each stage of the workflow might be implemented as a separate service. In such cases, all the services must coordinate with each other during the various steps of the business logic processing to achieve the desired goal. Standards are necessary for coordination among services. Such standards are in the process of being defined, but none has yet been universally accepted. Similar to those previously mentioned, various other standards for other areas, such as security and so forth, are currently being defined.

1.3.2 Security

It should come as no surprise to anyone, but security is just as important for Web services as it is for other enterprise applications. In fact, now that applications on the Web open an enterprise's business processes and data to distributed clients, security becomes an even more important factor.

Information systems security, while of utmost importance to IT managers and system architects, must also be handled with the proper balance. It is not only important to protect information assets to maximize their value, but care must be taken to not overprotect these assets to a degree that jeopardizes that very value. Traditionally, IT departments have maintained a relatively high level of control, if not complete control, over the environment of both servers and clients. When information assets are exposed in less-protected environments, such as through Web services, it becomes increasingly important to maintain tight security over the most sensitive assets, while allowing relatively easier access to other assets.

One of the difficulties in handling disparate systems is providing an integrated security model. Security needs to be compatible with existing mechanisms. In cases where customers need to access secure information, the mechanisms need to maintain high security (and user confidence) while remaining as unobtrusive and transparent as possible.

The key security issues for Web services concern authentication, authorization, and ensuring confidentiality. Web services standards for security are a high priority area for the community, but, as they are still evolving, they remain a work in progress. Chapter 7 examines these issues and provides some interim solutions.

1.3.3   Reliability, Availability, and Scalability

Web services are often about large-scale distributed applications. With these types of applications, the reliability, availability, and scalability of services of the underlying platform and its technologies are important considerations.

Reliability is the aspect of a Web service representing how well it maintains its service and service quality. Often, reliability is measured by the number of failures that occur in a given time period. For Web services, reliability may be more difficult to achieve because of the unreliable nature of the underlying transport, HTTP; HTTP provides only best-effort delivery and does not guarantee packet or in-order delivery. A Web service is considered more reliable the more easily and automatically it can handle changes in use patterns and system configurations.

Availability concerns whether the Web service is present or ready for immediate use. Does a client have to wait for the Web service, or is the client's request immediately handled? In other words, availability represents the probability that a service is available.

Web services that scale effectively can easily handle a large number of client interactions. For such Web services, the platform and technologies must efficiently manage system resources and services (such as database connections and transactions). The platform must also be able to handle XML parsing, which is done to validate a document's contents. XML parsing is a compute-intensive process that significantly affects performance. XML by itself entails a very verbose format that increases payload size significantly when compared to an equivalent binary format.

To achieve reliability, availability, and scalability, Web services should not only be flexible enough to run on any server configuration appropriate to anticipated client volumes, they should also be capable of easily switching configurations when necessary. A platform's support for clustered application deployment environments contributes to achieving many of these goals. It is also helpful when the platform can handle such changes without requiring the applications to be redesigned, recoded, or redeployed.

1.4 Typical Web Service Scenarios

Enterprise applications cover a wide spectrum of scenarios, such as interactions between business partners, supply chain management, inventory management, and even simple services (specialized converters, calculators, and so forth). Web services, when used strategically, can augment an application's functionality, but keep in mind that Web services are not an appropriate solution at every point in an application. While they do provide functional richness and interoperability, Web services may come at the price of increased performance overhead. Choosing when to implement a Web services-based solution comes down to addressing such issues as:

- Interoperability requirements for the enterprise application in a heterogeneous enterprise environment

- Integration requirements for those whose environments contain various enterprise information systems (EISs)

- Types of clients expected to be supported, such as J2EE applications, wireless devices, PDAs, and so forth

- Availability of tools to implement the solution

- Level of sacrifice, in terms of complexity and performance, that can be tolerated to achieve the advantages (interoperability, diverse client reach, and so forth) of Web services

This section looks at a typical enterprise scenario and identifies where a Web services solution might be appropriate. By no means does this section attempt to cover all scenarios suited for Web services. Rather, it tries to give the reader a flavor of the typical scenarios that might benefit from choosing Web services. Rather than continuing in the abstract, let's examine a sample enterprise application and see where in such an application it is beneficial to use Web services. That is, let's see where the use of Web services improves the application's functionality, its ease of use, or its ability to reach all types of clients.

Our sample scenario, called the Java™ Adventure Builder Reference application (referred to as adventure builder), is a fictitious enterprise that sells adventure packages for vacationers. This enterprise is considering going online. To do so, the enterprise needs to create a Web site, and it is considering having that site take advantage of the benefits of Web services. The enterprise is especially interested in using Web services to integrate with its numerous partners.

This enterprise

- Provides customers with a catalog of adventure packages

- Lets the customer build his or her particular trip experience, choosing accommodations, transportation, and scheduling various adventure activities, and finally booking the trip

- Provides customers with additional services, such as enabling them to track the status of their orders

For example, a customer might choose an adventure on Mt. Kilimanjaro. In addition to selecting accommodations, mode of transport, and preferred dates, the customer also can select from an assortment of adventures, such as mountain climbing, guided hiking tours of the volcanic peaks, a safari, and so forth. To achieve this, the enterprise might have in place non-Web-based applications or operations that do the following:

- Interact with clients who want to book adventures. There might be toll-free telephone numbers available to clients.

- Receive orders from clients and process the orders. Orders pass through a workflow, such as a workflow engine, during their various stages for completion.

- Keep track of client preferences, plus update clients regarding the status of an order. Customer relations management (CRM) is one such means for tracking clients.

- Verify and obtain approval for client payment.

- Interact with business partners—airlines, hotels, adventure or activity providers—so that the enterprise can provide a complete adventure package to the client.

When the developers of the adventure builder enterprise take it online, they implement individual modules for each function. (See Figure 1.1.) Let us see where Web services might fit in and where they might provide the enterprise with advantages in terms of integration and interoperability.

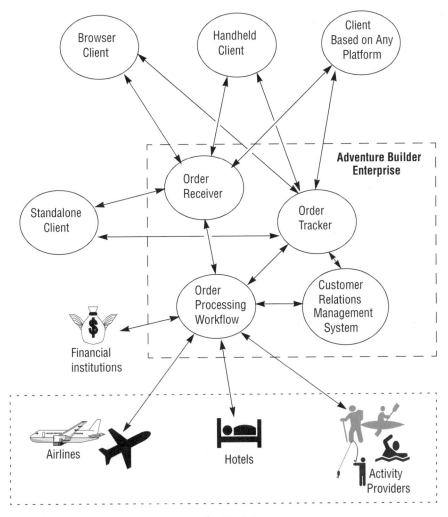

Figure 1.1 Adventure Builder Enterprise Modules

☐ Before proceeding, keep in mind that Web services basically help you to expose an interface to a software application or component that can be used by the client of that application or component, regardless of the client's platform.

Note: This sample scenario is used in the remainder of this book to illustrate specific design issues and recommendations.

1.4.1   Interacting with Business Partners

The adventure builder enterprise works with a number of partners to help it provide complete adventure packages to its customers. These partners range from small businesses, such as "mom and pop"-type shops that might arrange a fun activity in a locale, to large enterprises, such as major airlines and hotel chains. In effect, these partners fulfill various components of the travel packages ordered by customers.

Additionally, there is a two-way communication between adventure builder and its partners. The adventure builder enterprise communicates various orders to different partners. The partners, in turn, each bill the adventure builder enterprise for their costs. It is essential that the enterprise resolves the handling of this inter-partner communication when it goes online.

Web services can be an ideal way to integrate the enterprise with multiple partners for several reasons. Web services are more cost effective than electronic data interchange (EDI), currently the most common solution available for business partner interaction. EDI requires a significant up-front investment by all parties. While its large business partners may have an extensive EDI infrastructure in place, the adventure builder enterprise cannot expect its many small business partners to expend the resources to implement such an EDI infrastructure. Web services-based interaction is a good solution for small businesses that have no investment in an EDI infrastructure and more cost effective for larger enterprises with existing EDI infrastructures.

In addition, Web services can be used on a variety of hardware and software platforms. Existing and potential partners need not purchase or lease a particular hardware or software platform. Most likely, the partners can use their existing systems as long as these systems support Web services. Since many of the industry leaders cooperate on Web service standards and specifications, it is expected that the majority of platforms will support Web services.

Web services-based interaction gives the partners, especially the larger partners with significant technology infrastructure investments, a further advantage: They can use Web services to integrate their existing enterprise systems. Businesses that have integrated their existing systems with Web services offer an enhanced, more automated interaction experience for partners such as adventure builder. The result is an improved customer experience, cost saving, and increased interoperability.

1.4.2 Integrating with Existing Enterprise Information Systems

The adventure builder enterprise may have invested much time and resources in their existing enterprise information systems. The customer relations management system alone is a costly system that could have taken a significant amount of time and resources to implement and fine-tune to the enterprise's unique needs. The other enterprise information systems, too, may have been customized and tweaked so that they work efficiently within the unique combination of requirements and constraints of the adventure builder enterprise. Getting all these systems to work right is an evolving and expensive process. Although the adventure builder enterprise management is tempted by the advantages of some new technologies, they have invested too much in their existing systems to completely replace them with new systems.

Similarly, most enterprises have made extensive investments over the course of many years in information technology (IT) processing, data, and system resources. Often, most of this investment is in enterprise information systems (EISs), or what are sometimes referred to as legacy systems. Discarding existing systems is never easy. It means not only writing off money spent to install, use, and customize these systems, but also spending equivalent sums or more to install and customize new systems. There is also the disruption to the business itself, such as the lost productivity during the transition to the new system, and the potential changes in business processes that a new system may impose. Most businesses consider it more cost effective to evolve and enhance their existing information systems. As a result, enterprises are looking for solutions that let them not only stay current with the times but also evolve their infrastructure and integrate their existing systems with new systems.

Web services can efficiently meet this need to integrate existing technologies with new technologies. Since they are based on universally accepted, platform-independent standards, Web services make a natural integration layer. It is now possible to provide software to expose an existing EIS as a Web service. This makes it feasible for users who require access to that EIS to do so through its Web service.

1.4.3 Reaching Diverse Clients

Web services make it possible for an enterprise to make its functionality available to various types of clients. The adventure builder enterprise, to enhance the customer experience, can provide services such as customer order tracking and weather information at travel destination points, and the enterprise can ensure that these services are accessible by any type of client. Customers can get the information they want from anywhere, using almost any device. Some customers may use a Web browser to access these services, while others may prefer to use a more full-featured interface such as that of a rich client written with J2SE technology or Microsoft technologies. Other customers may use mobile devices, such as cell phones or PDAs, running on the Java™ 2 Platform Micro Edition (J2ME) environment. The customer experience is enhanced when end users have such a range of choices for accessing a service.

Web services are an ideal way to open these enterprise services to all types of clients. Since they expose a standard interface that is platform and technology independent, Web service-based features make it easy to develop clients on any platform that supports Web services.

1.4.4   Aggregation of Partner Data

Much of the adventure builder enterprise's interactions with its various business partners centers on obtaining and aggregating information from partners and other disparate sources. To provide a complete adventure package to its customers, adventure builder must obtain from its partners such information as the details of modes of travel, accommodations, and activities or adventures. This information is dynamic in nature, and the adventure builder enterprise needs these updates. For example, adventure builder needs to know which seats for a particular airline are available or which hotels have rooms available, and at what price. This information changes frequently, and it is important for the adventure builder enterprise to keep its data current.

The dynamic nature of the adventure builder enterprise's information extends beyond current availability of services. It is entirely possible that one or more of its partners may change its services, or even that a business partner ceases to exist. To maintain the best possible customer experience, the adventure builder enterprise needs to make available the most current package details possible. To do so, the adventure builder enterprise needs to maintain a dynamic catalog of its offerings. That is, adventure builder not only builds its catalog of adventure packages based on the services available from its various partners, but it may also periodically update its catalog of adventures, particularly when changes occur with its partners.

Web services enable a truly dynamic way to build and maintain this catalog of information. Furthermore, by incorporating its Web services with registry services, adventure builder can expand its network of suppliers and allow any number of suppliers or partners to participate at their own choosing. Once suppliers signal their participation through the registry, adventure builder can dynamically build its own catalog from the suppliers' offerings. Keep in mind, however, that a truly dynamic arrangement requires a set of legal and financial agreements to be in place beforehand.

1.5 J2EE 1.4: The Platform for Web Services

This section briefly describes the entire J2EE platform, providing an overview of the technologies that are part of the platform and the platform's benefits. The J2EE 1.4 platform, while it introduces new technologies for Web services, also builds upon its earlier technologies for its Web services support.

For more complete coverage of the earlier platform technologies, you should refer to the previous book in the Java BluePrint's series, *Designing Enterprise Applications with the J2EE Platform, Second Edition* (Addison-Wesley) and the Java BluePrints Web site: `http://java.sun.com/blueprints/`. (See "References and Resources" on page xx.)

1.5.1 J2EE Platform Overview

The J2EE platform is designed to provide server-side and client-side support for developing Web services and distributed, multi-tier enterprise applications. Let's briefly examine the main concepts underlying the architecture of the J2EE platform. (Readers familiar with the J2EE platform may want to skip this section.)

- **Multi-tier model**—The J2EE platform is architected to facilitate the deployment of multi-tier distributed applications and Web services. The platform defines different tiers, including a client tier, one or more middle tiers, and a back-end tier. It also defines a standard way for these tiers to communicate with each other. Because applications can communicate in a standard way, it is possible for an application's logic to reside in different tiers. Thus, applications can be deployed across different tiers in a distributed manner. Furthermore, the platform's multi-tier model enables various parts of an application to run on different systems. Each tier may also be assigned different and distinct responsibilities. This multi-tier development model also enables the platform to provide rich support to a wide variety of clients. The platform supports browser clients, wireless clients, rich Java-based GUI client, even non-Java clients.

- **Component-based development**—The J2EE platform supports component-based development of applications and services. The portions of application logic that reside on separate tiers can make use of the different components provided by the platform for each tier. Such component-based development encourages reusability, since components are discrete modules that can be reused by virtually any other component when needed. The platform can support a range of components for representing application business logic. This type of component-based development model also enables apportioning development responsibilities by skill set; that is, assigning different and distinct responsibilities to various developers based on their skill set. Such division by skill set helps to efficiently use developer skills.

- **Container-based component management**—To ensure that the components interact in a standard way, the platform introduces the concept of container-based component management. Components run within containers, which are standardized runtime environments that provide specific services to components and thus ensure application portability across platform implementations. In such a managed environment, containers interpose on all method calls and apply their services, which include standard session management, automated and declarable support for database transactions, security, standardized access to EISs, standardized deployment of applications (including the means to modify application behavior at deployment), and so forth. Components can expect these services to be available on any J2EE platform from any vendor. Along with this emphasis on standardization, the J2EE platform still remains open and flexible so that vendors can provide their own value-added support without compromising the portability of the application.

- **Support for the J2EE standard to promote portability**—The J2EE standard, which is defined through a set of related specifications—the Enterprise JavaBeans specification, the Java Servlet specification, the JavaServer Pages specification, Java API for XML Based RPC specification, among many others—define and ensure a platform architecture that enables development of distributed, portable, and interoperable enterprise applications and Web services. In addition to the specifications, several other technology deliverables support the J2EE standard, including the J2EE Compatibility Test Suite, the J2EE reference implementation, and the J2EE SDK. The J2EE Compatibility Test Suite (CTS) helps maximize the portability of applications by validating the specification compliance of a J2EE platform product. The J2EE reference implementation, a complete implementation of the J2EE standard provided by Sun Microsystems, represents an operational definition of the J2EE platform. It is used by licensees as the "gold standard" to determine what their product must do under a particular set of application circumstances. It is the standard platform for running the J2EE Compatibility Test Suite, and it can be used by developers to verify the portability of an application. The J2EE reference implementation is available in both binary and source code form.

- **Support for the WS-I standard for interoperability**—The Web Services Interoperability Organization (WS-I) promotes Web service interoperability across development platforms, operating systems, and programming languages, especially with the WS-I Basic Profile, which the J2EE 1.4 platform supports. Ensuring interoperability and portability starts with the specifications themselves. The J2EE 1.4 platform includes specifications and technologies that support Simple Object Access Protocol (SOAP), Web Services Definition Language (WSDL), and Universal Discovery, Description, and Integration (UDDI) specification. The platform includes technologies that enable standardized use of Web service specifications within the Java platform: Java™ API for XML-Based RPC (JAX-RPC), Web Services for J2EE (JSR-109), SOAP with Attachments API for Java (SAAJ), Java API for XML Registries (JAXR), and Java API for XML Processing (JAXP).

1.5.2 J2EE Platform Benefits

The J2EE platform, with features designed to expedite developing distributed and interoperable applications, offers Web services application developers these benefits:

- **Simplifies architecture and development**—The component-based J2EE development model enhances application development productivity because the components map well to the desired functionality of the application and service to be developed. Using tools, developers can configure application behavior at assembly or deployment, as required, knowing they can rely on the standardized interaction between components and the standard services provided by the container for the component.

- **Ensures support for emerging Web service standards**—The J2EE platform continues to evolve its support for Web service standards and the WS-I Basic

Profile. This ensures that application logic, whether new logic or enhancements to existing logic, developed using the standardized J2EE components can easily be exposed as Web services.

- **Ensures the development of portable and interoperable services**—The J2EE platform, since it supports both common J2EE and WS-I standards, ensures not only that applications are portable across J2EE implementations, but also that services are interoperable with any Web service implemented on any other platform that conforms to WS-I standards.

- **Allows for integration with existing information systems**—The J2EE platform provides industry-standard APIs, such as the J2EE Connector architecture, the JDBC API, Java Message Service, among others, for accessing EISs. Coupling these APIs with its support for Web services, the J2EE platform provides an excellent way to integrate existing EISs and make their data available to clients on heterogeneous platform environments.

- **Is scalable to meet demand variations**—J2EE containers provide a mechanism that supports simplified scaling of distributed applications with limited application development effort. J2EE containers provide transaction support, database connections, life cycle management, and other services that are both scalable and require no code from application developers.

- **Provides a flexible security model**—The J2EE security model is designed to be flexible, allowing component developers to declaratively specify component security requirements. Both Enterprise JavaBeans technology and Java Servlet APIs also provide programmatic security control.

In short, the J2EE standards and the J2EE brand have created a huge marketplace for servers, tools, and components. The J2EE brand on a server product ensures the consistent level of service fundamental to the goals of the J2EE platform. The J2EE standards encourage a lively marketplace for tools and components. Based on past experience coupled with the industry momentum behind Web services, all leading enterprise software vendors are expected to participate in the marketplace for J2EE 1.4 products.

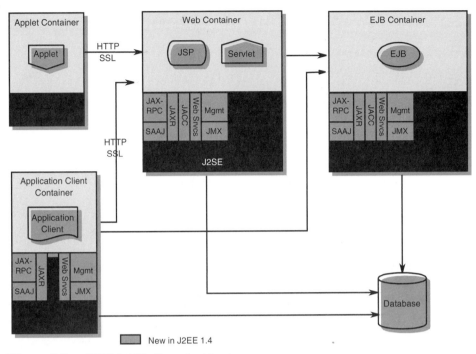

Figure 1.2 J2EE 1.4 Platform Architecture

1.5.3 J2EE Platform Technologies

The J2EE platform consists of technologies that support the development of distributed enterprise applications and services. These technologies fall into three broad categories: components, service, and communication. Figure 1.2 shows how these technologies interrelate. This section provides a brief overview of the J2EE 1.4 platform technologies. Refer to Chapter 2 for a more detailed discussion of these technologies.

1.5.3.1 Component Technologies

Developers use the platform's component technologies to create the essential parts of an enterprise application and a Web service, such as the business logic of the service. The approach of using component technologies to develop the essential parts of a service keeps development modular and promotes the reuse of modules. The various component technologies of the J2EE platform are as follows:

- **Client component**—The platform provides support for different types of clients to interact with components on the server side. *Applet clients* are Java-based clients that usually run from within a Web browser and have full access to the features of the J2SE platform. *Application clients* (often referred to as stand-alone clients) execute in their own containers and have full access to J2EE platform services such as JNDI lookups, asynchronous messaging, and so forth. These clients can directly interact with the Web and EJB components on the server-side of the application.

- **Web component**—Web components provide a response to a request received via HTTP. The J2EE platform defines two distinct Web component types. *Servlet components* extend the functionality of a Web server in a portable and efficient manner. With servlets, developers can map a set of URLs to a set of servlets. As a result of such mapping, an HTTP request to one of the URLs invokes the mapped servlet, which in turn processes the request and returns a response. Servlet components can also be exposed as Web services. *JSP components*, as well as servlet components, enable the generation of dynamic content.

- **Enterprise JavaBeans component**—Enterprise JavaBeans (EJB) components are designed specifically with business logic in mind. EJB components are scalable, transactional, and secure. *Session bean components* usually provide services to a single client, and their state cannot be recovered after a server crash. Furthermore, stateless session bean components can be exposed as Web services. *Entity bean components* are the object representation of data maintained in a data store. These components manage persistent data, either managing the persistence on their own or depending on the container to manage their persistence. *Message-driven bean components* enable clients to access business logic contained within enterprise bean components in an asynchronous manner. A *timer service* enables the implementation of timed operations.

Using these component technologies for implementing an application or service ensures the standardization of the application or service. Such standardization furthermore enables the reusability and portability of the application and service. Because they address different aspects of an enterprise application or service, using these components helps to divide development into different skill sets and make efficient use of different skills.

1.5.3.2 Platform and Container Services

The J2EE platform component technologies—the client, Web, and EJB components—depend on the support of the J2EE container to function properly. The J2EE platform standard, to ensure that components are portable, requires a conforming platform provider to make certain services available. Enterprise applications and Web services built with portable components and standard services are themselves assured of portability. Among the platform's required services are:

- **Naming service**—A naming service allows symbolic access to EIS resources and components within a naming environment. These components can be customized when assembled or deployed without requiring changes to the look-up source code.

- **Deployment service**—A deployment service allows changes to component behavior (such as transaction requirements and security requirements) at deployment without the need to change a component's source code.

- **Transaction service**—A transaction service frees the component developer from having to include code to handle such transactional issues as multi-user access and failure/recovery. A transaction service allows the transaction requirements for components to be specified when they are assembled.

- **Security service**—A security service ensures that components and resources are accessed by only those authorized for access. In addition, a security service provides authentication and confidentiality, among other services, for users.

1.5.3.3 Communication

The J2EE platform, in addition to specifying component technologies and platform services, also requires a set of standard communication technologies. These communication technologies bring the platform's components and services together, making the J2EE platform an integrated, standard platform for developing portable, interoperable enterprise applications and Web services.

- **Internet protocols**—The J2EE platform supports such standard, common Internet protocols as TCP/IP, HTTP, SSL, and so forth. These Internet protocols enable communication between components and between components and their clients.

- **Remote Method Invocation (RMI) protocols**—The J2EE platform supports the Java RMI. Java RMI relies on the Remote Method Invocation APIs, which use Java language interfaces to define remote interface objects. The platform uses IIOP to turn local method invocations into remote method invocations.

- **Messaging technologies**—In addition to its support for these Internet and RMI synchronous protocols, the J2EE platform supports technologies that enable asynchronous communication. Examples of these technologies are the Java Message Service API and the JavaMail API.

- **Web service technologies**—The J2EE platform also supports Web service-specific technologies and protocols that, along with the already mentioned technologies and protocols, standardize communication between J2EE components and J2EE clients. With the advent of Web services, which improve interoperability with non-Java clients, the J2EE platform supports Web service standards such as SOAP and UDDI using technologies such as Java API for XML-based RPC, Java API for XML Registries, and so forth.

1.6   Conclusion

The challenge to IT and computing professionals today is to efficiently develop and deploy distributed applications and Web services for use on both corporate intranets and over the Internet. Companies that can do this effectively are sure to gain strategic advantage in the information economy.

The Java 2 Platform, Enterprise Edition is a standard set of Java technologies that streamline the development, deployment, and management of Web services and enterprise applications. The J2EE platform provides a functionally complete environment, one in which it is possible to develop a large class of Web services and enterprise applications using J2EE technologies. Furthermore, developers can be assured that applications written for the J2EE platform will run on any J2EE-compatible server. Overall, the J2EE platform provides numerous benefits for organizations developing these Web service applications, including a simplified development model; industrial-strength scalability; support for existing information systems; choices in servers, tools, and components; and a simple, flexible security model.

By providing the ability to deploy component-oriented Web service endpoint and client applications in a platform-neutral manner, the J2EE platform gives fast-moving enterprises a significant and measurable competitive edge.

CHAPTER 2

Standards and Technologies

THIS chapter describes current, universally accepted Web Service standards and the J2EE platform's support for these standards. The Web services computing paradigm enables applications and services running on different platforms to easily communicate and interoperate with each other. To be so widely accepted, the paradigm must give service implementors flexibility in their implementation approach. Just as important, each such implementation must be assured that it can work with another implementation. Proven technologies facilitate Web service development, and these sorts of accepted standards enable interoperability.

2.1 Overview of Web Service Standards

Standards differ from technologies. Standards are a collection of specifications, rules, and guidelines formulated and accepted by the leading market participants. While these rules and guidelines prescribe a common way to achieve the standard's stated goal, they do not prescribe implementation details. Individual participants devise their own implementations of an accepted standard according to the standard's guidelines and rules. These various implementations of a standard by different vendors give rise to a variety of technologies. However, despite the implementation detail differences, the technologies can work together if they have been developed according to the standard's specifications.

For Web services to be successful, the Web service standards must be widely accepted. To enable such wide acceptance, the standards used for Web services and the technologies that implement those standards should meet the following criteria:

- A Web service should be able to service requests from any client regardless of the platform on which the client is implemented.

- A client should be able to find and use any Web service regardless of the service's implementation details or the platform on which it runs.

Standards establish a base of commonality and enable Web services to achieve wide acceptance and interoperability. Standards cover areas such as:

- **Common markup language for communication**—To begin with, service providers, who make services available, and service requestors, who use services, must be able to communicate with each other. Communication mandates the use of a common terminology, or language, through which providers and requestors talk to one another. A common markup language facilitates communication between providers and requestors, as each party is able to read and understand the exchanged information based on the embedded markup tags. Although providers and requestors can communicate using interpreters or translators, using interpreters or translators is impractical because such intermediary agents are inefficient and not cost effective. Web services use eXtensible Markup Language (XML) for the common markup language.

- **Common message format for exchanging information**—Although establishing a common markup language is important, by itself it is not sufficient for two parties (specifically, the service providers and service requestors) to properly communicate. For effective communication, the parties must be able to exchange messages according to an agreed-upon format. By having such a format, parties who are unknown to each other can communicate effectively. Simple Object Access Protocol (SOAP) provides a common message format for Web services.

- **Common service specification formats**—In addition to common message formats and markup language, there must be a common format that all service providers can use to specify service details, such as the service type, how to access the service, and so forth. A standard mechanism for specifying service details enables providers to specify their services so that any requestor can understand and use them. For example, Web Services Description Language (WSDL) provides Web services with common specification formats.

- **Common means for service lookup**—In the same way that providers need a common way to specify service details, service requestors must have a common way to look up and obtain details of a service. This is accomplished by having common, well-known locations where providers can register their service specifications and where requestors know to go to find services. By having these common, well-known locations and a standard way to access them, services can be universally accessed by all providers and requestors. Universal Description, Discovery, and Integration (UDDI) specification defines a common means for looking up Web services.

Although they do not exhaustively discuss these basic standards, the next sections provide enough information about the standards to enable further discussion about the J2EE technologies that implement them. For complete details, see the reference section at the end of this chapter. In addition to these basic standards, more complex Web services that implement enterprise-level processes need standards for security, transactions, process flow control, and so forth.

2.1.1 Extensible Markup Language

The eXtensible Markup Language (XML), a standard accepted throughout the industry, enables service providers and requestors to communicate with each other in a common language. XML is not dependent on a proprietary platform or technology, and messages in XML can be communicated over the Internet using standard Internet protocols such as HTTP. Because XML is a product of the World Wide Web Consortium (W3C) body, changes to it will be supported by all leading players. This ensures that as XML evolves, Web services can also evolve without backward compatibility concerns.

XML is a simple, flexible, text-based markup language. XML data is marked using tags enclosed in angled brackets. The tags contain the meaning of the data they mark. Such markup allows different systems to easily exchange data with each other. This differs from tag usage in HTML, which is oriented to displaying data. Unlike HTML, display is not inherent in XML. Code Example 2.1 shows the code from an XML document representing an individual's contact information.

```
<?xml version="1.0" encoding="ISO-8859-1" standalone="yes"?>
<ContactInformation>
    <Name>John Doe</Name>
    <Address>
        <Street>4140 Network Circle</Street>
```

```
        <City>Santa Clara</City>
        <State>California</State>
        <Country>USA</Country>
    </Address>
    <HomePhone>123-456-7890</HomePhone>
    <EMail>j2eeblueprints@sun.com</EMail>
</ContactInformation>
```

Code Example 2.1   XML Document Example

A Document Type Definition (DTD) or XML Schema Definition (XSD)
describes the structure of an XML document. It has information on the tags the
corresponding XML document can have, the order of those tags, and so forth. An
XML document can be validated against its DTD or its XSD. Validating an XML
document ensures that the document follows the structure defined in its DTD or
XSD and that it has no invalid XML tags. Thus, systems exchanging XML documents for some purpose can agree on a single DTD or XSD and validate all XML
documents received for that purpose against the agreed-upon DTD/XSD before
processing the document. Code Example 2.2 is the DTD for the XML document
in Code Example 2.1.

```
<!ELEMENT ContactInformation (Name, Address, HomePhone, EMail)>
<!ELEMENT Name (#PCDATA)>
<!ELEMENT Address (Street, City, State, Country)>
<!ELEMENT Street (#PCDATA)>
<!ELEMENT City (#PCDATA)>
<!ELEMENT State (#PCDATA)>
<!ELEMENT Country (#PCDATA)>
<!ELEMENT HomePhone (#PCDATA)>
<!ELEMENT EMail (#PCDATA)>
```

Code Example 2.2   Document Type Definition

Unfortunately, DTDs are an inadequate way to define XML document formats. For example, DTDs provide no real facility to express data types or complex
structural relationships. XML schema definitions standardize the format defini-

tions of XML documents. Code Example 2.4 shows the XSD schema for the
sample XML document in Code Example 2.3.

```
<?xml version="1.0" encoding="ISO-8859-1" standalone="yes"?>
<ContactInformation
        xmlns="http://simple.example.com/CInfoXmlDoc"
        xmlns:xsi="http://www.w3.org/2001/XMLSchema-instance"
        xsi:schemaLocation=
            "http://simple.example.com/CInfoXmlDoc
            file:./CInfoXmlDoc.xsd">
    <Name>John doe</Name>
    <Address>
        <Street>4140 Network Circle</Street>
        <City>Santa Clara</City>
        <State>California</State>
        <Country>USA</Country>
    </Address>
    <HomePhone>123-456-7890</HomePhone>
     <EMail>j2eeblueprints@sun.com</EMail>
</ContactInformation>
```

Code Example 2.3   XML Document

```
<?xml version="1.0" encoding="UTF-8"?>
<xsd:schema xmlns:xsd="http://www.w3.org/2001/XMLSchema"
    targetNamespace="http://simple.example.com/CInfoXmlDoc"
    xmlns=" http://simple.example.com/CInfoXmlDoc"
    elementFormDefault="qualified">
    <xsd:element name="ContactInformation">
        <xsd:complexType>
            <xsd:sequence>
                <xsd:element name="Name" type="xsd:string" />
                <xsd:element name="Address">
                    <xsd:complexType>
                        <xsd:sequence>
                            <xsd:element name="Street"
                                        type="xsd:string" />
                            <xsd:element name="City"
                                        type="xsd:string" />
```

```
            <xsd:element name="State"
                        type="xsd:string" />
            <xsd:element name="Country"
                        type="xsd:string" />
         </xsd:sequence>
       </xsd:complexType>
     </xsd:element>
     <xsd:element name="HomePhone" type="xsd:string" />
     <xsd:element name="EMail" type="xsd:string" />
   </xsd:sequence>
 </xsd:complexType>
</xsd:element>
</xsd:schema>
```

Code Example 2.4   XSD Schema

When considering XML schemas, it is important to understand the concept of XML namespaces. To enable using the same name with different meanings in different contexts, XML schemas may define a namespace. A *namespace* is a set of unique names that are defined for a particular context and that conform to rules specific for the namespace. Since a namespace is specific to a particular context, each namespace is unrelated to any other namespace. Thus, the same name can be used in different namespaces without causing a duplicate name conflict. XML documents, which conform to an XML schema and have multiple elements and attributes, often rely on namespaces to avoid a collision in tag or attribute names or to be able to use the same tag or attribute name in different contexts.

Technically speaking, an XML namespace defines a collection of names and is identified by a URI reference. (Notice in Code Example 2.4 the code `xmlns="http://simple.example.com/CInfoXmlDoc"`. Code such as this indicates that the XML schema defines a namespace for the various elements and attributes in the document.) Names in the namespace can be used as element types or attributes in an XML document. The combination of URI and element type or attribute name comprises a unique universal name that avoids collisions.

For example, in Code Example 2.4, there is a namespace that defines the `ContactInformation` document's element types, such as `Name` and `Address`. These element types are unique within the contact information context. If the document included another namespace context, such as `BankInformation` that defined its own `Name` and `Address` element types, these two namespaces would be separate and distinct. That is, a `Name` and `Address` used in the context of `BankInformation` would not conflict with a name and address used in the context of `ContactInformation`.

2.1.2 Simple Object Access Protocol

XML solves the need for a common language, and the Simple Object Access Protocol (SOAP) fills the need for a common messaging format. SOAP enables objects not known to one another to communicate; that is, to exchange messages. SOAP, a wire protocol similar to Internet Inter-ORB Protocol (IIOP) and Java Remote Method Protocol (JRMP), is a text-based protocol that uses an XML-based data encoding format and HTTP/SMTP to transport messages. SOAP is independent of both the programming language and the operational platform, and it does not require any specific technology at its endpoints, making it completely agnostic to vendors, platforms, and technologies. Its text format also makes SOAP a firewall-friendly protocol. Moreover, SOAP is backed by leading industrial players and can be expected to have universal support.

To enable message exchanges, SOAP defines an envelope, which contains a SOAP body, within which the message is included, and an optional SOAP-specific header. The whole envelope—body plus header—is one complete XML document. (See Figure 2.1.)

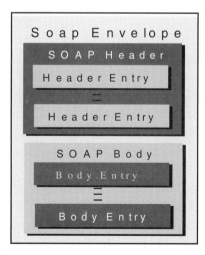

Figure 2.1 SOAP Message Structure

The header entries may contain information of use to recipients, and these header entries may also be of use to intermediate processors since they enable advanced features. The body, which contains the message contents, is consumed by the recipient. SOAP is agnostic about the message contents; the only restriction is that the message be in XML format.

Code Example 2.5 shows a simple but complete example of a SOAP request for obtaining a stock quote.

```
<SOAP-ENV:Envelope xmlns:SOAP-ENV="SoapEnvelopeURI"
        SOAP-ENV:encodingStyle="SoapEncodingURI">
    <SOAP-ENV:Header>
    </SOAP-ENV:Header>
    <SOAP-ENV:Body>
        <m:GetLastTradePrice xmlns:m="ServiceURI">
            <tickerSymbol>SUNW</tickerSymbol>
        </m:GetLastTradePrice>
    </SOAP-ENV:Body>
</SOAP-ENV:Envelope>
```

Code Example 2.5   Example SOAP Request

This example shows how a SOAP message is encoded using XML and illustrates some SOAP elements and attributes. All SOAP messages must have an `Envelope` element and must define two namespaces: One namespace connotes the SOAP envelope (`xmlns:SOAP-ENV`) and the other indicates the SOAP encoding (`SOAP-ENV:encodingStyle`). SOAP messages without proper namespace specification are considered invalid messages. The `encodingStyle` attribute is important, as it is used to specify serialization rules for the SOAP message. Moreover, there can be no DTD referrals from within SOAP messages.

While optional, the `Header` element when used should be the first immediate child after the `Envelope`. The `Header` element provides a way to extend the SOAP message by specifying additional information such as authentication and transactions. Specifying this additional information as part of the `Header` tells the message recipient how to handle the message.

There are many attributes that can be used in the SOAP `Header` element. For example, the `actor` attribute of the `Header` element enables a SOAP message to be passed through intermediate processes enroute to its ultimate destination. When the `actor` attribute is absent, the recipient is the final destination of the SOAP message. Similarly, many other attributes may be used. However, this chapter does not address these details.

The Body element, which must be present in all SOAP messages, must follow immediately after the Header element, if it is present. Otherwise, the Body element must follow immediately after the start of the Envelope element. The Body contains the specification of the actual request (such as method calls). The Fault element in the SOAP Body enables error handling for message requests.

Note that this chapter does not discuss details of Header elements, attributes, and other additional features, such as SOAP with attachments and binding HTTP, although they are part of the SOAP standard. Interested readers should refer to the SOAP specifications.

2.1.3 Registry Standards

The Universal Description, Discovery, and Integration (UDDI) specification defines a standard way for registering, deregistering, and looking up Web services. UDDI is a standards-based specification for Web service registration, description, and discovery. Similar to a telephone system's yellow pages, a UDDI registry's sole purpose is to enable providers to register their services and requestors to find services. Once a requestor finds a service, the registry has no more role to play between the requestor and the provider.

Figure 2.2 shows how UDDI enables dynamic description, discovery, and integration of Web services. A Web service provider registers its services with the UDDI registry. A Web service requestor looks up required services in the UDDI registry and, when it finds a service, the requestor binds directly with the provider to use the service.

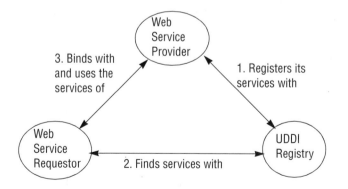

Figure 2.2   Role of a Registry in a Web Service

The UDDI specification defines an XML schema for SOAP messages and APIs for applications wanting to use the registry. A provider registering a Web service with UDDI must furnish business, service, binding, and technical information about the service. This information is stored in a common format that consists of three parts:

1. White pages—describe general business information such as name, description, phone numbers, and so forth

2. Yellow pages—describe the business in terms of standard taxonomies. This information should follow standard industrial categorizations so that services can be located by industry, category, or geographical location.

3. Green pages—list the service, binding, and service-specific technical information

The UDDI specification includes two categories of APIs for accessing UDDI services from applications:

1. Inquiry APIs—enable lookup and browsing of registry information

2. Publishers APIs—allow applications to register services with the registry

UDDI APIs behave in a synchronous manner. In addition, to ensure that a Web service provider or requestor can use the registry, UDDI uses SOAP as the base protocol. Note that UDDI is a specification for a registry, not a repository. As a registry it functions like a catalog, allowing requestors to find available services. A registry is not a repository because it does not contain the services itself.

2.1.4   Web Services Description Language

The Web Services Description Language (WSDL) defines a standard way for specifying the details of a Web service. It is a general-purpose XML schema that can be used to specify details of Web service interfaces, bindings, and other deployment details. By having such a standard way to specify details of a service, clients who have no prior knowledge of the service can still use that Web service.

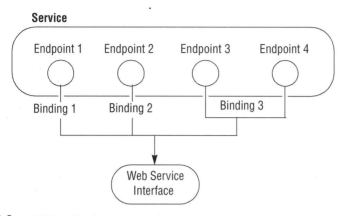

Figure 2.3 WSDL Service Description

WSDL specifies a grammar that describes Web services as a collection of communication endpoints, called ports. The data being exchanged are specified as part of messages. Every type of action allowed at an endpoint is considered an operation. Collections of operations possible on an endpoint are grouped together into port types. The messages, operations, and port types are all abstract definitions, which means the definitions do not carry deployment-specific details to enable their reuse.

The protocol and data format specifications for a particular port type are specified as a binding. A port is defined by associating a network address with a reusable binding, and a collection of ports define a service. In addition, WSDL specifies a common binding mechanism to bring together all protocol and data formats with an abstract message, operation, or endpoint. See Figure 2.3.

Code Example 2.6 shows a WSDL document for a weather Web service that returns a given city's weather information. The Web service, which uses SOAP as the communication protocol, expects to receive the city name as String type data and sends String type data as its response.

```
<?xml version="1.0" encoding="UTF-8"?>
<definitions name="WeatherWebService"
        targetNamespace="urn:WeatherWebService"
        xmlns:tns="urn:WeatherWebService"
        xmlns="http://schemas.xmlsoap.org/wsdl/"
        xmlns:xsd="http://www.w3.org/2001/XMLSchema"
```

```
                  xmlns:soap="http://schemas.xmlsoap.org/wsdl/soap/">
<types/>
<message name="WeatherService_getWeather">
    <part name="String_1" type="xsd:string"/>
</message>
<message name="WeatherService_getWeatherResponse">
    <part name="result" type="xsd:string"/>
</message>
<portType name="WeatherService">
    <operation name="getWeather" parameterOrder="String_1">
        <input message="tns:WeatherService_getWeather"/>
        <output
            message="tns:WeatherService_getWeatherResponse"/>
    </operation>
</portType>
<binding name="WeatherServiceBinding"
                        type="tns:WeatherService">
    <operation name="getWeather">
        <input>
            <soap:body use="literal"
                namespace="urn:WeatherWebService"/>
        </input>
        <output>
            <soap:body use="literal"
                namespace="urn:WeatherWebService"/>
        </output>
        <soap:operation soapAction=""/></operation>
    <soap:binding
            transport="http://schemas.xmlsoap.org/soap/http"
            style="rpc"/>
</binding>
<service name="WeatherWebService">
    <port name="WeatherServicePort"
                    binding="tns:WeatherServiceBinding">
        <soap:address
            location="http://mycompany.com/weatherservice"/>
    </port>
```

```
        </service>
    </definitions>
```

Code Example 2.6 WSDL Document for Weather Web Service

A complete WSDL document consists of a set of definitions starting with a root `definitions` element followed by six individual element definitions—`types`, `message`, `portType`, `binding`, `port`, and `service`—that describe the services.

- The `types` element defines the data types contained in messages exchanged as part of the service. Data types can be simple, complex, derived, or array types. Types, either schema definitions or references, that are referred to in a WSDL document's message element are defined in the WSDL document's type element.

- The `message` element defines the messages that the Web service exchanges. A WSDL document has a `message` element for each message that is exchanged, and the `message` element contains the data types associated with the message.

- The `portType` element specifies, in an abstract manner, operations and messages that are part of the Web service. A WSDL document has one or more `portType` definitions for each Web service it defines.

- The `binding` element binds the abstract port type, and its messages and operations, to a transport protocol and to message formats.

- The `service` and `port` elements together define the name of the Web service and, by providing a single address for binding, assign an individual endpoint for the service. A port can have only one address. The `service` element groups related ports together and, through its `name` attribute, provides a logical name for the service.

This description is for a simple WSDL document. Each element definition has various attributes and WSDL has additional features, such as fault handling. WSDL also specifies how to bind directly with HTTP/MIME, SMTP/MIME, and so forth, but these are beyond the scope of the current discussion. For more details, see the WSDL specification available at `http://www.w3c.org/TR/wsdl`.

2.1.5   Emerging Standards

So far we have examined existing standards, which meet the needs of simple Web services. Organizations that cross various industries have been formed to create and promote cross-platform standards. The Web Services Interoperability Organization (WS-I) is one such group. WS-I has published a WS-I Basic Profile that defines a set of cross-platform standards, such as those just examined, to promote and ensure interoperability. But other standards are required to address issues for Web services that handle complex business processes. These issues include strict security requirements, business processes interacting with other business processes and having long-lived transactions or transactions that span multiple business processes, or business processes nested within other processes. These business processes must also execute properly even when run on different platforms. Various standards bodies and organizations such as WS-I are currently working on these standards. Since these standards are still being defined and it is not yet clear which standards will be accepted as universal, we do not go into the details of emerging standards.

Now that we have examined the Web service standards, let's go on to see how J2EE supports these accepted standards.

2.2   J2EE: The Integrated Platform for Web Services

Starting with the J2EE 1.4 platform, with its main focus on Web services, the existing Java-XML technologies are integrated into a consolidated platform in a standard way, thereby allowing applications to be exposed as Web services through a SOAP/HTTP interface. The next sections briefly describe the Web service-specific additions made in the J2EE 1.4 platform. (Chapter 1 includes an overview of the J2EE 1.4 platform. See the J2EE 1.4 specification listed in "References and Resources" on page xx for complete information on the platform.)

This section is intended to give you an overview of the various Web service-specific additions in the J2EE platform. The next three chapters cover how to use these technologies in detail.

2.2.1 Java APIs for XML Processing

Java™ APIs for XML Processing (JAXP) is a vendor-neutral set of lightweight APIs for parsing or processing XML documents. Because XML is the common language enabling Web services, an XML parser is a necessity to process the messages—the XML documents—exchanged among Web services. Figure 2.4 depicts how the JAXP API abstracts the parser implementations from the user application.

Keep in mind that the JAXP API is not new to the J2EE 1.4 platform. It has been part of the earlier versions of both the J2EE and Java™ 2 Standard Edition (J2SE™) platforms. In the J2EE 1.4 platform implementation, JAXP has added support for XML schemas.

Although it has its own reference implementation, JAXP allows JAXP specification-conforming parsers from other vendors to be plugged in. JAXP falls back to parsing an XML document using its own implementation if no other implementation is provided. JAXP processes XML documents using the SAX or DOM models, and it permits use of XSLT engines during the document processing. (XSLT, which stands for eXtensible Stylesheet Language Transformation, is used for transforming XML documents from one format to another.)

The main JAXP APIs are available through the `javax.xml.parsers` package, which provides two vendor-agnostic factory interfaces—one interface for SAX processing and another for DOM processing. These factory interfaces allow the use of other JAXP implementations.

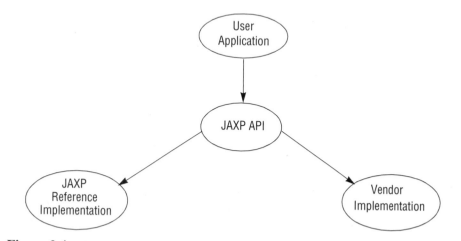

Figure 2.4   Using JAXP to Abstract Parser Implementations from User Application

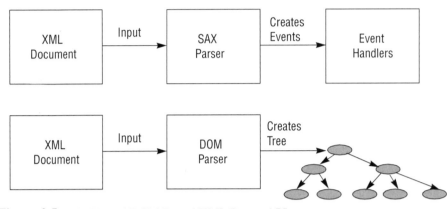

Figure 2.5   SAX- and DOM-Based XML Parser APIs

Figure 2.5 shows how the SAX and DOM parsers function. SAX processes documents serially, converting the elements of an XML document into a series of events. Each particular element generates one event, with unique events representing various parts of the document. User-supplied event handlers handle the events and take appropriate actions. SAX processing is fast because of its serial access and small memory storage requirements. Code Example 2.7 shows how to use the JAXP APIs and SAX to process an XML document.

```
public class AnAppThatUsesSAXForXMLProcessing
       extends DefaultHandler {

   public void someMethodWhichReadsXMLDocument() {

       // Get a SAX PArser Factory and set validation to true
       SAXParserFactory spf = SAXParserFactory.newInstance();
       spf.setValidating(true);

       // Create a JAXP SAXParser
       SAXParser saxParser = spf.newSAXParser();

       // Get the encapsulated SAX XMLReader
       xmlReader = saxParser.getXMLReader();

       // Set the ContentHandler of the XMLReader
```

```
            xmlReader.setContentHandler(this);

            // Tell the XMLReader to parse the XML document
            xmlReader.parse(XMLDocumentName);
        }
    }
```

Code Example 2.7   Using SAX to Process an XML Document

DOM processing creates a tree from the elements in the XML document. Although this requires more memory (to store the tree), this feature allows random access to document content and enables splitting of documents into fragments, which makes it easier to code DOM processing. DOM facilitates creations, changes, or additions to incoming XML documents. Code Example 2.8 shows how to use the JAXP APIs and DOM to process an XML document.

```
    public class AnAppThatUsesDOMForXMLProcessing {

        public void someMethodWhichReadsXMLDocument() {

            // Step 1: create a DocumentBuilderFactory
            DocumentBuilderFactory dbf =
                        DocumentBuilderFactory.newInstance();
            dbf.setValidating(true);
            // Step 2: create a DocumentBuilder that satisfies
            // the constraints specified by the DocumentBuilderFactory
            db = dbf.newDocumentBuilder();

            // Step 3: parse the input file
            Document doc = db.parse(XMLDocumentFile);

            // Parse the tree created - node by node
        }
    }
```

Code Example 2.8   Using DOM to Process an XML Document

2.2.2 Java™ API for XML-Based RPC

Java™ API for XML-based RPC (JAX-RPC) supports XML-based RPC for Java and J2EE platforms. It enables a traditional client-server remote procedure call (RPC) mechanism using an XML-based protocol. JAX-RPC enables Java technology developers to develop SOAP-based interoperable and portable Web services. Developers use the JAX-RPC programming model to develop SOAP-based Web service endpoints, along with their corresponding WSDL descriptions, and clients. A JAX-RPC-based Web service implementation can interact with clients that are not based on Java. Similarly, a JAX-RPC-based client can interact with a non-Java-based Web service implementation.

For typical Web service scenarios, using JAX-RPC reduces complexity for developers by:

- Standardizing the creation of SOAP requests and responses

- Standardizing marshalling and unmarshalling of parameters and other runtime and deployment-specific details

- Removing these SOAP creation and marshalling/unmarshalling tasks from a developer's responsibilities by providing these functions in a library or a tool

- Providing standardized support for different mapping scenarios, including XML to Java, Java to XML, WSDL-to-Java, and Java-to-WSDL mappings

JAX-RPC also defines standard mappings between WSDL/XML and Java, which enables it to support a rich type set. However, developers may use types that do not have standard type mappings. JAX-RPC defines a set of APIs for an extensible type mapping framework that developers can use for types with no standard type mappings. With these APIs, it is possible to develop and implement pluggable serializers and de-serializers for an extensible mapping. Figure 2.6 shows the high-level architecture of the JAX-RPC implementation.

A client application can make a request to a Web service in one of three ways. Chapter 5 contains detailed descriptions of these client access approaches.

1. Invoking methods on generated stubs—Based on the contents of a WSDL description of a service, tools can be used to generate stubs. These generated stubs are configured with all necessary information about the Web service and its endpoint. The client application uses the stubs to invoke remote methods available in the Web service endpoint.

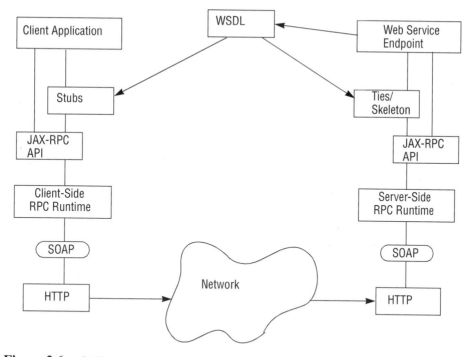

Figure 2.6 JAX-RPC Architecture

2. Using a dynamic proxy—A dynamic proxy supports a Web service endpoint. When this mode is used, there is no need to create endpoint-specific stubs for the client.

3. Using a dynamic invocation interface (DII)—In this mode, operations on target service endpoints are accessed dynamically based on an in-memory model of the WSDL description of the service.

No matter which mode is used, the client application's request passes through the client-side JAX-RPC runtime. The runtime maps the request's Java types to XML and forms a corresponding SOAP message for the request. It then sends the SOAP message across the network to the server.

On the server side, the JAX-RPC runtime receives the SOAP message for the request. The server-side runtime applies the XML to Java mappings, then maps the request to the corresponding Java method call, along with its parameters.

Note that a client of a JAX-RPC service may be a non-Java client. Also, JAX-RPC can interoperate with any Web service, whether that service is based on JAX-RPC or not. *Also note that developers need only deal with JAX-RPC APIs; all the details for handling SOAP happen under the hood.*

JAX-RPC supports three modes of operation:

1. Synchronous request–response mode—After a remote method is invoked, the service client's thread blocks until a return value or exception is returned.

2. One-way RPC mode—After a remote method is invoked, the client's thread is not blocked and continues processing. No return value or exception is expected on this call.

3. Non-blocking RPC invocation mode—A client invokes a remote procedure and continues in its thread without blocking. Later, the client processes the remote method return by performing a blocked receive call or by polling for the return value.

In addition, JAX-RPC, by specifying a standard way to plug in SOAP message handlers, allows both pre- and post-processing of SOAP requests and responses. These message handlers can intercept incoming SOAP requests and outgoing SOAP responses, allowing the service to do additional processing. See the JAX-RPC specification (listed in "References and Resources" on page xx) for more information on JAX-RPC.

Code Example 2.9 is an example of a JAX-RPC service interface for a simple service that provides weather information for a city.

```
public interface WeatherService extends Remote {
    public String getWeather(String city) throws RemoteException;
}
```

Code Example 2.9   JAX-RPC Service Endpoint Interface Example

Code Example 2.10 shows the implementation of the weather service interface using a Web component.

```
public class WeatherServiceImpl implements
                WeatherService, ServiceLifecycle {
```

```
    public void init(Object context) throws JAXRPCException {}

    public String getWeather(String city) {
        return ("Early morning fog clearing midday; " +
                "over all great day expected in " + city);
    }

    public void destroy() {}
}
```

Code Example 2.10 JAX-RPC Service Implementation

Code Example 2.11 shows how a client, using JAX-RPC to access this weather service.

```
.....
Context ic = new InitialContext();
Service svc = (Service)
        ic.lookup("java:comp/env/service/WeatherService");
WeatherSvcIntf port = (WeatherSvcIntf)
        svc.getPort(WeatherSvcIntf.class);
String info = port.getWeather("New York");
.....
```

Code Example 2.11 A Java/J2EE Client Accessing the Weather Service

These examples illustrate that a developer has to code very little configuration and deployment information. The JAX-RPC implementation handles the details of creating a SOAP request, handling the SOAP response, and so forth, thereby relieving the developer of these complexities.

2.2.3 Java™ API for XML Registries

Java™ API for XML Registries (JAXR), a Java API for accessing business registries, has a flexible architecture that supports UDDI, and other registry specifications (such as ebXML). Figure 2.7 illustrates the JAXR architecture.

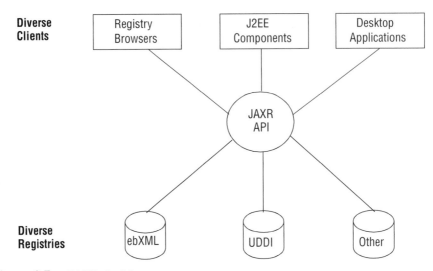

Figure 2.7   JAXR Architecture

A JAXR client, which can be a stand-alone Java application or a J2EE component, uses an implementation of the JAXR API provided by a JAXR provider to access business registries. A JAXR provider consists of two parts: a registry-specific JAXR provider, which provides a registry-specific implementation of the API, and a JAXR pluggable provider, which implements those features of the API that are independent of the type of registry. The pluggable provider hides the details of registry-specific providers from clients.

The registry-specific provider plugs into the pluggable provider, and acts on requests and responses between the client and the target registry. The registry-specific provider converts client requests into a form understood by the target registry and sends the requests to the registry provider using registry-specific protocols. It converts responses from the registry provider from a registry-specific format to a JAXR response, then passes the response to the client.

Refer to the JAXR specification for more information.

2.2.4   SOAP with Attachments API for Java™

SOAP with Attachments API for Java™ (SAAJ), which enables developers to produce and consume messages conforming to the SOAP 1.1 specification and SOAP with Attachments note, provides an abstraction for handling SOAP messages with attachments. Advanced developers can use SAAJ to have their applications operate directly with SOAP messages. Attachments may be complete XML documents, XML fragments, or MIME-type attachments. In addition, SAAJ allows developers to enable support for other MIME types. JAX technologies, such as JAX-RPC, internally use SAAJ to hide SOAP complexities from developers.

SAAJ allows the following modes of message exchanges:

- Synchronous request-response messaging—the client sends a message and then waits for the response

- One-way asynchronous messaging (also called fire and forget)—the client sends a message and continues with its processing without waiting for a response

Refer to the SAAJ specification for more information.

2.2.5 Web Service Technologies Integrated in J2EE Platform

Up to now, we have examined how the Java XML technologies support various Web service standards. Now let's see how the J2EE 1.4 platform combines these technologies into a standard platform that is portable and integrated. Not only are the Java XML technologies integrated into the platform, the platform also defines Web service-related responsibilities for existing Web and EJB containers, artifacts, and port components. The J2EE 1.4 platform ensures portability by integrating the Java XML technologies as extensions to existing J2EE containers, packaging formats, deployment models, and runtime services.

A Web service on the J2EE 1.4 platform may be implemented as follows:

- Using a JAX-RPC service endpoint—The service implementation is a Java class in the Web container. The service adheres to the Web container's servlet lifecycle and concurrency requirements.

- Using an EJB service endpoint—The service implementation is a stateless session bean in an EJB container. The service adheres to the EJB container's lifecycle and concurrency requirements.

In either case, the service is made portable with the definition of a port component, which provides the service's outside view for Web service implementation. A port component consists of:

- A WSDL document describing the Web service that its clients can use

- A service endpoint interface defining the Web service's methods that are available to clients

- A service implementation bean implementing the business logic of the methods defined in the service endpoint interface. The implementation may be either a Java class in the Web container or a stateless session bean in the EJB container.

Container-specific service interfaces, created by the J2EE container, provide static stub and dynamic proxies for all ports. A client of a J2EE platform Web service can be a Web service peer, a J2EE component, or a stand-alone application. It is not required that the client be a Web service or application implemented in Java.

How do clients use a J2EE platform Web service? Here is an example of a J2EE component that is a client of some Web service. Such a client uses JNDI to look up the service, then it accesses the Web service's port using methods defined in the `javax.xml.rpc.Service` interface. The client accesses the service's functionality using its service endpoint interface. A client that is a J2EE component needs only consider that the Web service implementation is stateless. Thus, the client cannot depend on the service holding state between successive service invocations. A J2EE component client does not have to know any other details of the Web service, such as how the service interface accesses the service, the service implementation, how its stubs are generated, and so forth.

Recall (from Code Example 2.9 and Code Example 2.10) what a Web service interface, such as the weather Web service, looks like when implemented as a JAX-RPC service endpoint on a J2EE platform. In contrast, Code Example 2.12 shows the equivalent EJB service endpoint implementation for the same weather service.

```
public class HelloService implements SessionBean {
    private SessionContext sc;

    public WeatherService(){}
```

```
    public void ejbCreate() {}
    public String getWeather(String city) {
        return ("Early morning fog clearing midday; " +
                "over all great day expected in " + city);
    }
    public void setSessionContext(SessionContext sc) {
        this.sc = sc;
    }
    public void ejbRemove() {}
    public void ejbActivate() {}
    public void ejbPassivate() {}
}
```

Code Example 2.12 EJB Service Endpoint Implementation for a Weather Service

Keep in mind that any client can use the code shown in Code Example 2.11 to access this weather service. This holds true

- Regardless of whether the service is implemented as a JAX-RPC service endpoint or an EJB service endpoint

- Regardless of whether the client is a servlet, an enterprise bean, or a standalone Java client

2.2.6   Support for WS-I Basic Profile

So far we have seen how the various Java technologies support Web service standards. We have also examined how these Java technologies have been integrated into the J2EE platform in a standard way to ensure portability of Web service implementations across J2EE platforms. Since ensuring interoperability among heterogeneous platforms is a primary force for Web services, the J2EE platform supports the WS-I Basic Profile.

As already seen in "Emerging Standards" on page 40, WS-I is an organization that spans industries and whose charter is to create and promote interoperability of Web services. WS-I has published the WS-I Basic Profile, which dictates how a set of Web service standards should be used together to ensure interoperability. The WS-I Basic Profile covers:

- Messaging standards (such as SOAP)

- Description and discovery standards (such as UDDI)

- Security

By supporting the WS-I Basic Profile, the J2EE platform is assured of providing an interoperable and portable platform for the development of Web services.

2.3   Other Java-XML Technologies

Up to now, we have discussed the Web service-specific technologies that are a mandatory part of the J2EE platform. As such, these technologies must be present in any J2EE implementation from any vendor. Apart from these, there are other Java-XML technologies that, while not a mandatory requirement of the J2EE platform, still prove very useful for implementing Web services. While there are a number of such technologies, we discuss here only those referenced throughout this book. One such non-mandatory but useful Java-XML technology is the Java Architecture for XML Binding (JAXB), which standardizes the representation of an XML document as an in-memory object.

As we have already seen, when two parties communicate by passing XML documents between them, the XML documents should follow some structure so that the communicating parties can understand the contents of the documents. XML document structure is defined using the standard schema facility for XML documents. Of course, while developers can use a DOM or SAX parser to parse such documents, it is much easier if the various parts of the XML documents are mapped or bound to in-memory objects that truly represent the document's intended meaning, as per the schema definition. In addition to using these objects, developers have access to the schema definitions as part of their logic. Such a facility is commonly called an XML data-binding facility. JAXB provides a good quality XML data-binding facility for the J2EE platform. Figure 2.8 shows the overall architecture of the JAXB data-binding facility.

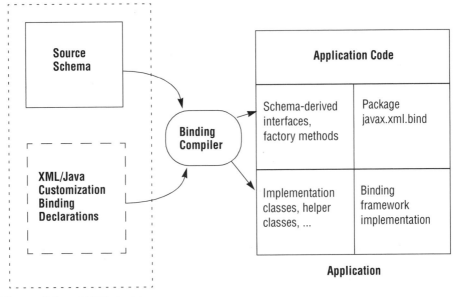

Figure 2.8 JAXB Architecture

JAXB consists of three main components:

- A **binding compiler** that creates Java classes (also called content classes) from a given schema. Complex type definitions within the schema are mapped to separate content classes, while simple types (such as attribute/element declarations) are mapped to fields within a content class. Developers use get and set methods (similar to JavaBeans get and set methods) to access and modify the object contents.

- A **binding framework** that provides runtime services—such as marshalling, unmarshalling, and validation—that can be performed on the contents classes.

- A **binding language** that describes binding of the schema to Java classes. This language enables a developer to override the default binding rules, thereby helping the developer to customize the content classes that are created by the binding compiler.

For more details on JAXB, refer to the JAXB specification available through the link provided in the next section.

Apart from JAXB, there are other emerging Java technologies that support Web service standards in terms of long-lived transactions, business process workflow, and so forth. At the time of this writing, they have not been finalized and hence will be dealt with in a future version of this book.

2.4   Conclusion

This chapter described the various Web service standards and the J2EE 1.4 platform technologies that support those standards in a portable and interoperable manner. It explained why such standards—including XML, SOAP, WSDL, and UDDI—are beneficial to developers, and briefly described each standard. It showed how the platform integrates existing Java and Web service/XML technologies to allow existing and new applications to be exposed as Web services.

In addition, this chapter described the different J2EE platform XML-related APIs, including JAXP, JAXR, JAX-RPC, and SAAJ. It described these technologies from a high-level architectural point of view, and, where appropriate, illustrated their use with sample code. It also showed how to implement a Web service on a J2EE platform using either a JAX-RPC or EJB service endpoint.

Table 2.1 summarizes the standards supported by the different J2EE platform technologies.

Table 2.1   J2EE Platform Web Service Support

Technology Name	Supporting Standard	Purpose
JAXP	XML schema	Enables processing of XML documents in a vendor neutral way; supports SAX and DOM models
JAX-RPC	SOAP	Enables exchange of SOAP requests and responses through an API that hides the complex SOAP details from the developers
JAXR	UDDI, ebXML	Enables accessing business registries with an API that supports any type of registry specification
SAAJ	SOAP with Attachments	Enables exchange of document-oriented XML messages using Java APIs

Table 2.1   J2EE Platform Web Service Support (*continued*)

Technology Name	Supporting Standard	Purpose
J2EE for Web Services	Integrates Java XML technologies into the J2EE platform; supports WS-I Basic Profile	Enables development and deployment of portable and interoperable Web services on the J2EE platform
JAXB (optional)	Standard in-memory representation of an XML document	Provides an XML data-binding facility for the J2EE platform

Now that you have a good grasp of the Web services technologies, you are ready to proceed with specific design and implementation issues. Chapter 3 describes how to design and implement an endpoint so that your application can make its functionality available as a Web service.

Service Endpoint Design

WEB services interact with clients to receive the clients' requests and return responses. In between the request and the response, a Web service applies appropriate business logic to process and fulfill a client's request. Designing an effective Web service starts with understanding the nature of the service to be provided—that is, how the service is going to interact with the client and how it is going to process and fulfill the client's request—coupled with how users of the service find and make their requests. This chapter examines Web services from the perspective of a service's interaction and processing functionality.

The chapter describes the key issues you must consider when designing a Web service, then shows how these considerations drive the design and implementation of a service's Web service interface and functionality. In particular, the chapter examines the interactions between a service and its clients and the business processing that the service performs. It illustrates these considerations by drawing from examples using three typical Web service scenarios.

The chapter covers most of the decisions that must be made when designing and implementing a Web service, including identifying the different possibilities that give rise to different solutions. It describes how to receive requests, delegate requests to business logic, formulate responses, publish a Web service, and handle document-based interactions.

Along the way, the chapter makes recommendations and offers some guidelines for designing a Web service. These recommendations and key points, marked with check boxes, include discussions of justifications and trade-offs. They are illustrated with the example service scenarios. Since Web services basically expose interoperable interfaces for new as well as existing applications, a large segment of the audience of this book may have existing applications for which they have already implemented the business logic. For that reason, and since the primary interest of most readers is on Web services, this chapter keeps its focus on Web service development and does not delve into the details of designing and implementing business logic.

3.1   Example Scenarios

Let's revisit the scenarios introduced in "Typical Web Service Scenarios" on page 11—the adventure builder enterprise scenario and the examples illustrating when Web services work well for an enterprise—from the point of view of designing a Web service. This chapter, rather than discussing design issues abstractly, expands these typical scenarios to illustrate important design issues and to keep the discussion in proper perspective.

In this chapter, we focus on three types of Web services:

1. An informational Web service serving data that is more often read than updated—clients read the information much more than they might update it. In our adventure builder example, a good scenario is a Web service that provides interested clients with travel-related information, such as weather forecasts, for a given city.

2. A Web service that concurrently completes client requests while dealing with a high proportion of shared data that is updated frequently and hence requires heavy use of EIS or database transactions. The airline reservation system partner to adventure builder is a good example of this type of Web service. Many clients can simultaneously send details of desired airline reservations, and the Web service concurrently handles and conducts these reservations.

3. A business process Web service whose processing of a client request includes starting a series of long-running business and workflow processes. Adventure builder enterprise's decision to build a service interface to partner travel agencies is a good example of this type of Web service. Through this service interface, partner agencies can offer their customers the same services offered in adventure builder's Web site. The partner agencies use adventure builder's business logic to fulfill their customer orders. A service such as this receives the details of a travel plan request from a partner agency, and then the service initiates a series of processes to reserve airlines, hotels, rental cars, and so forth for the specified dates.

Discussions of Web service design issues in this chapter include references to these examples and scenarios. However, the discussions use only appropriate characteristics of these scenarios as they pertain to a particular design issue, and they are not meant to represent a complete design of a scenario.

3.2   Flow of a Web Service Call

In a Web service scenario, a client makes a request to a particular Web service, such as asking for the weather at a certain location, and the service, after processing the request, sends a response to the client to fulfill the request. When both the client and the Web service are implemented in a Java environment, the client makes the call to the service by invoking a Java method, along with setting up and passing the required parameters, and receives as the response the result of the method invocation.

To help you understand the context within which you design Web services, let's first take a high-level view at what happens beneath the hood in a typical Web services implementation in a Java environment. Figure 3.1 shows how a Java client communicates with a Java Web service on the J2EE 1.4 platform.

Note: Figure 3.1 changes when a non-Java client interacts with a Java Web service. In such a case, the right side of the figure, which reflects the actions of the Web service, stays the same as depicted here, but the left side of the figure would reflect the actions of the client platform. When a Java client invokes a Web service that is on a non-Java platform, the right side of the figure changes to reflect the Web service platform and the left side, which reflects the actions of the client, remains as shown in the figure.

Once the client knows how to access the service, the client makes a request to the service by invoking a Java method, which is passed with its parameters to the client-side JAX-RPC runtime. With the method call, the client is actually invoking an operation on the service. These operations represent the different services of interest to clients. The JAX-RPC runtime maps the Java types to standard XML types and forms a SOAP message that encapsulates the method call and parameters. The runtime then passes the SOAP message through the SOAP handlers, if there are any, and then to the server-side service port.

The client's request reaches the service through a port, since a port provides access over a specific protocol and data format at a network endpoint consisting of a host name and port number.

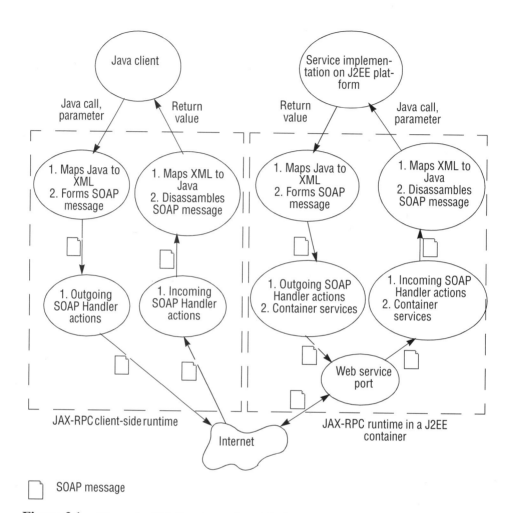

Figure 3.1   Flow of a Web Service on Java Platform

Before the port passes the request to the endpoint, it ensures that the J2EE container applies its declarative services (such as security checks) to the SOAP request. After that, any developer-written SOAP handlers in place are applied to the request. Note that SOAP handlers, which are optional, let developers apply application-specific processing logic common to all requests and responses that flow through this endpoint. After the handlers operate on the SOAP message, the message is passed to the service endpoint.

The J2EE container extracts the method call invoked by the client along with the parameters for the call, performs any XML-to-Java object mapping necessary, and hands the method to the Web service interface implementation for further processing. A similar set of steps happens when the service sends back its response.

Note: All the details between the method invocation and response just described happen under the hood. The platform shields the developer from these details. Instead, the developer deals only with typical Java programming language semantics, such as Java method calls, Java types, and so forth.

3.3 Key Web Services Design Decisions

Now that you understand what happens in a Web service interaction, let us look further at the issues involved in the design and implementation of a Web service. We first look at what goes into designing a Web service, examining the issues for which decisions are required and, when possible, making recommendations. (Similarly, Chapter 5 examines the issues to consider when designing a Web service client.) Before doing so, it is worthwhile to repeat this point:

❏ Web service technologies basically help you expose an interoperable interface for a new or an existing application. That is, you can add a Web service interface to an existing application to make it interoperable with other applications, or you can develop a completely new application that is interoperable from its inception.

It is important to keep in mind that designing Web service capabilities for an application is separate from designing the business logic of the application. In fact, you design the business logic of an application without regard to whether the application has a Web service interface. To put it another way, the application's business logic design is the same regardless of whether or not the application has a Web service interface. When you design a Web service interface for an application, you must consider those issues that pertain specifically to interoperability and Web services—and not to the business logic—and you make your design decisions based on these issues.

When designing a Web service, consider the logic flow for typical Web services and the issues they address. In general, a Web service:

- Exposes an interface that clients use to make requests to the service

- Makes a service available to partners and interested clients by publishing the service details

- Receives requests from clients

- Delegates received requests to appropriate business logic and processes the requests

- Formulates and sends a response for the request

Given this flow of logic, the following are the typical steps for designing a Web service.

1. Decide on the interface for clients. Decide whether and how to publish this interface.

You as the Web service developer start the design process by deciding on the interface your service makes public to clients. The interface should reflect the type and nature of the calls that clients will make to use the service. You should consider the type of endpoints you want to use—EJB service endpoints or JAX-RPC service endpoints—and when to use them. You must also decide whether you are going to use SOAP handlers. Last, but not least, since one reason for adding a Web service interface is to achieve interoperability, you must ensure that your design decisions do not affect the interoperability of the service as a whole.

Next, you decide whether you want to publish the service interface, and, if so, how to publish it. Publishing a service makes it available to clients. You can restrict the service's availability to clients you have personally notified about the service, or you can make your service completely public and register it with a public registry. Note that it is not mandatory for you to publish details of your service, especially when you design your service for trusted partners and do not want to let others know about your service. Keep in mind, too, that restricting service details to trusted partners does not by itself automatically ensure security. Effectively, you are making known the details about your service and its access only to partners rather than the general public.

2. Determine how to receive and preprocess requests.

Once you've decided on the interface and, if needed, how to make it available, you are ready to consider how to receive requests from clients. You need to design your service to not only receive a call that a client has made, but also to do any necessary preprocessing to the request—such as translating the request content to an internal format—before applying the service's business logic.

3. Determine how to delegate the request to business logic.

Once a request has been received and preprocessed, then you are ready to delegate it to the service's business logic.

4. Decide how to process the request.

Next, the service processes a request. If the service offers a Web service interface to existing business logic, then the work for this step may simply be to determine how the existing business logic interfaces can be used to handle the Web service's requests.

5. Determine how to formulate and send the response.

Last, you must design how the service formulates and sends a response back to the client. It's best to keep these operations logically together. There are other considerations to be taken into account before sending the response to the client.

6. Determine how to report problems.

Since Web services are not immune from errors, you must decide how to throw or otherwise handle exceptions or errors that occur. You need to address such issues as whether to throw service-specific exceptions or whether to let the underlying system throw system-specific exceptions. You must also formulate a plan for recovering from exceptions in those situations that require recovery.

After considering these steps, start designing your Web service by devising suitable answers to these questions:

- How will clients make use of your services? Consider what sort of calls clients may make and what might be the parameters of those calls.

- How will your Web service receive client requests? Consider what kind of end-points you are going to use for your Web service.

- What kind of common preprocessing, such as transformations, translations, and logging, needs to be done?

- How will the request be delegated to business logic?

- How will the response be formed and sent back?

- What kinds of exceptions will the service throw back to the clients, and when will this happen?

- How are you going to let clients know about your Web service? Are you going to publish your service in public registries, in private registries, or some way other than registries?

Before exploring the details of these design issues, let's look at a service from a high level. Essentially, a service implementation can be seen as having two layers: an interaction and a processing layer. (See Figure 3.2.)

❒   It is helpful to view a service in terms of layers: an interaction layer and a processing layer.

The service interaction layer consists of the endpoint interface that the service exposes to clients and through which it receives client requests. The interaction layer also includes the logic for how the service delegates the requests to business logic and formulates responses. When it receives requests from clients, the interaction layer performs any required preprocessing before delegating requests to the business logic. When the business logic processing completes, the interaction layer sends back the response to the client. The interaction layer may have additional responsibilities for those scenarios where the service expects to receive XML documents from clients but the business logic deals with objects. In these cases, you map the XML documents to equivalent object representations in the interaction layer before delegating the request to the business logic.

The service processing layer holds all business logic used to process client requests. It is also responsible for integrating with EISs and other Web services. In the case of existing applications adding a Web service interface, the existing application itself typically forms the service processing layer.

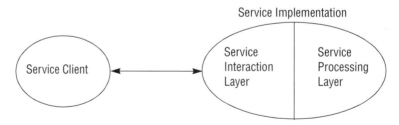

Figure 3.2   Layered View of a Web Service

Viewing your service implementation in terms of layers helps to:

- Clearly divide responsibilities
- Provide a common or single location for request processing (both pre- and post-processing) logic in the interaction layer
- Expose existing business logic as a Web service

To put this notion of a layered view in the proper context, let's look at an example such as adventure builder's business process Web service scenario. In this scenario, a partner travel agency uses adventure builder enterprise's Web service to build a travel itinerary for its clients. Through the service interface it exposes to these travel agencies, adventure builder enterprise receives business documents (in XML format) containing all required details for travel itinerary requests. Adventure builder uses its existing workflow systems to process and satisfy these partner requests. The interaction layer of adventure builder's exposed Web service interface validates these incoming business documents, then converts the incoming XML documents to its internal format or maps document content to Java objects. Once the conversion is finished, control passes to the workflow mechanisms in the processing layer where travel requests are completed. The interaction layer generates responses for completed travel requests, converts responses to XML documents or other appropriate formats, and ensures that responses are relayed to the partner agencies.

It is important to clarify the extent of the preprocessing performed at the interaction layer, since it differs from the JAX-RPC runtime processing. Adventure builder's interaction layer—its exposed Web service interface—applies service-specific preprocessing to requests coming in to the service. This service-specific preprocessing is performed only if required by the service logic, and it includes converting incoming XML documents to a suitable form or mapping the document contents to Java objects. This mapping of incoming XML documents to business objects is not the same as the JAX-RPC runtime mapping between XML documents and Java objects. Although the container performs the JAX-RPC runtime mapping for all requests and responses, the developer chooses the mapping of incoming XML documents to business objects.

❐ Although there are advantages, as noted previously, to viewing a service in terms of interaction and processing layers, a Web service may opt to merge these two layers into a single layer. There are times when multiple layers make a service unnecessarily complicated and, in these cases, it may be simpler to design the service as one layer. Typically, this happens in scenarios where the logic in either layer is too small to merit a separate layer.

The weather service scenario is one such service that might benefit from merging the interaction and processing layers into a single layer. This type of service does not need to preprocess incoming requests. A client request to the service for weather information simply includes a name or zip code to identify the location. The service looks up the location's weather information, forms a response containing the information, and returns it to the client. Since incoming requests require no preprocessing, a layered view of the weather service only complicates what otherwise should be a simple service.

3.4   Designing a Service's Interaction Layer

A service's interaction layer has several major responsibilities, and chief among them is the design of the interface the service presents to the client. Since clients access the service through it, the interface is the starting point of a client's interaction with the service. The interaction layer also handles other responsibilities, such as receiving client requests, delegating requests to appropriate business logic, and creating and sending responses. This section examines the responsibilities of the interaction layer and highlights some guidelines for its design.

3.4.1   Designing the Interface

There are some considerations to keep in mind as you design the interface of your Web service, such as issues regarding overloading methods, choosing the endpoint type, and so forth. Before examining these issues, decide on the approach you want to take for developing the service's interface definition.

Two approaches to developing the interface definition for a Web service are:

1. Java-to-WSDL—Start with a set of Java interfaces for the Web service and from these create the Web Services Description Language (WSDL) description of the service for others to use.

2. WSDL-to-Java—Start with a WSDL document describing the details of the Web service interface and use this information to build the corresponding Java interfaces.

How do these two approaches compare? Starting with Java interfaces and creating a WSDL document is probably the easier of the two approaches. With this approach, you need not know any WSDL details because you use vendor-provided tools to create the WSDL description. While these tools make it easy for you to generate WSDL files from Java interfaces, you do lose some control over the WSDL file creation.

❐ With the Java-to-WSDL approach, keep in mind that the exposed service interface may be too unstable from a service evolution point of view.

With the Java-to-WSDL approach, it may be hard to evolve the service interface without forcing a change in the corresponding WSDL document, and changing the WSDL might require rewriting the service's clients. These changes, and the accompanying instability, can affect the interoperability of the service itself. Since achieving interoperability is a prime reason to use Web services, the instability of the Java-to-WSDL approach is a major drawback. Also, keep in mind that different tools may use different interpretations for certain Java types (for example, `java.util.Date` might be interpreted as `java.util.Calendar`), resulting in different representations in the WSDL file. While not common, these representation variations may result in some semantic surprises.

On the other hand, the WSDL-to-Java approach gives you a powerful way to expose a stable service interface that you can evolve with relative ease. Not only does it give you greater design flexibility, the WSDL-to-Java approach also provides an ideal way for you to finalize all service details—from method call types and fault types to the schemas representing exchanged business documents—before you even start a service or client implementation. Although a good knowledge of WSDL and the WS-I Basic Profile is required to properly describe these Web services details, using available tools helps address these issues.

After you decide on the approach to take, you must still resolve other interface design details, which are described in the next sections.

3.4.1.1 Choice of the Interface Endpoint Type

In the J2EE platform, you have two choices for implementing the Web service interface—you can use a JAX-RPC service endpoint (also referred to as a Web tier endpoint) or an EJB service endpoint (also referred to as an EJB tier endpoint). Using one of these endpoint types makes it possible to embed the endpoint in the same tier as the service implementation. This simplifies the service implementation, because it obviates the need to place the endpoint in its own tier where the presence of the endpoint is solely to act as a proxy directing requests to other tiers that contain the service's business logic.

When you develop a new Web service that does *not* use existing business logic, choosing the endpoint type to use for the Web service interface is straight-forward. The endpoint type choice depends on the nature of your business logic—whether the business logic of the service is completely contained within either the Web tier or the EJB tier:

❒ Use a JAX-RPC service endpoint when the processing layer is within the Web tier.

❒ Use an EJB service endpoint when the processing layer is only on the EJB tier.

When you add a Web service interface to an existing application or service, you must consider whether the existing application or service preprocesses requests before delegating them to the business logic. If so, then keep the following guideline in mind:

❒ When you add a Web service interface for an existing application, choose an endpoint type suited for the tier on which the preprocessing logic occurs in the existing application. Use a JAX-RPC service endpoint when the preprocessing occurs on the Web tier of the existing application and an EJB service endpoint when preprocessing occurs on the EJB tier.

If the existing application or service does not require preprocessing of the incoming request, choose the appropriate endpoint that is present in the same tier as the existing business logic. Besides these major considerations for choosing an endpoint type, there are other, more subtle differences between an EJB service endpoint and a JAX-RPC service endpoint. You may find it helpful to keep in mind these additional points when choosing a Web service endpoint type:

• **Multi-threaded access considerations**—An EJB service endpoint, because it is implemented as a stateless session bean, need not worry about multi-threaded access since the EJB container is required to serialize requests to any particular instance of a stateless session bean. For a JAX-RPC service endpoint, on the other hand, you must do the synchronization yourself in the source code.

❑ A JAX-RPC service endpoint has to handle concurrent client access on its own, whereas the EJB container takes care of concurrent client access for an EJB service endpoint.

• **Transaction considerations**—The transactional context of the service implementation's container determines the transactional context in which a service implementation runs. Since a JAX-RPC service endpoint runs in a Web container, its transactional context is unspecified. There is also no declarative means to automatically start the transaction. Thus, you need to use JTA to explicitly demarcate the transaction.

On the other hand, an EJB service endpoint runs in the transaction context of an EJB container. You as the developer need to declaratively demarcate transactions. The service's business logic thus runs under the transactional context as defined by the EJB's `container-transaction` element in the deployment descriptor.

❑ If the Web service's business logic requires using transactions (and the service has a JAX-RPC service endpoint), you must implement the transaction-handling logic using JTA or some other similar facility. If your service uses an EJB service endpoint, you can use the container's declarative transaction services. By doing so, the container is responsible for handling transactions according to the setting of the deployment descriptor element `container-transaction`.

• **Considerations for method-level access permissions**—A Web service's methods can be accessed by an assortment of different clients, and you may want to enforce different access constraints for each method.

❑ When you want to control service access at the individual method level, consider using an EJB service endpoint rather than a JAX-RPC service endpoint.

Enterprise beans permit method-level access permission declaration in the deployment descriptor—you can declare various access permissions for different enterprise bean methods and the container correctly handles access to these methods. This holds true for an EJB service endpoint, since it is a stateless ses-

sion bean. A JAX-RPC service endpoint, on the other hand, does not have a
facility for declaring method-level access constraints, requiring you to do this
programmatically. See Chapter 7 for more information.

- **HTTP session access considerations**—A JAX-RPC service endpoint,
  because it runs in the Web container, has complete access to an `HttpSession`
  object. Access to an `HttpSession` object, which can be used to embed cookies
  and store client state, may help you build session-aware clients. An EJB
  service endpoint, which runs in the EJB container, has no such access to Web
  container state. However, generally HTTP session support is appropriate for
  short duration conversational interactions, whereas Web services often
  represent business processes with longer durations and hence need additional
  mechanisms. See "Correlating Messages" on page 359 for one such strategy.

3.4.1.2   Granularity of Service

Much of the design of a Web service interface involves designing the service's operations, or its methods. You first determine the service's operations, then define the
method signature for each operation. That is, you define each operation's parameters, its return values, and any errors or exceptions it may generate.

❒   It is important to consider the granularity of the service's operations when de-
      signing your Web service interface.

For those Web services that implement a business process, the nature of the
business process itself often dictates the service's granularity. Business processes
that exchange documents, such as purchase orders and invoices, by their nature
result in a Web service interface that is coarse grained. With more interactive Web
services, you need to carefully choose the granularity of these operations.

You should keep the same considerations in mind when designing the
methods for a Web service as when designing the methods of a remote enterprise
bean. This is particularly true not only regarding the impact of remote access on
performance but also with Web services; it is important with Web services
because there is an underlying XML representation requiring parsing and taking
bandwidth. Thus, a good rule is to define the Web service's interface for optimal
granularity of its operations; that is, find the right balance between coarse-grained
and fine-grained granularity.

❏ Generally, you should consolidate related fine-grained operations into more coarse-grained ones to minimize expensive remote method calls.

More coarse-grained service operations, such as returning catalog entries in sets of categories, keep network overhead lower and improve performance. However, they are sometimes less flexible from a client's point of view. While finer-grained service operations, such as browsing a catalog by products or items, offer a client greater flexibility, these operations result in greater network overhead and reduced performance.

❏ Keep in mind that too much consolidation leads to inefficiencies.

For example, consolidating logically different operations is inefficient and should be avoided. It is much better to consolidate similar operations or operations that a client is likely to use together, such as querying operations.

❏ When exposing existing stateless session beans as Web service endpoints, ensure that the Web service operations are sufficiently coarse grained.

If you are planning to expose existing stateless session beans as Web service endpoints, remember that such beans may not have been designed with Web services in mind. Hence, they may be too fine grained to be good Web service endpoints. You should consider consolidating related operations into a single Web service operation.

Good design for our airline reservation Web service, for example, is to expect the service's clients to send all information required for a reservation—destination, preferred departure and arrival times, preferred airline, and so forth—in one invocation to the service, that is, as one large message. This is far more preferable than to have a client invoke a separate method for each piece of information comprising the reservation. To illustrate, it is preferable to have clients use the interface shown in Code Example 3.1.

```
public interface AirlineTicketsIntf extends Remote {
    public String submitReservationRequest(
            AirReservationDetails details) throws RemoteException;
}
```

Code Example 3.1 Using Consolidation for Greater Efficiency (Recommended)

Code Example 3.1 combines logically-related data into one large message for a more efficient client interaction with the service. This is preferable to receiving the data with individual method calls, as shown in Code Example 3.2.

```
public interface AirlineTicketsIntf extends Remote {
    public String submitFlightInformation(FlightDetails fltInfo)
                    throws RemoteException;
    public String submitPreferredDates(Date depart, Date arrive)
                    throws RemoteException;
    // other similar methods
}
```

Code Example 3.2   Retrieving Data with Separate Method Calls (Not Recommended)

However, it might not be a good idea to combine in a single service invocation the same reservation with an inquiry method call.

Along with optimal granularity, you should consider data caching issues. Coarse-grained services involve transferring large amounts of data. If you opt for more coarse-grained service operations, it is more efficient to cache data on the client side to reduce the number of round trips between the client and the server.

3.4.1.3   Parameter Types for Web Service Operations

A Web service interface exposes a set of method calls to clients. When invoking a service interface method, a client may have to set values for the parameters associated with the call. When you design an interface's methods, choose carefully the types of these parameters. Keep in mind that a method call and its parameters are sent as a SOAP message between the client and the service. To be part of a SOAP message, parameters must be mapped to XML. When received at the client or service end, the same parameters must be mapped from XML to their proper types or objects. This section describes some guidelines to keep in mind when defining method call parameters and return values.

Note: Since each call potentially may return a value, the discussion in this section about parameter values applies equally to return values.

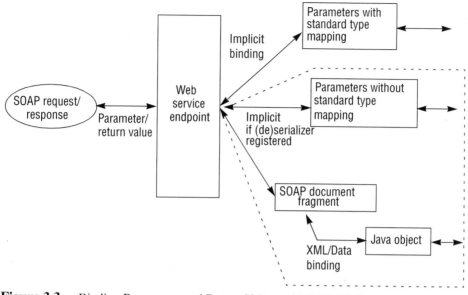

Figure 3.3   Binding Parameters and Return Values with JAX-RPC

Parameters for Web service method calls may be standard Java objects and types, XML documents, or even nonstandard types. Whether you use the Java-to-WSDL approach or the WSDL-to-Java approach, each type of parameter must be mapped to its XML equivalent in the SOAP message. Figure 3.3 shows how the binding happens for various types of parameters.

3.4.1.3.1 Java Objects as Parameters

Parameters for Web service calls can be standard Java types and objects. If you use the Java-to-WSDL approach, you specify the parameter types as part of the arguments of the method calls of your Java interface. If you use the WSDL-to-Java approach, you specify the parameter types as the `type` or `element` attributes of the `part` element of each `message` in your WSDL. The type of a parameter that you use has a significant effect on the portability and interoperability of your service.

The platform supports the following Java data types. (Refer to the JAX-RPC specification at `http://java.sun.com/xml/jaxrpc/` for the equivalent WSDL mappings for these Java data types.)

- Java primitive types `boolean`, `byte`, `short`, `int`, `long`, `float`, and `double`, along with their corresponding wrapper Java classes

- Standard Java classes: `String`, `Date`, `Calendar`, `BigInteger`, `BigDecimal`, `QName`, and `URI`

- Java arrays with JAX-RPC-supported Java types as members

- JAX-RPC value types—user-defined Java classes, including classes with JavaBeans™ component-like properties

❐ When designing parameters for method calls in a Web service interface, choose parameters that have standard type mappings. (See Figure 3.3.) Always keep in mind that the portability and interoperability of your service is reduced when you use parameter types that by default are not supported.

As Figure 3.3 shows, parameters that have standard type mappings are bound implicitly. However, the developer must do more work when using parameters that do not have standard type mappings. See "Handling Nonstandard Type Parameters" on page 76 for more details on using nonstandard Java types and possible side effects of such use.

Here are some additional helpful points to consider when you use Java objects with standard type mappings as parameters.

1. Many applications and services need to pass lists of objects. However, utilities for handling lists, such as `ArrayList` and `Collection`, to name a few, are not supported standard types. Instead, Java arrays provide equivalent functionality, and have a standard mapping provided by the platform.

2. JAX-RPC value types are user-defined Java classes with some restrictions. They have constructors and may have fields that are public, private, protected, static, or transient. JAX-RPC value types may also have methods, including set and get methods for setting and getting Java class fields.

   However, when mapping JAX-RPC value types to and from XML, there is no standard way to retain the order of the parameters to the constructors and other methods. Hence, avoid setting the JAX-RPC value type fields through the constructor. Using the get and set methods to retrieve or set value type fields avoids this mapping problem and ensures portability and interoperability.

3. The J2EE platform supports nested JAX-RPC value types; that is, JAX-RPC value types that reference other JAX-RPC value types within themselves. For

clarity, it is preferable to use this feature and embed value type references rather than to use a single flat, large JAX-RPC value type class.

4. The J2EE platform, because of its support for the SOAP message with attachment protocol, also supports the use of MIME-encoded content. It provides Java mappings for a subset of MIME types. (See Table 3.1.)

Table 3.1   Mapping of MIME Types

MIME Type	Java Type
`image/gif`	`java.awt.Image`
`image/jpeg`	`java.awt.Image`
`text/plain`	`java.lang.String`
`multipart/*`	`javax.mail.internet.MimeMultipart`
`text/xml` or `application/xml`	`javax.xml.transform.Source`

Since the J2EE container automatically handles mappings based on the Java types, using these Java-MIME mappings frees you from the intricacies of sending and retrieving documents and images as part of a service's request and response handling. For example, your service, if it expects to receive a GIF image with a MIME type of `image/gif`, can expect the client to send a `java.awt.Image` object. A sample Web service interface that receives an image might look like the one shown in Code Example 3.3:

```
import java.awt.Image;
public interface WeatherMapService extends Remote {
    public void submitWeatherMap(Image weatherMap)
                throws RemoteException, InvalidMapException;
}
```

Code Example 3.3   Receiving a `java.awt.Image` Object

In this example, the `Image` object lets the container implementation handle the image-passing details. The container provides `javax.activation.DataHandler` classes, which work with the Java Activation Framework to accomplish the Java-MIME and MIME-Java mappings.

❏ Considering this mapping between Java and MIME types, it is best to send images and XML documents that are in a Web service interface using the Java types shown in Table 3.1. However, you should be careful about the effect on the interoperability of your service. See "Interoperability" on page 86 for more details.

3.4.1.3.2 XML Documents as Parameters

There are scenarios when you want to pass XML documents as parameters. Typically, these occur in business-to-business interactions where there is a need to exchange legally binding business documents, track what is exchanged, and so forth. Exchanging XML documents as part of a Web service is addressed in a separate section—see "Handling XML Documents in a Web Service" on page 105 for guidelines to follow when passing XML documents as parameters.

3.4.1.3.3 Handling Nonstandard Type Parameters

JAX-RPC technology, in addition to providing a rich standard mapping set between XML and Java data types, also provides an extensible type mapping framework. Developers can use this framework to specify pluggable, custom serializers and deserializers that support nonstandard type mappings.

❏ Extensible type mapping frameworks, which developers may use to support nonstandard type mappings, are not yet a standard part of the J2EE platform.

Vendors currently can provide their own solutions to this problem. It must be emphasized that if you implement a service using some vendor's implementation-specific type mapping framework, then your service is not guaranteed to be portable and interoperable.

❏ Because of portability limitations, you should avoid passing parameters that require the use of vendor-specific serializers or deserializers.

Instead, a better way is to pass these parameters as SOAP document fragments represented as a DOM subtree in the service endpoint interface. (See Figure 3.3.) If so, you should consider binding (either manually or using JAXB) the SOAP fragments to Java objects before passing them to the processing layer to avoid tightly coupling the business logic with the document fragment.

3.4.1.4   Interfaces with Overloaded Methods

In your service interface, you may overload methods and expose them to the service's clients. Overloaded methods share the same method name but have different parameters and return values. If you do choose to use overloaded methods as part of your service interface, keep in mind that there are some limitations, as follows:

- If you choose the WSDL-to-Java approach, there are limitations to representing overloaded methods in a WSDL description. In the WSDL description, each method call and its response are represented as unique SOAP messages. To represent overloaded methods, the WSDL description would have to support multiple SOAP messages with the same name. WSDL version 1.1 does not have this capability to support multiple messages with the same name.

- If you choose the Java-to-WSDL approach and your service exposes overloaded methods, be sure to check how any vendor-specific tools you are using represent these overloaded methods in the WSDL description. You need to ensure that the WSDL representation of overloaded methods works in the context of your application.

Let's see how this applies in the weather service scenario. As the provider, you might offer the service to clients, letting them look up weather information by city name or zip code. If you use the Java-to-WSDL approach, you might first define the WeatherService interface as shown in Code Example 3.4.

```
public interface WeatherService extends Remote {
    public String getWeather(String city) throws RemoteException;
    public String getWeather(int zip) throws RemoteException;
}
```

Code Example 3.4   WeatherService Interface for Java-to-WSDL Approach

After you define the interface, you run the vendor-provided tool to create the WSDL from the interface. Each tool has its own way of representing the getWeather overloaded methods in the WSDL, and your WSDL reflects the particular tool you use. For example, if you use the J2EE 1.4 SDK from Sun Microsystems, its wscompile tool creates from the WeatherService interface the WSDL shown in Code Example 3.5.

```
<?xml version="1.0" encoding="UTF-8"?>
<definitions name="WeatherWebService" .......>
    <types/>
    <message name="WeatherService_getWeather">
        <part name="int_1" type="xsd:int"/>
    </message>
    <message name="WeatherService_getWeatherResponse">
        <part name="result" type="xsd:string"/>
    </message>
    <message name="WeatherService_getWeather2">
        <part name="String_1" type="xsd:string"/>
    </message>
    <message name="WeatherService_getWeather2Response">
        <part name="result" type="xsd:string"/>
    </message>
    ...
</definitions>
```

Code Example 3.5   Generated WSDL for `WeatherService` Interface

Notice that the WSDL represents the `getWeather` overloaded methods as two different SOAP messages, naming one `getWeather`, which takes an integer for the zip code as its parameter, and the other `getWeather2`, which takes a string parameter for the city. As a result, a client interested in obtaining weather information using a city name invokes the service by calling `getWeather2`, as shown in Code Example 3.6.

```
...
Context ic = new InitialContext();
WeatherWebService weatherSvc = (WeatherWebService)
        ic.lookup("java:comp/env/service/WeatherService");
WeatherServiceIntf port = (WeatherServiceIntf)
        weatherSvc.getPort(WeatherServiceIntf.class);
String returnValue = port.getWeather2("San Francisco");
...
```

Code Example 3.6   Using Weather Service Interface with Java-to-WSDL Approach

For example, to obtain the weather information for San Francisco, the client called port.getWeather2("San Francisco"). Keep in mind that another tool may very likely generate a WSDL whose representation of overloaded methods is different.

❑ You may want to avoid using overloaded methods in your Java interface altogether if you prefer to have only intuitive method names in the WSDL.

If instead you choose to use the WSDL-to-Java approach, your WSDL description might look as follows. (See Code Example 3.7.)

```
<?xml version="1.0" encoding="UTF-8"?>
<definitions name="WeatherWebService" ...>
    <types/>
    <message name="WeatherService_getWeatherByZip">
        <part name="int_1" type="xsd:int"/>
    </message>
    <message name="WeatherService_getWeatherByZipResponse">
        <part name="result" type="xsd:string"/>
    </message>
    <message name="WeatherService_getWeatherByCity">
        <part name="String_1" type="xsd:string"/>
    </message>
    <message name="WeatherService_getWeatherByCityResponse">
        <part name="result" type="xsd:string"/>
    </message>
    ...
</definitions>
```

Code Example 3.7   WSDL for Weather Service with Overloaded Methods Avoided

Since the messages in a WSDL file must have unique names, you must use different message names to represent methods that you would otherwise overload. These different message names actually convert to different method calls in your interface. Notice that the WSDL includes a method getWeatherByZip, which takes an integer parameter, and a method getWeatherByCity, which takes a string parameter. Thus, a client wishing to obtain weather information by city name from a `WeatherService` interface associated with the WSDL in Code Example 3.7 might invoke the service as shown in Code Example 3.8.

```
...
Context ic = new InitialContext();
WeatherWebService weatherSvc = (WeatherWebService)
        ic.lookup("java:comp/env/service/WeatherService");
WeatherServiceIntf port = (WeatherServiceIntf)
        weatherSvc.getPort(WeatherServiceIntf.class);
String returnValue = port.getWeatherByCity("San Francisco");
...
```

Code Example 3.8   Using Weather Service with WSDL-to-Java Approach

3.4.1.5   Handling Exceptions

Just like any Java or J2EE application, a Web service application may encounter an error condition while processing a client request. A Web service application needs to properly catch any exceptions thrown by an error condition and propagate these exceptions. For a Java application running in a single virtual machine, you can propagate exceptions up the call stack until reaching a method with an exception handler that handles the type of exception thrown. To put it another way, for non-Web service J2EE and Java applications, you may continue to throw exceptions up the call stack, passing along the entire stack trace, until reaching a method with an exception handler that handles the type of exception thrown. You can also write exceptions that extend or inherit other exceptions.

However, throwing exceptions in Web service applications has additional constraints that impact the design of the service endpoint. When considering how the service endpoint handles error conditions and notifies clients of errors, you must keep in mind these points:

- Similar to requests and responses, exceptions are also sent back to the client as part of the SOAP messages.

- Your Web service application should support clients running on non-Java platforms that may not have the same, or even similar, error-handling mechanisms as the Java exception-handling mechanism.

A Web service application may encounter two types of error conditions. One type of error might be an irrecoverable system error, such as an error due to a network connection problem. When an error such as this occurs, the JAX-RPC runtime on the client throws the client platform's equivalent of an irrecoverable system exception. For Java clients, this translates to a `RemoteException`.

A Web service application may also encounter a recoverable application error condition. This type of error is called a service-specific exception. The error is particular to the specific service. For example, a weather Web service might indicate an error if it cannot find weather information for a specified city.

To illustrate the Web service exception-handling mechanism, let's examine it in the context of the weather Web service example. When designing the weather service, you want the service to be able to handle a scenario in which the client requests weather information for a nonexistent city. You might design the service to throw a service-specific exception, such as `CityNotFoundException`, to the client that made the request. You might code the service interface so that the `getWeather` method throws this exception. (See Code Example 3.9.)

```
public interface WeatherService extends Remote {
    public String getWeather(String city) throws
            CityNotFoundException, RemoteException;
}
```

Code Example 3.9   Throwing a Service-Specific Exception

Service-specific exceptions like `CityNotFoundException`, which are thrown by the Web service to indicate application-specific error conditions, must be checked exceptions that directly or indirectly extend `java.lang.Exception`. They cannot be unchecked exceptions. Code Example 3.10 shows a typical implementation of a service-specific exception, such as for `CityNotFoundException`.

```
public class CityNotFoundException extends Exception {
    private String message;
    public CityNotFoundException(String message) {
        super(message);
        this.message = message;
    }
    public String getMessage() {
        return message;
```

```
        }
    }
```

Code Example 3.10 Implementation of a Service-Specific Exception

Code Example 3.11 shows the service implementation for the same weather service interface. This example illustrates how the service might throw `CityNotFoundException`.

```
public class WeatherServiceImpl implements WeatherService {
    public String getWeather(String city)
                              throws CityNotFoundException {
        if(!validCity(city))
            throw new CityNotFoundException(city + " not found");
        // Get weather info and return it back
    }
}
```

Code Example 3.11 Example of a Service Throwing a Service-Specific Exception

Chapter 5 describes the details of handling exceptions on the client side. (In particular, refer to "Handling Exceptions" on page 230.) On the service side, keep in mind how to include exceptions in the service interface and how to throw them. Generally, you want to do the following:

❏ Convert application-specific errors and other Java exceptions into meaningful service-specific exceptions and throw these service-specific exceptions to the clients.

Although they promote interoperability among heterogeneous platforms, Web service standards cannot address every type of exception thrown by different platforms. For example, the standards do not specify how Java exceptions such as `java.io.IOException` and `javax.ejb.EJBException` should be returned to the client. As a consequence, it is important for a Web service—from the service's interoperability point of view—to not expose Java-specific exceptions (such as those just mentioned) in the Web service interface. Instead, throw a service-specific exception. In addition, keep the following points in mind:

- You cannot throw nonserializable exceptions to a client through the Web service endpoint.

- When a service throws `java` or `javax` exceptions, the exception type and its context information are lost to the client that receives the thrown exception. For example, if your service throws a `javax.ejb.FinderException` exception to the client, the client may receive an exception named `FinderException`, but its type information may not be available to the client. Furthermore, the type of the exception to the client may not be the same as the type of the thrown exception. (Depending on the tool used to generate the client-side interfaces, the exception may even belong to some package other than `javax.ejb`.)

As a result, you should avoid directly throwing `java` and `javax` exceptions to clients. Instead, when your service encounters one of these types of exceptions, wrap it within a meaningful service-specific exception and throw this service-specific exception back to the client. For example, suppose your service encounters a `javax.ejb.FinderException` exception while processing a client request. The service should catch the `FinderException` exception, and then, rather than throwing this exception as is back to the client, the service should instead throw a service-specific exception that has more meaning for the client. See Code Example 3.12.

```
...
try {
    // findByPrimaryKey
    // Do processing
    // return results
} catch (javax.ejb.FinderException fe) {
    throw new InvalidKeyException(
        "Unable to find row with given primary key");
}
```

Code Example 3.12 Converting an Exception into a Service-Specific Exception

❐ Exception inheritances are lost when you throw a service-specific exception.

You should avoid defining service-specific exceptions that inherit or extend other exceptions. For example, if `CityNotFoundException` in Code Example 3.10

extends another exception, such as `RootException`, then when the service throws `CityNotFoundException`, methods and properties inherited from `RootException` are *not* passed to the client.

❐   The exception stack trace is not passed to the client.

The stack trace for an exception is relevant only to the current execution environment and is meaningless on a different system. Hence, when a service throws an exception to the client, the client does not have the stack trace explaining the conditions under which the exception occurred. Thus, you should consider passing additional information in the message for the exception.

Web service standards make it easier for a service to pass error conditions to a client in a platform-independent way. While the following discussion may be of interest, it is not essential that developers know these details about the J2EE platform's error-handling mechanisms for Web services.

As noted previously, error conditions are included within the SOAP messages that a service returns to clients. The SOAP specification defines a message type, called `fault`, that enables error conditions to be passed as part of the SOAP message yet still be differentiated from the request or response portion. Similarly, the WSDL specification defines a set of operations that are possible on an endpoint. These operations include `input` and `output` operations, which represent the request and response respectively, and an operation called `fault`.

A SOAP `fault` defines system-level exceptions, such as `RemoteException`, which are irrecoverable errors. The WSDL `fault` denotes service-specific exceptions, such as `CityNotFoundException`, and these are recoverable application error conditions. Since the WSDL `fault` denotes a recoverable error condition, the platform can pass it as part of the SOAP response message. Thus, the standards provide a way to exchange fault messages and map these messages to operations on the endpoint.

Code Example 3.13 shows the WSDL code for the same weather Web service example. This example illustrates how service-specific exceptions are mapped just like input and output messages are mapped.

```
<?xml version="1.0" encoding="UTF-8"?>
<definitions ...>
   ...
   <message name="WeatherService_getWeather">
      <part name="String_1" type="xsd:string"/>
```

```
    </message>
    <message name="WeatherService_getWeatherResponse">
        <part name="result" type="xsd:string"/>
    </message>
    <message name="CityNotFoundException">
        <part name="CityNotFoundException"
                    element="tns:CityNotFoundException"/>
    </message>
    <portType name="WeatherService">
        <operation name="getWeather" parameterOrder="String_1">
            <input message="tns:WeatherService_getWeather"/>
            <output message=
                    "tns:WeatherService_getWeatherResponse"/>
            <fault name="CityNotFoundException"
                    message="tns:CityNotFoundException"/>
        </operation>
    </portType>
    ...
</definitions>
```

Code Example 3.13 Mapping a Service-Specific Exception in WSDL

3.4.1.6   Use of Handlers

As discussed in Chapter 2, and as shown in Figure 3.1, JAX-RPC technology enables you to plug in SOAP message handlers, thus allowing processing of SOAP messages that represent requests and responses. Plugging in SOAP message handlers gives you the capability to examine and modify the SOAP requests before they are processed by the Web service and to examine and modify the SOAP responses before they are delivered to the client.

Handlers are particular to a Web service and are associated with the specific port of the service. As a result of this association, the handler's logic applies to all SOAP requests and responses that pass through a service's port. Thus, you use these message handlers when your Web service must perform some SOAP message-specific processing common to all its requests and responses. Because handlers are common to all requests and responses that pass through a Web service endpoint, keep the following guideline in mind:

❐   It is not advisable to put in a handler business logic or processing particular to specific requests and responses.

You cannot store client-specific state in a handler: A handler's logic acts on all requests and responses that pass through an endpoint. However, you may use the handler to store port-specific state, which is state common to all method calls on that service interface. Note also that handlers execute in the context of the component in which they are present.

❐   Do not store client-specific state in a handler.

Also note that handlers work directly on the SOAP message, and this involves XML processing. You can use handlers to pass client-specific state through the message context. (See "Passing Context Information on Web Service Calls" on page 366.)

❐   Use of handlers can result in a significant performance impact for the service as a whole.

Use of handlers could potentially affect the interoperability of your service. See the next section on interoperability. Keep in mind that it takes advanced knowledge of SOAP message manipulation APIs (such as SAAJ) to correctly use handlers. To avoid errors, Web service developers should try to use existing or vendor-supplied handlers. Using handlers makes sense primarily for writing system services such as auditing, logging, and so forth.

3.4.1.7   Interoperability

A major benefit of Web services is interoperability between heterogeneous platforms. To get the maximum benefit, you want to design your Web service to be interoperable with clients on any platform, and, as discussed in Chapter 2, the Web Services Interoperability (WS-I) organization helps in this regard. WS-I promotes a set of generic protocols for the interoperable exchange of messages between Web services. The WS-I Basic Profile promotes interoperability by defining and recommending how a set of core Web services specifications and standards (including SOAP, WSDL, UDDI, and XML) can be used for developing interoperable Web services.

In addition to the WS-I protocols, other groups, such as SOAPBuilders Interoperability group (see `http://java.sun.com/wsinterop/sb/index.html`), provide common testing grounds that make it easier to test the interoperability of various SOAP implementations. This has made it possible for various Web services technology vendors to test the interoperability of implementations of their standards. When you implement your service using technologies that adhere to the WS-I Basic Profile specifications, you are assured that such services are interoperable.

Apart from these standards and testing environments, you as the service developer must design and implement your Web service so that maximum interoperability is possible. For maximum interoperability, you should keep these three points in mind:

1. The two messaging styles and bindings supported by WSDL

2. The WS-I support for attachments

3. The most effective way to use handlers

WSDL supports two types of messaging styles: `rpc` and `document`. The WSDL `style` attribute indicates the messaging style. (See Code Example 3.14.) A `style` attribute set to `rpc` indicates a RPC-oriented operation, where messages contain parameters and return values, or function signatures. When the `style` attribute is set to `document`, it indicates a document-oriented operation, one in which messages contain documents. Each operation style has a different effect on the format of the body of a SOAP message.

Along with operation styles, WSDL supports two types of serialization and deserialization mechanisms: a `literal` and an `encoded` mechanism. The WSDL `use` attribute indicates which mechanism is supported. (See Code Example 3.14.) A `literal` value for the `use` attribute indicates that the data is formatted according to the abstract definitions within the WSDL document. The `encoded` value means data is formatted according to the encodings defined in the URI specified by the `encodingStyle` attribute. Thus, you can choose between an rpc or document style of message passing and each message can use either a literal or encoded data formatting.

❐ Because the WS-I Basic Profile 1.0, to which J2EE1.4 platform conforms, supports only literal bindings, you should avoid encoded bindings.

❑   Literal bindings cannot represent complex types, such as objects with circular
     references, in a standard way.

Code Example 3.14 shows a snippet from the WSDL document illustrating
how the sample weather service specifies these bindings.

```
<?xml version="1.0" encoding="UTF-8"?>
<definitions .......>
<binding name="WeatherServiceBinding" type="tns:WeatherService">
    <operation name="getWeather">
        <input>
            <soap:body use="literal"
                        namespace="urn:WeatherWebService"/>
        </input>
        <output>
            <soap:body use="literal"
                        namespace="urn:WeatherWebService"/>
        </output>
        <soap:operation soapAction=""/></operation>
        <soap:binding style="rpc"
                transport="http://schemas.xmlsoap.org/soap/http" />
    </binding>
    <service .....>
</definitions>
```

Code Example 3.14 Specifying WSDL Bindings

It is important to keep in mind these message styles and bindings, particularly
when you design the interface using the WSDL-to-Java approach and when you
design the WSDL for your service. When you use the Java-to-WSDL approach,
you rely on the vendor-provided tools to generate the WSDL for your Java interfaces, and they can be counted on to create WS-I-compliant WSDL for your service. However, note that some vendors may expect you to specify certain options
to ensure the creation of a WS-I-compliant WSDL. For example, the J2EE 1.4
SDK from Sun Microsystems provides a `wscompile` tool, which expects the developer to use the `-f:wsi` flag to create the WS-I-compliant WSDL for the service. It
is also a good idea to check the WSDL document itself to ensure that whatever
tool you use created the document correctly.

Regarding the second issue, you should note that the WS-I Basic Profile 1.0 (which is the profile supported by the J2EE 1.4 platform) does not address attachments. The section, "Parameter Types for Web Service Operations" on page 72, which discussed Java-MIME type mappings provided by the J2EE platform, advised that an efficient design is to use these mappings to send images and XML documents within a completely Java environment. Because the WS-I Basic Profile, version 1.0 does not address attachments, a Web service that uses these mappings may not be interoperable with clients on a non-Java platform.

❏ Since the WS-I Basic Profile 1.0 specification does not address attachments, a Web service using the Java-MIME mappings provided by the J2EE platform is not guaranteed to be interoperable.

Since most Web services rely on an exchange of business documents, and interoperability is not always guaranteed, it is important that you properly understand the options for handling XML documents. The section, "Exchanging XML Documents" on page 107, explains the various options available to Web services for exchanging XML documents in an interoperable manner. It should also be noted that the next version of the WS-I Basic Profile specification addresses a standard way to send attachments, and later versions of the J2EE platforms will incorporate this.

Last is the issue of handlers. Handlers, which give you access to SOAP messages, at the same time impose major responsibilities on you.

❏ When using handlers, you must be careful not to change a SOAP message to the degree that the message no longer complies with WS-I specifications, thereby endangering the interoperability of your service.

This ends the discussion of considerations for designing a Web service interface. The next sections examine other responsibilities of the interaction layer, such as receiving and delegating requests and formulating responses.

3.4.2 Receiving Requests

The interaction layer, through the endpoint, receives client requests. The platform maps the incoming client requests, which are in the form of SOAP messages, to method calls present in the Web service interface.

❐ Before delegating these incoming client requests to the Web service business
    logic, you should perform any required security validation, transformation of
    parameters, and other required preprocessing of parameters.

As noted in "Parameter Types for Web Service Operations" on page 72 and
elsewhere, Web service calls are basically method calls whose parameters are
passed as either Java objects, XML documents (`javax.xml.transform.Source`
objects), or even SOAP document fragments (`javax.xml.soap.SOAPElement`
objects).

❐ For parameters that are passed as Java objects (such as `String`, `int`, JAX-RPC
    value types, and so forth), do the application-specific parameter validation and
    map the incoming objects to domain-specific objects in the interaction layer
    before delegating the request to the processing layer.

You may have to undertake additional steps to handle XML documents that
are passed as parameters. These steps, which are best performed in the interaction
layer of your service, are as follows:

  1. The service endpoint should validate the incoming XML document against its
     schema. For details and guidelines on how and when to validate incoming
     XML documents, along with recommended validation techniques, refer to
     "Validating XML Documents" on page 139.

  2. When the service's processing layer and business logic are designed to deal
     with XML documents, you should transform the XML document to an inter-
     nally supported schema, if the schema for the XML document differs from the
     internal schema, before passing the document to the processing layer.

  3. When the processing layer deals with objects but the service interface receives
     XML documents, then, as part of the interaction layer, map the incoming XML
     documents to domain objects before delegating the request to the processing
     layer. For details and guidelines on mapping techniques for incoming XML
     documents, refer to "Mapping Schemas to the Application Data Model" on
     page 143.

❐ It is important that these three steps—validation of incoming parameters or
    XML documents, translation of XML documents to internal supported sche-

mas, and mapping documents to domain objects—be performed as close to the service endpoint as possible, and certainly in the service interaction layer.

A design such as this helps to catch errors early, and thus avoids unnecessary calls and round-trips to the processing layer. Figure 3.4 shows the recommended way to handle requests and responses in the Web service's interaction layer.

The Web service's interaction layer handles all incoming requests and delegates them to the business logic exposed in the processing layer. When implemented in this manner, the Web service interaction layer has several advantages, since it gives you a common location for the following tasks:

- Managing the handling of requests so that the service endpoint serves as the initial point of contact

- Invoking security services, including authentication and authorization

- Validating and transforming incoming XML documents and mapping XML documents to domain objects

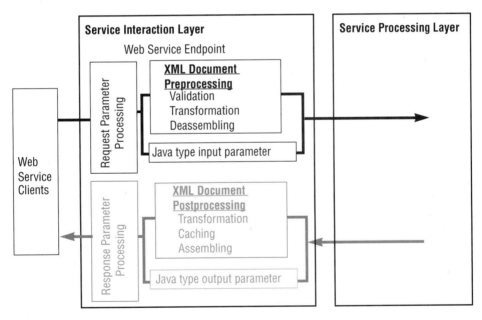

Figure 3.4   Web Service Request Processing

- Delegating to existing business logic

- Handling errors

It is generally advisable to do all common processing—such as security checks, logging, auditing, input validation, and so forth—for requests at the interaction layer as soon as a request is received and before passing it to the processing layer.

3.4.3   Delegating Web Service Requests to Processing Layer

After designing the request preprocessing tasks, the next step is to design how to delegate the request to the processing layer. At this point, consider the kind of processing the request requires, since this helps you decide how to delegate the request to the processing layer. All requests can be categorized into two large categories based on the time it takes to process the request, namely:

- A request that is processed in a short enough time so that a client can afford to block and wait to receive the response before proceeding further. In other words, the client and the service interact in a synchronous manner such that the invoking client blocks until the request is processed completely and the response is received.

- A request that takes a long time to be processed, so much so that it is not a good idea to make the client wait until the processing is completed. In other words, the client and the service interact in an asynchronous manner such that the invoking client need not block and wait until the request is processed completely.

Note: When referring to request processing, we use the terms synchronous and asynchronous from the point of view of when the client's request processing completes fully. Keep in mind that, under the hood, an asynchronous interaction between a client and a service might result in a synchronous invocation over the network, since HTTP is by its nature synchronous. Similarly, SOAP messages sent over HTTP are also synchronous.

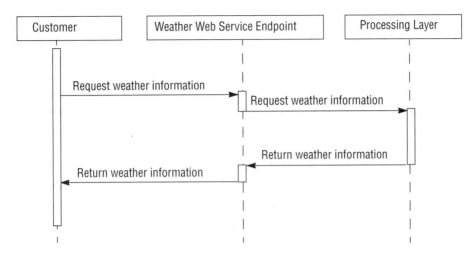

Figure 3.5   Weather Information Service Interaction

The weather information service is a good example of a synchronous interaction between a client and a service. When it receives a client's request, the weather service must look up the required information and send back a response to the client. This look-up and return of the information can be achieved in a relatively short time, during which the client can be expected to block and wait. The client continues its processing only after it obtains a response from the service. (See Figure 3.5.)

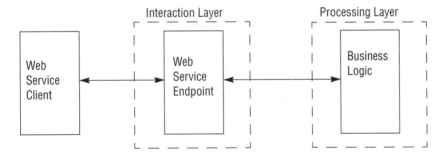

Figure 3.6   Synchronous Interaction Between Client and Service

A Web service such as this can be designed using a service endpoint that receives the client's request and then delegates the request directly to the service's appropriate logic in the processing layer. The service's processing layer processes the request and, when the processing completes, the service endpoint returns the response to the client. (See Figure 3.6.)

Code Example 3.15 shows the weather service interface performing some basic parameter validation checks in the interaction layer. The interface also gets required information and passes that information to the client in a synchronous manner:

```
public class WeatherServiceImpl implements
                    WeatherService, ServiceLifecycle {

    public void init(Object context) throws JAXRPCException {....}

    public String getWeather(String city)
                        throws CityNotFoundException {

        /** Validate parameters **/
        if(!validCity(city))
            throw new CityNotFoundException(....);

        /** Get weather info form processing layer and **/
        / **return results **/
        return (getWeatherInfoFromDataSource(city));
    }

    public void destroy() {....}
}
```

Code Example 3.15   Performing a Synchronous Client Interaction

Now let's examine an asynchronous interaction between a client and a service. When making a request for this type of service, the client cannot afford to wait for the response because of the significant time it takes for the service to process the request completely. Instead, the client may want to continue with some other processing. Later, when it receives the response, the client resumes whatever processing initiated the service request. Typically in these types of services, the content of the request parameters initiates and determines the processing workflow—the steps to fulfill the request—for the Web service. Often, fulfilling a request requires multiple workflow steps.

The travel agency service is a good example of an asynchronous interaction between a client and a service. A client requests arrangements for a particular trip by sending the travel service all pertinent information (most likely in an XML document). Based on the document's content, the service performs such steps as verifying the user's account, checking and getting authorization for the credit card, checking accommodations and transportation availability, building an itinerary, purchasing tickets, and so forth. Since the travel service must perform a series of often time-consuming steps in its normal workflow, the client cannot afford to pause and wait for these steps to complete.

Figure 3.7 shows one recommended approach for asynchronously delegating these types of Web service requests to the processing layer. In this architecture, the client sends a request to the service endpoint. The service endpoint validates the incoming request in the interaction layer and then delegates the client's request to the appropriate processing layer of the service. It does so by sending the request as a JMS message to a JMS queue or topic specifically designated for this type of request.

❑ Delegating a request to the processing layer through JMS *before* validating the request should be avoided.

Validation ensures that a request is correct. Delegating the request before validation may result in passing an invalid request to the processing layer, making error tracking and error handling overly complex. After the request is successfully delegated to the processing layer, the service endpoint may return a correlation identifier to the client. This correlation identifier is for the client's future reference and may help the client associate a response that corresponds to its previous request. If the business logic is implemented using enterprise beans, message-driven beans in the EJB tier read the request and initiate processing so that a response can ultimately be formulated.

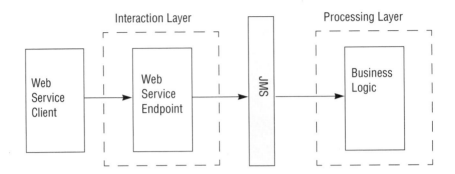

Figure 3.7   Asynchronous Interaction Between Client and Service

Figure 3.8 shows how the travel agency service might implement this interaction, and Code Example 3.16 shows the actual code that might be used.

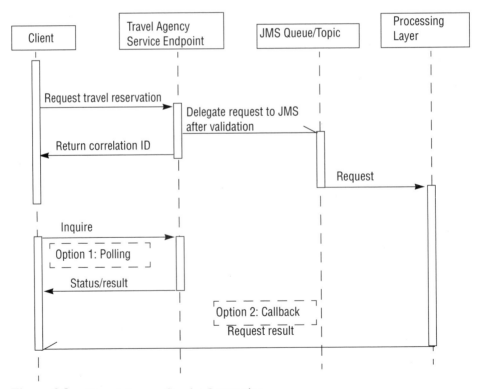

Figure 3.8   Travel Agency Service Interaction

In Figure 3.8, the vertical lines represent the passage of time, from top to bottom. The vertical rectangular boxes indicate when the entity (client or service) is busy processing the request or waiting for the other entity to complete processing. The half arrow type indicates asynchronous communication and the dashed vertical line indicates that the entity is free to work on other things while a request is being processed.

```java
public class ReservationRequestRcvr {
    public ReservationRequestRcvr() throws RemoteException {....}

    public String receiveRequest(Source reservationDetails) throws
                        RemoteException, InvalidRequestException{

        /** Validate incoming XML document **/
        String xmlDoc = getDocumentAsString(reservationDetails);
        if(!validDocument(xmlDoc))
            throw new InvalidRequestException(...);

        /** Get a JMS Queue and delegate the incoming request **/
        /** to the queue **/
        QueueConnectionFactory queueFactory =
            serviceLocator.getQueueConnectionFactory(....);
        Queue reservationRequestQueue =
                    serviceLocator.getQueue(...);
        QueueConnection connection =
            queueFactory.createQueueConnection();
        QueueSession session = connection.createQueueSession(false,
                    Session.AUTO_ACKNOWLEDGE);
        QueueSender queueSender = session.createSender(queue);
        TextMessage message = session.createTextMessage();
        message.setText(xmlDoc);
        queueSender.send(message);
        /** Generate and return a correlation identifier **/
        return generateCorrelationID();
    }
}
```

Code Example 3.16 Implementing Travel Agency Service Interaction

One question remains: How does the client get the final result of its request? The service may make the result of the client's request available in one of two ways:

- The client that invoked the service periodically checks the status of the request using the correlation identifier that was provided at the time the request was submitted. This is also known as polling, and it appears as Option 1 in Figure 3.8.

- Or, if the client itself is a Web service peer, the service calls back the client's service with the result. The client may use the correlation identifier to relate the response with the original request (Option 2 in Figure 3.8).

Often this is decided by the nature of the service itself. For example, if the service runs a business process workflow, the workflow requires the service to take appropriate action after processing the request.

3.4.4   Formulating Responses

After you delegate the request to the business logic portion of the application, and the business logic completes its processing, you are ready for the next step: to form the response to the request.

❏   You should perform response generation, which is simply constructing the method call return values and output parameters, on the interaction layer, as close as possible to the service endpoint.

This permits having a common location for response assembly and XML document transformations, particularly if the document you return to the caller must conform to a different schema from the internal schema. Keeping this functionality near the endpoint lets you implement data caching and avoid extra trips to the processing layer. (See Figure 3.9.).

Consider response generation from the weather information service's point-of-view. The weather information service may be used by a variety of client types, from browsers to rich clients to handheld devices. A well-designed weather information service would render its responses in formats suitable for these different client types.

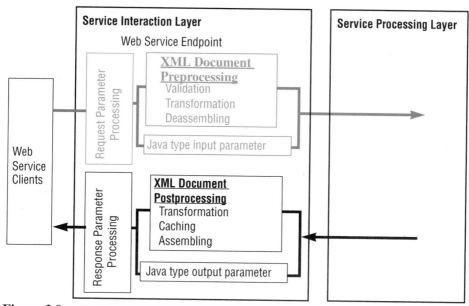

Figure 3.9   Web Service Response Processing

However, it is not good design to have a different implementation of the service's logic for each client type. Rather, it is better to design a common business logic for all client types. Then, in the interaction layer, transform the results per client type for rendering. It is thus important to consider the above guidelines, especially when your service has a common processing logic but potentially has different response rendering needs to fit its varied client types.

3.5   Processing Layer Design

The processing layer is where the business logic is applied to a Web service request. Recall that Web service is an interoperable way to expose new or existing applications. Hence, regardless of the means you use to expose your application's functionality, the business logic design issues are the same. You must still design the business logic by considering such issues as using enterprise beans, exposing a local or a remote EJB interface model, using container-managed or bean-managed persistence, and so forth.

❐   The issues and considerations for designing an application's processing or
     business logic layer, such as whether to perform this logic in the Web or EJB
     tier, are the same whether or not you use a Web service.

We do not address these business logic design issues here, since much of this
discussion has already been covered in the book *Designing Enterprise Applications with the J2EE™ Platform, Second Edition*, and you can refer to that book for
general guidelines and recommendations. You should also refer to the BluePrints
Web site at `http://java.sun.com/blueprints` for recommendations on designing
an application's business processing logic.

In addition to these general guidelines, there are some specific issues to keep
in mind when designing the processing layer of a Web service.

• **Keep the processing layer independent of the interaction layer**. By keeping
  the layers independent and loosely coupled, the processing layer remains generic and can support different types of clients, such as Web service clients,
  classic Web clients, and so forth. To achieve loose coupling between the layers, consider using delegate classes that encapsulate the access to business
  components.

• **Bind XML documents to Java objects in the interaction layer**. There are
  times when your Web service expects to receive from a client an XML document containing a complete request, but the service's business logic has no
  need to operate on the document. On these occasions, it is recommended that
  the interaction layer bind the XML document contents to Java objects before
  passing the request to the processing layer. Since the processing logic does not
  have to perform the XML-to-Java conversion, a single processing layer can
  support XML documents that rely on different schemas. This also makes it
  easy to support multiple versions of an XML schema.

Keep in mind that your processing logic can operate on the contents of an
XML document received from a client. Refer to "Handling XML Documents in a
Web Service" on page 105, which highlights issues to consider when you pass
XML documents to your business processing logic.

Depending on your application scenario, your processing layer may be
required to work with other Web service peers to complete a client's request. If so,
your processing layer effectively becomes a client of another Web service. Refer
to Chapter 5 for guidelines on Web service clients. In other circumstances, your

processing layer may have to interact with EISs. For these cases, refer to Chapter 6 for guidelines.

3.6   Publishing a Web Service

Up to now, this chapter has covered guidelines for designing and implementing your Web service. Just as important, your Web service needs to be accessible to its intended clients. Recall that some Web services are intended for use by the general public. Other Web services are intended to be used only between trusted business partners (inter-enterprise), and still others are intended for use just within an enterprise (intra-enterprise).

Regardless of whether a service is to be accessible to the public, other enterprises, or even within a single enterprise, you must first make the details about the Web service—its interface, parameters, where the service is located, and so forth—accessible to clients. You do so by making a description of the Web service available to interested parties. As noted in "Web Services Description Language" on page 36, WSDL is the standard language for describing a service. Making this WSDL description available to clients enables them to use the service.

Once the WSDL is ready, you have the option to publish it in a registry. The next section describes when you might want to publish the WSDL in a registry. If you make the WSDL description of your service available in a public registry, then a Java-based client can use the JAXR APIs to look up the description of your service and then use the service. For that matter, a client can use the same JAXR APIs to look up the description of any Web service with an available WSDL description. This section examines registries from the point of view of a service developer.

3.6.1   Publishing a Service in a Registry

Publishing a service in a registry is one method of making the service available to clients. If you decide to publish your service in a registry, you decide on the type of registry to use based on the likely usage scenarios for your service. Registries run the gamut from public registries to corporate registries available only within a single enterprise.

❏   You may want to register Web services for general public consumption on a well-known public registry.

When you make your service available through a public registry, you essentially open the service's accessibility to the widest possible audience. When a service is registered in a public registry, any client, even one with no prior knowledge of the service, may look up and use the service. Keep in mind that the public registry holds the Web service description, which consists not only of the service's WSDL description but also any XML schemas referenced by the service description. In short, your Web service must publish its public XML schemas and any additional schemas defined in the context of the service. You also *must* publish on the same public registry XML schemas referred to by the Web service description.

❏   When a Web service is strictly for intra-enterprise use, you may publish a Web service description on a corporate registry within the enterprise.

❏   You do not need to use a registry if all the customers of your Web services are dedicated partners and there is an agreement among the partners on the use of the services. When this is the case, you can publish your Web service description—the WSDL and referenced XML schemas—at a well-known location with the proper access protections.

3.6.2   Understanding Registry Concepts

When considering whether to publish your service via a registry, it is important to understand some of the concepts, such as repositories and taxonomies, that are associated with registries.

Public registries are not repositories. Rather than containing complete details on services, public registries contain only details about what services are available and how to access these services. For example, a service selling adventure packages cannot register its complete catalog of products. A registry can only store the type of service, its location, and information required to access the service. A client interested in a service must first discover the service from the registry and then bind with the service to obtain the service's complete catalog of products. Once it obtains the service's catalog, the client can ascertain whether the particular service meets its needs. If not, the client must go back to the registry and repeat the discovery and binding process—the client looks in the registry for some other service that potentially offers what it wants, binds to that service, obtains and assesses its catalog, and so forth. Since this process, which is not insignificant, may have to be repeated several times, it is easy to see that it is important to register a service under its proper taxonomy.

❐ Register a service under the proper taxonomy.

It is important to register your service under the proper taxonomies. When you want to publish your service on a registry, either a public or corporate registry, you must do so against a taxonomy that correctly classifies or categorizes your Web service. It is important to decide on the proper taxonomy, as this affects the ease with which clients can find and use your service. Several well-defined industry standard taxonomies exist today, such as those defined by organizations such as the North American Industry Classification System (NAICS).

Using existing, well-known taxonomies gives clients of your Web service a standard base from which to search for your service, making it easy for clients to find your service. For example, suppose your travel business provides South Sea island-related adventure packages as well as alpine or mountaineering adventures. Rather than create your own taxonomy to categorize your service, clients can more easily find your service if you publish your service description using two different standard taxonomies: one taxonomy for island adventures and another for alpine and mountaineering adventures.

You can publish your Web service in more than one registry. To further help clients find your service, it is also a good idea to publish in as many applicable categories as possible. For example, a travel business selling adventure packages might register using a product category taxonomy as well as a geographical taxonomy. This gives clients a chance to use optimal strategies for locating a service. For example, if multiple instances of a service exist for a particular product, the client might further refine its selection by considering geographical location and choosing a service close to its own location. Using the travel business service as an example, such a service might register under the taxonomies for types of adventure packages (island and mountaineering), as well as under the taxonomies for the locales in which the adventure packages are provided (Mount Kilimanjaro or Tahiti), thus making it as easy as possible for a prospective client to locate its services.

3.6.3 Registry Implementation Scenarios

Once you decide to publish your service and establish the taxonomies that best identify your service, you are ready to implement your decisions. Before doing so, you may find it helpful to examine some of the registry implementation scenarios that you may encounter.

When a registry is used, we have seen that the service provider publishes the Web service description on a registry and clients discover and bind to the Web service to use its services. In general, a client must perform three steps to use a Web service:

1. The client must determine how to access the service's methods, such as determining the service method parameters, return values, and so forth. This is referred to as discovering the service definition interface.

2. The client must locate the actual Web service; that is, find the service's address. This is referred to as discovering the service implementation.

3. The client must be bound to the service's specific location, and this may occur on one of three occasions:

   - When the client is developed (called static binding)
   - When the client is deployed (also called static binding)
   - During runtime (called dynamic binding)

These three steps may produce three scenarios. The particular scenario depends on when the binding occurs and whether the client is implemented solely for a specific service or is a generic client. The following paragraphs describe these scenarios. (See Table 3.2 for a summary.) They also note important points you should consider when designing and implementing a Web service. (Chapter 5 considers these scenarios from the point of view of a client.)

- Scenario 1: The Web service has an agreement with its partners and publishes its WSDL description and referenced XML schemas at a well-known, specified location. It expects its client developers to know this location. When this is the case, the client is implemented with the service's interface in mind. When it is built, the client is already designed to look up the service interface directly rather than using a registry to find the service.

- Scenario 2: Similar to scenario 1, the Web service publishes its WSDL description and XML schemas at a well-known location, and it expects its partners to either know this location or be able to discover it easily. Or, when the partner is built, it can use a tool to dynamically discover and then include either the service's specific implementation or the service's interface definition, along with its specific implementation. In this case, binding is static because the partner is built when the service interface definition and implementation are already known to it, even though this information was found dynamically.

- Scenario 3: The service implements an interface at a well-known location, or it expects its clients to use tools to find the interface at build time. Since the Web service's clients are generic clients—they are not clients designed solely to use this Web service—you must design the service so that it can be registered in a registry. Such generic clients dynamically find a service's specific implementation at runtime using registries. Choose the type of registry for the service—either public, corporate, or private—depending on the types of its clients—either general public or intra-enterprise—its security constraints, and so forth.

Table 3.2   Discovery-Binding Scenarios for Clients

Scena rios	Discover Service Interface Definition	Discover Service Implementation	Binding to Specific Location
1	None	None	Static
2	None or dynamic at build time	Dynamic at build time	Static
3	None or dynamic at build time	Dynamic at runtime	Dynamic at build time

3.7   Handling XML Documents in a Web Service

Up to now, this chapter addressed issues applicable to all Web service implementations. There are additional considerations when a Web service implementation expects to receive an XML document containing all the information from a client, and which the service uses to start a business process to handle the request. There are several reasons why it is appropriate to exchange documents:

- Documents, especially business documents, may be very large, and as such, they are often sent as a batch of related information. They may be compressed independently from the SOAP message.

- Documents may be legally binding business documents. At a minimum, their original form needs to be conserved through the exchange and, more than likely, they may need to be archived and kept as evidence in case of disagreement.

For these documents, the complete infoset of the original document should be preserved, including comments and external entity references (as well as the referred entities).

- Some application processing requires the complete document infoset, including comments and external entity references. As with the legally binding documents, it is necessary to preserve the complete infoset, including comments and external entity references, of the original document.

- When sent as attachments, it is possible to handle documents that may conform to schemas expressed in languages not supported by the Web service endpoint or that are prohibited from being present within a SOAP message infoset (such as the Document Type Declaration `<!DOCTYPE>` for a DTD-based schema).

For example, consider the travel agency Web service, which typically receives a client request as an XML document containing all information needed to arrange a particular trip. The information in the document includes details about the customer's account, credit card status, desired travel destinations, preferred airlines, class of travel, dates, and so forth. The Web service uses the documents contents to perform such steps as verifying the customer's account, obtaining authorization for the credit card, checking accommodations and transportation availability, building an itinerary, and purchasing tickets.

In essence, the service, which receives the request with the XML document, starts a business process to perform a series of steps to complete the request. The contents of the XML document are used throughout the business process. Handling this type of scenario effectively requires some considerations in addition to the general ones for all Web services.

❏ Good design expects XML documents to be received as `javax.xml.transform.Source` objects. See "Exchanging XML Documents" on page 107, which discusses exchanging XML documents as parameters. Keep in mind the effect on interoperability (see "Interoperability" on page 86).

❏ It is good design to do the validation and any required transformation of the XML documents as close to the endpoint as possible. Validation and transformation should be done before applying any processing logic to the document content. See Figure 3.4 and the discussion on receiving requests in "Receiving Requests" on page 89.

❐ It is important to consider the processing time for a request and whether the client waits for the response. When a service expects an XML document as input and starts a lengthy business process based on the document contents, then clients typically do not want to wait for the response. Good design when processing time may be extensive is to delegate a request to a JMS queue or topic and return a correlation identifier for the client's future reference. (Recall Figure 3.7 on page 96 and its discussion.)

The following sections discuss other considerations.

3.7.1   Exchanging XML Documents

As noted earlier, there are times when you may have to exchange XML documents as part of your Web service and such documents are received as parameters of a method call. The J2EE platform provides three ways to exchange XML documents.

The first option is to use the Java-MIME mappings provided by the J2EE platform. See Table 3.1 on page 75. With this option, the Web service endpoint receives documents as `javax.xml.transform.Source` objects. (See Code Example 3.3 on page 75.) Along with the document, the service endpoint can also expect to receive other JAX-RPC arguments containing metadata, processing requirements, security information, and so forth. When an XML document is passed as a `Source` object, the container automatically handles the document as an attachment—effectively, the container implementation handles the document-passing details for you. This frees you from the intricacies of sending and retrieving documents as part of the endpoint's request/response handling.

❐ Passing XML documents as `Source` objects is the most effective option in a completely Java-based environment (one in which all Web service clients are based on Java). However, sending documents as `Source` objects may not be interoperable with non-Java clients. (As already noted in the section "Interoperability" on page 86, standard ways to exchange attachments are currently being formulated. Future versions of the J2EE platform will incorporate these standards once they are final.)

The second option is to design your service endpoint such that it receives documents as `String` types. Code Example 3.17 shows the WSDL description for a service that receives documents as String types, illustrating how the WSDL maps the XML document.

```
<?xml version="1.0" encoding="UTF-8"?>
<definitions ...>
    <types/>
    <message name="PurchaseOrderService_submitPurchaseOrder">
        <part name="PurchaseOrderXMLDoc" type="xsd:string"/>
    </message>
    <message
            name="PurchaseOrderService_submitPurchaseOrderResponse">
        <part name="result" type="xsd:string"/>
    </message>
    <portType name="PurchaseOrderService">
        <operation name="submitPurchaseOrder"
                            parameterOrder="PurchaseOrderXMLDoc">
            <input
            message="tns:PurchaseOrderService_submitPurchaseOrder"/>
            <output message=
            "tns:PurchaseOrderService_submitPurchaseOrderResponse"/>
        </operation>
    </portType>
    ...
</definitions>
```

Code Example 3.17   Mapping XML Document to `xsd:string`

Code Example 3.18 shows the equivalent Java interface for the WSDL shown in Code Example 3.17.

```
public interface PurchaseOrderService extends Remote {
    public String submitPurchaseOrder(String poDocument)
            throws RemoteException, InvalidOrderException;
}
```

Code Example 3.18   Receiving an XML Document as a `String` object

If you are developing your service using the Java-to-WSDL approach, and the service must exchange XML documents and be interoperable with clients on any platform, then passing documents as `String` objects may be your only option.

❑ There may be a performance drawback to sending an XML document as a String object: As the document size grows, the String equivalent size of the document grows as well. As a result, the payload size of the message you send also grows. In addition, the XML document loses its original format since sending a document as a String object sends it in a canonical format.

The third option is to exchange the XML document as a SOAP document fragment. With this option, you map the XML document to xsd:anyType in the service's WSDL file.

❑ It is recommended that Web services exchange XML documents as SOAP document fragments because passing XML documents in this manner is both portable across J2EE implementations and interoperable with all platforms.

❑ To pass SOAP document fragments, you must implement your service using the WSDL-to-Java approach.

For example, the travel agency service receives an XML document representing a purchase order that contains all details about the customer's preferred travel plans. To implement this service, you define the WSDL for the service and, in the WSDL, you map the XML document type as xsd:anyType. See Code Example 3.19.

```
<?xml version="1.0" encoding="UTF-8"?>
<definitions ...>
    <types/>
    <message name="PurchaseOrderService_submitPurchaseOrder">
        <part name="PurchaseOrderXMLDoc" type="xsd:anyType"/>
    </message>
    <message
            name="PurchaseOrderService_submitPurchaseOrderResponse">
        <part name="result" type="xsd:string"/>
    </message>
    <portType name="PurchaseOrderService">
        <operation name="submitPurchaseOrder"
                        parameterOrder="PurchaseOrderXMLDoc">
            <input
            message="tns:PurchaseOrderService_submitPurchaseOrder"/>
            <output message=
```

```
                  "tns:PurchaseOrderService_submitPurchaseOrderResponse"/>
            </operation>
        </portType>
        ...
    </definitions>
```

Code Example 3.19   Mapping XML document to `xsd:anyType`

A WSDL mapping of the XML document type to `xsd:anyType` requires the platform to map the document parameter as a `javax.xml.soap.SOAPElement` object. For example, Code Example 3.20 shows the Java interface generated for the WSDL description in Code Example 3.19.

```
public interface PurchaseOrderService extends Remote {
    public String submitPurchaseOrder(SOAPElement
                        purchaseOrderXMLDoc) throws RemoteException;
}
```

Code Example 3.20   Java Interface for WSDL in Code Example 3.19

In this example, the `SOAPElement` parameter in `submitPurchaseOrder` represents the SOAP document fragment sent by the client. For the travel agency service, this is the purchase order. The service can parse the received SOAP document fragment using the `javax.xml.soap.SOAPElement` API. Or, the service can use JAXB to map the document fragment to a Java `Object` or transform it to another schema. A client of this Web service builds the purchase order document using the client platform-specific API for building SOAP document fragments—on the Java platform, this is the `javax.xml.soap.SOAPElement` API—and sends the document as one of the Web service's call parameters.

When using the WSDL-to-Java approach, you can directly map the document to be exchanged to its appropriate schema in the WSDL. The corresponding generated Java interface represents the document as its equivalent Java `Object`. As a result, the service endpoint never sees the document that is exchanged in its original document form. It also means that the endpoint is tightly coupled to the document's schema: Any change in the document's schema requires a corresponding change to the endpoint. If you do not want such tight coupling, consider using `xsd:anyType` to map the document.

3.7.2 Separating Document Manipulation from Processing Logic

When your service's business logic operates on the contents of an incoming XML document, the business processing logic must at a minimum read the document, if not modify the document. By separating the document manipulation logic from the processing logic, a developer can switch between various document manipulation mechanisms without affecting the processing logic. In addition, there is a clear division between developer skills.

❏ It is a good practice to separate the XML document manipulation logic from the business logic.

The "Abstracting XML Processing from Application Logic" section on page 155 provides more information on how to accomplish this separation and its merits.

3.7.3 Fragmenting XML Documents

When your service's business logic operates on the contents of an incoming XML document, it is a good idea to break XML documents into logical fragments when appropriate. When the processing logic receives an XML document that contains all information for processing a request, the XML document usually has well-defined segments for different entities, and each segment contains the details about a specific entity.

❏ Rather than pass the entire document to different components handling various stages of the business process, it's best if the processing logic breaks the document into fragments and passes only the required fragments to other components or services that implement portions of the business process logic.

See "Fragmenting Incoming XML Documents" on page 153 for more details on fragmentation.

3.7.4 Using XML

XML, while it has many benefits, also has performance disadvantages. You should weigh the trade-offs of passing XML documents through the business logic processing stages. The pros and cons of passing XML documents take on greater significance when the business logic implementation spans multiple containers. Refer to

Chapter 5, specifically the section entitled "Use XML Judiciously" on page 194, which provides guidelines on this issue. Following these guidelines may help minimize the performance overhead that comes with passing XML documents through workflow stages.

Also, when deciding on an approach, keep in mind the costs involved for using XML and weigh them along with the recommendations on parsing, validation, and binding documents to Java objects. See Chapter 4 for a discussion of these topics.

3.7.5   Using JAXM and SAAJ Technologies

The J2EE platform provides an array of technologies—including mandatory technologies such as JAX-RPC and SAAJ and optional technologies such as Java™ API for XML Messaging (JAXM)—that enable message and document exchanges with SOAP. Each of these J2EE technologies offers a different level of support for SOAP-based messaging and communication. (See Chapter 2 for the discussion on JAX-RPC and SAAJ.)

An obvious question that arises is: Why not use JAXM or SAAJ technologies in scenarios where you have to pass XML documents? If you recall:

- SAAJ lets developers deal directly with SOAP messages, and is best suited for point-to-point messaging environments. SAAJ is better for developers who want more control over the SOAP messages being exchanged and for developers using handlers.

- JAXM defines an infrastructure for guaranteed delivery of messages. It provides a way of sending and receiving XML documents and guaranteeing their receipt, and is designed for use cases that involve storing and forwarding XML documents and messages.

SAAJ is considered more useful for advanced developers who thoroughly know the technology and who must deal directly with SOAP messages.

Using JAXM for scenarios that require passing XML documents may be a good choice. Note, though, that JAXM is optional in the J2EE 1.4 platform. As a result, a service developed with JAXM may not be portable. When you control both end points of a Web service, it may make more sense to consider using JAXM.

3.8   Deploying and Packaging a Service Endpoint

Up to now, we have examined Web services on the J2EE platform in terms of design, development, and implementation. Once you complete the Web services implementation, you must write its deployment descriptors, package the service with all its components, and deploy the service.

❐   Developers should, if at all possible, use tools or IDEs to develop a Web ser-
     vice. These Web service development tools and IDEs automatically create the
     proper deployment descriptors for the service and correctly handle the packag-
     ing of the service—steps necessary for a service to operate properly. Further-
     more, tools and IDEs hide these details from the developer.

Although you can expect your development tool to perform these tasks for you, it is good to have a conceptual understanding of the J2EE 1.4 platform deployment descriptor and packaging structure, since they determine how a service is deployed on a J2EE server and the service's availability to clients. This section, which provides a conceptual overview of the deployment and packaging details, is not essential reading. Nonetheless, you may find it worthwhile to see how these details contribute to portable, interoperable Web services.

3.8.1   Service Information in the Deployment Descriptors

To successfully deploy a service, the developer provides the following information.

- Deployment-related details of the service implementation, including the Web
  service interface, the classes that implement the Web service interface, and so
  forth.

- Details about the Web services to be deployed, such as the ports and mappings

- Details on the WSDL port-to-port component relationship

More specifically, the deployment descriptor contains information about a service's port and associated WSDL. Recall from "Web Service Technologies Integrated in J2EE Platform" on page 49:

- A port component (also called a port) gives a view of the service to clients such that the client need not worry about how the service has been implemented.

- Each port has an associated WSDL.

- Each port has an associated service endpoint (and its implementation). The endpoint services all requests that pass through the location defined in the WSDL port address.

To begin, the service implementation declares its deployment details in the appropriate module-specific deployment descriptors. For example, a service implementation that uses a JAX-RPC service endpoint declares its details in the WEB-INF/web.xml file using the servlet-class element. (See Code Example 3.21.)

```
<web-app ...>
    ...
    <servlet>
        <description>Endpoint for Some Web Service</description>
        <display-name>SomeWebService</display-name>
        <servlet-name>SomeService</servlet-name>
        <servlet-class>com.a.b.c.SomeServiceImpl</servlet-class>
        <load-on-startup>0</load-on-startup>
    </servlet>
    <servlet-mapping>
        <servlet-name>SomeService</servlet-name>
        <url-pattern>/webservice/SomeService</url-pattern>
    </servlet-mapping>
    ...
</web-app>
```

Code Example 3.21 web.xml File for a JAX-RPC Service Endpoint

Note that when you have a service that functions purely as a Web service using JAX-RPC service endpoints, some specifications in the web.xml file, such as <error-page> and <welcome-file-list>, have no effect.

A service implementation that uses an EJB service endpoint declares its deployment details in the file META-INF/ejb-jar.xml using the session element. (See Code Example 3.22.)

```
<ejb-jar ...>
    <display-name>Some Enterprise Bean</display-name>
    <enterprise-beans>
        <session>
            <ejb-name>SomeBean</ejb-name>
            <service-endpoint>com.a.b.c.SomeIntf</service-endpoint>
            <ejb-class>com.a.b.c.SomeServiceEJB</ejb-class>
            <session-type>Stateless</session-type>
            <transaction-type>Container</transaction-type>
        </session>
    </enterprise-beans>
    ...
</ejb-jar>
```

Code Example 3.22 `ejb-jar.xml` File for an EJB Service Endpoint

Next, the details of the port are specified. The Web service deployment descriptor, called `webservices.xml`, defines and declares the structural details for the port of a Web service. This file contains the following information:

- A logical name for the port that is also unique among all port components (`port-component-name` element)

- The service endpoint interface for the port (`service-endpoint-interface` element)

- The name of the class that implements the service interface (`service-impl-bean` element)

- The WSDL file for the service (`wsdl-file` element)

- A QName for the port (`wsdl-port` element)

- A correlation between WSDL definitions and actual Java interfaces and definitions using the mapping file (`jaxrpc-mapping-file` element)

- Optional details on any handlers

The reference to the service implementation bean, specified using the `service-impl-bean` element in `webservices.xml`, is either a `servlet-link` or an `ejb-link` depending on whether the endpoint is a JAX-RPC or EJB service endpoint. This link element associates the Web service port to the actual endpoint implementation defined in either the web.xml or ejb-jar.xml file.

The JAX-RPC mapping file, which is specified using the jaxrpc-mapping-file element in webservices.xml, keeps details on the relationships and mappings between WSDL definitions and corresponding Java interfaces and definitions. The information contained in this file, along with information in the WSDL, is used to create stubs and ties for deployed services.

Thus, the Web services deployment descriptor, webservices.xml, links the WSDL port information to a unique port component and from there to the actual implementation classes and Java-to-WSDL mappings. Code Example 3.23 is an example of the Web services deployment descriptor for our sample weather Web service, which uses a JAX-RPC service endpoint.

```
<webservices ...>
    <description>Web Service Descriptor for weather service
    </description>
    <webservice-description>
        <webservice-description-name>
            WeatherWebService
        </webservice-description-name>
        <wsdl-file>
            WEB-INF/wsdl/WeatherWebService.wsdl
        </wsdl-file>
        <jaxrpc-mapping-file>
            WEB-INF/WeatherWebServiceMapping.xml
        </jaxrpc-mapping-file>
        <port-component>
            <description>port component description</description>
            <port-component-name>
                WeatherServicePort
            </port-component-name>
            <wsdl-port xmlns:weatherns="urn:WeatherWebService">
                weatherns:WeatherServicePort
            </wsdl-port>
            <service-endpoint-interface>
                endpoint.WeatherService
            </service-endpoint-interface>
            <service-impl-bean>
                <servlet-link>WeatherService</servlet-link>
```

```
        </service-impl-bean>
      </port-component>
    </webservice-description>
  </webservices>
```

Code Example 3.23   Weather Web Service Deployment Descriptor

3.8.2   Package Structure

Once the service implementation and deployment descriptors are completed, the following files should be packaged into the appropriate J2EE module:

- The WSDL file

- The service endpoint interface, including its implementation and dependent classes

- The JAX-RPC mapping file, which specifies the package name containing the generated runtime classes and defines the namespace URI for the service. See Code Example 5.21 on page 242.

- The Web service deployment descriptor

The type of endpoint used for the service implementation determines the type of the J2EE module to use.

❐   The appropriate J2EE module for a service with a JAX-RPC service endpoint is a WAR file. A service using an EJB service endpoint must be packaged in an EJB-JAR file.

The package structure is as follows:

- WSDL files are located relative to the root of the module.

- The service interface, the service implementation classes, and the dependent classes are packaged just like any other J2EE component.

- The JAX-RPC mapping file is located relative to the root of the module (typically in the same place as the module's deployment descriptor).

- The Web service deployment descriptor location depends on the type of service endpoint, as follows:

  - For an EJB service endpoint, the Web service deployment descriptor is packaged in an EJB-JAR in the META-INF directory as `META-INF/webservice.xml`

  - For a JAX-RPC service endpoint, the deployment descriptor is packaged in a WAR file in the WEB-INF directory as `WEB-INF/webservices.xml`.

See Figure 3.10, which shows a typical package structure for a Web service using an EJB endpoint. Figure 3.11 shows the typical structure for a Web service using a JAX-RPC endpoint.

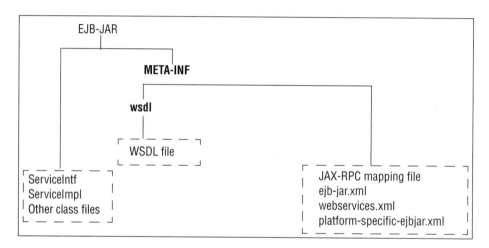

Figure 3.10   Package Structure for EJB Endpoint

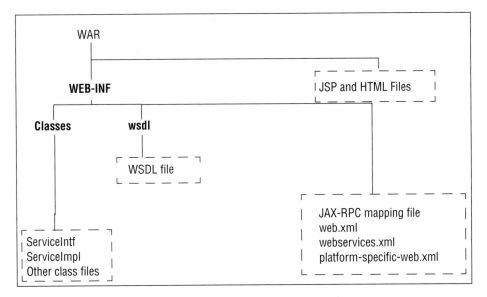

Figure 3.11   Package Structure for JAX-RPC Service Endpoint

3.9   Conclusion

This chapter began with a description of Web service fundamentals. It described the underlying flow of a typical Web service on the Java platform, showing how the various components making up clients and services pass requests and responses among themselves. The chapter also described some example scenarios, which it used to illustrate various concepts. Once the groundwork was set, the chapter discussed the key design decisions that a Web service developer needs to make, principally the design of a service as an interaction and a processing layer. It traced how to go about making design decisions and recommending good design choices for specific scenarios.

The next chapter focuses on developing Web service clients.

CHAPTER 4

XML Processing

W EB service applications often pass information using XML documents. Application developers whose applications accept XML documents must understand how best to extract information from these XML documents and use that information in their business processing. They must also understand how to assemble XML documents from the results of this business processing.

This chapter provides an extensive coverage of XML document handling. To make it more manageable, you may want to concentrate on the sections of particular interest to you. These sections are as follows:

- "XML Overview" on page 122—Provides an overview of basic XML concepts. If you are not familiar with XML, this section provides a concise summary of key XML concepts and technologies. Even if you do know XML well, you may want to skim this part since it highlights issues important for designing XML-based applications.

- "Outline for Handling XML Documents" on page 128—Describes how applications typically handle XML documents.

- "Designing XML-Based Applications" on page 131—Covers such design topics as receiving and sending XML documents, validating XML documents, mapping XML documents to data objects, applying business logic on documents or objects, and keeping business processing logic separate from XML processing logic. This discussion also includes recommendations that help determine how to best design an XML-based application. Architects and application designers should find this section of particular interest.

- "Implementing XML-Based Applications" on page 164—Provides guidelines for developers on how best to implement XML-based applications. This section includes an in-depth discussion of the various XML-processing technologies that developers can use to implement their applications. It covers the advantages and disadvantages of the principal XML programming models and provides recommendations for when you should consider using each of the models.

- "Performance Considerations" on page 182—Outlines guidelines for maximizing performance. This section makes specific recommendations for approaches developers can take to keep performance at an acceptable level.

Many of these concepts for designing XML-based applications are generic in nature; they apply to any application handling XML documents. Since Web services are XML-based applications, these concepts especially apply to the design of Web service endpoints and clients. The chapter emphasizes the design considerations that should be kept in mind when developing Web service endpoints and clients.

Although it presents the basic XML concepts, this chapter assumes that you have a working knowledge of the XML processing technologies, especially SAX, DOM, XSLT, and JAXB. (Refer to Chapter 2 for more details on these technologies.) Whenever possible, the chapter uses the scenarios introduced in Chapter 1 to illustrate various points.

4.1   XML Overview

While you may already be familiar with XML, it is important to understand XML concepts from the point of view of applications handling XML documents. With this knowledge, you are in a better position to judge the impact of your design decisions on the implementation and performance of your XML-based applications.

Essentially, XML is a markup language that enables hierarchical data content extrapolated from programming language data structures to be represented as a marked-up text document. As a markup language, XML uses tags to mark pieces of data. Each tag attempts to assign meaning to the data associated with it; that is, transform the data into information. If you know SGML (Standard Generalized Markup Language) and HTML (HyperText Markup Language), then XML will look familiar to you. XML is derived from SGML and also bears some resemblance to HTML, which is also a subset of SGML. But unlike HTML, XML focuses on representing data rather than end-user presentation. While XML aims to separate data from presentation, the end-user presentation of XML data is nevertheless specifically addressed by additional XML-based technologies in rich and various ways.

Although XML documents are not primarily intended to be read by users, the XML specification clearly states as one of its goals that "XML documents should be human-legible and reasonably clear." This legibility characteristic contributed to XML's adoption. XML supports both computer and human communications, and it ensures openness, transparency, and platform-independence compared to a binary format.

A grammar along with its vocabulary (also called a schema in its generic acception) defines the set of tags and their nesting (the tag structure) that may be allowed or that are expected in an XML document. In addition, a schema can be specific to a particular domain, and domain-specific schemas are sometimes referred to as markup vocabularies. The Document Type Definition (DTD) syntax, which is part of the core XML specification, allows for the definition of domain-specific schemas and gives XML its "eXtensible" capability. Over time, there have been an increasing number of these XML vocabularies or XML-based languages, and this extensibility is a key factor in XML's success. In particular, XML and its vocabularies are becoming the lingua franca of business-to-business (B2B) communication.

In sum, XML is a metalanguage used to define other markup languages. While tags help to describe XML documents, they are not sufficient, even when carefully chosen, to make a document completely self-describing. Schemas written as DTDs, or in some other schema language such as the W3C XML Schema Definition (XSD), improve the descriptiveness of XML documents since they may define a document's syntax or exact structure. But even with the type systems introduced by modern schema languages, it is usually necessary to accompany an XML schema with specification documents that describe the domain-specific semantics of the various XML tags. These specifications are intended for application developers and others who create and process the XML documents. Schemas are necessary for specifying and validating the structure and, to some extent, the content of XML documents. Even so, developers must ultimately build the XML schema's tag semantics into the applications that produce and consume the documents. However, thanks to the well-defined XML markup scheme, intermediary applications such as document routers can still handle documents partially or in a generic way without knowing the complete domain-specific semantics of the documents.

The handling of the following XML document concepts may have a significant impact on the design and performance of an XML-based application:

- **Well-formedness**—An XML document needs to be well formed to be parsed. A well-formed XML document conforms to XML syntax rules and constraints, such as:

  - The document must contain exactly one root element, and all other elements are children of this root element.

  - All markup tags must be balanced; that is, each element must have a start and an end tag.

  - Elements may be nested but they must not overlap.

  - All attribute values must be in quotes.

- **Validity**—According to the XML specification, an XML document is considered valid if it has an associated DTD declaration and it complies with the constraints expressed in the DTD. To be valid, an XML document must meet the following criteria:

  - Be well-formed

  - Refer to an accessible DTD-based schema using a Document Type Declaration: `<!DOCTYPE>`

  - Conform to the referenced DTD

  With the emergence of new schema languages, the notion of validity is extended beyond the initial specification to other, non-DTD-based schema languages, such as XSD. For these non-DTD schemas, the XML document may not refer explicitly to the schema, though it may only contain a hint to the schema to which it conforms. The application is responsible for enabling the validation of the document. Regardless of any hints, an application may still forcefully validate this document against a particular schema. (See "Validating XML Documents" on page 139.)

- **Logical and physical forms**—An XML document has one logical form that may be laid out potentially in numerous physical forms. The physical form (or forms) represent the document's storage layout. The physical form consists of storage units called entities, which contain either parsed or unparsed data. Parsed entities are invoked by name using entity references. When parsed, the reference is replaced by the contents of the entity, and this replacement text becomes an integral part of the document. The logical form is the entire document regardless of its physical or storage layout.

An XML processor, in the course of processing a document, may need to find the content of an external entity—this process is called entity resolution. The XML processor may know some identifying information about the external entity, such as its name, system, or public identifier (in the form of a URI: URL or URN), and so forth, which it can use to determine the actual location of the entity. When performing entity resolution, the XML processor maps the known identifying information to the actual location of the entity. This mapping information may be accessible through an entity resolution catalog.

4.1.1   Document Type and W3C XML Schema Definitions

Originally, the Document Type Definition (DTD) syntax, which is part of the core XML 1.0 specification and became a recommendation in 1998, allowed for the definition of domain-specific schemas. However, with the growth in the adoption of XML (particularly in the B2B area), it became clear that the DTD syntax had some limitations. DTD's limitations are:

- It uses a syntax that does not conform to other XML documents.

- It does not support namespaces. However, with some cleverness, it is possible to create namespace-aware DTD schemas.

- It cannot express data types. With DTD, attribute values and character data in elements are considered to be text (or character strings).

To address these shortcomings, the W3C defined the XML Schema Definition language (XSD). (XSD became an official recommendation of the W3C in 2001.) XSD addresses some of the shortcomings of DTD, as do other schema languages, such as RELAX-NG. In particular, XSD:

- Is itself an application of XML based on the XML specification—An XML schema can be written and manipulated just like an XML document.

- Supports namespaces—By supporting namespaces, XSD allows for modular schema design and permits the composition of XSD schema definitions. It particularly solves the problem of conflicting tag names, which can often occur with modularization.

- Supports data types—XSD provides a type system that supports type derivation and restriction, in addition to supporting various built-in simple types, such as integer, float, date, and time.

The following convention applies to the rest of the chapter: The noun "schema" or "XML schema" designates the grammar or schema to which an XML document must conform and is used regardless of the actual schema language (DTD, XSD, and so forth). **Note:** While XSD plays a major role in Web services, Web services may still have to deal with DTD-based schemas because of legacy reasons.

As an additional convention, we use the word "serialization" to refer to XML serialization and deserialization. We explicitly refer to Java serialization when referring to serialization supported by the Java programming language. Also note that we may use the terms "marshalling" and "unmarshalling" as synonyms for XML serialization and deserialization. This is the same terminology used by XML data-binding technologies such as JAXB.

4.1.2   XML Horizontal and Vertical Schemas

XML schemas, which are applications of the XML language, may apply XML to horizontal or vertical domains. Horizontal domains are cross-industry domains, while vertical domains are specific to types of industries. Specific XML schemas have been developed for these different types of domains, and these horizontal and vertical applications of XML usually define publicly available schemas.

Many schemas have been established for horizontal domains; that is, they address issues that are common across many industries. For example, W3C specifications define such horizontal domain XML schemas or applications as Extensible HyperText Markup Language (XHTML), Scalable Vector Graphics (SVG), Mathematical Markup Language (MathML), Synchronized Multimedia Integration Language (SMIL), Resource Description Framework (RDF), and so forth.

Likewise, there are numerous vertical domain XML schemas. These schemas or applications of XML define standards that extend or apply XML to a vertical domain, such as e-commerce. Typically, groups of companies in an industry develop these standards. Some examples of e-commerce XML standards are Electronic Business with XML (ebXML), Commerce XML (CXML), Common Business Language (CBL), and Universal Business Language (UBL).

When designing an enterprise application, developers often may define their own custom schemas. These custom schemas may be kept private within the enterprise. Or, they may be shared just with those partners that intend to exchange data with the application. It is also possible that these custom schemas may be publicly exposed. Such custom schemas or application-specific schemas are defined either from scratch or, if appropriate, they may reuse where possible existing horizontal or vertical schema components. Note that publishing schemas in order to share them among partners can be implemented in various ways, including publishing the schemas along with Web service descriptions on a registry (see "Publishing a Web Service" on page 101).

4.1.3   Other Specifications Related to XML

For those interested in exploring further, here is a partial list of the many specifications that relate to XML.

- Document Object Model (DOM)—The Document Object Model is an interface, both platform and language neutral, that lets programs and scripts dynamically process XML documents. Using DOM, programs can access and update the content, structure, and style of documents.

- Xpath—The Xpath specification defines an expression language for navigating and processing an XML source document, including how to locate elements in an XML document.

- eXtensible Stylesheet Language Transformations (XSLT)—This specification, which is a subset of eXtensible Stylesheet Language (XSL), describes how to transform XML documents between different XML formats as well as non-XML formats.

- Namespaces—This specification describes how to associate a URI with tags, elements, attribute names, and data types in an XML document, to resolve ambiguity when elements and attributes have the same names.

- XML Information Set—This specification, often referred to as Infoset, provides the definitions for information in XML documents that are considered well formed according to the Namespaces criteria.

- Canonical XML—This specification addresses how to resolve syntactic variations between the XML 1.0 and the Namespaces specifications to create the physical, canonical representation of an XML document.

4.2   Outline for Handling XML Documents

An XML-based application, and in particular a Web service application, may consume or produce XML documents, and such an application may implement three distinct processing phases:

1. The application consumes an XML document.

2. The application applies its business logic on information retrieved from the document.

3. The application produces an XML document for response.

Generally speaking, an XML-based application exposes an interface that is defined in terms of the schemas for the XML documents that it consumes and produces as well as by the communication or interaction policies of the application. In the case of a Web service, a Web Services Description Language (WSDL) document describes this interface, and this document refers to the XML schemas to which the exchanged documents conform.

Let's examine the steps for handling XML documents. (See Figure 4.1.) The first phase, consuming XML incoming documents or XML input processing, consists of the following steps:

1. **Parse and optionally validate the document**—Parse and validate the incoming document against the schema to which the document should conform.

2. **Transform the document**—If necessary, transform the document from its conforming schema to the internally supported schema.

3. **Disassemble the document or pass it as is to the next phase**—Disassembling a document consists of these steps:

   - Search the incoming document for relevant information. The information can be recognized by using the embedded tags or its expected location within the document.

   - Extract the relevant information once it is located.

   - Optionally, map the retrieved information to domain-specific objects.

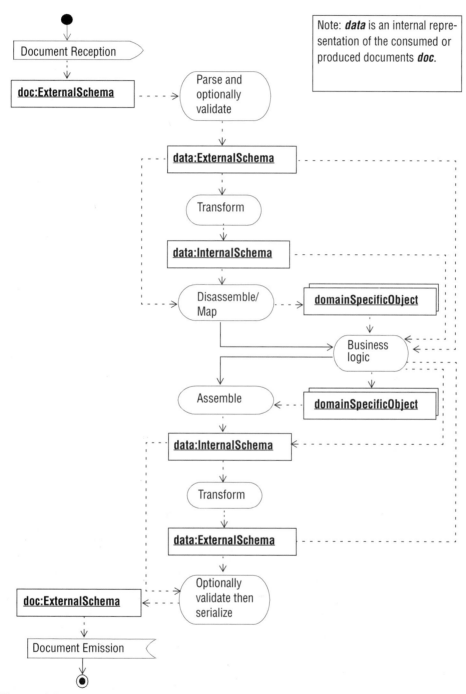

Figure 4.1   Activity Diagram Modeling Typical Steps for Handling XML Documents

In the second phase, the application applies the business logic. This entails actually processing the input information retrieved from the XML document. Such processing is considered document-centric when the logic handles the document directly, or object-centric when the logic is applied to domain-specific objects to which the retrieved information has been mapped. As a result of this processing, the application may generate XML output information, which is the third phase.

The steps for this third phase, XML output processing, mirror that of XML input processing. Producing XML output consists of the following steps:

1. **Assemble the document**—Assemble the output document from the results of applying the application's logic.

2. **Transform the document**—If necessary, transform the document from the internally supported schema to the appropriate external vertical schemas.

3. **Optionally validate, then serialize, the document**—Validating prior to serializing the output document is often considered optional.

It is quite possible that an XML-based application may only implement some of these phases, generally those that apply to its services. For example, some applications use XML just for configuration purposes, and these applications may only consume XML documents. Other applications just generate device-targeted content, and these applications may only produce XML documents (Wireless Markup Language, HTML, SVG, and so forth). E-commerce applications, on the other hand, may both consume and produce XML documents.

There are also applications that specialize in particular operations, such as those that specialize in transformations, in which case they perform only their intended operations. For instance, an application's function might be to select and apply a transformation to a document based on the processing requirements passed with the document, thus producing one or more new documents. In this example, the application's logic may consist only of the style sheet selection logic.

Developers implementing applications with a document-centric processing model—where the business logic itself handles the documents—may find that document handling is more entangled with the business logic. In particular, the steps that may intermingle with the business logic are those to disassemble the consumed documents and assemble the output document. These cases require careful handling. See "Abstracting XML Processing from Application Logic" on page 155.

Clients, whether a Web service peer or a rich client interacting with an end user, implement processes, such as the process just presented, for handling XML documents either submitted along with requests to a service or received as responses. Sometimes the application logic of human-facing rich clients may have to deal with the presentation of received documents to the end user rather than with business logic processing.

Note that real-world enterprise applications may have several instances of this abstract process to handle documents with unrelated schemas or documents with unrelated purposes. Moreover, these processes can actually be implemented to span one or more layers of an enterprise application. In particular, in the case of a Web service endpoint, these phases can be implemented in both the interaction and processing layers, depending on the processing model used by the Web service. See the discussion on a Web services layered architecture in "Key Web Services Design Decisions" on page 61.

4.3   Designing XML-Based Applications

There are a number of considerations to keep in mind when designing XML-based applications, particularly Web service applications. For one, you may need to design an XML schema specific for your domain. You also need to consider how your application intends to receive and send documents, and how and when to go about validating those documents. It is also important to separate the XML document processing from the application's business logic processing. ("Choosing Processing Models" on page 151 discusses in more detail separating XML document from business logic processing.)

Whether you design your own domain-specific schema or rely on standard vertical schemas, you still must understand the dynamics of mapping the application's data model to the schema. You also need to consider the processing model, and whether to use a document-centric model or an object-centric model.

These issues are discussed in the next sections.

4.3.1   Designing Domain-Specific XML Schemas

Despite the availability of more and more vertical domain schemas, application developers still may have to define application-specific XML schemas that must be agreed upon and shared between interoperating participants. With the introduction of modern schema languages such as XSD, which introduced strong data typing and type derivation, XML schema design shares many of the aspects of object-oriented design especially with respect to modularization and reuse.

The design of domain-specific XML schemas breaks down according to the definition of XML schema types, their relationship to other types, and any constraints to which they are subjected. The definitions of such XML schema types, relationships, and constraints are typically the result of the analysis of the application domain vocabulary (also called the business vocabulary). As much as possible, schema designers should leverage already-defined public vertical domain schema definitions to promote greater acceptance and interoperability among intended participants. The designers of new schemas should keep interoperability concerns in mind and try to account for reuse and extensibility. Figure 4.2 shows the UML model of a typical XML schema.

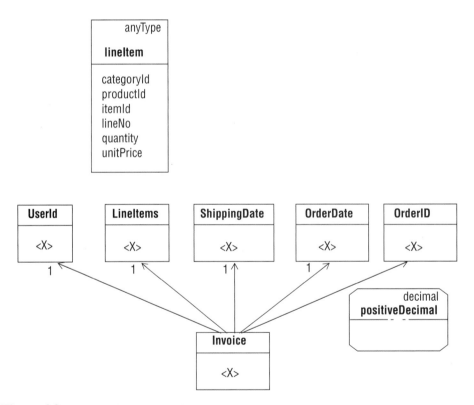

Figure 4.2   Model for an XML Schema (`Invoice.xsd`)

The strong similarity between object-oriented design and XML schema design makes it possible to apply UML modelling when designing XML schemas. Designers can use available software modelling tools to model XML schemas as UML class diagrams and, from these diagrams, to generate the actual schemas in a target schema language such as XSD. Code Example 4.1 shows an example of a schema based on XSD.

```xml
<?xml version="1.0" encoding="UTF-8"?>

<xsd:schema xmlns:xsd="http://www.w3.org/2001/XMLSchema" ...>
    <xsd:element name="Invoice">
        <xsd:complexType>
            <xsd:sequence>
                <xsd:element name="OrderId" type="xsd:string" />
                ...
                <xsd:element name="ShippingDate" type="xsd:date" />
                <xsd:element name="LineItems">
                    <xsd:complexType>
                        <xsd:sequence>
                            <xsd:element type="lineItem" minOccurs="1"
                            maxOccurs="unbounded" />
                        </xsd:sequence>
                    </xsd:complexType>
                    <xsd:unique name="itemIdUniqueness">
                        <xsd:selector xpath="LineItem"/>
                        <xsd:field xpath="@itemId"/>
                    </xsd:unique>

                </xsd:element>
            </xsd:sequence>
        </xsd:complexType>
    </xsd:element>

    <xsd:complexType name="lineItem">
        <xsd:attribute name="categoryId" type="xsd:string"
        use="required" />
        ...
        <xsd:attribute name="unitPrice" type="positiveDecimal"
        use="required" />
```

```
    </xsd:complexType>

    <xsd:simpleType name="positiveDecimal">
        <xsd:restriction base="xsd:decimal">
            <xsd:minInclusive value="0.0" />
        </xsd:restriction>
    </xsd:simpleType>
</xsd:schema>
```

Code Example 4.1   An Invoice XSD-Based Schema (`Invoice.xsd`)

To illustrate, consider the Universal Business Language (UBL) library, which provides a standard library of XML business documents, such as purchase orders, invoices, and so forth. UBL is a conceptual model of a collection of object classes and associations, called business information entities (BIES). These entities are organized into specific hierarchies, from which specific document types are assembled. As a result, UBL is:

- An XML-based business language

- Built on existing electronic data interchange (EDI) and XML business-to-business schemas or vocabularies

- Applicable across industry sectors and electronic trade domains

- Designed to be modular, reusable, and extensible

Additionally, as with any software design, there must be a balance between reusability, maintainability, and performance. This holds true both for the design of the XML schema itself and the logical and physical layout of the XML documents or schema instances. For example, consider a schema that reuses type and element definitions from other schemas. Initially loading this schema may require numerous network connections to resolve these external definitions, resulting in a significant performance overhead. Although this issue is well understood, and some XML-processing technologies may provide solutions in the form of XML entity catalogs, the developer may have to explicitly address this issue. Similarly, dynamically-generated instance of a document may be laid out such that it uses external entity references to include static or less dynamic fragments rather than embedding these fragments. This arrangement may potentially require the consumer of this document to issue many network connections to retrieve these different fragments. Although this sort of modularization and inclusion may lead to significant network overhead, it does allow consumers of document schemas and instances to more finely tune caching mechanisms. See "Performance Considerations" on page 182.

Generally, document schema design and the layout of document instances closely parallel object-oriented design. In addition, design strategies exist that identify and provide well-defined solutions to common recurring problems in document schema design.

Keep the following recommendations in mind when designing an XML schema:

❑ Adopt and develop design patterns, naming conventions, and other best practices similar to those used in object-oriented modelling to address the issues of reuse, modularization, and extensibility.

❑ Leverage existing horizontal schemas, and vertical schemas defined within your industry, as well as the custom schemas already defined within your enterprise.

❑ Do not solely rely on self-describing element and attribute names. Comment and document custom schemas.

❑ Use modelling tools that support well-known schema languages such as XSD.

Keep in mind that reusing schemas may enable the reuse of the corresponding XML processing code.

4.3.2   Receiving and Sending XML Documents

XML schemas of documents to be consumed and produced are part of the overall exposed interface of an XML-based application. The exposed interface encompasses schemas of all documents passed along with incoming and outgoing messages regardless of the message-passing protocol—SOAP, plain HTTP, or JMS.

Typically, an application may receive or return XML documents as follows:

• Received through a Web service endpoint: either a JAX-RPC service endpoint or EJB service endpoint if the application is exposed as a Web service. (See Chapter 3 for more information.)

- Returned to a Web service client: if the application is accessing a Web service through JAX-RPC. (See Chapter 5 for more details.)

- Through a JMS queue or topic (possibly attached to a message-driven bean in the EJB tier) when implementing a business process workflow or implementing an asynchronous Web service architecture. (See "Delegating Web Service Requests to Processing Layer" on page 92.)

Note that a generic XML-based application can additionally receive and return XML documents through a servlet over plain HTTP.

Recall from Chapter 3 that a Web service application must explicitly handle certain XML schemas—schemas for SOAP parameters that are not bound to Java objects and schemas of XML documents passed as attachments to SOAP messages. Since the JAX-RPC runtime passes SOAP parameter values (those that are *not* bound to Java objects) as SOAPElement document fragments, an application can consume and process them as DOM trees—and even programmatically bind them to Java objects—using XML data-binding techniques such as JAXB. Documents might be passed as attachments to SOAP messages when they are very large, legally binding, or the application processing requires the complete document infoset. Documents sent as attachments may also conform to schemas defined in languages not directly supported by the Web service endpoint.

Code Example 4.2 and Code Example 4.3 illustrate sending and receiving XML documents.

```
public class SupplierOrderSender {
    private SupplierService_Stub supplierService;

    public SupplierOrderSender(URL serviceEndPointURL) {
        // Create a supplier Web service client stub
        supplierService = ...
        return;
    }
    // Submits a purchase order document to the supplier Web service
    public String submitOrder(Source supplierOrder)
        throws RemoteException, InvalidOrderException {
        String trackingNumber
            = supplierService.submitOrder(supplierOrder);
        return trackingNumber;
```

```
        }
    }
```

Code Example 4.2   Sending an XML Document Through a Web Service Client Stub

```
public class SupplierServiceImpl implements SupplierService, ... {

    public String submitOrder(Source supplierOrder)
        throws InvalidOrderException, RemoteException {
        SupplierOrderRcvr supplierOrderRcvr
            = new SupplierOrderRcvr();
        // Delegate the processing of the incoming document
        return supplierOrderRcvr.receive(supplierOrder);
    }
}
```

Code Example 4.3   Receiving an XML Document Through a Web Service Endpoint

JAX-RPC passes XML documents that are attachments to SOAP messages as abstract `Source` objects. Thus, you should assume no specific implementation—`StreamSource`, `SAXSource`, or `DOMSource`—for an incoming document. You should also not assume that the underlying JAX-RPC implementation will validate or parse the document before passing it to the Web service endpoint. The developer should programmatically ensure that the document is valid and conforms to an expected schema. (See the next section for more information about validation.) The developer should also ensure that the optimal API is used to bridge between the specific `Source` implementation passed to the endpoint and the intended processing model. See "Use the Most Appropriate API" on page 184.

Producing XML documents that are to be passed as attachments to SOAP operations can use any XML processing model, provided the resulting document can be wrapped into a `Source` object. The underlying JAX-RPC is in charge of attaching the passed document to the SOAP response message. For example, Code Example 4.4 and Code Example 4.5 show how to send and receive XML documents through a JMS queue.

```
public class SupplierOrderRcvr {
    private QueueConnectionFactory queueFactory;
```

```
    private Queue queue;

    public SupplierOrderRcvr() throws RemoteException {
        queueFactory = ...; // Lookup queue factory
        queue = ...; // Lookup queue
        ...
    }

    public String receive(Source supplierOrder)
            throws InvalidOrderException {
        // Preprocess (validate and transform) the incoming document
        String document = ...
        // Extract the order id from the incoming document
        String orderId = ...
        // Forward the transformed document to the processing layer
        // using JMS
        QueueConnection connection
            = queueFactory.createQueueConnection();
        QueueSession session = connection.createQueueSession(...);
        QueueSender queueSender = session.createSender(queue);
        TextMessage message = session.createTextMessage();
        message.setText(document);
        queueSender.send(message);
        return orderId;
    }
}
```

Code Example 4.4   Sending an XML Document to a JMS Queue

```
public class SupplierOrderMDB
        implements MessageDrivenBean, MessageListener {
    private OrderFulfillmentFacadeLocal poProcessor = null;

    public SupplierOrderMDB() {}

    public void ejbCreate() {
        // Create a purchase order processor
        poProcessor = ...
    }
```

```
        // Receives the supplier purchase order document from the
        // Web service endpoint (interaction layer) through a JMS queue
        public void onMessage(Message msg) {
            String document = ((TextMessage) msg).getText();
            // Processes the XML purchase order received by the supplier
            String invoice = poProcessor.processPO(document);
            ...
        }
    }
}
```

Code Example 4.5   Receiving an XML Document Through a JMS Queue

There are circumstances when a Web service may internally exchange XML documents through a JMS queue or topic. When implementing an asynchronous architecture, the interaction layer of a Web service may send XML documents asynchronously using JMS to the processing layer. Similarly, when a Web service implements a workflow, the components implementing the individual stages of the workflow may exchange XML documents using JMS. From a developer's point of view, receiving or sending XML documents through a JMS queue or topic is similar in principle to the case of passing documents as SOAP message attachments. XML documents can be passed through a JMS queue or topic as text messages or in a Java-serialized form when those documents can be bound to Java objects.

4.3.3   Validating XML Documents

Once a document has been received or produced, a developer may—and most of the time must—validate the document against the schema to which it is supposed to conform. Validation, an important step in XML document handling, may be required to guarantee the reliability of an XML application. An application may legitimately rely on the parser to do the validation and thus avoid performing such validation itself.

However, because of the limited capabilities of some schema languages, a valid XML document may still be invalid in the application's domain. This might happen, for example, when a document is validated using DTD, because this schema language lacks capabilities to express strongly-typed data, complex unicity, and cross-reference constraints. Other modern schema languages, such as XSD, more rigorously—while still lacking some business constraint expressiveness—narrow the set of valid document instances to those that the business logic can effectively process. Regardless of the schema language, even when performing XML validation, the application is responsible for enforcing any uncovered domain-specific constraints that the document may nevertheless violate. That is, the application may have to perform its own business logic-specific validation in addition to the XML validation.

To decide where and when to validate documents, you may take into account certain considerations. Assuming a system—by system we mean a set of applications that compose a solution and that define a boundary within which trusted components can exchange information—one can enforce validation according to the following observations. (See Figure 4.3.)

1. Documents exchanged within the components of the system may not require validation.

2. Documents coming from outside the system, especially when they do not originate from external trusted sources, must be validated on entry.

3. Documents coming from outside the system, once validated, may be exchanged freely between internal components without further validation.

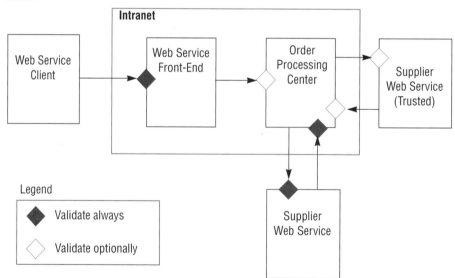

Figure 4.3   Validation of Incoming Documents

For example, a multitier e-business application that exchanges documents with trading partners through a front end enforces document validity at the front end. Not only does it check the validity of the document against its schema, but the application also ensures that the document type is a schema type that it can accept. It then may route documents to other applications or servers so that the proper services can handle them. Since they have already been validated, the documents do not require further validation. In a Web service, validation of incoming documents is typically performed in the interaction layer. Therefore, the processing layer may not have to validate documents it receives from the interaction layer.

Some applications may have to receive documents that conform to different schemas or different versions of a schema. In these cases, the application cannot do the validation up front against a specific schema unless the application is given a directive within the request itself about which schema to use. If no directive is included in the request, then the application has to rely on a hint provided by the document itself. Note that to deal with successive versioning of the same schema—where the versions actually modify the overall application's interface—it sometimes may be more convenient for an application to expose a separate endpoint for each version of the schema.

To illustrate, an application must check that the document is validated against the expected schema, which is not necessarily the one to which the document declares it conforms. With DTD schemas, this checking can be done only after validation. When using DOM, the application may retrieve the system or public identifier (SystemID or PublicID) of the DTD to ensure it is the identifier of the schema expected (Code Example 4.6), while when using SAX, it can be done on the fly by handling the proper event. With JAXP 1.2 and XSD (or other non-DTD schema languages), the application can specify up-front the schema to validate against (Code Example 4.7); the application can even ignore the schema referred to by the document itself.

```
public static boolean checkDocumentType(Document document,
        String dtdPublicId) {
    DocumentType documentType = document.getDoctype();
    if (documentType != null) {
        String publicId = documentType.getPublicId();
        return publicId != null && publicId.equals(dtdPublicId);
    }
```

```
        return false;
    }
```

Code Example 4.6   Ensuring the Expected Type of a DTD-Conforming Document

```
public static final String W3C_XML_SCHEMA
    = "http://www.w3.org/2001/XMLSchema";
public static final String JAXP_SCHEMA_LANGUAGE
    = "http://java.sun.com/xml/jaxp/properties/schemaLanguage";
public static final String JAXP_SCHEMA_SOURCE
    = "http://java.sun.com/xml/jaxp/properties/schemaSource";

public static SAXParser createParser(boolean validating,
        boolean xsdSupport, CustomEntityResolver entityResolver,
        String schemaURI) throws ... {
    // Obtain a SAX parser from a SAX parser factory
    SAXParserFactory parserFactory
        = SAXParserFactory.newInstance();
    // Enable validation
    parserFactory.setValidating(validating);
    parserFactory.setNamespaceAware(true);
    SAXParser parser = parserFactory.newSAXParser();
    if (xsdSupport) { // XML Schema Support
        try {
            // Enable XML Schema validation
            parser.setProperty(JAXP_SCHEMA_LANGUAGE,
                W3C_XML_SCHEMA);
            // Set the validating schema to the resolved schema URI
            parser.setProperty(JAXP_SCHEMA_SOURCE,
                entityResolver.mapEntityURI(schemaURI));
        } catch(SAXNotRecognizedException exception) { ... }
    }
    return parser;
}
```

Code Example 4.7   Setting the Parser for Validation in JAXP 1.2

When relying on the schemas to which documents internally declare they are conforming (through a DTD declaration or an XSD hint), for security and to avoid external malicious modification, you should keep your own copy of the schemas and validate against these copies. This can be done using an entity resolver, which is an interface from the SAX API (`org.xml.sax.EntityResolver`), that forcefully maps references to well-known external schemas to secured copies.

To summarize these recommendations:

❏ Validate incoming documents at the system boundary, especially when documents come from untrusted sources.

❏ When possible, enforce validation up-front against the supported schemas.

❏ When relying on internal schema declarations (DTD declaration, XSD hint, and so forth):

    ❏ Reroute external schema references to secured copies.

    ❏ Check that the validating schemas are supported schemas.

4.3.4 Mapping Schemas to the Application Data Model

After defining the application interface and the schemas of the documents to be consumed and produced, the developer has to define how the document schemas relate or map to the data model on which the application applies its business logic. We refer to these document schemas as external schemas. These schemas may be specifically designed to meet the application's requirements, such as when no preexisting schemas are available, or they may be imposed on the developer. The latter situation, for example, may occur when the application intends to be part of an interacting group within an industry promoting standard vertical schemas. (For example, UBL or ebXML schemas.)

4.3.4.1 Mapping Design Strategies

Depending on an application's requirements, there are three main design strategies or approaches for mapping schemas to the application data model. (See Figure 4.4.)

1. An "out-to-in" approach—The developer designs the internal data model based on the external schemas.

2. A "meet-in-the-middle" approach—The developer designs the data model along with an internal generic matching schema. Afterwards, the developer de-

fines transformations on the internal schema to support the external schemas.

3. An "in-to-out" approach, or legacy adapter—This approach is actually about how to map an application data model to schemas. The developer designs the exposed schema from an existing data model.

Figure 4.4, Figure 4.5, and Figure 4.6 show the sequencing of the activities involved at design time and the artifacts (schemas and classes) used or produced by these activities. The figures also show the relationships between these artifacts and the runtime entities (documents and objects), as well as the interaction at runtime between these entities.

The first approach (Figure 4.4), which introduces a strong dependency between the application's data model and logic and the external schemas, is suitable only for applications dedicated to supporting a specific interaction model. A strong dependency such as this implies that evolving or revising the external schemas impacts the application's data model and its logic.

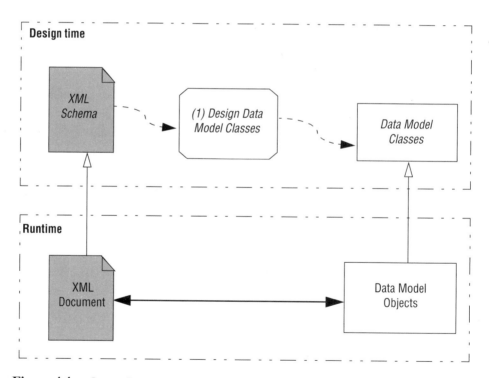

Figure 4.4   Out-to-In Approach for Mapping Schemas to the Data Model Classes

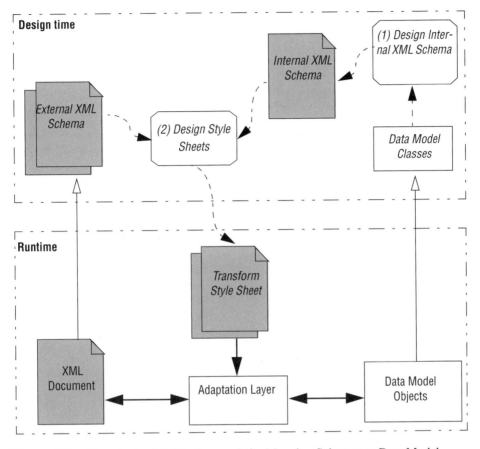

Figure 4.5   Meet-in-the-Middle Approach for Mapping Schemas to Data Model
Classes

The second approach (Figure 4.5), which introduces a transformation or adaptation layer between the application's data model and logic and the external schemas, is particularly suitable for applications that may have to support different
external schemas. Having a transformation layer leaves room for supporting additional schemas and is a natural way to account for the evolution of a particular
schema. The challenge is to devise an internal schema that is sufficiently generic
and that not only shields the application from external changes (in number and
revision) but also allows the application to fully operate and interoperate. Typically, such an internal schema either maps to a minimal operational subset or
common denominator of the external schemas, or it maps to a generic, universal

schema of the application's domain. (UBL is an example of the latter case.) The developer must realize that such an approach has some limitations—it is easier to transform from a structure containing more information to one with less information than the reverse. Therefore, the choice of the generic internal schema is key to that approach. Code Example 4.8 shows how to use a stylesheet to transform an external, XSD-based schema to an internal, DTD-based schema.

```xml
<?xml version="1.0" encoding="UTF-8"?>

<xsl:stylesheet xmlns:xsl="http://www.w3.org/1999/XSL/Transform"
    xmlns:so="http://blueprints.j2ee.sun.com/SupplierOrder"
    xmlns:li="http://blueprints.j2ee.sun.com/LineItem"
    xmlns:xsi="http://www.w3.org/2001/XMLSchema-instance"
    version="1.0">

    <xsl:output method="xml" indent="yes" encoding="UTF-8"
        doctype-public="-//Sun Microsystems, Inc. -
            J2EE Blueprints Group//DTD SupplierOrder 1.1//EN"
        doctype-system="/com/sun/j2ee/blueprints/
            supplierpo/rsrc/schemas/SupplierOrder.dtd" />

    <xsl:template match="/">
        <SupplierOrder>
            <OrderId><xsl:value-of select="/
            so:SupplierOrder/so:OrderId" /></OrderId>
            <OrderDate><xsl:value-of select="/
                so:SupplierOrder/so:OrderDate" /></OrderDate>
            <xsl:apply-templates select=".//
            so:ShippingAddress|.//li:LineItem"/>
        </SupplierOrder>
    </xsl:template>

    <xsl:template match="/so:SupplierOrder/
            so:ShippingAddress">
        ...
    </xsl:template>

    <xsl:template match="/so:SupplierOrder/so:LineItems/
            li:LineItem">
```

```
    . . .
    </xsl:template>
</xsl:stylesheet>
```

Code Example 4.8   Stylesheet for Transforming from External XSD-Based Schema to
Internal DTD-Based Schema

Normally, developers should begin this design process starting from the application's interface definition plus the XML schemas. In some situations, a developer may have to work in reverse; that is, start from the inside and work out. See the third approach, shown in Figure 4.6.

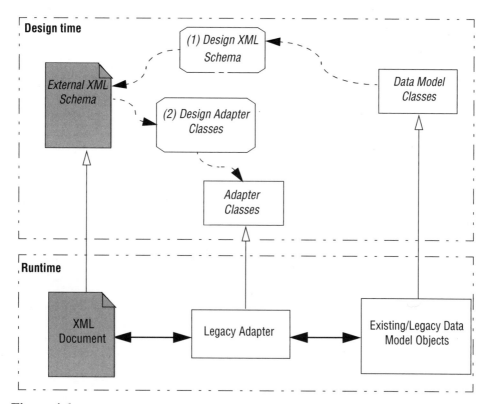

Figure 4.6   Legacy Adapter (In-to-Out) Approach for Mapping Schemas to Data
Model Classes

The developer may have to use the application's data model to create a set of matching schemas, which would then be exposed as part of the application's interface. This third approach is often used when existing or legacy applications need to expose an XML-based interface to facilitate a loosely coupled integration in a broader enterprise system. This technique is also known as legacy adapters or wrappers. In these cases, the application's implementation determines the interface and the schemas to expose. In addition, this approach can be combined with the meet-in-the-middle approach to provide a proper adaptation layer, which in turn makes available a more interoperable interface that is, an interface that is not so tightly bound to the legacy application. See Chapter 6 for more information on application integration.

4.3.4.2   Flexible Mapping

In complement to these approaches, it is possible to map complete documents or map just portions of documents. Rather than a centralized design for mapping from an external schema to a well-defined internal schema, developers can use a decentralized design where components map specific portions of a document to an adequate per-component internal representation. Different components may require different representations of the XML documents they consume or produce. Such a decentralized design allows for flexible mapping where:

- A component may not need to know the complete XML document. A component may be coded against just a fragment of the overall document schema.

- The document itself may be the persistent core representation of the data model. Each component maps only portions of the document to transient representation in order to apply their respective logic and then modifies the document accordingly.

- Even if the processing model is globally document-centric (see "Choosing Processing Models" on page 151), each component can—if adequate—locally implement a more object-centric processing model by mapping portions of the document to domain-specific objects.

- Each component can handle the document using the most effective or suitable XML processing technique. (See "Choosing an XML Processing Programming Model" on page 164.)

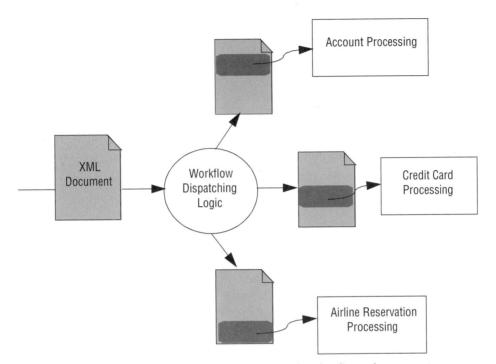

Figure 4.7   Flexible Mapping Applied to a Travel Service Scenario

This technique is particularly useful for implementing a document-oriented workflow where components exchange or have access to entire documents but only manipulate portions of the documents. For example, Figure 4.7 shows how a PurchaseOrder document may sequentially go through all the stages of a workflow. Each stage may process specific information within the document. A credit card processing stage may only retrieve the CreditCard element from the PurchaseOrder document. Upon completion, a stage may "stamp" the document by inserting information back into the document. In the case of a credit card processing stage, the credit card authorization date and status may be inserted back into the PurchaseOrder document.

4.3.4.3   XML Componentization

For a document-centric processing model, especially when processing documents in the EJB tier, you may want to create generic, reusable components whose state is serializable to and from XML. (See "Designing Domain-Specific XML Schemas" on page 131.) For example, suppose your application works with an Address entity bean whose instances are initialized with information retrieved from various XML documents, such as purchase order and invoice documents. Although the XML documents conform to different schemas, you want to use the same component—the same Address bean—without modification regardless of the underlying supported schema.

A good way to address this issue is to design a generic XML schema into which your component state can be serialized. From this generic schema, you can generate XML-serializable domain-specific or content objects that handle the serialization of your component state.

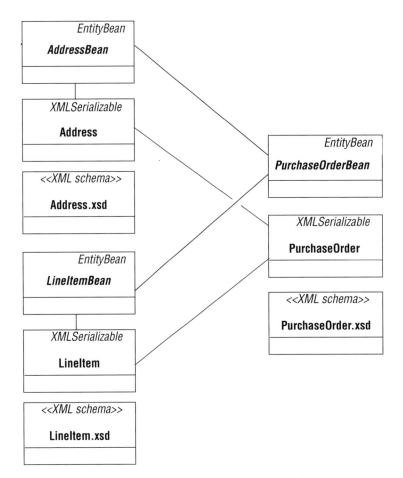

Figure 4.8   Composite XML-Serializable Component

You can generate the content objects manually or automatically by using XML data-binding technologies such as JAXB. Furthermore, you can combine these XML-serializable components into composite entities with corresponding composite schemas.

When combined with the "meet-in-the-middle" approach discussed previously, you can apply XSLT transformations to convert XML documents conforming to external vertical schemas into your application's supported internal generic schemas. Transformations can also be applied in the opposite direction to convert documents from internal generic schemas to external vertical schemas.

For example, Figure 4.8, which illustrates XML componentization, shows a `PurchaseOrderBean` composite entity and its two components, `AddressBean` and `LineItemBean`. The schemas for the components are composed in the same way and form a generic composite schema. Transformations can be applied to convert the internal generic composite `PurchaseOrder` schema to and from several external vertical schemas. Supporting an additional external schema is then just a matter of creating a new stylesheet.

4.3.5 Choosing Processing Models

An XML-based application may either apply its business logic directly on consumed or produced documents, or it may apply its logic on domain-specific objects that completely or partially encapsulate the content of such documents. Domain-specific objects are Java objects that may not only encapsulate application domain-specific data, but may also embody application domain-specific behavior.

An application's business logic may directly handle documents it consumes or produces, which is called a document-centric processing model, if the logic:

- Relies on both document content and structure

- Is required to punctually modify incoming documents while preserving most of their original form, including comments, external entity references, and so forth

In a document-centric processing model, the document processing may be entangled with the business logic and may therefore introduce strong dependencies between the business logic and the schemas of the consumed and produced documents—the "meet-in-the-middle" approach (discussed in "Mapping Schemas to the Application Data Model" on page 143) may, however, alleviate this problem. Moreover, the document-centric processing model does not promote a clean separation between business and XML programming skills, especially when an application developer who is more focused on the implementation of the business logic must additionally master one or several of the XML processing APIs.

There are cases that require a document-centric processing model, such as:

- The schema of the processed documents is only partially known and therefore cannot be completely bound to domain-specific objects; the application edits only the known part of the documents before forwarding them for further processing.

- Because the schemas of the processed documents may vary or change greatly, it is not possible to hard-code or generate the binding of the documents to domain-specific objects; a more flexible solution is required, such as one using DOM with XPath.

A typical document-centric example is an application that implements a data-driven workflow: Each stage of the workflow processes only specific information from the incoming document contents, and there is no central representation of the content of the incoming documents. A stage of the workflow may receive a document from an earlier stage, extract information from the document, apply some business logic on the extracted information, and potentially modify the document before sending it to the next stage.

Generally, it is best to have the application's business logic directly handle documents only in exceptional situations, and to do so with great care. You should instead consider applying the application's business logic on domain-specific objects that completely or partially encapsulate the content of consumed or produced documents. This helps to isolate the business logic from the details of XML processing.

Keep in mind that schema-derived classes, which are generated by JAXB and other XML data-binding technologies (see "XML Data-Binding Programming Model" on page 169), usually completely encapsulate the content of a document. While these schema-derived classes isolate the business logic from the XML processing details—specifically parsing, validating, and building XML documents—they still introduce strong dependencies between the business logic and the schemas of the consumed and produced documents. Because of these strong dependencies, and because they may still retain some document-centric characteristics (especially constraints), applications may still be considered document centric when they apply business logic directly on classes generated by XML data-binding technologies from the schemas of consumed and produced documents. To change to a pure object-centric model, the developer may move the dependencies on the schemas down by mapping schema-derived objects to domain-specific objects. The domain-specific object classes expose a constant, consistent interface to the business logic but internally delegate the XML processing details to the schema-derived classes. Overall, such a technique reduces the coupling between the business logic and the schema of the processed documents. "Abstracting XML Processing from Application Logic" on page 155 discusses a generic technique for decoupling the business logic and the schema of the processed documents.

A pure object-centric processing model requires XML-related issues to be kept at the periphery of an application—that is, in the Web service interaction layer closest to the service endpoint, or, for more classical applications, in the Web tier. In this case, XML serves only as an additional presentation media for the application's inputs and outputs. When implementing a document-oriented workflow in the processing layer of a Web service, or when implementing the asynchronous Web service interaction layer presented in "Delegating Web Service Requests to Processing Layer" on page 92, an object-centric processing model may still be enforced by keeping the XML-related issues within the message-driven beans that exchange documents.

Note that the object- and document-centric processing models may not be exclusive of one another. When using the flexible mapping technique mentioned earlier, an application may be globally document-centric and exchange documents between its components, and some components may themselves locally process part of the documents using an object-centric processing model. Each component may use the most adequate processing model for performing its function.

4.3.6 Fragmenting Incoming XML Documents

When your service's business logic operates on the contents of an incoming XML document, it is a good idea to break XML documents into logical fragments when appropriate. The processing logic receives an XML document containing all information for processing a request. However, the XML document usually has well-defined segments for different entities, and each segment contains the details about a specific entity.

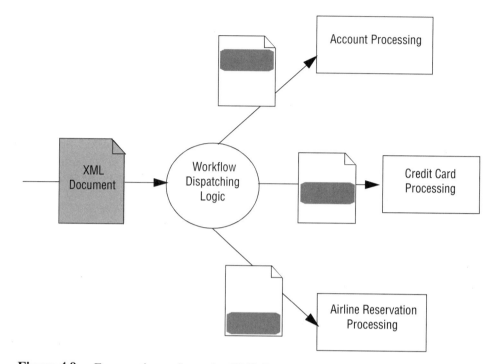

Figure 4.9   Fragmenting an Incoming XML Document for a Travel Service

❒   Rather than pass the entire document to different components handling various
     stages of the business process, it's best if the processing logic breaks the doc-
     ument into fragments and passes only the required fragments to other compo-
     nents or services that implement portions of the business process logic.

Figure 4.9 shows how the processing layer might process an XML document
representing an incoming purchase order for a travel agency Web service. The
document contains details such as account information, credit card data, travel
destinations, dates, and so forth. The business logic involves verifying the
account, authorizing the credit card, and filling the airline and hotel portions of the
purchase order. It is not necessary to pass all the document details to a business
process stage that is only performing one piece of the business process, such as
account verification. Passing the entire XML document to all stages of the business process results in unnecessary information flows and extra processing. It is
more efficient to extract the logical fragments—account fragment, credit card

fragment, and so forth—from the incoming XML document and then pass these individual fragments to the appropriate business process stages in an appropriate format (DOM tree, Java object, serialized XML, and so forth) expected by the receiver.

While it is complementary to most of the mapping design strategies presented in "Mapping Design Strategies" on page 143, this technique is best compared against the flexible mapping design strategy. (See "Flexible Mapping" on page 148.) Flexible mapping advocates a decentralized mapping approach: Components or stages in a workflow each handle the complete incoming document, but each stage only processes the appropriate part of the document. Fragmenting an incoming document can be viewed as a centralized implementation of the flexible mapping design. Fragmenting an incoming document, by suppressing redundant parsing of the incoming document and limiting the exchanges between stages to the strictly relevant data, improves performance over a straightforward implementation of flexible mapping. However, it loses some flexibility because the workflow dispatching logic is required to specifically know about (and therefore depend on) the document fragments and formats expected by the different stages.

Fragmenting a document has the following benefits:

- It avoids extra processing and exchange of superfluous information throughout the workflow.

- It maximizes privacy because it limits sending sensitive information through the workflow.

- It centralizes some of the XML processing tasks of the workflow and therefore simplifies the overall implementation of the workflow.

- It provides greater flexibility to workflow error handling since each stage handles only business logic-related errors while the workflow dispatching logic handles document parsing and validation errors.

4.3.7   Abstracting XML Processing from Application Logic

As mentioned earlier, the developer of an XML-based application and more specifically of a Web service application, may have to explicitly handle XML in the following layers of the application:

- In the interaction layer of a Web service in order to apply some pre- or post-processing, such as XML validation and transformation to the exchanged documents. (See "Receiving Requests" on page 89 and "Formulating Responses" on page 98.) Moreover, when the processing layer of a Web service implements an object-centric processing model, the interaction layer may be required to map XML documents to or from domain-specific objects before delegating to the processing layer by using one of the three approaches for mapping XML schemas to the application data model presented in "Mapping Schemas to the Application Data Model" on page 143.

* In the processing layer of a Web service when implementing a document-centric processing model. (See "Handling XML Documents in a Web Service" on page 105.) In such a case, the processing layer may use techniques such as flexible mapping or XML componentization. See "Flexible Mapping" on page 148 and "XML Componentization" on page 149.

With the object-centric processing model—when XML document content is mapped to domain-specific objects—the application applies its business logic on the domain-specific objects rather than the documents. In this case, only the interaction logic may handle documents. However, in the document-centric model, the application business logic itself may directly have to handle the documents. In other words, some aspects of the business model may be expressed in terms of the documents to be handled.

There are drawbacks to expressing the business model in terms of the documents to be handled. Doing so may clutter the business logic with document processing-related logic, which should be hidden from application developers who are more focused on the implementation of the business logic. It also introduces strong dependencies between the document's schemas and the business logic, and this may cause maintainability problems particularly when handling additional schemas or supporting new versions of an original schema (even though those are only internal schemas to which documents originally conforming to external schemas have been converted). Additionally, since there are a variety of APIs that support various XML processing models, such a design may lock the developer into one particular XML-processing API. It may make it difficult, and ineffective from a performance perspective, to integrate components that use disparate processing models or APIs.

The same concerns—about maintainability in the face of evolution and the variety of XML processing models or APIs—apply to some extent for the logic of the Web service interaction layer, which may be in charge of validating exchanged documents, transforming them from external schemas to internal schemas and, in some cases, mapping them to domain-specific objects.

For example, consider a system processing a purchase order that sends the order to a supplier warehouse. The supplier, to process the order, may need to translate the incoming purchase order from the external, agreed-upon schema (such as an XSD-based schema) to a different, internal purchase order schema (such as a DTD-based schema) supported by its components. Additionally, the supplier may want to map the purchase order document to a purchase order business object. The business logic handling the incoming purchase order must use an XML-processing API to extract the information from the document and map it to the purchase order entity. In such a case, the business logic may be mixed with the document-handling logic. If the external purchase order schema evolves or if an additional purchase order schema needs to be supported, the business logic will be impacted. Similarly, if for performance reasons you are required to revisit your choice of the XML-processing API, the business logic will also be impacted. The initial choice of XML-processing API may handicap the integration of other components that need to retrieve part or all of the purchase order document from the purchase order entity.

The design shown in Figure 4.10, which we refer to as the XML document editor (XDE) design, separates application logic (business or interaction logic) from document processing logic. Following a design such as this helps avoid the problems just described.

The term "Editor" used here refers to the capability to programmatically create, access, and modify—that is, edit—XML documents. The XML document editor design is similar to the data access object design strategy, which abstracts database access code from a bean's business logic.

The XML document editor implements the XML document processing using the most relevant API, but exposes only methods relevant to the application logic. Additionally, the XML document editor should provide methods to set or get documents to be processed, but should not expose the underlying XML processing API. These methods should use the abstract `Source` class (and `Result` class) from the JAXP API, in a similar fashion as JAX-RPC, to ensure that the underlying XML-processing API remains hidden. If requirements change, you can easily switch to a different XML processing technique without modifying the application logic. Also, a business object (such as an enterprise bean) that processes XML documents through an XML document editor should itself only expose accessor methods that use the JAXP abstract `Source` or `Result` class. Moreover, a business object or a service endpoint can use different XML document editor design strategies, combined with other strategies for creating factory methods or abstract factories (strategies for creating new objects where the instantiation of those objects is deferred to a subclass), to uniformly manipulate documents that conform to different schemas. The business object can invoke a factory class to create instances of different XML document editor implementations depending on the schema of the processed document. This is an alternate approach to applying transformations for supporting several external schemas.

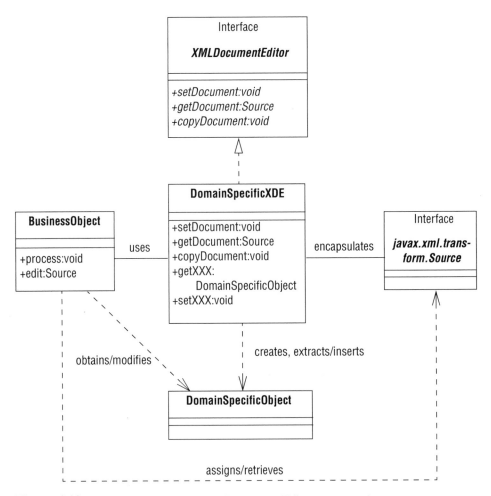

Figure 4.10   Basic Design of an XML Document Editor

Figure 4.10 shows the class diagram for a basic XML document editor design, while Figure 4.11 shows the class diagram for an XML document editor factory design. You should consider using a similar design in the following situations:

- When you want to keep the business objects focused on business logic and keep code to interact with XML documents separate from business logic code.

- In a similar way, when you want to keep the Web service endpoints focused on interaction logic and keep code to pre- and post-process XML documents separate from interaction logic code.

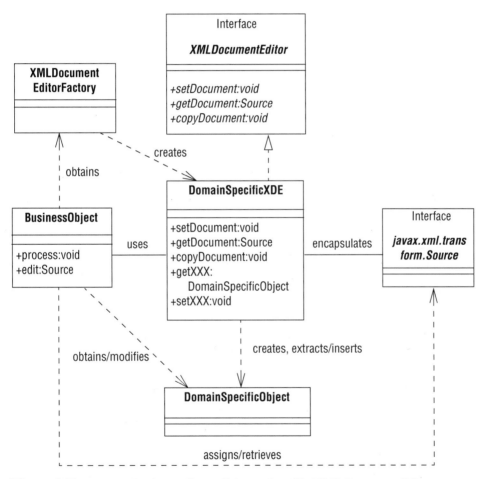

Figure 4.11 Factory Design to Create Schema-Specific XML Document Editors

- When you want to implement a flexible mapping design where each component may manipulate a common document in the most suitable manner for itself.

- When requirements might evolve (such as a new schema to be supported or a new version of the same schema) to where they would necessitate changes to the XML-processing implementation. Generally, you do not want to alter the application logic to accommodate these XML-processing changes. Additionally, since several XML-processing APIs (SAX, DOM, XSLT, JAXB technology, and so forth) may be relevant, you want to allow for subsequent changes to later address such issues as performance and integration.

- When different developer skill sets exist. For example, you may want the business domain and XML-processing experts to work independently. Or, you may want to leverage particular skill sets within XML-processing techniques.

Figure 4.12 and Code Example 4.9 give an example of a supplier Web service endpoint using an XML document editor to preprocess incoming purchase order documents.

```
public class SupplierOrderXDE extends
            XMLDocumentEditor.DefaultXDE {
    public static final String DEFAULT_ENCODING = "UTF-8";
    private Source source = null;
    private String orderId = null;

    public SupplierOrderXDE(boolean validating, ...) {
        // Initialize XML processing logic
    }
    // Sets the document to be processed
    public void setDocument(Source source) throws ... {
        this.source = source;
    }
    // Invokes XML processing logic to validate the source document,
    // extract its orderId, transform it into a different format,
    // and copy the resulting document into the Result object
    public void copyDocument(Result result) throws ... {
        orderId = null;
        // XML processing...
    }
```

```java
    // Returns the processed document as a Source object
    public Source getDocument() throws ... {
        return new StreamSource(new StringReader(
            getDocumentAsString()));
    }
    // Returns the processed document as a String object
    public String getDocumentAsString() throws ... {
        ByteArrayOutputStream stream = new ByteArrayOutputStream();
        copyDocument(new StreamResult(stream));
        return stream.toString(DEFAULT_ENCODING);
    }
    // Returns the orderId value extracted from the source document
    public String getOrderId() {
        return orderId;
    }
}
```

Code Example 4.9   Supplier Service Endpoint Using XML Document Editor

❏ To summarize, it is recommended that you use a design similar to the XML Document Editor presented above to abstract and encapsulate all XML document processing. In turn, the business object or service endpoint using such a document editor only invokes the simple API provided by the document editor. This hides all the complexities and details of interacting with the XML document from the business object clients.

As noted earlier, this design is not limited to the document-centric processing model where the application applies its business logic on the document itself. In an object-centric processing model, document editors can be used by the Web service interaction layer closest to the service endpoint, to validate, transform, and map documents to or from domain-specific objects. In this case, using the document editor isolates the interaction logic from the XML processing logic.

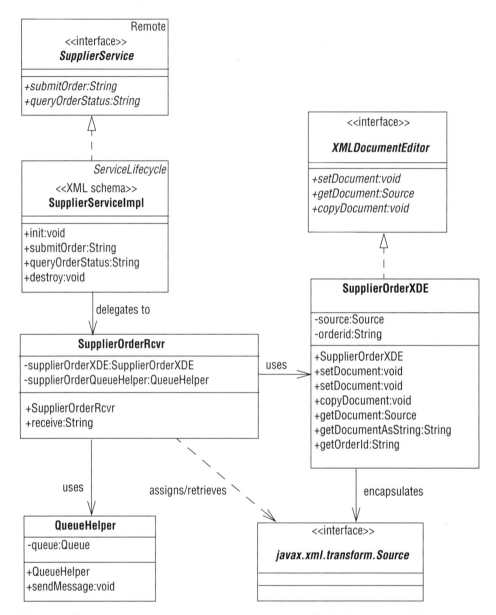

Figure 4.12   Class Diagram of Supplier Service Using XML Document Editor

4.3.8 Design Recommendation Summary

When you design an XML-based application, specifically one that is a Web service, you must make certain decisions concerning the processing of the content of incoming XML documents. Essentially, you decide the "how, where, and what" of the processing: You decide the technology to use for this process, where to perform the processing, and the form of the content of the processing.

In summary, keep in mind the following recommendations:

❐ When designing application-specific schemas, promote reuse, modularization, and extensibility, and leverage existing vertical and horizontal schemas.

❐ When implementing a pure object-centric processing model, keep XML on the boundary of your system as much as possible—that is, in the Web service interaction layer closest to the service endpoint, or, for more classical applications, in the presentation layer. Map document content to domain-specific objects as soon as possible.

❐ When implementing a document-centric processing model, consider using the flexible mapping technique. This technique allows the different components of your application to handle XML in a way that is most appropriate for each of them.

❐ Strongly consider validation at system entry points of your processing model—specifically, validation of input documents where the source is not trusted.

❐ When consuming or producing documents, as much as possible express your documents in terms of abstract `Source` and `Result` objects that are independent from the actual XML-processing API you are using.

❐ Consider a "meet-in-the-middle" mapping design strategy when you want to decouple the application data model from the external schema that you want to support.

❐ Abstract XML processing from the business logic processing using the XML document editor design strategy. This promotes separation of skills and independence from the actual API used.

4.4   Implementing XML-Based Applications

You must make some decisions when formulating the implementation of an XML-based application. Briefly, you have to choose the XML programming models for your application. Note that multiple programming models are available and these models may be relevant for different situations—models may be complementary or even competing. As such, your application may use different models, sometimes even in conjunction with one another. That is, you may have to combine programming models in what may be called XML processing pipelines.

You may also have to consider and address other issues. For example, you may have to determine how to resolve external entity references in a uniform way across your application regardless of the programming models used.

4.4.1   Choosing an XML Processing Programming Model

A J2EE developer has the choice of four main XML processing models, available through the following APIs:

1. Simple API for XML Parsing (SAX), which provides an event-based programming model

2. Document Object Model (DOM), which provides an in-memory tree-traversal programming model

3. XML data-binding, which provides an in-memory Java content class-bound programming model

4. eXtensible Stylesheet Language Transformations (XSLT), which provides a template-based programming model

The most common processing models are SAX and DOM. These two models along with XSLT are available through the JAXP APIs. (See "Java APIs for XML Processing" on page 41.) The XML data binding model is available through the JAXB technology. (See "Emerging Standards" on page 40.)

Processing an XML document falls into two categories. Not only does it encompass parsing a source XML document so that the content is available in some form for an application to process, processing also entails writing or producing an XML document from content generated by an application. Parsing an XML representation into an equivalent data structure usable by an application is often called deserialization, or unmarshalling. Similarly, writing a data structure to an equivalent XML representation is often called serialization or marshalling. Some processing models support both processing types, but others, such as SAX, do not.

❏ Just as you would avoid manually parsing XML documents, you should avoid manually constructing XML documents. It is better to rely on higher-level, reliable APIs (such as DOM, and DOM-like APIs, or JAXB technology) to construct XML documents, because these APIs enforce the construction of well-formed documents. In some instances, these APIs also allow you to validate constructed XML documents.

Now let's take a closer look at these XML processing APIs.

4.4.1.1 SAX Programming Model

When you use SAX to process an XML document, you have to implement event handlers to handle events generated by the parser when it encounters the various tokens of the markup language. Because a SAX parser generates a transient flow of these events, it is advisable to process the source document in the following fashion. Intercept the relevant type of the events generated by the parser. You can use the information passed as parameters of the events to help identify the relevant information that needs to be extracted from the source document. Once extracted from the document, the application logic can process the information.

Typically, with SAX processing, an application may have to maintain some context so that it can logically aggregate or consolidate information from the flow of events. Such consolidation is often done before invoking or applying the application's logic. The developer has two choices when using SAX processing:

1. The application can "on the fly" invoke the business logic on the extracted information. That is, the logic is invoked as soon as the information is extracted or after only a minimal consolidation. With this approach, referred to as stream processing, the document can be processed in one step.

2. The application invokes the business logic after it completes parsing the document and has completely consolidated the extracted information. This approach takes two steps to process a document.

Note that what we refer to as consolidated information may in fact be domain-specific objects that can be directly passed to the business logic.

Stream processing (the first approach) lets an application immediately start processing the content of a source document. Not only does the application not have to wait for the entire document to be parsed, but, in some configurations, the application does not have to wait for the entire document to be retrieved. This includes retrieving the document from an earlier processing stage when implementing pipelines, or even retrieving the document from the network when exchanging documents between applications.

Stream processing, while it offers some performance advantages, also has some pitfalls and issues that must be considered. For instance, a document may appear to be well-formed and even valid for most of the processing. However, there may be unexpected errors by the end of the document that cause the document to be broken or invalid. An application using stream processing notices these problems only when it comes across erroneous tokens or when it cannot resolve an entity reference. Or, the application might realize the document is broken if the input stream from which it is reading the document unexpectedly closes, as with an end-of-file exception. Thus, an application that wants to implement a stream processing model may have to perform the document parsing and the application's business logic within the context of a transaction. Keeping these operations within a transaction leverages the container's transaction capabilities: The container's transaction mode accounts for unexpected parsing errors and rolls back any invalidated business logic processing.

With the second approach, parsing the document and applying business logic are performed in two separate steps. Before invoking the application's business logic, the application first ensures that the document and the information extracted from the document are valid. Once the document data is validated, the application invokes the business logic, which may be executed within a transaction if need be.

The SAX programming model provides no facility to produce XML documents. However, it is still possible to generate an XML document by initiating a properly balanced sequence of events—method calls—on a custom serialization handler. The handler intercepts the events and, using an XSLT identity transformation operation, writes the events in the corresponding XML syntax. The difficulty for the application developer lies in generating a properly balanced sequence of events. Keep in mind, though, that generating this sequence of events is prone to error and should be considered only for performance purposes.

SAX generally is very convenient for extracting information from an XML document. It is also very convenient for data mapping when the document structure maps well to the application domain-specific objects—this is especially true when only part of the document is to be mapped. Using SAX has the additional benefit of avoiding the creation of an intermediate resource-consuming representation. Finally, SAX is good for implementing stream processing where the business logic is invoked in the midst of document processing. However, SAX can be tedious to use for more complex documents that necessitate managing sophisticated context, and in these cases, developers may find it better to use DOM or JAXB.

In summary, consider using the SAX processing model when any of the following circumstances apply:

- You are familiar with event-based programming.

- Your application only consumes documents without making structural modifications to them.

- The document must only be processed one time.

- You have to effectively extract and process only parts of the document.

- Memory usage is an issue or documents may potentially be very large.

- You want to implement performant stream processing, such as for dealing with very large documents.

- The structure of a document and the order of its information map well to the domain-specific objects or corresponds to the order in which discrete methods of the application's logic must be invoked. Otherwise, you may have to maintain rather complicated contexts.

Note that the SAX model may not be the best candidate for application developers who are more concerned about implementing business logic.

4.4.1.2   DOM Programming Model

With the DOM programming model, you write code to traverse a tree-like data structure created by the parser from the source document. Typically, processing the XML input data is done in a minimum of two steps, as follows:

1. The DOM parser creates a tree-like data structure that models the XML source document. This structure is called a DOM tree.

2. The application code walks the DOM tree, searching for relevant information that it extracts, consolidates, and processes further. Developers can use consol-

idated information to create domain-specific objects. The cycle of searching for, extracting, and processing the information can be repeated as many times as necessary because the DOM tree persists in memory.

There are limitations to the DOM model. DOM was designed to be both a platform- and language-neutral interface. Because of this, the Java binding of the DOM API is not particularly Java friendly. For example, the binding does not use the `java.util.Collection` API. Generally, DOM is slightly easier to use than the SAX model. However, due to the awkwardness of DOM's Java binding, application developers who are focused on the implementation of the business logic may still find DOM difficult to use effectively. For this reason, similarly with SAX, application developers should be shielded as much as possible from the DOM model.

In addition, the DOM API prior to version level 3 does not support serialization of DOM trees back to XML. Although some implementations do provide serialization features, these features are not standard. Thus, developers should instead rely on XSLT identity transformations, which provide a standard way to achieve serialization back to XML.

Java developers can also use other technologies, such as JDOM and dom4j, which have similar functionality to DOM. The APIs of these technologies tend to be more Java-friendly than DOM, plus they interface well with JAXP. They provide a more elaborate processing model that may alleviate some of DOM's inherent problems, such as its high memory usage and the limitation of processing document content only after a document has been parsed.

Although not yet standard for the Java platform (not until JAXP 1.3), the Xpath API enables using it in conjunction with the DOM programming model. (The Xpath API can be found along with some DOM implementations such as Xerces or dom4j.) Developers use Xpath to locate and extract information from a source document's DOM tree. By allowing developers to specify path patterns to locate element content, attribute values, and subtrees, Xpath not only greatly simplifies, but may even eliminate, tree-traversal code. Since Xpath expressions are strings, they can be easily parameterized and externalized in a configuration file. As a result, developers can create more generic or reusable document processing programs.

To sum up, consider using DOM when any of these circumstances apply:

❏ You want to consume or produce documents.

❏ You want to manipulate documents and need fine-grained control over the document structure that you want to create or edit.

❏ You want to process the document more than once.

❏ You want random access to parts of the document. For example, you may want to traverse back and forth within the document.

❏ Memory usage is not a big issue.

❏ You want to implement data binding but you cannot use JAXB technology because the document either has no schema or it conforms to a DTD schema definition rather than to an XSD schema definition. The document may also be too complex to use SAX to implement data binding. (See "SAX Programming Model" on page 165.)

❏ You want to benefit from the flexibility of Xpath and apply Xpath expressions on DOM trees.

4.4.1.3   XML Data-Binding Programming Model

The XML data-binding programming model, contrary to the SAX and DOM models, allows the developer to program the processing of the content of an XML document without being concerned with XML document representations (infosets).

Using a binding compiler, the XML data-binding programming model, as implemented by JAXB, binds components of a source XSD schema to schema-derived Java content classes. JAXB binds an XML namespace to a Java package. XSD schema instance documents can be unmarshalled into a tree of Java objects (called a content tree), which are instances of the Java content classes generated by compiling the schema. Applications can access the content of the source documents using JavaBeans-style get and set accessor methods. In addition, you can create or edit an in-memory content tree, then marshal it to an XML document instance of the source schema. Whether marshalling or unmarshalling, the developer can apply validation to ensure that either the source document or the document about to be generated satisfy the constraints expressed in the source schema.

The steps for using JAXB technology schema-derived classes to process an incoming XML document are very simple, and they are as follows:

1. Set up the JAXB context (`JAXBContext`) with the list of schema-derived packages that are used to unmarshal the documents.

2. Unmarshal an XML document into a content tree. Validation of the document is performed if enabled by the application.

3. You can then directly apply the application's logic to the content tree. Or, you can extract and consolidate information from the content tree and then apply the application's logic on the consolidated information. As described later, this consolidated information may very well be domain-specific objects that may expose a more adequate, schema-independent interface.

This programming model also supports serialization to XML, or marshalling a content tree to an XML format. Marshalling of a document has the following steps:

1. Modify an existing content tree, or create a new tree, from the application's business logic output.

2. Optionally, validate in-memory the content tree against the source schema. Validation is performed in-memory and can be applied independently of the marshalling process.

3. Marshal the content tree into an XML document.

There are various ways a developer can design an application with the schema-derived classes that JAXB generates:

1. The developer may use them directly in the business logic, but, as noted in "Choosing Processing Models" on page 151, this tightly binds the business logic to the schemas from which the classes were generated. This type of usage shares most of the issues of a document-centric processing model.

2. The developer can use the schema-derived classes in conjunction with an object-centric processing model:

   a. The developer may design domain-specific classes whose instances will be populated from the content objects created by unmarshalling an XML document, and vice versa.

   b. The developer may design domain-specific classes, which inherit from the schema-derived classes, and define additional domain-oriented methods. The problem with this design is that these classes are tightly coupled to the implementation of the schema-derived classes, and they may also expose the methods from the schema-derived classes as part of the domain-specific class. Additionally, as a side effect, if the developer is not careful, this may result in tightly binding the business logic to the schemas from which the classes were generated.

c. The developer can use aggregation or composition and design domain-specific classes that only expose domain-oriented methods and delegate to the schema-derived classes. Since the domain-specific classes only depend on the interfaces of the schema-derived classes, the interfaces of the domain-specific classes may therefore not be as sensitive to changes in the original schema.

Note that when no well-defined schema or variable in nature (abstract) or in number (including new schema revisions) is available, JAXB may be cumbersome to use due to the tight coupling between the schemas and the schema-derived classes. Also note that the more abstract the schema, the less effective the binding.

Consider using the XML data-binding programming model, such as JAXB, when you have any of the following conditions:

❑ You want to deal directly with plain Java objects and do not care about, nor want to handle, document representation.

❑ You are consuming or producing documents.

❑ You do not need to maintain some aspects of a document, such as comments and entity references. The JAXB specification does not require giving access to the underlying document representation (infoset). For example, the JAXB reference implementation is based on SAX 2.0 and therefore does not maintain an underlying document representation. However, other implementations may be layered on top of a DOM representation. A developer may fall back on this DOM representation to access unexposed infoset elements.

❑ You want to process the content tree more than once.

❑ You want random access to parts of the document. For example, you may want to traverse back and forth within the document.

❑ Memory usage may be less of an issue. A JAXB implementation, such as the standard implementation, creates a Java representation of the content of a document that is much more compact than the equivalent DOM tree. The standard implementation is layered on top of SAX 2.0 and does not maintain an additional underlying representation of the source document. Additionally, where DOM represents all XML schema numeric types as strings, JAXB's standard implementation maps these values directly to much more compact Java numeric data types. Not only does this use less memory to represent the same content, the JAXB approach saves time, because converting between the two representations is not necessary.

❏   You previously were implementing XML data-binding manually with DOM, and an XSD schema definition is available.

4.4.1.4   XSLT Programming Model

XSLT is a higher-level processing model than the SAX, DOM, and XML data-binding models. Although developers can mimic XSLT by implementing transformations programmatically on top of SAX, DOM, or the XML data-binding model, XSLT does not compare with other processing models and should be regarded as complementary, to be used along with these other models.

XSLT implements a functional declarative model as opposed to a procedural model. This requires skills that are quite different from Java programming skills. For the most part, XSLT requires developers to code rules, or templates, that are applied when specified patterns are encountered in the source document. The application of the rules adds new fragments or copies fragments from the source tree to a result tree. The patterns are expressed in the Xpath language, which is used to locate and extract information from the source document.

Instead of writing Java code (as with SAX, DOM, and the XML data-binding model), developers using XSLT principally write style sheets, which are themselves XML documents. (Invoking the XSLT engine, however, does require the developer to write Java code.) Compared to the other programming models, XSLT programming gives developers the sort of flexibility that comes with scripting. In an XML-based application, XSLT processing is usually used along with the other three processing models. The XSLT API available with JAXP provides an abstraction for the source and result of transformations, allowing the developer not only the ability to chain transformations but also to interface with other processing models, such as SAX, DOM, and JAXB technology. To interface with SAX and DOM, use the classes `SAXSource`, `SAXResult`, `DOMSource`, and `DOMResult` provided by JAXP. To interface with JAXB, use the classes `JAXBSource` and `JAXBResult`.

By definition, XSLT supports not only processing XML input documents but it also can output XML documents. (Other output methods include text, HTML, and so forth.) Note that although the DOM version level 2 API does not support serialization—that is, transformation of a DOM tree to an XML document—the JAXP implementation of XSLT addresses the serialization of a DOM tree using an identity transformer. An identity transformer copies a source tree to a result tree and applies the specified output method, thus solving the serialization problem in an easy, implementation-independent manner. For example, to output in XML, the output method is set to xml. XSLT can also be used to serialize to XML from DOM trees, SAX events, and so forth.

Consider using XSLT when any of the following circumstances apply:

❐ You want to change the structure, insert, remove, rename, or filter content of an XML document.

❐ You potentially have more than one transformation for the same document. Although one transformation can be hand coded using another API, multiple transformations, because of the scripting nature of style sheets, are better done using XSLT transformations.

❐ You have to perform complex transformations. Because of XSLT's functional declarative model, it is easier to design complex transformations by coding individual rules or templates than by hard-coding procedures.

❐ You want the ability to be flexible and leave room for future changes in the schemas of documents you are processing.

❐ You want to process documents that contain a significant amount of data to minimize performance overhead.

❐ You need to transform a document for non-interactive presentation or in batch mode. The performance overhead of transformation is usually less of an issue with non-interactive presentations. Such a document might be a purchase order or an invoice, for example.

❐ You must support multiple external schemas but you want to internally program only against a generic schema (schema adapter).

❏ You want to promote the separation of skills between XML transformation style sheet developers and business logic developers.

❏ In general, when you must deal with non-interactive presentation or you must integrate various XML data sources or perform XML data exchanges.

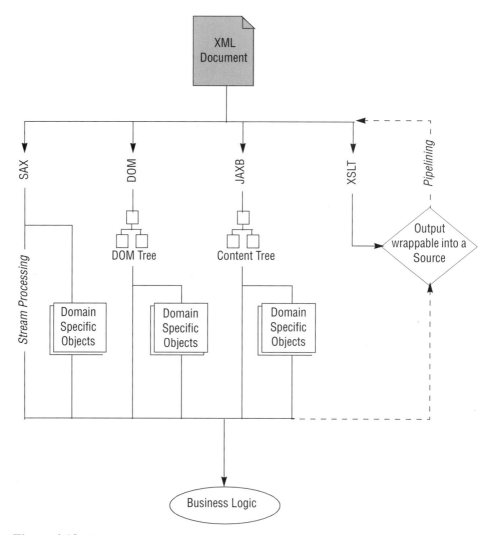

Figure 4.13 Programming Models and Implied Intermediary Representations

4.4.1.5   Recommendation Summary

In summary, choose the programming model and API processing according to your needs. If you need to deal with the content and structure of the document, consider using DOM and SAX because they provide more information about the document itself than JAXB usually does. On the other hand, if your focus is more on the actual, domain-oriented objects that the document represents, consider using JAXB, since JAXB hides the details of unmarshalling, marshalling, and validating the document. Developers should use JAXB—XML data-binding—if the document content has a representation in Java that is directly usable by the application (that is, close to domain-specific objects).

DOM, when used in conjunction with XPath, can be a very flexible and powerful tool when the focus is on the content and structure of the document. DOM may be more flexible than JAXB when dealing with documents whose schemas are not well-defined.

Finally, use XSLT to complement the three other processing models, particularly in a pre- or post-processing stage.

Figure 4.13 summarizes the different programming models from which the developer can choose and highlights the intermediary representations (which have a direct impact on performance) implied by each of them. Table 4.1 summarizes the features of the three most prevalent XML programming models.

Table 4.1   DOM, SAX, and XML Data-Binding Programming Models

DOM	SAX	XML Data-Binding
Tree traversal model	Event-based model	Java-bound content tree model
Random access (in-memory data structure) using generic (application independent) API	Serial access (flow of events) using parameters passed to events	Random access (in-memory data structure) using Java-Beans style accessors

Table 4.1   DOM, SAX, and XML Data-Binding Programming Models (*continued*)

DOM	SAX	XML Data-Binding
High memory usage (The document is often completely loaded in memory, though some techniques such as deferred or lazy DOM node creation may lower the memory usage.)	Low memory usage (only events are generated)	Intermediate memory usage (The document is often completely loaded in memory, but the Java representation of the document is more effective than a DOM representation. Nevertheless, some implementations may implement techniques to lower the memory usage.)
To edit the document (processing the in-memory data structure)	To process parts of the document (handling relevant events)	To edit the document (processing the in-memory data structure)
To process multiple times (document loaded in memory)	To process the document only once (transient flow of events)	To process multiple times (document loaded in memory)
Processing once the parsing is finished	Stream processing (start processing before the parsing is finished, and even before the document is completely read)	Processing once the parsing is finished

4.4.2   Combining XML Processing Techniques

The JAXP API provides support for chaining XML processings: The JAXP `javax.xml.Source` and `javax.xml.Result` interfaces constitute a standard mechanism for chaining XML processings. There are implementations of these two interfaces for DOM, SAX, and even streams; JAXB and other XML processing technologies, such as JDOM and dom4j, provide their own implementations as well.

Basically, XML processings can be chained according to two designs:

- The first design wraps the result of one processing step into a `Source` object that can be processed by the next step. XML processing techniques that can produce an in-memory representation of their results, such as DOM and JAXB, lend themselves to this design. This design is often called "batch sequential" because each processing step is relatively independent and each runs to completion until the next step begins.

- The second design, called "stream processing" or "pipes and filters," creates a chain of filters and each filter implements a processing step. XML processing techniques such as SAX work well with this design.

The two designs can, of course, be combined. When combined, transformations and identity transformations become handy techniques to use when the result of a processing step cannot be directly wrapped into a Source object compatible with the next step. JAXP also provides support for chaining transformations with the use of javax.xml.transform.sax.SAXTransformerFactory.

Code Example 4.10 illustrates an XML processing pipeline that combines SAX and XSLT to validate an incoming purchase order document, extract on-the-fly the purchase order identifier, and transform the incoming document from its external, XSD-based schema to the internal, DTD-based schema supported by the business logic. The code uses a SAX filter chain as the Source of a transformation. Alternatively, the code could have used a SAXTransformerFactory to create an org.xml.sax.XMLFilter to handle the transformation and then chain it to the custom XMLFilter, which extracts the purchase order identifier.

```
public class SupplierOrderXDE extends
        XMLDocumentEditor.DefaultXDE {
    public static final String DEFAULT_ENCODING = "UTF-8";
    private XMLFilter filter;
    private Transformer transformer;
    private Source source = null;
    private String orderId = null;

    public SupplierOrderXDE(boolean validating, ...) {
        // Create a [validating] SAX parser
        SAXParser parser = ...;
        filter = new XMLFilterImpl(parser.getXMLReader()) {
            // Implements a SAX XMLFilter that extracts the OrderID
            // element value and assigns it to the orderId attribute
        };
        // Retrieve the style sheet as a stream
        InputStream stream = ...;
        // Create a transformer from the stylesheet
        transformer = TransformerFactory.newInstance()
            .newTransformer(new StreamSource(stream));
    }
    // Sets the document to be processed
```

```
public void setDocument(Source source) throws ... {
    this.source = source;
}
// Builds an XML processing pipeline (chaining a SAX parser and
// a style sheet transformer) which validates the source document
// extracts its orderId, transforms it into a different format,
// and copies the resulting document into the Result object
public void copyDocument(Result result) throws ... {
    orderId = null;
    InputSource inputSource
        = SAXSource.sourceToInputSource(source);
    SAXSource saxSource = new SAXSource(filter, inputSource);
    transformer.transform(transformer, saxSource, result);
}
// Returns the processed document as a Source object
public Source getDocument() throws ... {
    return new StreamSource(new StringReader(
        getDocumentAsString()));
}
// Returns the processed document as a String object
public String getDocumentAsString() throws ... {
    ByteArrayOutputStream stream = new ByteArrayOutputStream();
    copyDocument(new StreamResult(stream));
    return stream.toString(DEFAULT_ENCODING);
}
// Returns the orderId value extracted from the source document
public String getOrderId() {
    return orderId;
}
}
```

Code Example 4.10   Combining SAX and XSLT to Perform XML Processing Steps

4.4.3   Entity Resolution

As mentioned earlier in this chapter, XML documents may contain references to other external XML fragments. Parsing replaces the references with the actual content of these external fragments. Similarly, XML schemas may refer to external type definitions, and these definitions must also be accessed for the schema to be completely interpreted. (This is especially true if you follow the modular design recommendations suggested in "Designing Domain-Specific XML Schemas" on page 131.) In both cases, an XML processor, in the course of processing a document or a schema, needs to find the content of any external entity to which the document or schema refers. This process of mapping external entity references to their actual physical location is called entity resolution. Note that entity resolution recursively applies to external entity references within parsed external entities.

Entity resolution is particularly critical for managing the XML schemas upon which your application is based. As noted in "Validating XML Documents" on page 139, the integrity and the reliability of your application may depend on the validation of incoming documents against specific schemas—typically the very same schemas used to initially design your application. Your application usually cannot afford for these schemas to be modified in any way, whether by malicious modifications or even legitimate revisions. (For revisions, you should at a minimum assess the impact of a revision on your application.)

Therefore, you may want to keep your own copies of the schemas underlying your application and redirect references to these copies. Or you may want to redirect any such references to trusted repositories. A custom entity resolution allows you to implement the desired mapping of external entity references to actual trusted physical locations. Moreover, implementing an entity catalog—even as simple as the one presented in Code Example 4.12—gives you more flexibility for managing the schemas upon which your application depends. Note that to achieve our overall goal, the entity catalog must itself be adequately protected. Additionally, redirecting references to local copies of the schemas may improve performance when compared to referring to remote copies, especially for remote references across the Internet. As described in "Reduce the Cost of Referencing External Entities" on page 189, performance can be improved further by caching in memory the *resolved* entities.

Code Example 4.11 illustrates an entity resolver that implements an interface from the SAX API (`org.xml.sax.EntityResolver`). The entity resolver uses a simple entity catalog to map external entity references to actual locations. The entity catalog is simply implemented as a `Properties` file that can be loaded from a URL (see Code Example 4.12). When invoked, this entity resolver first tries to use the catalog to map the declared public identifier or URI of the external entity to an actual physical location. If this fails—that is, if no mapping is defined in the catalog for this public identifier or URI—the entity resolver uses the declared system identifier or URL of the external entity for its actual physical location. In both cases, the resolver interprets the actual physical location either as an URL or, as a fall-back, as a Java resource accessible from the class path of the entity resolver class. The latter case allows XML schemas to be bundled along with their dependent XML processing code. Such bundling can be useful when you must absolutely guarantee the consistency between the XML processing code and the schemas.

```
public class CustomEntityResolver implements EntityResolver {
    private Properties entityCatalog = null;

    public CustomEntityResolver(URL entityCatalogURL)
            throws IOException {
        entityCatalog = new Properties(entityCatalog);
        entityCatalog.load(entityCatalogURL.openStream());
    }
    // Opens the physical location as a plain URL or if this fails, as
    // a Java resource accessible from the class path.
    private InputSource openLocation(String location)
            throws IOException {
        URL url = null;
        InputStream entityStream = null;
        try { // Wellformed URL?
            url = new URL(location);
        } catch (MalformedURLException exception) { ... }
        if (url != null) { // Wellformed URL.
            try { // Try to open the URL.
                entityStream = url.openStream();
            } catch (IOException exception) { ... }
        }
        if (entityStream == null) { // Not a URL or not accessible.
            try { // Resource path?
                String resourcePath = url != null
                    ? url.getPath() : location;
                entityStream
                    = getClass().getResourceAsStream(resourcePath);
            } catch (Exception exception1) { ... }
        }
        if (entityStream != null) { // Readable URL or resource.
            InputSource source = new InputSource(entityStream);
            source.setSystemId(location);
```

```
                return source;
            }
        return null;
    }
    // Maps an external entity URI or Public Identifier to a
    // physical location.
    public String mapEntityURI(String entityURI) {
        return entityCatalog.getProperty(entityURI);
    }


    public InputSource resolveEntity(String entityURI,
            String entityURL) {
        InputSource source = null;
        try {
            // Try first to map its URI/PublicId using the catalog.
            if (entityURI != null) {
                String mappedLocation = mapEntityURI(entityURI);
                if (mappedLocation != null) {
                    source = openLocation(mappedLocation);
                    if (source != null) { return source; }
                }
            }
            // Try then to access the entity using its URL/System Id.
            if (entityURL != null) {
                source = openLocation(entityURL);
                if (source != null) { return source; }
            }
        }
    } catch (Exception exception) { ... }
        return null; // Let the default entity resolver handle it.
    }
}
```

Code Example 4.11 Entity Resolver Using a Simple Entity Catalog

```
# DTD Public Indentifier to physical location (URL or resource path)
-//Sun Microsystems, Inc. -
 J2EE Blueprints Group//DTD LineItem 1.0//EN: /com/sun/j2ee/blue-
prints/xmldocuments/rsrc/schemas/LineItem.dtd
```

```
-//Sun Microsystems, Inc. -
 J2EE Blueprints Group//DTD Invoice 1.0//EN: /com/sun/j2ee/blue-
prints/xmldocuments/rsrc/schemas/Invoice.dtd
# XSD URI to physical location (URL or resource path)
http\://blueprints.j2ee.sun.com/LineItem: /com/sun/j2ee/blue-
prints/xmldocuments/rsrc/schemas/LineItem.xsd
http\://blueprints.j2ee.sun.com/Invoice: /com/sun/j2ee/blue-
prints/xmldocuments/rsrc/schemas/Invoice.xsd
```

Code Example 4.12   A Simple Entity Catalog

Although simple implementations such as Code Example 4.11 solve many of the common problems related to external entity management, developers should bear in mind that better solutions are on the horizon. For example, organizations such as the Oasis Consortium are working on formal XML catalog specifications. (See the Web site `http://www.oasis-open.org` for more information on entity resolution and XML catalogs.)

In summary, you may want to consider implementing a custom entity resolution—or, even better, resort to a more elaborate XML catalog solution—in the following circumstances:

❐ To protect the integrity of your application against malicious modification of external schemas by redirecting references to secured copies (either local copies or those on trusted repositories)

❐ During design and, even more so, during production, to protect your application against unexpected, legitimate evolution of the schemas upon which it is based. Instead, you want to defer accounting for this evolution until after you have properly assessed their impact on your application.

❐ To improve performance by maintaining local copies of otherwise remotely accessible schemas.

4.5   Performance Considerations

It is important to consider performance when processing XML documents. XML document processing—handling the document in a pre- or post-processing stage to an application's business logic—may adversely affect application performance because such processing is potentially very CPU, memory, and input/output or network intensive.

Why does XML document processing potentially impact performance so significantly? Recall that processing an incoming XML document consists of multiple steps, including parsing the document; optionally validating the document against a schema (this implies first parsing the schema); recognizing, extracting, and directly processing element contents and attribute values; or optionally mapping these components to other domain-specific objects for further processing. These steps must occur before an application can apply its business logic to the information retrieved from the XML document. Parsing an XML document often requires a great deal of encoding and decoding of character sets, along with string processing. Depending on the API that is used, recognition and extraction of content may consist of walking a tree data structure, or it may consist of intercepting events generated by the parser and then processing these events according to some context. An application that uses XSLT to preprocess an XML document adds more processing overhead before the real business logic work can take place. When the DOM API is used, it creates a representation of the document—a DOM tree—in memory. Large documents result in large DOM trees and corresponding consumption of large amounts of memory. The XML data-binding process has, to some extent, the same memory consumption drawback. Many of these constraints hold true when generating XML documents.

There are other factors with XML document processing that affect performance. Often, the physical and logical structures of an XML document may be different. An XML document may also contain references to external entities. These references are resolved and substituted into the document content during parsing, but prior to validation. Given that the document may originate on a system different from the application's system, and external entities—and even the schema itself—may be located on remote systems, there may be network overhead affecting performance. To perform the parsing and validation, external entities must first be loaded or downloaded to the processing system. This may be a network intensive operation, or require a great deal of input and output operations, when documents have a complex physical structure.

In summary, XML processing is potentially CPU, memory, and network intensive, for these reasons:

- It may be CPU intensive. Incoming XML documents need not only to be parsed but also validated, and they may have to be processed using APIs which may themselves be CPU intensive. It is important to limit the cost of validation as much as possible without jeopardizing the application processing and to use the most appropriate API to process the document.

- It may be memory intensive. XML processing may require creating large numbers of objects, especially when dealing with document object models.

- It may be network intensive. A document may be the aggregation of different external entities that during parsing may need to be retrieved across the network. It is important to reduce as much as possible the cost of referencing external entities.

Following are some guidelines for improving performance when processing XML documents. In particular, these guidelines examine ways of improving the CPU, memory, and input/output or network consumption.

4.5.1   Limit Parsing of Incoming XML Documents

In general, it is best to parse incoming XML documents only when the request has been properly formulated. In the case of a Web service application, if a document is retrieved as a Source parameter from a request to an endpoint method, it is best first to enforce security and validate the meta information that may have been passed as additional parameters with the request.

In a more generic messaging scenario, when a document is wrapped inside another document (considered an envelope), and the envelope contains meta information about security and how to process the inner document, you may apply the same recommendation: Extract the meta information from the envelope, then enforce security and validate the meta information before proceeding with the parsing of the inner document. When implementing a SAX handler and assuming that the meta information is located at the beginning of the document, if either the security or the validation of the meta information fails, then the handler can throw a SAX exception to immediately abort the processing and minimize the overall impact on performance.

4.5.2   Use the Most Appropriate API

It's important to choose the most appropriate XML processing API for your particular task. In this section, we look at the different processing models in terms of the situations in which they perform best and where their performance is limited.

In general, without considering memory consumption, processing using the DOM API tends to be slower than processing using the SAX API. This is because

DOM may have to load the entire document into memory so that the document can be edited or data retrieved, whereas SAX allows the document to be processed as it is parsed. However, despite its initial slowness, it is better to use the DOM model when the source document must be edited or processed multiple times.

You should also try to use JAXB whenever the document content has a direct representation, as domain-specific objects, in Java. If you don't use JAXB, then you must manually map document content to domain-specific objects, and this process often (when SAX is too cumbersome to apply—see page 166) requires an intermediate DOM representation of the document. Not only is this intermediate DOM representation transient, it consumes memory resources and must be traversed when mapping to the domain-specific objects. With JAXB, you can automatically generate the same code, thus saving development time, and, depending on the JAXB implementation, it may not create an intermediate DOM representation of the source document. In any case, JAXB uses less memory resources as a JAXB content tree is by nature smaller than an equivalent DOM tree.

When using higher-level technologies such as XSLT, keep in mind that they may rely on lower-level technologies like SAX and DOM, which may affect performance, possibly adversely.

When building complex XML transformation pipelines, use the JAXP class `SAXTransformerFactory` to process the results of one style sheet transformation with another style sheet. You can optimize performance—by avoiding the creation of in-memory data structures such as DOM trees—by working with SAX events until at the last stage in the pipeline.

As an alternative, you may consider using APIs other than the four discussed previously. JDOM and dom4j are particularly appropriate for applications that implement a document-centric processing model and that must manipulate a DOM representation of the documents.

JDOM, for example, achieves the same results as DOM but, because it is more generic, it can address any document model. Not only is it optimized for Java, but developers find JDOM easy to use because it relies on the Java `Collection` API. JDOM documents can be built directly from, and converted to, SAX events and DOM trees, allowing JDOM to be seamlessly integrated in XML processing pipelines and in particular as the source or result of XSLT transformations.

Another alternative API is dom4j, which is similar to JDOM. In addition to supporting tree-style processing, the dom4j API has built-in support for Xpath. For example, the `org.dom4j.Node` interface defines methods to select nodes according to an Xpath expression. dom4j also implements an event-based processing model so that it can efficiently process large XML documents. When Xpath expressions are matched during parsing, registered handlers can be called back, thus allowing you to immediately process and dispose of parts of the document without waiting for the entire document to be parsed and loaded into memory.

When receiving documents through a service endpoint (either a JAX-RPC or EJB service endpoint) documents are parsed as abstract Source objects. As already noted, do not assume a specific implementation—StreamSource, SAXSource, or DOMSource—for an incoming document. Instead, you should ensure that the optimal API is used to bridge between the specific Source implementation passed to the endpoint and the intended processing model. Keep in mind that the JAXP XSLT API does not guarantee that identity transformations are applied in the most effective way. For example, when applying an identity transformation from a DOM tree to a DOM tree, the most effective way is to return the source tree as the result tree without further processing; however, this behavior is not enforced by the JAXP specification.

A developer may also want to implement stream processing for the application so that it can receive the processing requirements as part of the SOAP request and start processing the document before it is completely received. Document processing in this manner improves overall performance and is useful when passing very large documents. Extreme caution should be taken if doing this, since there is no guarantee that the underlying JAX-RPC implementation will not wait to receive the complete document before passing the Source object to the endpoint and that it will effectively pass a Source object that allows for stream processing, such as StreamSource or SAXSource. The same holds true when implementing stream processing for outgoing documents. While you can pass a Source object that allows for stream processing, there is no guarantee on how the underlying JAX-RPC implementation will actually handle it.

4.5.3   Choose Effective Parser and Style Sheet Implementations

Each parser and style sheet engine implementation is different. For example, one might emphasize functionality, while another performance. A developer might want to use different implementations depending on the task to be accomplished. Consider using JAXP, which not only supports many parsers and style sheet engines, but also has a pluggability feature that allows a developer to swap between implementations and select the most effective implementation for an application's requirements.

When you use JAXP, you can later change the underlying parser implementation without having to change application code.

4.5.3.1 Tune Underlying Parser and Style Sheet Engine Implementations

The JAXP API defines methods to set and get features and properties for configuring the underlying parser and style sheet engine implementations. A particular parser, document builder, or transformer implementation may define specific features and properties to switch on or off specific behaviors dedicated to performance improvement. These are separate from such standard properties and features, such as the `http://xml.org/sax/features/validation` feature used to turn validation on or off.

For example, Xerces defines a deferred expansion feature called `http://apache.org/xml/features/dom/defer-node-expansion`, which enables or disables a lazy DOM mode. In lazy mode (enabled by default), the DOM tree nodes are lazily evaluated, their creation is deferred: They are created only when they are accessed. As a result, DOM tree construction from an XML document returns faster since only accessed nodes are expanded. This feature is particularly useful when processing only parts of the DOM tree. Grammar caching, another feature available in Xerces, improves performance by avoiding repeated parsing of the same XML schemas. This is especially useful when an application processes a limited number of schemas, which is typically the case with Web services.

Use care when setting specific features and properties to preserve the interchangeability of the underlying implementation. When the underlying implementation encounters a feature or a property that it does not support or recognize, the `SAXParserFactory`, the `XMLReader`, or the `DocumentBuilderFactory` may throw these exceptions: a `SAXNotRecognizedException`, a `SAXNotSupportedException`, or an `IllegalArgumentException`. Avoid grouping unrelated features and properties, especially standard versus specific ones, in a single `try/catch` block. Instead, handle exceptions independently so that optional specific features or properties do not prevent switching to a different implementation. You may design your application in such a way that features and properties specific to the underlying implementations may also be defined externally to the application, such as in a configuration file.

4.5.3.2   Reuse and Pool Parsers and Style Sheets

An XML application may have to process different types of documents, such as documents conforming to different schemas. A single parser may be used (per thread of execution) to handle successively documents of different types just by reassigning the handlers according to the source documents to be processed. Parsers, which are complex objects, may be pooled so that they can be reused by other threads of execution, reducing the burden on memory allocation and garbage collection. Additionally, if the number of different document types is large and if the handlers are expensive to create, handlers may be pooled as well. The same considerations apply to style sheets and transformers.

Parsers, document builders, and transformers, as well as style sheets, can be pooled using a custom pooling mechanism. Or, if the processing occurs in the EJB tier, you may leverage the EJB container's instance pooling mechanism by implementing stateless session beans or message-driven beans dedicated to these tasks. Since these beans are pooled by the EJB container, the parsers, document builders, transformers, and style sheets to which they hold a reference are pooled as well.

Style sheets can be compiled into `javax.xml.transform.Templates` objects to avoid repeated parsing of the same style sheets. `Templates` objects are thread safe and are therefore easily reusable.

4.5.4   Reduce Validation Cost

Not only is it important, but validation may be required to guarantee the reliability of an XML application. An application may legitimately rely on the parser's validation so that it can avoid double-checking the validity of document contents. Validation is an important step of XML processing, but keep in mind that it may affect performance.

Consider the trusted and reliable system depicted in Figure 4.14. This system is composed of two loosely coupled applications. The front-end application receives XML documents as part of requests and forwards these documents to the reservation engine application, which is implemented as a document-centric workflow.

Although you must validate external incoming XML documents, you can exchange freely—that is, without validation—internal XML documents or already validated external XML documents. In short, you need to validate only at the system boundaries, and you may use validation internally only as an assertion mechanism during development. You may turn validation off when in production and looking for optimal performance.

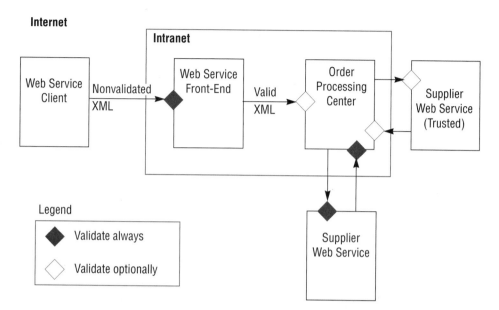

Figure 4.14 Validating Only When Necessary

In other words, when you are both the producer and consumer of XML documents, you may use validation as an assertion mechanism during development, then turn off validation when in production. Additionally, during production validation can be used as a diagnostic mechanism by setting up validation so that it is triggered by fault occurrences.

4.5.5 Reduce the Cost of Referencing External Entities

Recall that an XML document may be the aggregation of assorted external entities, and that these entities may need to be retrieved across the network when parsing. In addition, the schema may also have to be retrieved from an external location. External entities, including schemas, must be loaded and parsed even when they are not being validated to ensure that the same information is delivered to the application regardless of any subsequent validation. This is especially true with respect to default values that may be specified in an incoming document schema.

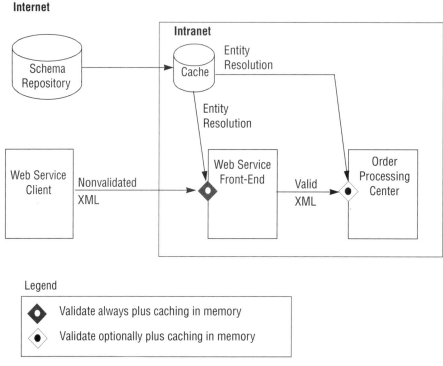

Figure 4.15   An Architecture for Caching External Entities

There are two complementary ways to reduce the cost of referencing external entities:

1. **Caching using a proxy cache**—You can improve the efficiency of locating references to external entities that are on a remote repository by setting up a proxy that caches retrieved, external entities. However, references to external entities must be URLs whose protocols the proxy can handle. (See Figure 4.15, which should be viewed in the context of Figure 4.14.)

2. **Caching using a custom entity resolver**—SAX parsers allow XML applications to handle external entities in a customized way. Such applications have to register their own implementation of the `org.xml.sax.EntityResolver` interface with the parser using the `setEntityResolver` method. The applications are then able to intercept external entities (including schemas) before they are parsed. Similarly, JAXP defines the `javax.xml.transform.URIResolver` inter-

face. Implementing this interface enables you to retrieve the resources referred to in the style sheets by the `xsl:import` or `xsl:include` statements. For an application using a large set of componentized style sheets, this may be used to implement a cache in much the same way as the `EntityResolver`. You can use `EntityResolver` and `URIResolver` to implement:

- A caching mechanism in the application itself, or
- A custom URI lookup mechanism that may redirect system and public references to a local copy of a public repository.

You can use both caching approaches together to ensure even better performance. Use a proxy cache for static entities whose lifetime is greater than the application's lifetime. This particularly works with public schemas, which include the version number in their public or system identifier, since they evolve through successive versions. A custom entity resolver may first map public identifiers (usually in the form of a URI) into system identifiers (usually in the form of an URL). Afterwards, it applies the same techniques as a regular cache proxy when dealing with system identifiers in the form of an URL, especially checking for updates and avoiding caching dynamic content. Using these caching approaches often results in a significant performance improvement, especially when external entities are located on the network. Code Example 4.13 illustrates how to implement a caching entity resolver using the SAX API.

```java
import java.util.Map;
import java.util.WeakHashMap;
import java.lang.ref.SoftReference;
import org.xml.sax.*;

public class CachingEntityResolver implements EntityResolver {
    public static final int MAX_CACHE_ENTRY_SIZE = ...;
    private EntityResolver parentResolver;
    private Map entities = new WeakHashMap();

    static private class Entity {
        String name;
        byte[] content;
    }

    public CachingEntityResolver(EntityResolver parentResolver) {
        this.parentResolver = parentResolver;
```

```
        buffer = new byte[MAX_CACHE_ENTRY_SIZE];
    }

    public InputSource resolveEntity(String publicId,
        String systemId) throws IOException, SAXException {
        InputStream stream = getEntity(publicId, systemId);
        if (stream != null) {
            InputSource source = new InputSource(stream);
            source.setPublicId(publicId);
            source.setSystemId(systemId);
            return source;
        }
        return null;
    }

    private InputStream getEntity(String publicId, String systemId)
            throws IOException, SAXException {
        Entity entity = null;
        SoftReference reference
            = (SoftReference) entities.get(systemId);
        if (reference != null) {
            // Got a soft reference to the entity,
            // let's get the actual entity.
            entity = (Entity) reference.get();
        }
        if (entity == null) {
            // The entity has been reclaimed by the GC or was
            // never created, let's download it again! Delegate to
            // the parent resolver that implements the actual
            // resolution strategy.
            InputSource source
                = parentResolver.resolveEntity(publicId, systemId);
            if (source != null) {
                return cacheEntity(publicId, systemId,
                    source.getByteStream());
            }
            return null;
        }
        return new ByteArrayInputStream(entity.content);
```

```
        }
        // Attempts to cache an entity; if it's too big just
        // return an input stream to it.
        private InputStream cacheEntity(String publicId,
                String systemId, InputStream stream) throws IOException {
            stream = new BufferedInputStream(stream);
            int count = 0;
            for (int i = 0; count < buffer.length; count += i) {
                if ((i = stream.read(buffer, count,
                    buffer.length - count)) < 0) { break; }
            }
            byte[] content = new byte[count];
            System.arraycopy(buffer, 0, content, 0, count);
            if (count != buffer.length) {
                // Cache the entity for future use, using a soft reference
                // so that the GC may reclaim it if it's not referenced
                // anymore and memory is running low.
                Entity entity = new Entity();
                entity.name = publicId != null ? publicId : systemId;
                entity.content = content;
                entities.put(entity.name, new SoftReference(entity));
                return new ByteArrayInputStream(content);
            }
            // Entity too big to be cached.
            return new SequenceInputStream(
                new ByteArrayInputStream(content), stream);
        }
    }
```

Code Example 4.13 Using SAX API to Implement a Caching Entity Resolver

4.5.6   Cache Dynamically Generated Documents

Dynamically generated documents are typically assembled from values returned from calls to business logic. Generally, it is a good idea to cache dynamically generated XML documents to avoid having to refetch the document contents, which entails extra round trips to a business tier. This is a good rule to follow when the data is predominantly read only, such as catalog data. Furthermore, if applicable, you can cache document content (DOM tree or JAXB content tree) in the user's session on the interaction or presentation layer to avoid repeatedly invoking the business logic.

However, you quickly consume more memory when you cache the result of a user request to serve subsequent, related requests. When you take this approach, keep in mind that it must not be done to the detriment of other users. That is, be sure that the application does not fail because of a memory shortage caused by holding the cached results. To help with memory management, use soft references, which allow more enhanced interaction with the garbage collector to implement caches.

When caching a DOM tree in the context of a distributed Web container, the reference to the tree stored in an HTTP session may have to be declared as `transient`. This is because `HttpSession` requires objects that it stores to be Java serializable, and not all DOM implementations are Java serializable. Also, Java serialization of a DOM tree may be very expensive, thus countering the benefits of caching.

4.5.7   Use XML Judiciously

Using XML documents in a Web services environment has its pluses and minuses. XML documents can enhance Web service interoperability: Heterogeneous, loosely coupled systems can easily exchange XML documents because they are text documents. However, loosely coupled systems must pay the price for this ease of interoperability, since the parsing that these XML documents require is very expensive. This applies to systems that are loosely coupled in a technical and an enterprise sense.

Contrast this with tightly coupled systems. System components that are tightly coupled can use standard, nondocument-oriented techniques (such as RMI) that are far more efficient in terms of performance and require far less coding complexity. Fortunately, with technologies such as JAX-RPC and JAXB you can combine the best of both worlds. Systems can be developed that are internally tightly coupled and object oriented, and that can interact in a loosely coupled, document-oriented manner.

Generally, when using XML documents, follow these suggestions:

☐ Rely on XML protocols, such as those implemented by JAX-RPC and others, to interoperate with heterogeneous systems and to provide loosely coupled integration points.

☐ Avoid using XML for unexposed interfaces or for exchanges between components that should be otherwise tightly coupled.

Direct Java serialization of domain-specific objects is usually faster than XML serialization of an equivalent DOM tree or even the Java serialization of the DOM tree itself (when the DOM implementation supports such a Java serialization). Also, direct Java serialization of the domain-specific objects usually results in a serialized object form that is smaller than the serialized forms of the other two approaches. The Java serialization of the DOM tree is usually the most expensive in processing time as well as in memory footprint; therefore it should be used with extreme care (if ever), especially in an EJB context where serialization occurs when accessing remote enterprise beans. When accessing local enterprise beans, you can pass DOM tree or DOM tree fragments without incurring this processing expense. Table 4.2 summarizes the guidelines for using XML for component interactions.

To summarize, when implementing an application which spans multiple containers, keep the following points in mind (also see Table 4.2).

☐ For remote component interaction, Java objects are efficient, serialized XML —although expensive—may be used for interoperability. DOM is very expensive, and Java serialization of DOM trees is not always supported.

☐ For local component interaction, Java objects are the most efficient and DOM may be used when required by the application processing model. However, serialized XML is to be avoided.

☐ Bind to domain-specific Java objects as soon as possible and process these objects rather than XML documents.

Table 4.2   Guidelines for Using XML Judiciously for Component Interaction

Data Passing Between Components	Remote Components	Local Components
Java Objects	Efficient	Highly efficient (Fine-grained access}
Document Object Model	Very expensive, nonstandard serialization	Only for document-centric architectures
Serialized XML	Expensive, but interoperable	No reason to serialize XML for local calls

4.6   Conclusion

This chapter covered much of the considerations a developer should keep in mind when writing applications, particularly Web services-based applications, that use XML documents. Once these issues and considerations are understood, then a developer can make informed decisions about not only how to design and implement these XML-based applications, but if the applications should even be based on XML. In a sense, the developer is encouraged to ask this question first: "Should this application be based on XML?"

Once the developer decides that XML is appropriate for the application, then the next task is for the developer to design a sound and balanced architecture. Such an architecture should rely on XML only for what XML is good at. That is, the architecture should use XML for open, inter-application communication, configuration descriptions, information sharing, and especially for accessing domains for which public XML schemas exist. At the same time, XML may not be the appropriate solution of choice when application interfaces are not exposed publicly or for exchanging information between components that should be communicating in a tightly coupled manner.

The chapter also considered the factors a developer must weigh when deciding where and how to perform XML processing. Should XML processing be limited to the interaction layer of a Web service as a pre- or post-processing stage of the business logic, or should the business logic itself be expressed in terms of

XML processing? The chapter further helped clarify when it makes sense to implement an object-centric processing model or a document-centric processing model.

These decisions determine the developer's choice among the different XML-processing APIs and implementations. Furthermore, the chapter described the performance trade-offs among these different processing techniques and compared performance with functionality and ease of use. It indicated situations where and why one technique might be superior to another and helped delineate the rationale for these choices.

CHAPTER 5

Client Design

W EB services take the Web client model to the next level. Developers can write far more powerful clients whose interaction with Web services provides a rich client experience. In this environment, client developers need not have control over the server portion of an application, yet they can still write powerful, rich client applications. This chapter focuses on using the Java platform to design and develop Web services-based clients.

Clients can take advantage of Web services to obtain a wide range of functions or services. To a client, a Web service is a black box: The client does not have to know how the service is implemented or even who provides it. The client primarily cares about the functionality—the service—provided by the Web service. Examples of Web services include order tracking services, information lookup services, and credit card validation services. Various clients running on different types of platforms can all access these Web services.

One of the principal reasons for implementing Web services is to achieve interoperability. Clients can access Web services regardless of the platform or operating system upon which the service is implemented. Not only is the service's platform of no concern to the client, the client's implementation language is completely independent of the service.

Web service clients can take many forms, from full-blown J2EE applications, to rich client applications, even to light-weight application clients, such as wireless devices. In short, there are many different types of clients that can talk to Web services. The Java platform provides excellent support for writing Web service clients. Web services also provide clients a standardized approach to access services through firewalls. Such access extends the capabilities of clients. Clients accessing Web services also remain more loosely coupled to the service.

We start by looking at the different means for communicating with Web services and applications, and then examine some typical scenarios where using Web services-based clients make sense. From there, the chapter discusses the different types of clients that use Web services, particularly highlighting the different design considerations for the principal Java clients: J2EE, J2SE, and J2ME clients. Then the chapter addresses the steps for developing these client applications, from locating a service through handling errors. It also covers the communication APIs that client applications can employ to access a service. Included in this discussion are recommendations and guidelines to help developers choose the optimal approach. The chapter concludes with guidelines for packaging client applications.

5.1   Choosing a Communication Technology

Web services are only one of several ways for a client to access an application service. For example, Java applications may access application services using RMI/IIOP, JMS, or Web services. There are advantages and disadvantages with each of these communication technologies, and the developer must weigh these considerations when deciding on the client application design.

Interoperability is the primary advantage for using Web services as a means of communication. Web services give clients the ability to interoperate with almost any type of system and application, regardless of the platform on which the system or application runs. In addition, the client can use a variety of technologies for this communication. Furthermore, different client types—such as handheld devices, desktop browsers, or rich GUI clients—running on different platforms and written in different languages may be able to access the same set of services. Some applications may be designed such that their functionality is only accessible via a Web service.

Web services use HTTP as the transport protocol, which enables clients to operate with systems through firewalls. The service's WSDL document enables clients and services that use very different technologies to map and convert their respective data objects. For services and clients that are based on JAX-RPC, the JAX-RPC runtime handles this mapping transparently.

Let's look at the different communication approaches that are available to a J2EE client to access a service, including Web services, RMI/IIOP, and Java Message Service. Clients can easily use the JAX-RPC-generated stub classes to access a Web service. Although not as fast from a performance perspective as other technologies (such as RMI/IIOP), JAX-RPC gives clients greater flexibility and supports more types of clients.

J2EE application clients may also use RMI/IIOP to make remote calls over the network on application business logic. RMI/IIOP is often used for clients operating in intranet environments, where there is a greater degree of control over the client's deployment and the J2EE server. While these controlled environments provide a client container that handles the communication security, passing through firewalls can be problematic. RMI/IIOP provides clients with secure access to the application business logic while at the same time taking care of the details of the client and server communication and marshalling and demarshalling parameters.

Java Message Service (JMS) is another means for J2EE clients to communicate with server applications. JMS provides a means for asynchronous communication. Applications using JMS are better suited to a setting that is behind a firewall, since messaging systems generally do not work well on the Internet. (Often, messaging systems are not even exposed on the Internet.) Not only must developers have some knowledge of how to work with messaging systems, such as how to set up and use topics or queues, but the messaging system mechanisms must already be in place.

Although Web services provide a standard way to exchange XML documents over HTTP, you can use nonstandard approaches as well. Communication using the HTTP protocol requires only a simple infrastructure to send and receive messages. However, the client application must be able to parse the XML documents representing the messages. Parsing involves mapping the XML data to the client application's object model. When using this means of communication, the developer at a minimum needs to write code to send and receive the documents over HTTP as well as to parse the document data. If such communication must also be secure, developers would have to include code that uses Secure Socket Layer (SSL), making the development task more difficult. However, this means of communication may be sufficient, particularly in a closed environment or when clients are applets. Care should be taken if using this approach, since it is not standard.

5.2　Scenarios for Web Services-Based Client Applications

Developers typically write clients to access preexisting Web services—that is, public or private Web services. At times, the same developers may simultaneously develop both the service and its clients. Regardless of this, client developers should rely on the WSDL service description for their knowledge of the service details. In addition, developers may use a variety of technologies and APIs for developing these clients. They may develop clients using J2EE technologies, often called J2EE clients, or they may use the standard Java (J2SE and J2ME) technologies, or even non-Java technologies.

Before delving into the details of client development, let's examine several Web service client scenarios. Although different, each scenario is based on accessing the same Web service. The scenarios are as follows:

- J2EE component—In this scenario, a J2EE component accesses a Web service. The J2EE component receives results from the service, and it formats these results so that it can be read or displayed by a browser.

- J2SE client—A J2SE client may access the same Web service as the J2EE component. However, the J2SE client provides a more detailed view of the results returned from the service.

- J2ME client—A J2ME client, such as a client application running on a mobile device or PDA, gives a user the freedom to access the same Web service from places other than his or her office. In addition, the user can work offline with the results returned from the service.

- Non-Java client—A non-Java client accesses the same Web service using SOAP over HTTP.

Figure 5.1 shows how these different types of clients might access the same purchase order tracking Web service interface. All clients, regardless of their platform, rely on the Web service's WSDL document, which uses a standard format to describe the service's location and its operations. Clients need to know the information in the WSDL document—such as the URL of the service, types of parameters, and port names—to understand how to communicate with a particular service.

It is important to note that none of the clients communicate directly with a Web service. Each client type relies on a runtime—either a JAX-RPC or SOAP runtime—through which it accesses the service. From the developer's perspective, the client's use of a runtime is kept nearly transparent. However, good design dictates that a developer still modularize the Web service access code, plus consider issues related to remote calls and handling remote exceptions. These points are addressed later. (See "Locating and Accessing a Service" on page 219 and "Handling Exceptions" on page 230.)

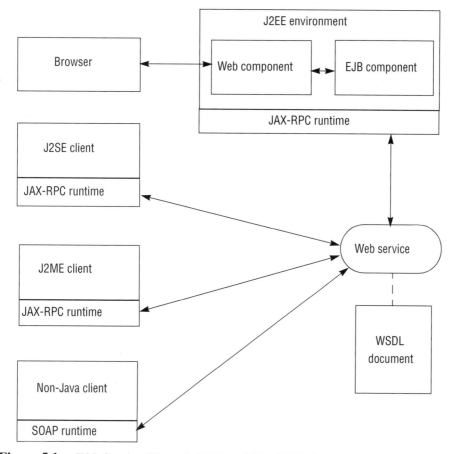

Figure 5.1 Web Service Clients in J2EE and Non-J2EE Environments

Browser-based applications rely on J2EE components, which act as clients of the Web service. These clients, referred to as J2EE clients, are J2EE components that access a Web service, and the JAX-RPC runtime in turn handles the communication with the Web service. The J2EE environment shields the developer from the communication details. J2EE clients run in either an EJB container or a Web container, and these containers manage the client environment.

Stand-alone clients—which may be J2SE clients, J2ME clients, or clients written in a language other than Java—communicate to the Web service through the JAX-RPC runtime or the SOAP runtime. Stand-alone clients are outside the J2EE environment. Because they don't have a J2EE EJB container or Web container to manage the environment, stand-alone clients require more work from the developer.

Although each type of client works well, developers must deal with an increasing level of complexity if they work directly with the JAX-RPC or SOAP runtimes. The advantage of the J2EE environment is that it shields developers from some of the complexity associated with developing Web services, such as the look up of the service and the life-cycle management of objects used to access a service. In the J2EE environment, a developer uses JNDI to look up a service in much the same way as he or she might use other Java APIs, such as JDBC or JMS.

Given that many types of clients can access Web services, how do you determine which type of client is best for your application? To make this determination, you must consider how end users and the application expect to use the service. You should also weigh the pros and cons of each client type, and consider that each type of client has its own unique characteristics that may make it appropriate (or not appropriate) for a specific application task. Thus, you should consider the characteristics of the different client types as well as the communication mechanisms available to each client type when deciding which client type to use to access a Web service. The following general guidelines should help with this decision:

- ❒ **J2EE clients**—J2EE clients have good access to Web services. J2EE clients have other advantages provided by the J2EE platform, such as declarative security, transactions, and instance management. J2EE clients may also access Web services from within a workflow architecture, and they may aggregate Web services.

- ❒ **J2SE clients**—Generally, J2SE clients are best when you need to provide a rich interface or when you must manipulate large sets of data. J2SE clients may also work in a disconnected mode of operation.

- ❒ **J2ME clients**—J2ME clients are best for applications that require remote and immediate access to a Web service. J2ME clients may be restricted to a limited set of interface components. Like J2SE clients, J2ME clients may also work in a disconnected mode of operation.

Now that we have looked at some sample Web service scenarios, let's examine in more detail the different types of clients that use Web services.

5.2.1 Designing J2EE Clients

As already noted, the J2EE 1.4 platform provides an environment that supports client application access to Web services. In a J2EE environment the deployment descriptors declaratively define the client-side Web service configuration information. The deployer may change this configuration information at deployment. In addition, the J2EE platform handles the underlying work for creating and initializing the access to the Web services.

The J2EE platform provides many other technologies in addition to supporting Web services. Developers can obtain a richer set of functionality by using these other services, such as Web and EJB components, in addition to Web services for their client applications.

For example, consider a browser client that accesses an order tracking Web service via a Web component. (See Figure 5.2.) The Web component presents a browser page to the end user, who enters an order identifier to a form displayed in its browser. The browser client passes this order identifier to a Web component, which accesses the order tracking Web service and retrieves the order information. The Web component converts the retrieved information to an HTML page and returns the formatted page to the browser client for presentation to the end user.

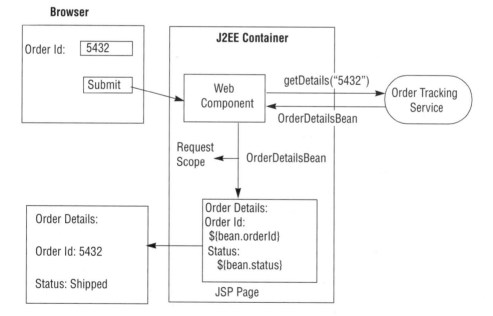

Figure 5.2 Web Tier Component Calling a Web Service

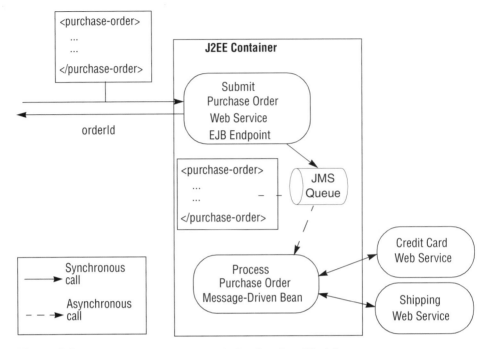

Figure 5.3   EJB Components and Web Services in a Workflow

In this example, a Web component calls the order tracking service and, when it receives a response from the service, it puts the results in a Java Beans component (OrderDetailsBean) that is within the request scope. The Web component uses a JSP to generate an HTML response, which the container returns to the browser that made the original request.

It is also possible to write J2EE clients using EJB components. (See Figure 5.3.) These EJB components may themselves be Web service endpoints as well as clients of other Web services. Often, EJB components are used in a workflow to provide Web services with the additional support provided by an EJB container—that is, declarative transactional support, declarative security, and life-cycle management.

Figure 5.3 demonstrates a workflow scenario: a Web service endpoint used in combination with a message-driven bean component to provide a workflow operation that runs asynchronously once the initial service starts. The Web service endpoint synchronously puts the purchase order in a JMS message queue and returns an orderId to the calling application. The message-driven bean listens for messages delivered from the JMS queue. When one arrives, the bean retrieves the message and initiates the purchase order processing workflow. The purchase order is processed asynchronously while the Web service receives other purchase orders.

In this example, the workflow consists of three additional stages performed by separate Web services: a credit card charging service, a shipping service, and a service that sends an order confirmation. The message-driven bean aggregates the three workflow stages. Other systems within an organization may provide these services and they may be shared by many applications.

5.2.2 Designing J2SE Clients

Unlike the J2EE environment, developers of non-J2EE clients are responsible for much of the underlying work to look up a service and to create and maintain instances of classes that access the service. Since they cannot rely on a container, these developers must create and manage their own services and ensure the availability of all runtime environments needed to access the Web services.

J2SE clients, such as desktop applications developed using the Swing API, have the capability to do more processing and state management than other clients. This type of application client can provide a rich GUI application development environment that includes document editing and graphical manipulation. However, there are some points that should be kept in mind when considering J2SE clients:

- Long-running applications—Using J2SE is particularly good for Web service clients that run for extended periods of time. Because these applications run for long periods, developers must consider that both the client and the Web service may need to maintain the state of at least some of the data. It is possible to embed conversational state within each method invocation, if required by the service's use case.

- Using a rich graphical user interface (GUI) for complex data—J2SE clients can provide users with a rich view of data. Such a rich interface might permit a user to navigate and modify offline a large set of data returned by a service. The client can later update the Web service with any changes to the data.

- Requiring only intermittent network access—J2SE client can use Web services without needing to maintain continuous network access, relieving some of the burden on a network. Care must be taken to ensure data consistency between the service and the client.

- Requiring complex computations on the client—J2SE clients are well-suited for performing complex mathematical calculations, as well as operations that update data, and then submitting the results to a service. For example, these clients have better resources for image manipulation, and they can relieve the server of this burden. Thus, J2SE clients can provide a better environment than a service for a user's interaction with data sets.

For example, a J2SE application may contain a rich GUI used to update catalog information. The user can manipulate attributes as well as graphical data using the application's GUI screens. When the user finishes, the application submits new or updated catalog data to the catalog service.

J2SE applications may be deployed using Java Web Start technology. Java Web Start simplifies deployment in large enterprise environments by ensuring that clients have available the proper versions of the Java Runtime Environment and all necessary libraries.

❑ Whenever possible, use Java Web Start to provide a standardized means of deployment for J2SE clients.

❑ When designing a Web service client, try to keep Web service access code separate from GUI code.

❑ Since J2SE clients may operate in either a connected or disconnected mode, when developing these clients keep in mind issues related to maintenance of state and client and service synchronization.

5.2.3   J2ME Clients

Java 2 Platform, Micro Edition (J2ME) clients may interact remotely with a Web service. However, since J2ME clients have limited GUI capabilities compared to J2SE clients, consider using J2ME clients when mobility and remote access are requirements. Also consider using this type of client when immediacy of access is important.

For example, Figure 5.4 shows a J2ME client running on a cell phone and accessing an order tracking service. The client does not need an elaborate GUI or set of widgets to interact with the Web service.

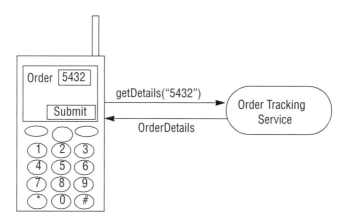

Figure 5.4   J2ME Client Accessing Web Service

J2ME clients may access Web services using a subset of the JAX-RPC API. When accessing Web services, J2ME clients should consider network connection and bandwidth issues, offline versus connected operation, and GUI and processing limitations.

Networks supporting J2ME devices may not always provide consistent connectivity. Applications using such networks must consider connection failure, or sporadic connectivity, and be designed so that recovery is possible.

Additionally, the bandwidths for many networks supporting J2ME devices limit the rate at which data can be exchanged. Applications need to be designed to limit their data exchange rate to that allowed by the network and to consider the cost that these limitations imply. Care must also be taken to deal with network latency to keep the user experience acceptable. Since Web services do not specify a level of service for message delivery, the client application must take this into account and provide support for message delivery failures.

Keep in mind that J2ME network providers may charge for network usage by the kilobyte. J2ME-targeted applications may be expensive for the user unless care is taken to limit the data transferred.

Applications for J2ME devices may work in an offline, or disconnected, mode as well as an online, or connected, mode. When working in an offline mode, applications should collect data and batch it into requests to the Web service, as well as obtain data from the service in batches. Consideration should be given to the amount of data that is passed between the Web service and the client.

Applications for J2ME devices have a standard, uniform set of GUI widgets available for manipulating data, such as the liquid crystal display UI that is part of MIDP 1.0 and MIDP 2.0. Plus, each device type may have its own set of widgets. Such widgets have different abilities for validating data prior to accessing a service.

J2ME devices, while capable of small computations and data validation, have limited processing capabilities and memory constraints. Client applications need to consider the types of data exchanged and any pre- and post-processing required. For example, J2ME devices have limited support for XML document processing and are not required to perform XML document validation.

In summary, keep the following considerations in mind when designing J2ME clients.

❏ **Connectivity and bandwidth limitations**—J2ME clients may have limited bandwidth, intermittent disconnects, and fees for connection usage.

❏ **Processing power**—The processing capabilities of a Web service client should be considered in its design.

❏ **State maintenance**—J2ME clients may operate in a connected or disconnected mode, requiring the maintenance of state and synchronization between client and service.

5.3   Developing Client Applications to Use a Web Service

All client applications follow certain steps to use a Web service. In brief, they must first look up or locate the service, make a call to the service, and process any returned data. The choice of communication mode determines much of the details for performing these steps.

An application can communicate with a service using stubs, dynamic proxies, or the dynamic invocation interface (DII) `Call` interface. (The next section explains these modes.) With these modes, a developer relies on some form of client-side proxy class (stub, dynamic proxy, or a DII interface) representing a Web service to access the service's functionality. The client developer decides which representation to use based on the WSDL availability, the service's endpoint address, and the use cases for the service.

After deciding on a communication mode, developers need to do the following when designing and developing client applications:

1. **Assess the nature and availability of the service and the service description.**

   Typically, the first step is to determine the location of the Web service's WSDL document and choose a communication mode. If you are using stubs or dynamic proxies, you must first locate and gain access to the full WSDL document representing the Web service, since you develop the client application from the stubs and supporting files generated from the WSDL. If you have access to only a partial WSDL file, then use DII, since DII lets you locate the service at runtime . See "Communication Modes for Accessing a Service" on page 212 for more information.

2. **Create a client-side Web service delegate.**

   - If applicable, generate the necessary stubs and support classes—Generated classes may not be portable across implementations. If portability is important, limit your use of vendor-specific method calls in the stub classes.

   - Locate the service—Depending on the communication mode, there are different ways to locate a service. See "Locating and Accessing a Service" on page 219.

   - Configure the stub or Call objects—See "Stubs and Call Configuration" on page 223.

3. **Invoke the service.**

   - When using stubs and dynamic proxies, invocations are synchronous. Use DII if you choose to have a one-way call.

   - Handle parameters, return values, and exceptions.

4. **Present the view.**

   Often the client may need to generate a view for end users. There are different ways clients can handle the presentation to the user of the Web service response. In some cases, a service sends its response as an XML document, and this document may be transformed or mapped to a suitable format for presentation. Web tier clients might pass the service response to a Web component such as JSP and let the component apply a transformation to the XML document or otherwise handle the returned data. EJB tier clients may themselves apply XSLT transformations to the returned content to create the target content, which they then pass to a Web component.

   The following sections examine some of the considerations for designing and implementing client applications.

5.3.1   Communication Modes for Accessing a Service

To best determine the communication mode for your client application, you need to know the answers to the following two questions. Is the Web service's full WSDL document known? Is the endpoint address for the Web service known?

As indicated, there are three principal modes for a client application's communication with a Web service: stub, dynamic proxy, and dynamic invocation interface (DII). By a communication mode, we mean the APIs for programmatically accessing a service via the `javax.xml.rpc.Service` interface. Clients using either the stubs or dynamic proxies to access a service require the prior definition of a service endpoint interface. Note that when we refer to the service endpoint interface, which is the interface between the stub and dynamic proxy clients and the JAX-RPC API and stub, we are referring to the interface that represents the client's view of a Web service.

When using stubs, a JAX-RPC runtime tool generates during development static stub classes that enable the service and the client to communicate. The stub, which sits between the client and the client representation of the service endpoint interface, is responsible for converting a request from a client to a SOAP message and sending it to the service. The stub also converts responses from the service endpoint, which it receives as SOAP messages, to a format understandable by the client. In a sense, a stub is a local object that acts as a proxy for the service endpoint.

Dynamic proxies provides the same functionality as the stubs, but do so in a more dynamic fashion. Stubs and dynamic proxies both provide the developer access to the `javax.xml.rpc.Stub` interface, which represents a service endpoint. With both models, it is easy for a developer to program against the service endpoint interface, particularly because the JAX-RPC runtime does much of the communication work behind the scenes. The dynamic proxy model differs from the stub model principally because the dynamic proxy model does not require code generation during development.

DII is a call interface that supports a programmatic invocation of JAX-RPC requests. Using DII, a client can call a service or a remote procedure on a service without knowing at compile time the exact service name or the procedure's signature. A DII client can discover this information at runtime and can dynamically look up the service and its remote procedures.

When using DII, clients can dynamically access a service at runtime. The stubs rely on a tool that uses the WSDL file to create the service endpoint interface, plus generate stub and other necessary classes. These generated classes eliminate the need for the developer to use the JAX-RPC APIs directly. By contrast, the dynamic proxy and DII approaches both require the developer to use the JAX-RPC APIs.

5.3.1.1 Using Stub Communication

J2EE clients should use generated stubs to access services, especially for services with fairly static interfaces. Stub communication easily allows Java access to a Web service. This is the recommended approach for accessing services and their WSDL files when they are unlikely to change over time.

Figure 5.5 shows how a client application might access a Web service using a stub generated by a tool prior to the client's deployment and compilation. The WSDL file for the service served as input to the tool. The client-side service endpoint interface, which implements the service endpoint interface on the client-side of the communication channel, provides the client view of the Web service.

The stub, which implements the client-side service endpoint interface, acts as a proxy to the Web service for the client; that is, the stub is the client's view of the Web service. The tool that generates the stub class also generates all necessary helper classes for accessing the service. These helper classes define the parameters for calls to the service and the service's return values, ensuring that the parameters and return values are all of the proper types expected by the JAX-RPC runtime. To generate these stub and helper classes, the tool relies on the WSDL document as well as a JAX-RPC mapping file. The mapping file supplies information regarding the Java-to-XML bindings, such as the correct package name for generated classes.

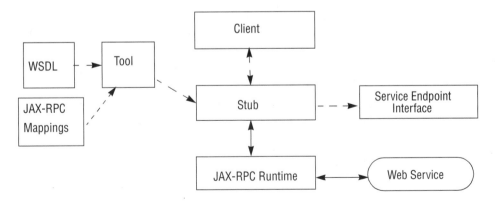

Figure 5.5   Stub Communication Model

The J2ME environment differs somewhat. Applications in J2ME environments can use only stubs to access Web services, and stubs are portable for J2ME devices. The JAX-RPC profile for J2ME environments does not support dynamic proxies and DII.

Although at this time stubs are not portable across J2EE implementations, the next version of JAX-RPC is expected to address this portability issue.

❏　Using stubs, especially in a Java environment, is often the easiest because the developer can work with generated class files representing the service method call parameters and return values. However, the greater dependencies between the client and the Web service may lead to problems if the service interface changes frequently. This mode also requires that stub classes be generated before compiling the application.

5.3.1.2　Using Dynamic Proxy Communication

The dynamic proxies are similar in many ways to the stubs previously described. However, unlike stubs, the client developer needs only the client-side interface that matches the service endpoint interface. That is, clients using dynamic proxies program to an interface that ensures the client application is portable across other JAX-RPC runtime implementations. Developers using dynamic proxies must create Java classes to serve as JAX-RPC value types—these classes have an empty constructor and set methods for each field, similar to JavaBeans classes.

The dynamic proxy is based on the service endpoint interface, its WSDL document, and a JAX-RPC mapping file (similar to the stubs model). (See Figure 5.6.) Client applications can access the Web service ports using the `javax.xml.rpc.Service` method `getPort`.

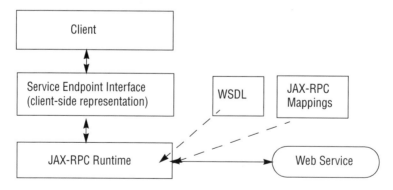

Figure 5.6　Accessing a Service Using a Dynamic Proxy

Note in Figure 5.6 that a client accesses a Web service via the client-side representation of the service endpoint interface, while the JAX-RPC runtime handles the work of communicating with the respective service. A developer programs against an interface, which provides a flexible way to access a service in a portable fashion.

❑ Consider using the dynamic proxy approach if portability is important to your application, since this approach uses the service's endpoint interface to communicate with a service at runtime. Dynamic proxy communication is the most portable mode across JAX-RPC implementations.

❑ Because of how they access a service at runtime, dynamic proxies may have additional overhead when calls are made.

5.3.1.3   Using DII Call Interface

A client application may also dynamically access a Web service by locating the service at runtime from a registry. The client does not know about the service when it is compiled; instead, the client discovers the service's name from a JAXR registry at runtime. Along with the name, the client discovers the required parameters and return values for making a call to the service. Using a dynamic invocation interface, the client locates the service and calls it at runtime.

Generally, using DII is more difficult for a developer. A developer must work with a more complex interface than with stubs or dynamic proxies. Not only does this interface require more work on the part of the developer, it is more prone to class cast exceptions. In addition, the DII approach may have slower access. A developer may choose to use the DII approach when a complete WSDL document is not available or provided, particularly when the WSDL document does not specify ports. The DII approach is more suitable when used within a framework, since from within a framework, client applications can generically and dynamically access services with no changes to core application code.

Figure 5.7 shows how a client uses the JAXR API to look up the endpoint WSDL for a service in a registry. The client uses the information from the registry to construct a `javax.xml.rpc.Call`, which it uses to access the Web service.

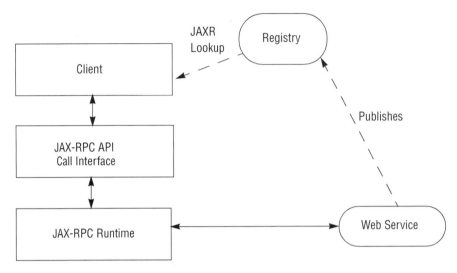

Figure 5.7   DII Call Interface

Using the DII Call interface allows a client application to define at runtime
the service name and the operations it intends to call on the service, thus giving
the client the benefit of loosely coupling its code with that of the service. The
client is less affected by changes to the service, whether those changes involve
access to the service or data requirements. In addition, the DII communication
model permits Web service access code to be standardized among a set of clients
and reused as a component.

❏ DII involves more work than stubs or dynamic proxies and should be used
   sparingly. You may consider using this mode if a service changes frequently.

5.3.1.4   Summary of Communication Model Guidelines

Table 5.1 summarizes the communication models for Web service clients.

Table 5.1   Client Communication Modes

Client Considerations	Stub	Dynamic Proxy	DII
Portable client code across JAX-RPC implementations	Yes, in the J2EE platform when an application uses a neutral means for accessing the stubs. (For an example, see Code Example 5.2.) Since stubs are bound to a specific JAX-RPC runtime, reliance on JAX-RPC-specific access to a stub may not behave the same on all platforms. Stub code needs to be generated for an application.	Yes	Yes
Requires generation of code using a tool	Yes	No. A tool may be used to generate JAX-RPC value types required by a service endpoint interface (but not serializers and other artifacts).	No
Ability to programmatically change the service endpoint URL	Yes, but the WSDL must match that used to generate the stub class and supporting classes.	Yes, but the client-side service endpoint interface must match the representation on the server side.	Yes
Supports service-specific exceptions	Yes	Yes	No. All are `java.rmi.Remote` exceptions. Checked exceptions cannot be used when calls are made dynamically.

Table 5.1   Client Communication Modes (*continued*)

Client Considerations	Stub	Dynamic Proxy	DII
Supports one way communication mode	No	No	Yes
Supports the ability to dynamically specify JAX-RPC value types at runtime	No. Developer must program against a service endpoint interface.	No. Developer must program against a service endpoint interface.	Yes. However, returns Java objects which the developer needs to cast to application-specific objects as necessary.
Supported in J2ME platform	Yes	No	No
Supported in J2SE and J2EE platforms	Yes	Yes	Yes
Requires WSDL	No. A service end-point interface may generate a stub class along with information concerning the protocol binding.	No. A partial WSDL (one with the service port element undefined) may be used.	No. Calls may be used when partial WSDL or no WSDL is specified. Use of methods other than the `createCall` method on the `Call` interface may result in unexpected behavior in such cases.

Choose the communication mode for your client application after considering the following:

❏   J2EE clients should use stubs. Stubs are easiest for developers to use. Keep in mind, however, that with stubs you might lose some portability across JAX-RPC implementations.

❏   J2EE components acting as clients should use dynamic proxies when portability is a requirement. Since dynamic proxies do not require a JAX-RPC mapping file, some ambiguity may occur, and this may result in unexpected behavior when calling a service.

❏   DII is the most difficult to use of the three approaches. Only consider using DII if you need the runtime ability to look up operations.

❏   All J2SE and J2ME clients should use stubs if at all possible.

5.3.2 Locating and Accessing a Service

Locating a service differs depending on the client. Client applications that run in J2EE environments use the JNDI `InitialContext.lookup` method to locate a service, whereas a J2SE client can use the `javax.xml.rpc.ServiceFactory` class or an implementation-specific stub to locate a service. Clients use the `javax.xml.rpc.Service` interface API to access a Web service. A stub implements the service interface.

Code Example 5.1 shows how an application in a J2EE environment might use a stub to access a service. The application locates the service using a JNDI `InitialContext.lookup` call. The JNDI call returns an `OpcOrderTrackingService` object, which is a stub.

```
Context ic = new InitialContext();
OpcOrderTrackingService opcOrderTrackingSvc =
        (OpcOrderTrackingService) ic.lookup(
        "java:comp/env/service/OpcOrderTrackingService");
OrderTrackingIntf port =
        opcOrderTrackingSvc.getOrderTrackingIntfPort();
OrderDetails od = port.getOrderDetails(orderId);
```

Code Example 5.1   Accessing a Service with a Stub in a J2EE Environment

Because it depends on the generated stub classes, the client code in Code Example 5.1 is not the recommended strategy for using stubs. Although this example works without problems, JAX-RPC gives you a neutral way to access a service and obtain the same results. By using the JAX-RPC `javax.xml.rpc.Service` interface method `getPort`, you can access a Web service in the same manner regardless of whether you use stubs or dynamic proxies. The `getPort` method returns either an instance of a generated stub implementation class or a dynamic proxy, and the client can then uses this returned instance to invoke operations on the service endpoint.

The `getPort` method removes the dependencies on generated service-specific implementation classes. When this method is invoked, the JAX-RPC runtime selects a port and protocol binding for communicating with the port, then configures the returned stub that represents the service endpoint interface. Furthermore, since the J2EE platform allows the deployment descriptor to specify multiple ports for a service, the container, based on its configuration, can choose the best available protocol binding and port for the service call. (See Code Example 5.2.)

```
Context ic = new InitialContext();
Service service = (Service)ic.lookup(
        "java:comp/env/service/OpcPurchaseOrderService");
PurchaseOrderIntf port = (PurchaseOrderIntf)service.getPort(
        PurchaseOrderIntf.class);
```

Code Example 5.2   Looking Up a Port Using a Stub or Dynamic Proxy

Code Example 5.2 illustrates how a J2EE client might use the Service interface getPort method. Rather than cast the JNDI reference to the service implementation class, the code casts the JNDI reference to a javax.xml.rpc.Service interface. Using the Service interface in this manner reduces the dependency on generated stub classes. The client developer, by invoking the getPort method, uses the client-side representation of the service endpoint interface to look up the port. After obtaining the port, the client may make any calls desired by the application on the port.

❏ When using stubs or dynamic proxies, the recommended strategy to reduce the dependency on generated classes is to use the java.xml.rpc.Service interface and the getPort method as a proxy for the service implementation class.

❏ A client developer should not circumvent the J2EE platform's management of a service. A client should not create or destroy a Web service port. Instead, a client should use the standard J2EE mechanisms, such as those shown in Code Example 5.2.

❏ A client developer should not assume that the same port instance for the service is used for all calls to the service. Port instances are stateless, and the J2EE platform is not required to return a previously used port instance to a client.

An application in a non-J2EE environment uses a stub to make a Web services call in a different manner. The client application accesses a stub for a service using the method getOrderTrackingIntfPort on the generated implementation class, OpcOrderTrackingService_Impl, which is specific to each JAX-RPC runtime. J2SE or J2ME clients use these generated _Impl files because they do not have access to the naming services available to clients in a J2EE environment through JNDI APIs. See Code Example 5.3.

```
Stub stub = (Stub)(new OpcOrderTrackingService_Impl().
    getOrderTrackingIntfPort());
OrderTrackingIntf port = (OrderTrackingIntf)stub;
```

Code Example 5.3   Accessing a Service with a Stub in J2SE and J2ME Environments

In addition, a J2SE or J2ME client can access a service by using the javax.xml.rpc.ServiceFactory class to instantiate a stub object. Code Example 5.4 shows how a J2SE client might use a factory to locate the same order tracking service.

```
ServiceFactory factory = ServiceFactory.newInstance();
Service service = factory.createService(new QName(
    "urn:OpcOrderTrackingService", "OpcOrderTrackingService"));
```

Code Example 5.4   Looking Up a Service in J2SE and J2ME Environments

Similarly, Code Example 5.5 shows how a J2SE application might use a dynamic proxy instead of a stub to access a service.

```
...
ServiceFactory sf = ServiceFactory.newInstance();
String wsdlURI =
        "http://localhost:8001/webservice/OtEndpointEJB?WSDL";
URL wsdlURL = new URL(wsdlURI);
Service ots = sf.createService(wsdlURL,
        new QName("urn:OpcOrderTrackingService",
        "OpcOrderTrackingService"));
```

```
OrderTrackingIntf port = (
        OrderTrackingIntf)ots.getPort(new QName(
        "urn:OpcOrderTrackingService", "OrderTrackingIntfPort"),
        OrderTrackingIntf.class);
    ...
```

Code Example 5.5   J2SE Client Dynamic Proxy Service Lookup

Code Example 5.5 illustrates how a J2SE client might program to interfaces that are portable across JAX-RPC runtimes. It shows how a J2SE client uses a `ServiceFactory` to look up and obtain access to the service, represented as a `Service` object. The client uses the qualified name, or `QName`, of the service to obtain the service's port. The WSDL document defines the `QName` for the service. The client needs to pass as arguments the `QName` for the target service port and the client-side representation of the service endpoint interface.

By contrast, Code Example 5.6 shows how a J2EE client might use a dynamic proxy to look up and access a service. These two examples show how much simpler it is for J2EE clients to look up and access a service than it is for J2SE clients, since a JNDI lookup from the `IntialContext` of an existing service is much simpler than configuring the parameters for `ServiceFactory`. The J2EE client just invokes a `getPort` call on the client-side representation of the service endpoint interface.

```
Context ic = new InitialContext();
Service ots =
        (Service) ic.lookup(
        "java:comp/env/service/OpcOrderTrackingService");
OrderTrackingIntf port = (OrderTrackingIntf)ots.getPort(
    OrderTrackingIntf.class);
```

Code Example 5.6   Using a Dynamic Proxy in a J2EE Environment

A J2SE client using the DII approach might implement the code shown in Code Example 5.7 to look up the same service at runtime. DII communication supports two invocation modes: synchronous and one way, also called fire and forget. Both invocation modes are configured with the `javax.xml.rpc.Call` object. Note that DII is the only communication model that supports one-way invocation. Code Example 5.7 illustrates using the DII approach for locating and accessing a service. It shows how the Call interface used by DII is configured with the property values required to access the order tracking Web service. The values set for these properties may have been obtained from a registry. Keep in mind that using DII is complex and often requires more work on the part of the client developer.

```
Service service = //get service
QName port = new QName("urn:OpcOrderTrackingService",
        "OrderTrackingIntfPort");
Call call = service.createCall(port);
call.setTargetEndpointAddress(
        "http://localhost:8000/webservice/OtEndpointEJB");
call.setProperty(Call.SOAPACTION_USE_PROPERTY,
        new Boolean(true));
call.setProperty(Call.SOAPACTION_URI_PROPERTY,"");
call.setProperty(ENCODING_STYLE_PROPERTY, URI_ENCODING);
QName QNAME_TYPE_STRING = new QName(NS_XSD, "string");
call.setReturnType(QNAME_TYPE_STRING);
call.setOperationName(
new QName(BODY_NAMESPACE_VALUE "getOrderDetails"));
call.addParameter("String_1", QNAME_TYPE_STRING,
        ParameterMode.IN);
String[] params = {orderId};
OrderDetails = (OrderDetails)call.invoke(params);
```

Code Example 5.7   J2SE Client Using DII to Access a Web Service

5.3.3   Stubs and Call Configuration

Developers may want to configure an instance of a stub or a Call interface prior to invoking a service or may prefer to allow the configuration to take place dynamically at runtime. Often, the developer configures the stub or Call interface prior to invoking the service when the service requires basic authentication. For example, a J2SE client application needs to set a user name and password in the stub or Call just before invoking the service; the service requires these two fields so that it can authenticate the client. In other cases, the developer may want flexibility in specifying the endpoint address to use for a particular service, depending on network availability and so forth. The developer might configure this endpoint address dynamically at runtime.

Stubs may be configured statically or dynamically. A stub's static configuration is set from the WSDL file description at the time the stub is generated. Instead of using this static configuration, a client may use methods defined by the javax.xml.rpc.Stub interface to dynamically configure stub properties at runtime. Two methods are of particular interest: _setProperty to configure stub properties and _getProperty to obtain stub property information. Clients can use these methods to obtain or configure such properties as the service's endpoint address, user name, and password.

Generally, it is advisable to cast vendor-specific stub implementations into a javax.xml.rpc.Stub object for configuration. This ensures that configuration is done in a portable manner and that the application may be run on other JAX-RPC implementations with minimal changes, if any.

Code Example 5.8 shows how a J2EE client might use Stub interface methods to look up and set the endpoint address of a Web service.

```
Service opcPurchaseOrderSvc =
        (Service) ic.lookup(AdventureKeys.PO_SERVICE);
PurchaseOrderIntf port =
        opcPurchaseOrderSvc.getPort(PurchaseOrderIntf.class);
((Stub)port)._setProperty(Stub.ENDPOINT_ADDRESS_PROPERTY,
    "http://localhost:8000/webservice/PoEndpointEJB");
```

Code Example 5.8   Setting Properties on a Stub

In a J2EE environment, the J2EE container reserves the right to use two security-related properties for its own purposes. As a result, J2EE clients using any of the three communication modes (stub, dynamic proxy, or DII) should not configure these two security properties:

```
javax.xml.rpc.security.auth.username
javax.xml.rpc.security.auth.password
```

However, J2SE developers do need to set these two security properties if they invoke a Web service that requires basic authentication. When using DII, the client application may set the properties on the `Call` interface. See Code Example 5.7, which illustrates setting these properties.

❑ J2EE client developers should avoid setting properties other than the `javax.xml.rpc.endpoint.address` property.

❑ Avoid setting nonstandard properties if it is important to achieve portability among JAX-RPC runtimes. Nonstandard properties are those whose property names are *not* preceded by `javax.xml.rpc`.

❑ Avoid using `javax.xml.rpc.session.maintain` property. This property pertains to a service's ability to support sessions. Unless you have control over the development of both the client and the endpoint, such as when both are developed within the same organization, you cannot be sure that the Web service endpoints support sessions, and you may get into trouble if you set this property incorrectly.

5.3.4 WSDL-to-Java Type Mapping

When working with Web services, there may be differences between the SOAP-defined types (defined in the WSDL document) used by the service and the Java-defined types used by the client application. To handle these different types, a client of a Web service cannot use the normal approach and import remote classes. Instead, the client must map the WSDL types to Java types to obtain the parameter and return types used by the service. Once the types are mapped, the client has the correct Java types to use in its code.

Generally, the JAX-RPC runtime handles the mapping of parameters, exceptions, and return values to JAX-RPC types. When a client invokes a service, the JAX-RPC runtime maps parameter values to their corresponding SOAP representations and sends an HTTP request containing a SOAP message to the service. When the service responds to the request, the JAX-RPC runtime receives this SOAP response and maps the return values to Java objects or standard types. If an exception occurs, then the runtime maps the `WSDL:fault` to a Java exception, or to a `javax.rmi.RemoteException` if a `soap:fault` is encountered. (This is discussed further in "Handling Exceptions" on page 230).

The JAX-RPC runtime supports the following standard value types: `String`, `BigInteger`, `Calender`, `Date`, `boolean`, `byte`, `short`, `int`, `long`, `float`, `double`, and arrays of these types. Services can return mime types as images mapped to the `java.awt.Image` class and XML text as `javax.xml.transform.Source` objects.

(The WSDL Basic Profile 1.0 does not support `javax.xml.transform.Source` objects as mime types. As a result, you should avoid this usage until it is supported by a future WSDL version.) A service may also return complex types, and these are mapped to Java `Object` representations. For more information, see "Parameter Types for Web Service Operations" on page 72.

When stubs are used, the JAX-RPC WSDL-to-Java mapping tool maps parameter, exception, and return value types into the generated classes using information contained in the developer-provided WSDL document. Complex types defined within a WSDL document are represented by individual Java classes, as are faults. A WSDL-to-Java mapping tool included with the JAX-RPC runtime also generates classes to serialize and deserialize these values to XML. The JAX-RPC runtime uses these generated classes to serialize parameter values into a SOAP message and deserialize return values and exceptions.

❐   Use WSDL-to-Java tools to generate support classes, even if using the dynamic proxy or DII approach.

Whenever possible, developers should try to use a tool to do the WSDL-to-Java mapping, since a tool correctly handles the WSDL format and mapping semantics. Note that the Java objects generated by these mapping tools contain empty constructors and get and set methods for elements. You should use the empty constructor to create an instance of the object and set any field or element values using the corresponding set methods. JAX-RPC does not guarantee that it will correctly map values created as part of the constructor to the corresponding fields.

Although not advisable, it is possible for a developer to work without the benefit of a mapping tool, if none are available. However, without such mapping tools the scope of the developer's work greatly expands. For example, just to compile the client code, the developer must understand the WSDL for a service and generate by hand Java classes that match the parameter and return types defined in the WSDL document or, in the case of a dynamic proxy, the client-side representation of the service endpoint interface. These classes must be set up properly so that the JAX-RPC runtime can match SOAP message types to the corresponding Java objects.

5.3.5 Processing Return Values

J2EE applications generally use Web components to generate returned data for display. For example, a client accessing an order tracking service might display tracking information in a Web page using an HTML browser. The J2EE component may take the values returned from the Web service and handle them just like any other Java object. For example, a Web component in a J2EE client application might query the status of an order from an order tracking service, which returns these values within a JavaBeans-like object. The client component places the returned object in the request scope and uses a JSP to display its contents. (See Code Example 5.9.)

```
<html>
Order ID: ${bean.orderId}
Status: ${bean.status} <br>
Name: ${bean.givenName} ${bean.familyName} <br>
</html>
```

Code Example 5.9   JSP for Generating an HTML Document

The J2EE platform has a rich set of component technologies for generating Web content, including JavaServer Pages (JSP) technology for generating HTML content and Java Standard Tag Libraries (JSTL). JSTL is a set of tags that assist a client developer in formatting JSPs. For example, JSTL provides additional tags for looping, database access, object access, and XSLT stylesheet transformations. The current version of JSP (2.0), along with future versions, provides an expression language that allows a developer to access bean properties. Together, developers can use JSTL and JSP technologies to generate HTML documents from data retrieved from a service. For example, a developer might generate the following HTML document for the order details (see Code Example 5.10). This HTML document is returned to the HTML browser client that requested the service.

```
<html>
    Order: 54321<br>
    Status: SHIPPED<br>
```

```
    Name: Duke Smith<br>
</html>
```

Code Example 5.10   HTML Document

A different use case might be EJB components using returned data in a workflow. For example, as the workflow progresses, they may provide order tracking
updates by formatting the tracking data in HTML and attaching it to an e-mail
message sent to the customer. Unless the initial request originated from a Web tier
client, EJB components in a workflow situation do not have Web-tier technologies
such as JSP available to them. Furthermore, the order tracking service may return
results as XML documents, requiring EJB components to apply XSL transformations to these documents. Code Example 5.11 shows an XML document containing the returned data from the service.

```
<orderdetails>
    <id>54321</id>
    <status>SHIPPED</status>
    <shippinginfo>
        <family-name>Smith</family-name>
        <given-name>Duke</given-name>
    </shippinginfo>
</orderdetails>
```

Code Example 5.11   Data Returned as XML Document

An EJB component may use the XSL stylesheet shown in Code Example 5.12
to transform an order details XML document to the same HTML document as in
Code Example 5.10. This HTML document may be attached to an e-mail message
and sent to a customer. XSLT transformations may also be used to transform a
document into multiple formats for different types of clients.

```
<xsl:stylesheet version='1.0'
    xmlns:xsl='http://www.w3.org/1999/XSL/Transform'>

<xsl:output method="html"/>
<xsl:template match="text()"/>
```

```
<xsl:template match="orderdetails">
  <html>
  Order: <xsl:value-of select="id/text()"/><br/>
  <xsl:apply-templates/>
  </html>
</xsl:template>

<xsl:template match="shippinginfo">
 Name: <xsl:value-of select="given-name/text()"/>
        <xsl:text> </xsl:text>
        <xsl:value-of select="family-name/text()"/>
 <br/>
</xsl:template>

<xsl:template match="status">
 Status: <xsl:value-of select="text()"/><br/>
</xsl:template>
</xsl:stylesheet>
```

Code Example 5.12 XSL Stylesheet

Technologies for handling and transforming XML documents are also available to Web components such as servlets or JSPs. Web components may use custom tag components, XSL, or the JAXP APIs to handle XML documents. (For more information on handling XML documents, see Chapter 4.)

❏ Generally, whenever possible client developers should use JSP to generate responses by a service and to present the data as a view to clients (such as browsers that use Web tier technologies).

❏ For clients in a non-Web tier environment where JSP technology is not available, developers should use XSLT transformations.

Developers can use JSP technology to access content in XML documents and to build an HTML page from the XML document contents. Code Example 5.13 shows how JSP technology makes it easy to parse XML content and build an HTML page from the order detail contents shown in Code Example 5.11.

```
<%@ taglib prefix="x" uri="/WEB-INF/x-rt.tld" %>
<x:parse xml="${orderDetailsXml}" var="od" scope="application"/>
<html>
   Order:<x:out select="$od/orderdetails/id"/><br>
   Status:<x:out select="$od/orderdetails/status"/><br>
   Name:<x:out select="$od/orderdetails/shippinginfo/given-name"/>
        <x:out select="$od/orderdetails/shippinginfo/family-name"/>
</html>
```

Code Example 5.13 JSP Generating a Web Service Response

In this example, the J2EE application first places the order details document received from the service in the request scope using the key `orderDetailsXML`. The next lines are JSP code that use the `x:out` JSTL tag to access the order details XML content. These lines of code select fields of interest (such as order identifier, status, and name fields) using XPath expressions, and convert the data to HTML for presentation to a browser client. The JSP code relies on JSTL tags to access these portions of the order details document. For example, the JSTL tag `x:out`, which uses XPath expressions, accesses the order identifier, status, and name fields in the order details document. When the JSP processing completes, the result is identical to the HTML page shown in Code Example 5.10.

5.3.6 Handling Exceptions

Two types of exceptions occur for client applications that access Web services: system exceptions and service-specific exceptions, which are thrown by a service endpoint. System exceptions are thrown for such conditions as passing incorrect parameters when invoking a service method, service inaccessibility, network error, or some other error beyond the control of the application. Service exceptions, which are mapped from faults, are thrown when a service-specific error is encountered. The client application must deal with both types of exceptions.

5.3.6.1 System Exceptions

System exceptions generally involve unanticipated errors—such as a network timeout or an unavailable or unreachable server—that occur when invoking a Web service. Although system exceptions are usually out of the control of the client developer, you should still be aware that these errors may occur, and you should have a strategy for your client application to deal with these situations. For example, with these types of errors, it may be useful to have the client application prompt the user to retry the operation or redirect the user to an alternative service, if possible. Many times the only solution is to display the exception occurrence to the end user. Sometimes it may be appropriate to translate the system exception to an unchecked exception and devise a global way to handle them. The exact solution is particular to each application and situation.

System exceptions, which the client receives as `RemoteException`, arise from a variety of reasons. Often system exceptions happen because of network failures or server errors. They also may be the result of a SOAP fault. Since a `RemoteException` usually contains an explanation of the error, the application can use that message to provide its own error message to the user and can prompt the user for an appropriate action to take. If an EJB component client is doing its work on behalf of a Web tier client, the EJB client should throw an exception to the Web tier client. The Web tier client notifies the user, giving the user a chance to retry the action or choose an alternative action.

When communicating using stubs, most system exceptions involve network issues or the configuration of the stub. A configuration error is thrown from the `_getProperty` and `_setProperty` methods as a `javax.xml.rpc.JAXRPCException` and indicates a property name that is not supported or is invalid, a property setting value that is not allowed, or a type mismatch.

When using a dynamic proxy, the `getPort` method may throw a `javax.xml.rpc.ServiceException` if the WSDL document has insufficient metadata to properly create the proxy.

A client may receive several different exceptions when using the DII `Call` interface. A client may receive a `RemoteException` if a network failure occurs. A client may also be thrown a `javax.xml.rpc.JAXRPCException` if the `Call` set methods use invalid property names or try to set properties with invalid values.

For example, a client application accessing an order tracking service may want to use an alternative service or endpoint if it receives a `RemoteException` indicating the unavailability of the service.

Web components may leverage the servlet error messaging system and map the `RemoteException` to some exception handling instructions in the `web.xml` file. The client can throw its own `javax.servlet.ServletException` and can display a general application error message. It is possible to extend `ServletException` to create a set of application-specific exceptions for different errors. It may also use the file to define a specific error JSP to handle the error, as shown in Code Example 5.14.

```
<error-page>
    <exception-type>java.lang.Runtime</exception-type>
    <location>/order_tracking_system_exception.jsp</location>
</error-page>
```

Code Example 5.14   Using the Servlet Error Messaging System

Although they do not directly interact with the user, workflow clients implemented as EJB components can benefit from transactional processing, particularly if using container-managed transactions. However, since you cannot assume that the Web service is also transactional, you might have to manually back out some of your changes if other Web services are involved in the processing. Keep in mind that backing out changes can be difficult to accomplish and is prone to problems.

An J2EE component that receives a RemoteException when accessing a service may retry connecting to the service a set number of times. If none of the retries are successful, then the client can log an error and quit the workflow. Or, the client may forward the unit of work to another process in the workflow and let that component access the same service at a later point or use a different service. EJB component-based clients using DII may locate an alternative service using the JAXR API from a registry.

5.3.6.2   Service Exceptions

Service exceptions occur when a Web service call results in the service returning a fault. A service throws such faults when the data presented to it does not meet the service criteria. For example, the data may be beyond boundary limits, it may duplicate other data, or it may be incomplete. These exceptions are defined in the service's WSDL file as operation elements, and they are referred to as wsdl:fault elements. These exceptions are checked exceptions in client applications. For example, a client accessing the order tracking service may pass to the service an order identifier that does not match orders kept by the service. The client may receive an OrderNotFoundException, since that is the error message defined in the WSDL document:

```
<fault name="OrderNotFoundException"
        message="tns:OrderNotFoundException"/>
```

This exception-mapping mechanism may not be used with DII, since this communication mode returns all exceptions as `java.rmi.RemoteException`. Note that there is no guarantee that the JAX-RPC runtime system will throw a `ServiceException` for a specific `wsdl:fault` error. The runtime may instead throw a `javax.xml.rpc.soap.SOAPFaultException` runtime exception.

Use the JAX-RPC tools to map faults to Java objects. (See "WSDL-to-Java Type Mapping" on page 225.) These tools generate the necessary parameter mappings for the exception classes and generate the necessary classes for the mapping. Generated exceptions classes extend `java.lang.Exception`. The client application developer is responsible for catching these checked exceptions in a try/catch block. The developer should also try to provide the appropriate application functionality to recover from such exceptions. For example, an order tracking client might include the code shown in Code Example 5.15 to handle cases where a matching order is not found. The order tracking service threw an `OrderNotFoundException`, and the client presented the user with a GUI dialog indicating that the order was not found.

```
try {
    OrderDetails od = service.getOrderDetails(orderId);
} catch (OrderNotFoundException onx) {
    JOptionPane.showMessageDialog(gui,
        "Order Not found with Order ID " + orderId, "Error",
        JOptionPane.ERROR_MESSAGE);
}
```

Code Example 5.15 J2SE Client Displaying an Error

A J2EE Web component client may handle the exception using the facilities provided by the J2EE environment. The client may wrap the application exception and throw an unchecked exception, such as a `javax.servlet.ServletException`, or it may map the exception directly to an error page in the Web deployment descriptor. In Code Example 5.16, the client maps the `OrderNotFoundException` directly to a JSP. Clients should always provide human-readable messages and give the user the ability to return to an entry page.

```
<error-page>
    <exception-type>com.sun.blueprints.adventure.
        OrderNotFoundException</exception-type>
```

```
<location>/order_not_found_exception.jsp</location>
</error-page>
```

Code Example 5.16 Using the Servlet Error Mechanism

Notice that using the servlet error mechanism in this way tightly binds the Web application client to the service. If the service changes the faults it throws, or any of the fault parameters, the client is directly affected.

❐ Client developers should isolate service-specific exceptions as much as possible by wrapping them in their own application-specific exceptions to keep the client application from being too closely tied to a service. This is especially important when the service is outside the control of the client developer or if the service changes frequently. A client may require refactoring when a service changes because the stubs and supporting Java object representations of the exceptions were generated statically.

Client developers may also generalize exception handling and instead handle all exceptions in a single point in the application. Keeping exception handling to one place in an application reduces the need to include code for handling exceptions throughout the application.

```
try {
    OrderDetails od = stub.getOrderDetails(orderId);
} catch (OrderNotFoundException onx) {
    RuntimeException re= new RuntimeException(onx);
}
```

Code Example 5.17 Generalized Exception Processing

In Code Example 5.17, the exception thrown as a result of the Web service call is set as the cause of the runtime exception. This technique, known as chaining exceptions, produces a better stack trace and helps to more clearly display the root cause of the exception. Chaining exceptions in conjunction with the servlet error mechanism shown in Code Example 5.16 may provide a generalized means of displaying service exceptions.

Boundary checking can help prevent service exceptions. For example, a client of an order tracking service might first check that an order identifier is a five-digit integer, or that its value falls within a certain range. While the JAX-RPC API ensures that types are correct, the application developer is responsible for checking boundary limitations.

Clients in a J2EE environment that present HTML content can use JavaScript to validate boundaries before sending requests to a service. Clients using an HTML interface should ensure that types for entered values are correct, since HTML parameters are all treated as `String` objects.

❑ Do boundary checking and other validations on the client side so that Web service calls and round-trips to the server are kept to a minimum.

5.4 General Considerations

There are some general considerations that Web service client developers might want to keep in mind. In particular, developers need to be aware of the issues regarding conversational state. Also included in this section are some guidelines for improving or enhancing the user experience, and a short discussion of server-side design considerations. Last, there is an explanation of how to package client applications.

5.4.1 Managing Conversational State

Clients should view Web services as stateless and should assume that a service endpoint retains no knowledge of previous client interactions. However, some use cases may require a client to make a sequence of calls to a service to accomplish a given operation.

It is best if the client application maintains state when circumstances require this. The client may manipulate this retained state when not online. There are ways for a client to identify itself across multiple calls to a service and manage its state to keep it in sync with state on the server.

5.4.1.1 Coordinating State with a Service Endpoint

There are certain situations where the client may want to have its conversational state managed by the service endpoint. A client application, for example, may have only minimal processing capabilities and insufficient memory resources to adequately store its conversational state during a session interaction with a service. For a service endpoint to maintain conversational state with its clients, the endpoint must be designed with this in mind.

Often, such endpoints are designed to use a unique, nonreplicable token to identify communication from a specific client, much like browsers use the cookie mechanism. The service endpoint and the client application pass the token between them with each call during their conversation. Code Example 5.18 shows the definition of an order management service endpoint's methods for retrieving and updating a purchase order. Each method includes a token parameter, clientToken, that identifies the specific client. The client application creates a unique token and passes it to the service endpoint when invoking these methods. When it receives the method invocation, the service endpoint identifies the client and persists its state. In this example, notice that the endpoint can identify the purchase order because the same client token is passed when retrieving and updating the purchase order.

```
public interface OrderManagementSEI extends Remote {
    public void updatePurchaseOrder(PurchaseOrder po,
            String clientToken) throws RemoteException;
    public PurchaseOrder getPurchaseOrder(String id,
            String clientToken) throws RemoteException;
}
```

Code Example 5.18   Service Endpoint Interface Methods with Unique Tokens

When an EJB component is the basis for a service endpoint, the EJB component can persist conversational state to a data store during the session. The service endpoint may still be designed to use tokens, and such tokens may represent the primary key of an entity bean. In this case, the endpoint designer must be sure to clean up stale session data from the persistent store. This can be done using a time stamp on the entity bean holding the conversational state and a timer bean to track elapsed time. An endpoint that does not properly clean up stale session data might eventually persist a large amount of data.

A client developer whose application interacts with an endpoint that stores conversational state needs to have detailed knowledge of the endpoint's token requirements and the state maintained by the endpoint. In addition, the developer needs detailed knowledge of the timeout, if one exists. This coordination between the client and endpoint makes them tightly coupled. As such, developers should use this approach only when a tightly coupled situation is acceptable or required, or when the client and service endpoint responsibilities are clearly documented.

5.4.1.2 Synchronizing Shared State among Clients

There are times when multiple Web service clients share state among themselves. Such shared state may be read only or it may be state that is updated. Read-only state does not require synchronization—since clients are retrieving data only, they may poll the service at intervals and obtain current data. However, it is possible for other Web clients to concurrently update shared data. Data consistency is an issue when one or more clients may be manipulating the same data at the same time.

An example use case that illustrates sharing modifiable state among Web service clients might be purchase order management client application. The application accesses a set of purchase orders that require manual approval. After the user manually processes these orders offline, the application uploads them to the service. It is conceivable that two such client applications may each download some of the same purchase orders, and some of these orders may be changed independent of each other. After the first client application uploads its changed data to the service, there is a data consistency problem if the second application tries to upload its modified data.

To prevent such inconsistencies, the client developer should keep certain considerations in mind. The developer can detect data inconsistency using techniques such as time-stamp checking or checksum analysis before uploading modified data, and this may require cooperation from the service endpoint. Data locking is another technique to avoid simultaneous changes to the same data. A service endpoint could throw a service-specific exception indicating that data has been modified by another client and might be out of sync. The client application can be designed to overwrite the service endpoint copy, or it can ask the user to re-enter the data. Both client and service endpoint developers need to ensure that their respective applications handle such inconsistencies properly.

5.4.2 Enhancing User Experience

The dynamics of the user interface play a large role in determining the quality of a user's experience. J2SE clients have the advantage of drawing on a rich set of APIs, in particular the Swing APIs, to make the user experience the highest quality possible. These APIs give J2SE clients the ability to query a Web service in the background, by invoking the Web service in a different thread, and then updating the user interface when the information is received. The client is able to continue its interaction with the user until the service returns the information. With other types of clients, the user is often left with what appears to be a frozen screen or a nonfunctional or locked application, since the client application blocks during the call to the Web service. In short, the user does not know whether the application is still alive.

A J2SE client can use the SwingUtilities.invokeLater method to make the call to the service in a separate thread, and thus to achieve a better user experience. (See Code Example 5.19.) This method takes a single argument of an object implementing the Runnable interface. When the invokeLater method is invoked, the J2SE platform creates another thread to run in background mode by invoking the run method on the Runnable class.

```
private void trackOrder() {
    setStatus("Tracking Order " + getOrderId());
    GetOrderDetails gd = new GetOrderDetails(this);
    SwingUtilities.invokeLater(gd);
}

class GetOrderDetails implements Runnable {
    private OTClientGUI gui;
    private String orderId;
    boolean done = false;

    GetOrderDetails(OTClientGUI gui) {
        this.gui = gui;
        this.orderId = gui.getOrderId();
    }

public void run() {
    if (!done) {
        try {
            gui. setStatus("Looking for Order " + orderId);
            OrderDetails od = WSProcessor.getOrderDetails(orderId);
            if (od != null) {
                gui.setDetails(od);
            }
        } catch (OrderNotFoundException ex) {
            gui.clearDetails();
```

```
        gui.setStatus("");
        JOptionPane.showMessageDialog(gui,
            "Order Not found with Order ID " + orderId,
            "Error",
            JOptionPane.ERROR_MESSAGE);
    } catch (Exception ex) {
        // do nothing for now
    }
    gui.setStatus("Completed lookup for order ID " + orderId);
    SwingUtilities.invokeLater(this);
    done = true;
    }
  }
}
```

Code Example 5.19 J2SE Client Using `SwingUtils.invokeLater`

This example illustrates how a J2SE client can use the J2SE platform APIs to enhance the user experience. In this example, the user has selected an option to track an order currently being handled by the Web service. That option calls the `invokeLater` method, which in turn invokes a class implementing the `Runnable` interface. This class, using a callback mechanism, updates the user with messages indicating the status of the Web service call and details pertaining to the order being tracked. If the order is not found, the code handles displaying to the user a suitable error message indicating the exception.

Note: More information is available on the `SwingUtilities` API, along with using threads and GUIs with J2SE clients. You can find this information at `http://java.sun.com/docs/books/tutorial/uiswing/misc/threads.html`.

5.4.3   Server-Side Design Considerations for Clients

It should be clear by now that client developers and service endpoint providers do not operate in a vacuum. When it is known that the target client environment is based on JAX-RPC, the service endpoint developer can provide prepackaged libraries and server-side documentation. These libraries should contain all files, such as the client-side representation of the service endpoint interface and its dependent classes, that are necessary to access the service. The library can include additional façade classes that simplify the client view of the service and potentially shield the client from some future changes to the service. These façade classes help a client developer to not only access the service in a standardized manner, but may also improve their understanding of the service endpoint so as to develop better clients.

More extensive HTML documentation of a service covering parameters required by the service, return values, and exceptions helps developers better interact with the service. This information should go beyond what is included in the WSDL document.

5.4.4   Packaging

To access a service, a stand-alone client requires a runtime environment. For J2SE clients, the runtime must be packaged with the application. J2EE clients rely on the JAX-RPC runtime.

J2ME clients do not need to package the JAX-RPC runtime with the applications. Although stubs do need to be packaged with an application, the stubs are portable across JAX-RPC runtimes. The portability of stubs is critical because J2ME clients cannot generate or compile stub implementation code, and thus must rely on more dynamic provisioning.

This section discusses packaging issues for the different types of clients.

5.4.4.1   J2EE Clients

Web service clients running in a J2EE environment require some basic artifacts, as follows:

- Service reference—A `service-ref` element in the deployment descriptor

- Mapping file—A JAX-RPC mapping file

- WSDL document

- Service endpoint interface—A stub or dynamic proxy

- Generated classes

The `service-ref` element, part of the general J2EE 1.4 schema, contains information about a service. Web, EJB, and J2EE application client module deployment descriptors use this element to locate the JAX-RPC mapping files as well as the service's WSDL file. The service reference element maps a service to a JNDI resource name and also specifies the service endpoint interface for those clients using stubs and dynamic proxies. (Clients using DII do not need to specify the service endpoint interface.) It also specifies the WSDL file for the service (its location is given relative to the root of the package) and the qualified name for the service in the WSDL file. If a WSDL file is required, the element specifies a JAX-RPC mapping file. The mapping file's location is also relative to the package root. Code Example 5.20 is an example of a service reference:

```
<service-ref>
    <description>OPC OT Service Client</description>
    <service-ref-name>service/OpcOrderTrackingService
    </service-ref-name>
    <service-interface>
        com.sun.j2ee.blueprints.adventure.web.actions.
            OpcOrderTrackingService
    </service-interface>
    <wsdl-file>WEB-INF/wsdl/OpcOrderTrackingService.wsdl
    </wsdl-file>
    <jaxrpc-mapping-file>WEB-INF/opc-ot-jaxrpc-mapping.xml
    </jaxrpc-mapping-file>
    <service-qname
        xmlns:servicens="urn:OpcOrderTrackingService">
            servicens:OpcOrderTrackingService
    </service-qname>
</service-ref>
```

Code Example 5.20 web.xml Fragment for Web Service Reference

The JAX-RPC mapping file specifies the package name containing the generated runtime classes and defines the namespace URI for the service. (See Code Example 5.21.)

```
<java-wsdl-mapping xmlns="http://java.sun.com/xml/ns/j2ee"
xmlns:xsi="http://www.w3.org/2001/XMLSchema-instance"
xsi:schemaLocation="http://java.sun.com/xml/ns/j2ee ht
    tp://www.ibm.com/webservices/xsd/j2ee_jaxrpc_mapping_1_1.xsd"
version="1.1">
<package-mapping>
    <package-type>com.sun.j2ee.blueprints.adventure.web.actions
</package-type>
```

```
<namespaceURI>urn:OpcOrderTrackingService</namespaceURI>
</package-mapping>
</java-wsdl-mapping>
```

Code Example 5.21   JAX-RPC Mapping File

WSDL files, including partial WSDL files, are packaged within clients. Their location is dependent on the type of module. Since clients using DII do not require a WSDL file, they leave the `wsdl-file` element portion of the `service-ref` element undefined and they must not specify the `jaxrpc-mapping-file` element.

For a web application archive (WAR) file, the WSDL file is in the `WEB-INF/wsdl` directory. (See Figure 5.8.) For an EJB endpoint as well as a J2EE application client, the WSDL file is in the directory `MET-INF/wsdl`. (See Figure 5.9.) Both directories are relative to the root directory of the application module.

For Web tier clients, a `service-ref` element in the `web.xml` file contains the location of the JAX-RPC mapping file, `client-jaxrpc-mapping-file.xml`. The service endpoint interface (if provided) is either a class file in the `WEB-INF/classes` directory or it is packaged in a JAR file in the `WEB-INF/lib` directory. Generated classes are located in the same directory.

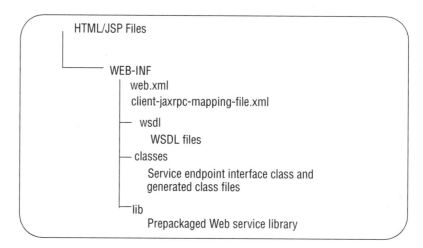

Figure 5.8   Web Application Module Packaging

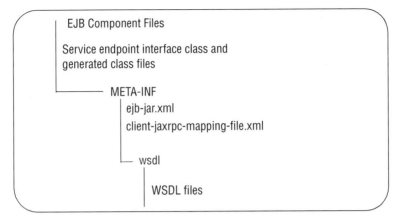

Figure 5.9   EJB Module Packaging

For EJB tier client components, the `service-ref` element is defined in the deployment descriptor of the `ejb-jar.xml` file and the `client-jaxrpc-mapping-file.xml` mapping file. The WSDL files are in a `META-INF/wsdl` directory. The service endpoint interface as well as generated class files are stored in the module's root directory.

The client developer should ensure that the `resource-ref` definition in the client deployment descriptor is correct and that the JAX-RPC mapping file is packaged in the correct module.

5.4.4.2   J2SE Clients

J2SE clients using stubs or dynamic proxies should package the service endpoint interface with the application client, and they should be referenced by the class path attribute of the package's manifest file. J2SE clients also must provide a JAX-RPC runtime. For example, a J2SE client is packaged along with its supporting classes or with references to these classes. (See Figure 5.10.) The service endpoint interface as well as the necessary generated files may be provided in a separate JAR file.

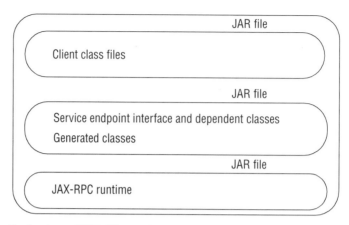

Figure 5.10   Packaging a J2SE Client with Web Service Library

Figure 5.10 shows how to package a J2SE client in a modular manner. The classes specific for Web service access are kept in a separate JAR file referenced via a class path dependency. Packaged this way, a client can swap out the service endpoint access without having to change the core client code. The service access classes may also be shared by different application clients accessing the same service. A developer utilizing a prepackaged service interface may also be able to develop a Web service client with less knowledge of a service.

5.4.4.3   J2ME Clients

Two optional packages, both of which are extensions of the J2ME platform, enable Web services in the J2ME platform by providing runtime support for XML processing and JAX-RPC communication. (Note that although XML processing capabilities are not provided in the J2ME platform, they are required for JAX-RPC communication.)

A J2ME client application developer must package certain resources with a J2ME application. First, J2ME applications are packaged in a MIDlet format. A MIDlet is a Java Archive (JAR) file that contains class files, application resources, and a manifest file (`manifest.mf`), which contains application attributes.

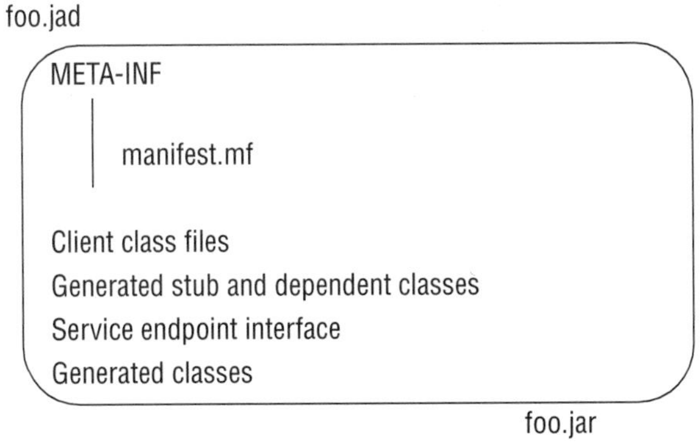

Figure 5.11   Packaging a MIDlet Web Service Client Application

A developer may also provide an external Java Application Descriptor (JAD) file for the MIDlet. A JAD file provides the J2ME environment with additional information about the application, such as the location of the application's MIDlet file. A JAD file's attributes mirror those found in the manifest file, but the JAD file takes precedence over the manifest file. Furthermore, a developer or deployer may override application attributes in the JAD file. Figure 5.11 describes the packaging for a Web service MIDlet client application.

The foo.jar MIDlet file contains the client application classes and the respective artifacts generated by the J2ME Web service development tools, as well as a manifest file. A foo.jad file describes the foo.jar MIDlet. Similar to the J2EE platform, the J2ME platform with the optional Web service packages provides the resources required for Web service communication.

5.5   Conclusion

This chapter described the different types of clients that may access Web services and the issues faced by developers of these clients. It highlighted the differences between clients running in a J2EE environment from clients running in the J2SE and J2ME environments, and how these differences affect the design of a client application.

The chapter described the three communication modes available to clients: stubs, dynamic proxy, and dynamic invocation interface. These three modes form the basis for a client's access to a Web service. For each communication mode, the chapter discussed the steps for implementing Web service clients. It provided detailed discussions from how to locate and access a service through handling errors thrown by a service.

The chapter also described how to package different types of clients and discussed managing conversational state. It also provided guidelines for improving the overall end user experience.

The next chapter talks about XML in depth, since XML places a large role in Web services.

CHAPTER **6**

Enterprise Application Integration

ENTERPRISE information systems—the collection of relational and legacy database systems, enterprise resource planning (ERP) systems, and mainframe transaction processing systems—provide the critical information infrastructure for an enterprise's business processes. These varied systems hold the information that an enterprise needs to carry out its daily operations. It is essential that new applications developed for an enterprise be able to integrate with these enterprise information systems (EIS).

EIS integration has always been of great importance, and this has given rise to enterprise application integration, or EAI. EAI enables an enterprise to integrate its existing applications and systems, plus it enables the addition of new technologies and applications. Enterprises must leverage their existing systems and resources even as they adopt new technologies. Considering the cost already invested in these existing systems, no business can afford to discard them. Plus, since these systems often contain valuable data needed by the enterprise, the enterprise is not likely to disrupt them. Yet, at the same time, enterprises continually grow and require new applications. To keep their businesses growing and to remain cost effective, enterprises must integrate their existing systems with these new applications and not replace existing systems with new applications written from scratch. The emergence of Web-based architectures and Web services adds impetus for enterprises to integrate their EISs and expose them to the Web.

The emergence of the Web and Web services is not the only factor driving the need for integration. More and more, enterprises are either merging or acquiring other enterprises. Such mergers and acquisitions usually entail merging and combining two divergent information technology (IT) systems. Not only are the IT systems different, but, as a further challenge, they each may have standardized on using different integration technologies within their respective environments. Emerging Web services standards are another factor driving Web services-based EAI. These standards are making it possible to integrate heterogeneous systems easily and cost effectively.

In today's environment, a typical enterprise has a multitude of existing applications running on diverse platforms and operating systems. Although these applications may very well rely on the same or similar data, they keep that data in different formats. Thus, the integration problem encompasses both data and system platforms.

These are but a few examples of the complexities that enterprise application integration must address. Not only must EAI handle integrating applications, it must also address integrating data and technologies so that enterprises can easily share business processes and data.

Using several scenarios, this chapter illustrates key integration considerations. It describes the J2EE 1.4 platform technologies that help with integration and presents some integration design approaches and guidelines.

6.1   Integration Requirements and Scenarios

Before delving in the details of the technologies, it is helpful to illustrate the major concerns for integrating enterprise information systems and to get a sense of the extent of the EAI problem. We discuss three types of integration scenarios: data integration, application integration, and business process integration. Often, an enterprise's integration needs span these different types.

6.1.1   Typical Integration Scenarios

Data integration involves integrating existing data living in different enterprise systems, and it often occurs when an enterprise relies on multiple types of database systems. For example, some database systems may be relational, others may be hierarchical or based on objects, and still others may be file based or even legacy stores. As an illustration, a newly developed Web-based order management system might have to integrate with an existing customer order database. Data integration involves not only integrating different data systems, but it also entails integrating different informational or data models.

Application integration involves integrating new applications with existing or legacy applications. Since an enterprise's business relies on the continuity of its existing applications, it is important to integrate the new applications with minimal disruptions. Integrating with home-grown legacy applications presents a bigger challenge, since these systems have no vendor-provided or off-the-shelf adapter layers. Not only do you have to write the adapter layers yourself, these home-grown applications may be more idiosyncratic, with an architecture that is more opaque and difficult to understand.

Business process integration involves integrating an enterprise's existing systems to support a set of business processes. A *business process* is a series of (often asynchronous) steps that together complete a business task or function. For example, the adventure builder enterprise has a business process for fulfilling purchase orders submitted to its order processing center. The order fulfillment business process includes such steps as validating a customer's credit card, communicating with various suppliers to fill different parts of an order, and notifying the customer of the order status at various stages of processing.

Integration is often accomplished by exchanging documents, which more and more are XML documents, among business processes according to defined business rules. The different processes transform the documents by applying their individual business rules, and then they route the documents to other processes. Good examples are business processes that do such things as handle purchase orders and invoices, or incorporate supplier catalogs. Each such business process runs a workflow that interacts with other entities, either internal or external.

6.1.2   Example Integration Scenarios

Examining some typical scenarios helps to bring these integration requirements into better perspective. We use the scenarios present in our adventure builder enterprise example for illustration. One common integration scenario is that of the adventure builder enterprise, which may want to make its inventory available online to expand its customer reach. The enterprise may have existing applications and databases—for example, catalog and inventory databases, along with order processing and customer relationship management (CRM) systems—for its business. These systems and databases need to be enhanced to accommodate the e-store.

Adventure builder enterprise purchases and customizes the CRM package, but its order processing system may be homegrown. As much as possible, the enterprise wants to reduce software duplication and keep its infrastructure costs to a minimum. To that end, it may want to use these same systems to handle the e-store business, especially since its existing customers may also buy products through the online store. Adventure builder enterprise also wants to leverage its customer service department and have these same specialists service both types of customers: store front as well as online. Adventure builder enterprise expects to include additional databases relevant for the Web site only.

This scenario illustrates an application and data integration problem. The enterprise's existing databases store information needed by the e-store, which may need to update these databases. The databases have existing security settings, plus protocols for transactions. The vendor for the CRM system may have provided a J2EE connector that could be used to plug the CRM system into the enterprise's J2EE application server. However, the order processing system, since it is home-grown, may have no such support.

Figure 6.1 illustrates the scenario of this application with respect to the EISs that it uses. This example scenario touches upon many of the integration requirements that pertain to all enterprises. Because it is open to anyone on the Internet, the adventure builder Web site may potentially have a large number of users, making scalability and performance important issues. Security is an important consideration, since adventure builder's Web site handles customer data that it must keep private. The enterprise has the further challenge of ensuring that its legacy systems are not stretched beyond their capabilities and that heterogeneous platforms may host the EIS systems.

The enterprise relies on an order fulfillment center to process orders placed through the e-store Web site. A separate department owns the order fulfillment center, and it uses its own set of databases separate from the e-store's Web site. To keep the two data models decoupled, orders flowing between the e-store and the order fulfillment center are kept in XML format. Communication is also asynchronous, allowing clients to continue their own work while an order is processed. In essence, the order fulfillment center initiates a business process whenever it receives an order. The business process, following a set of automated rules, interacts with several systems in a workflow to complete or fulfill the order with no human intervention. Part of the workflow includes sending confirming e-mails to customers and keeping records for administrative reports.

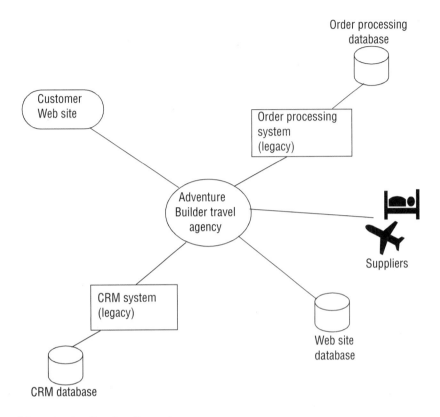

Figure 6.1 An Application Scenario

The order fulfillment center interacts with external business partners to complete its workflow. For example, the order fulfillment center might rely on a separate credit card billing service to process its customer billing. Some of its products may be supplied directly by another vendor. The order fulfillment process initiates multiple business processes for each external business with which it interacts.

Let's look at a different integration scenario. A human resources application, designed for internal use only, may have a similar scenario to an e-store, since it concerns a new application that uses existing enterprise assets. However, the application's internal use limits the scalability, performance, and security concerns. The principal concerns with internal applications such as this are fast delivery time, platform heterogeneity, and the capacity to grow the application and support multiple types of clients as the enterprise expands. The application may also want single sign-on for users across various security domains, but, at the same time, permit access only to employees whose proper access privileges adhere to company-wide rules.

Internal applications may also provide some limited mobile functionality; that is, they need to be accessible from mobile devices such as PDAs and cellphones. For example, a travel expense tracking application may want to allow employees who are on the road to keep track of their expense records. Likewise, enterprises whose departments are geographically scattered may find it more efficient for employees to use the Internet for internal communications. Web service interfaces are particularly useful in these situations, although there are the additional concerns of distributed and multiple security domains.

Often, systems developed for internal use rely on home-grown legacy systems. While systems bought from third-party vendors may be integrated using standard connectors supplied by their vendors or third parties, this is not true for homegrown systems. These homegrown, or one-off, applications must still be integrated with other applications in the enterprise and accessed from a Web browser.

6.2   J2EE Integration Technologies

Now that we have examined some common integration scenarios, let's look at the technologies that are available on the J2EE 1.4 platform to help with these issues. The J2EE platform provides a set of EIS integration technologies that address the EIS integration problem. These include relational database integration technologies (such as JDBC, Enterprise JavaBeans technology container-managed persistence, and Java Data Objects), messaging technologies (such as Java Message Service and message-driven beans), EIS access technologies (particularly the J2EE Connector architecture), Web services, and XML technologies for manipulating documents.

Let's briefly examine some of the available integration technologies. The section "Integration Design Approaches" on page 263 maps these technologies to different integration problems, illustrating when and how to use them most effectively.

6.2.1 Relational Database Integration Technologies

Relational database management systems (RDBMS) are the most prevalent form of enterprise data store. The J2EE platform provides three technologies for integrating data in RDBMS:

- JDBC—Developers can use the JDBC APIs to access relational data in a tabular form.

- Enterprise JavaBeans container-managed persistence (CMP)—Developers use container-managed persistence to do object-relational (O/R) mapping. By mapping database table data to Java objects, developers can deal with an object view of the data rather than a tabular, relational view. CMP also encapsulates the objects into higher-level managed components with transactional and security features.

- Java Data Objects (JDO)—An O/R mapping technology that generates Java classes as opposed to components. Note that JDO is optional in the J2EE 1.4 platform. Since it is optional, your application server may not support JDO, or it may support JDO in a nonstandard manner.

"Data Mapping in EAI Applications" on page 274 explains when it is better to use JDBC, enterprise beans, or JDO.

6.2.1.1 JDBC

The JDBC API defines a standard Java API for integration with relational database systems. A Java application uses the JDBC API for obtaining a database connection, retrieving database records, executing database queries and stored procedures, and performing other database functions.

Many application component providers use the JDBC API for accessing relational databases to manage persistent data for their applications.

The JDBC API has two parts: a client API for direct use by developers to access relational databases and a standard, system-level contract between J2EE servers and JDBC drivers for supporting connection pooling and transactions. Developers do not use the contract between J2EE servers and JDBC drivers directly. Rather, J2EE server vendors use this contract to provide pooling and transaction services to J2EE components automatically. Note that, according to the JDBC 3.0 specification, the JDBC system-level contracts can be the same as the Connector architecture system contracts. Conceptually, JDBC drivers are pluggable resource adapters and may be packaged as J2EE Connector resource adapters.

6.2.1.2   EJB Container-Managed Persistence

Container-managed persistence (CMP), which is a resource manager–independent data access API for entity beans, has been expanded and enhanced in the J2EE 1.4 platform. CMP technology enables applications to be easily integrated with various databases or resource managers, plus it enhances portability.

CMP shields the developer from the details of the underlying data store. The developer does not need to know how to persist or retrieve data to or from a particular data store, since the EJB container handles these tasks. Instead, the developer need only indicate what data or state needs to be stored persistently.

In addition, a developer uses the same API—that is, the EJB CMP methods—regardless of the underlying type of resource manager. The same entity bean can thus be used with any type of resource manager or database schema. The technology makes it possible to develop enterprise beans that can be customized at deployment to work with existing data. That is, the same bean implementation can be deployed to work with many different customer data schemes. The mapping done at deployment may vary for each customer set up, but the bean itself is the same. Since the EJB container generates suitable data access code for each situation, the bean developer does not have to know or care about the underlying resource manager-specific code. Furthermore, since it has complete control over managing persistence, the container can optimize database access for better performance.

The J2EE 1.4 platform includes the most up-to-date EJB specification and CMP technology. Rather than declaring persistent variables in a bean's implementation, developers include abstract get and set accessor methods for persistent variables. Persistent variables are thus treated similarly to JavaBeans properties. Developers do not provide an implementation for these accessor methods since they are abstract methods; instead, the EJB container provides the method implementations.

The CMP architecture also includes container-managed relationships, which allows multiple entity beans to have relationships among themselves. Container-managed relationships are handled in much the same way as container-managed persistence. The bean implementation merely provides get and set accessor methods for these fields, and the container provides the method implementations. Similarly, the developer specifies the relationships in the deployment descriptor.

6.2.1.3   Java Data Objects

Java Data Objects (JDO) is an API that provides a standard, interface-based Java model abstraction of persistence. Application developers can use the JDO API to directly store Java domain model instances into a persistent store, such as a database. You may consider JDO as one alternative to using JDBC or enterprise beans with container-managed persistence. Keep in mind, however, that JDO is not standard in the J2EE 1.4 platform.

There are some benefits to using JDO. Since JDO keeps applications independent or insulated from the underlying database, application developers can focus on their domain object model and not have to be concerned with the persistence details, such as the field-by-field storage of objects. JDO also ensures that the application uses the optimal data access strategies for best performance.

It is not unusual to compare JDO to enterprise beans with container-managed persistence, since both provide object-relational mapping capabilities. The principal difference is that JDO maps database relationships to plain Java objects, while EJB CMP maps relationships to transactional components managed by a container. EJB CMP essentially provides a higher layer of service than JDO. Some J2EE application servers, such as the J2EE 1.4 platform SDK, internally use JDO to implement enterprise bean container-managed persistence.

6.2.2   Messaging Technologies

Messaging systems allow unrelated applications to communicate asynchronously and reliably. Not only do the communicating parties not have to be closely tied to each other, they can also remain relatively anonymous.

The J2EE platform provides the Java Message Service (JMS) API, which is a standard Java API defined for enterprise messaging systems. Along with JMS, the J2EE platform also provides message-driven beans. Message-driven beans are EJB components that consume and process asynchronous messages delivered via JMS or some other messaging system.

Let's take a look at messaging technologies in general, then examine two J2EE-specific technologies: Java Message Service and message-driven beans.

6.2.2.1   Overview of Messaging Technologies

Prior to the advent of Web services, developers often chose messaging systems (called MOM for Message Oriented Middleware) to create an integration architecture. With a messaging system, two systems can communicate with each other by sending messages. Such messages, which are delivered asynchronously, typically consist of two parts: one part—the message body—contains the business data and the other part—the message header—contains routing information. Since messages are sent asynchronously, the sender does not have to wait for the message to be delivered to the receiver.

There are two common messaging styles: point-to-point, and publish and subscribe. A point-to-point messaging style is used when messages are sent to only one receiver. The recipient receives messages sent to it through a queue specifically set up for the receiver. A message sender sends messages to this queue, and the recipient retrieves (and removes) its messages from the queue. Publish and subscribe, on the other hand, is intended to be used when there can be multiple recipients of a message. Rather than a queue, this style uses a topic. Messages are sent—or, more correctly, published—to the topic, and all receivers interested in these messages subscribe to the topic. Any message published to a topic can be received by any receiver that has subscribed to the topic. See Figure 6.2.

In addition, a typical MOM system has a message router that is responsible for ensuring message delivery (according to the agreed-upon quality of service) to the receiver. The message router uses the message header information to determine where and how to route the message contents.

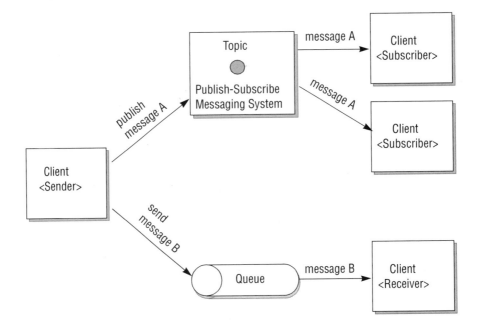

Figure 6.2   Messaging System Queues and Topics

When used for integration, an enterprise very likely requires that all participating EIS systems communicate with each other by sending messages via the messaging system. As a result, enterprises typically standardize on one vendor for their MOM system, and they use that vendor's adapters to accommodate their various EISs. In return, enterprises using messaging systems gain the benefits of asynchronous messaging calls: Messages are queued and delivered when the target system is available without constraining the sending system. The asynchronicity of messaging systems means that communicating applications need not be currently running to receive messages. This protects the communicating applications from system failures and other types of partial outages, conditions that are not uncommon in network situations.

Messaging systems also bring a dynamic quality to EIS systems. Components can be added or removed to the network without affecting other systems. Systems do not need to have their throughputs perfectly match since they can interact with the messaging system at their own pace. For example, if one application sends messages more rapidly than the receiving application can retrieve these messages, the messaging system keeps these messages in the queue indefinitely. As a result, good overall throughput is achieved since each part of the system can work at its optimum capacity.

Furthermore, messaging technology is considered a fairly mature technology. Most MOM systems provide a number of quality of service features, such as reliable once and only once delivery, load balancing, scalability, fault tolerance, and transactional support.

However, the proprietary nature of MOM systems results in some significant disadvantages. Since they use proprietary protocols over the network, it is usually more difficult to mix and match MOM products from different vendors. Although messaging systems decouple the sender and receiver and permit communicating parties to run on different hardware and software platforms, they fall short of achieving true interoperability because they tie developers to their proprietary APIs to send and receive messages. As a result, application developers must customize their applications for different MOM systems.

6.2.2.2 Java Message Service

The Java Message Service (JMS) API, a standard Java API defined for enterprise messaging systems, can be used across different types of messaging systems. A Java application uses the JMS API to connect to an enterprise messaging system. Once connected, the application uses the facilities of the underlying enterprise messaging system (through the API) to create messages and to communicate asynchronously with one or more peer applications.

For the J2EE 1.4 platform, JMS includes some enhancements. In particular, the addition of common interfaces enables you to use the JMS API so that it is not specific to either a point-to-point or publish-subscribe domain. A JMS provider may also use the J2EE Connector architecture to integrate more closely with an application server. (The section "EIS Access Technologies" on page 259 discusses the J2EE Connector architecture.)

In many ways, JMS is to messaging systems what JDBC is to database systems. Just as JDBC provides a standard interface to many database systems, JMS provides a standard API for MOM systems. In fact, JMS changed the proprietary nature of MOM systems by providing a standard Java API that interfaces with any MOM system. The developer now writes to this standard API rather than to individual, proprietary APIs. The J2EE platform further simplified—and made more portable—the integration of a MOM system with a J2EE application server.

Similar to its support for JDBC, the J2EE platform has added support to JMS for a connection-oriented operational style: Developers can look up a factory and a connection in the same way. Like JDBC, JMS supports transactions and can continue JTA transactions started by either a Web or EJB component.

6.2.2.3   Message-Driven Beans

Message-driven beans, which are EJB components that receive incoming enterprise messages from a messaging provider, contain the logic for processing these messages. The business logic of a message-driven bean—which may include initiating a workflow, performing a computation, or sending a message—may be driven by the contents of the message itself or merely the receipt of the message.

Message-driven beans are particularly useful in situations where messages need to be automatically delivered and asynchronous messaging is desired. They enable applications to be integrated in a loosely coupled, but still reliable, fashion. Message-driven beans are also useful when the delivery of a message should be the event initiating a workflow process or when a specific message must trigger a subsequent action.

When an application produces and sends a message to a particular message destination queue or topic, the EJB container activates the corresponding message-driven bean (from the pool of available message-driven beans). The activated bean instance consumes the message from the message destination. Since they are stateless, any instance of a matching type of message-driven bean can handle the message.

Implementing a message-driven bean is straightforward. The bean developer extends the `javax.ejb.MessageDrivenBean` interface and a message listener interface for the bean—the message listener interface corresponds to the enterprise's messaging system. For enterprises using JMS, the developer extends the `javax.jms.MessageListener` interface. A developer may embed business logic to handle particular messages within the `MessageListener` methods. For example, when a message-driven bean consumes JMS messages, the developer codes the message-handling business logic within the `onMessage` method. When a message appropriate for this bean arrives at a message destination, the EJB container invokes the message-driven bean's `onMessage` method.

With message-driven beans, you can make the invocation of the bean part of a transaction. That is, you can ensure that the message delivery from the message destination to the message-driven bean is part of any subsequent transactional work initiated by the bean's logic. If problems occur with the subsequent logic causing the transaction to roll back, the message delivery also rolls back—and the message is redelivered to another message-driven bean instance.

6.2.3 EIS Access Technologies

The J2EE 1.4 platform includes the J2EE Connector architecture, a technology designed specifically for accessing enterprise information systems (EISs). The Connector architecture simplifies integrating diverse EISs into the platform, since each EIS can use the same, single resource adapter to integrate with all compliant J2EE servers.

The J2EE Connector architecture provides a standard architecture for integrating J2EE applications with existing EISs and applications, and particularly for data integration with non-relational databases. The Connector architecture enables adapters for external EISs to be plugged into the J2EE application server. Enterprise applications can use these adapters to support and manage secure, transactional, and scalable, bi-directional communication with EISs. The EIS vendor knows that its adapter will work with all J2EE-compliant application servers, and the compliant J2EE server can connect to multiple EISs. See Figure 6.3.

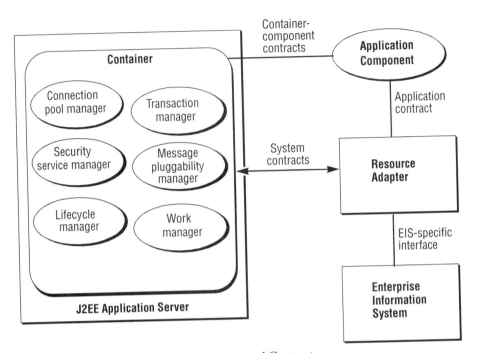

Figure 6.3   Connector Architecture System and Contracts

The earlier version of the Connector architecture focused on synchronous integration with EISs, while the current version that is part of J2EE 1.4 extends this core functionality to support asynchronous integration. That is, it supports both outbound and inbound message-driven integration that is protocol independent.

A *resource adapter* is a J2EE component that implements the Connector API for a specific EIS. Communication between a J2EE application and an EIS occurs through this resource adapter. In a sense, think of a resource adapter as analogous to a JDBC driver, since it provides a standard API for access between the J2EE server and the external resource.

The J2EE Connector architecture, through its contracts, establishes a set of rules for EIS integration. The J2EE application server and an EIS resource adapter collaborate, through a set of system-level contracts, to keep security, transaction, and connection mechanisms transparent to the application components. Application components and resource adapters rely on the application-level contract for their communication.

The application-level contract defines the API used by a client to access a resource adapter for an EIS. This API may be the Common Client Interface (CCI), which is a generic API for accessing multiple heterogeneous EISs, or it may be a resource adapter-specific API.

The initial release of the Connector architecture, which is part of the J2EE 1.3 platform, established three system-level contracts, as follows:

- Connection management contract—Supports connection pooling to an underlying EIS, an important requirement for scalable applications.

- Transaction management contract—Supports local and global transactions, and enables management of (global) transactions across multiple EISs.

- Security management contract—Enables secure interchanges between an EIS and a J2EE application server and protects EIS-managed resources.

The most recent release (version 1.5) of the Connector architecture expanded the capabilities of resource adapters. This release expanded the transaction support for a resource adapter. Previously, a transaction had to start from an enterprise bean on the J2EE application server, and it remained in force during operations on the EIS. Now, transactions can start on the EIS and be imported to the application server. The J2EE Connector architecture specifies how to propagate the transaction context from the EIS to the application server. The Connector architecture also specifies the container's role in completing a transaction and how it should handle data recovery after a crash.

The current version also specifies additional system-level contracts to the initial three contracts just noted. These new contracts are:

- Messaging "pluggability" contract—Extends the capabilities of message-driven beans so that they can handle messages from any message provider rather than being limited to handling only JMS messages. By following the APIs for message handling and delivery specified in this contract, an EIS or message provider can plug its own custom or proprietary message provider into a J2EE container. JAXM is a good example of this type of message provider.

- Work management contract—Enables the J2EE application server to manage threads for resource adapter, ensuring that resource adapters use threads properly. When a resource adapter improperly uses threads, such as when it creates too many threads or fails to release threads, it can cause problems for the entire application server environment. Poor thread handling by a resource adapter can inhibit server shutdown and impact performance. To alleviate this problem, the work management contract enables the application server to pool and reuse threads, similar to pooling and reusing connections.

In addition, the work management contract gives resource adapters more flexibility for using threads. The resource adapter can specify the execution context for a thread. The contract allows a requesting thread to block—stop its own execution—until a work thread completes. Or, a requesting thread can block while it waits to get a work thread; when the application server provides a work thread, both the requesting and work threads execute in parallel. Yet another option, a resource adapter can submit the work for the thread to a queue and have it execute at some later point; the adapter continues its own execution without waiting further. Thus, a resource adapter and a thread may execute in conjunction with each other or independently, using a listener mechanism, if need be, to notify the resource adapter that the work thread has completed.

- Lifecycle management contract—Enables an application server to manage the lifecycle of a resource adapter. With this contract, the application server has a mechanism to bootstrap a resource adapter instance at deployment or at server startup, and to notify the adapter instance when it is undeployed or when the server is shutting down.

6.2.4   Web Service and XML Technologies

Although messaging systems provide many of the same EAI advantages as Web services, Web services go a step further. Principally, Web services support multiple vendors and the ability to go through firewalls using Internet standards. Web services also support a flexible XML format.

The J2EE 1.4 platform provides a rich set of Web service APIs and XML document-manipulating technologies. The Web service APIs—JAX-RPC, JAXR, SAAJ, JAXB, and JAXP—provide standard Java APIs for integrating applications and other systems. A Java application can use these APIs to obtain and use a Web service. These APIs are particularly useful when an application or system exposes a Web service layer explicitly for integration purposes.

There are also a number of XML-related APIs and facilities in the Java language (and the J2EE 1.4 platform) that can be applied to integration problems. They permit you to define an interface data model, manipulate disparate documents, and perform transformations between data types. These XML APIs give you the ability to structure a data model for passing data among different systems.

Chapter 2 discusses these technologies in greater depth.

6.3 Integration Design Approaches

The J2EE 1.4 platform provides several technologies for integration, and you can combine them to fit your integration requirements. These technologies, together with the other platform capabilities, give you a rich platform for designing an integration solution. IT architects face the challenge of combining the technologies in the most effective and flexible manner possible to create an integration architecture that can adapt to changing business needs and strategies.

Often, enterprises attempt integration as a "one-off" solution—that is, they treat each integration problem as a unique instance with its own special solution. With this type of approach, an enterprise integrates each system in an individual, custom manner—not the most efficient or effective integration approach. It is far better to have an integration architecture that grows with the needs of the enterprise. The J2EE platform, with its extensive support for Web services, makes such an architecture possible. A J2EE application server acts as the universal connector between the EIS systems and new EAI applications. (This chapter uses the term EAI applications to refer to applications specially designed to solve the problems of integrating enterprise applications.) In a sense, the J2EE application server is the integration hub. The data model in the application server becomes the canonical agreed-upon data model to which all others—EISs and new EAI applications—adapt. Figure 6.4 shows how this might look from a high level.

A good integration architecture consists of a set of "integration layers" each of which provide certain quality of services. By integration layer we mean the interface or endpoint at which distinct systems intersect. Enterprise architects and software developers must decide how to implement these various integration layers in the most suitable manner. Generally, the requirements of each situation drive the choice of integration layer. For example, the adventure builder enterprise uses Web services as the integration layer for its supply chain. As a result, all interactions with its suppliers must happen through the Web service interfaces.

❑ The integration layer defines the interface between the EIS systems and new applications, thus exposing an EIS system to an application.

❑ An integration layer needs to be the stable point in your system—the fixed standard against which new applications are programmed. While both the new application and the existing EIS may change, the integration layer should remain the same. Otherwise, changes in one place will require changes to numerous dependent systems.

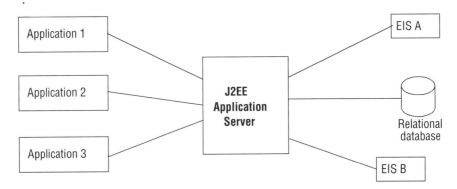

Figure 6.4   J2EE Application Server as Integration Hub

Integration approaches vary, and often the situation dictates the best approach. In some situations, the integration approach is fairly obvious. For example, when a client requires a tightly coupled interaction with a relational database, clearly the JDBC API is the design strategy to use. Similarly, another design strategy uses the J2EE Connector architecture for data integration with non-relational databases. These two design strategies are particularly appropriate when the client requires an API for connecting, querying, and updating a database with transactional semantics. Other situations require you to combine technologies to meet the integration requirements. You might use connectors on top of a non-relational database, but then, based on the client requirements, you might add a Web service layer on top of the connector.

It is helpful to view the process of formulating an integration approach as three separate tasks (each requiring a design and implementation phase):

- Decide on the integration layer, including where it should be located and what form it should take. With the J2EE platform, various integration layers are possible, including connectors, enterprise beans, JMS, and Web services. Remember that you want the integration layer to be such that other applications or systems can evolve easily.

- Decide how to adapt each EIS to the integration layer.

- Decide how to write new applications against these integration layers.

Keep in mind that an important reason for using an integration layer is the services it provides for distribution. Usually, EISs are located on different physical machines, or they may be run as separate processes. To integrate these EISs, you need to use a distributed technology. J2EE application servers are an excellent choice for integration because they can handle multiple protocols for distributed computing: Internet Inter-ORB Protocol (IIOP), messaging, HTTP and Web services. In addition, J2EE application servers can handle native EIS protocols through connectors. These native protocols include proprietary protocols used by ERP and database vendors, among others.

Figure 6.5 shows the integration design approaches that are possible with the J2EE technologies.

Note: This figure uses dashed lines to represent asynchronous calls, such as sending a JMS message. The solid lines show synchronous calls, which are made either through EJB or Web service APIs. The three applications, which are shown on the left side of the diagram, are new EAI applications that you might be writing. The right side of the diagram shows some of the existing EIS systems that need to be integrated with the EAI applications.

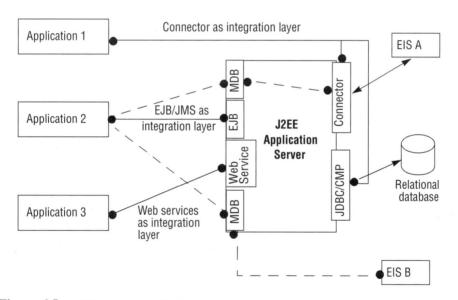

Figure 6.5   EIS Integration Design Approaches

Since it requires very tight coupling with EIS A, EAI application 1 bypasses the J2EE application server but reuses the connector layer. Application 2 needs to use some business logic present in the application server. As a result, it does not want to access the EIS directly. Application 2 instead uses a combination of synchronous and asynchronous calls to the EJB tier. These calls (to enterprise beans and message-driven beans) access EIS A and the relational database through JDBC, EJB container-managed persistence, or connectors. EIS B also generates asynchronous messages for implementing the business logic, and these messages must be delivered to a message-driven bean. Application 3 uses the least tightly coupled interface, Web services, and it accesses available functionality through a Web service interface. The Web service internally uses the business logic stored in the J2EE application server. (In the next sections we take a closer look at these different EAI design approaches and then provide some guidelines for implementing these approaches.)

Let's see how you might apply this strategy to the adventure builder enterprise. The adventure builder enterprise decides to use several layers for integration:

1. Web services as an integration layer for its supply chain.

2. Web services as an integration layer for communicating among different departments. For example, the adventure builder Web site uses a Web service to send an order to the order processing center.

3. EJB/JMS components as the integration layer with EISs. The order processing center integrates EISs within its department using JMS. Hence, the order processing center fulfills an order using JMS and EJB technologies for integrating its various EIS systems, customer relations management, billing systems, and so forth.

6.3.1   Web Services Approach

One approach for EAI is to use a Web service as the integration layer. With this approach, an enterprise's EIS systems expose their functionality by implementing Web services. They make their Web service interfaces available to other applications by providing WSDL descriptions of them. In addition, the integration layer may also include XML schemas for the documents used as parameters and return values. Essentially, the WSDL description of the service interface and document schemas becomes the integration layer, or the point of stability.

Developers who use the Web service approach for integration can leverage the advantages of Web services. Developers can write new enterprise applications with any technology that supports Web services, and the applications may be run on a variety of hardware and software platforms. However, this approach falls short when the new applications have certain additional requirements, such as transactional semantics or stringent security requirements. We discuss how to handle these issues in subsequent sections.

The adventure builder application is a good example of the Web services approach. As noted, the adventure builder enterprise uses Web services for integrating its supply chain. (Chapter 8 discuss the exact structure of the application, but here we highlight those details that pertain to integration.) The adventure builder architects decide, in consultation with the suppliers, on the schemas for the documents that they intend to exchange. (See "Designing Domain-Specific XML Schemas" on page 131.) Since their business depends on this exchange of documents—the adventure builder application sends purchase orders to various suppliers who fulfill adventure requests, and, in turn, the suppliers invoice adventure builder—the adventure builder enterprise and the suppliers need to agree on schemas that describe the content of these documents. For example, a lodging supplier might use an invoice document schema. Code Example 6.1 shows an example document corresponding to that schema. Similar schemas are defined for other kinds of suppliers, such as activity and airline suppliers.

```xml
<?xml version="1.0" encoding="UTF-8"?>
<Invoice xmlns="http://java.sun.com/blueprints/ns/invoice"
    xmlns:xsi="http://www.w3.org/2001/XMLSchema-instance"
    xsi:schemaLocation="http://java.sun.com/blueprints/ns/invoice
http://java.sun.com/blueprints/schemas/invoice-lodging.xsd">
    <ID>1234</ID>
    <OPCPoId>AB-j2ee-1069278832687</OPCPoId>
    <SupplierId>LODGING_INVOICE</SupplierId>
    <status>COMPLETED</status>
    <HotelId>LODG-6</HotelId>
    <HotelAddress>1234 Main Street, Sometown 12345, USA
    </HotelAddress>
<CancelPolicy>No Cancelations 24 hours prior</CancelPolicy>
</Invoice>
```

Code Example 6.1   Lodging Supplier Invoice

Similarly, the architects standardize on the WSDL to use for invoices when fulfilling an order. Suppliers, such as airlines, hotels, and activity providers, use these schemas and WSDL descriptions when interacting with the adventure builder enterprise. Code Example 6.2 shows the WSDL for the Web service endpoint to which the suppliers send their invoices.

The WSDL shown in Code Example 6.2 provides a single operation, submitDocument, which has a single xsd:anyType parameter representing the invoice XML document and which returns a single string value indicating a confirmation. The use of xsd:anyType enables an endpoint to receive multiple types of invoice documents with one method. See "Exchanging XML Documents" on page 107. A WSDL document normally begins with the type definitions that it uses, such as the exception type InvalidDocumentException. (For brevity, the code sample omits these type definitions.) The WSDL code then describes the SOAP messages used in the SOAP request and reply calls that correspond to the submitDocument method. It also describes a WSDL port corresponding to the JAX-RPC interface for receiving invoices, plus it binds the port to the HTTP protocol and indicates the RPC-literal binding. Finally, the WSDL code defines the name of the service and the URL at which the service is available. (For a more detailed explanation of a WSDL document, see "Web Services Description Language" on page 36.)

```
<?xml version="1.0" encoding="UTF-8"?>
<definitions name="WebServiceBroker" targetNamespace= ...>
    ...
    <message name="BrokerServiceIntf_submitDocument">
        <part name="Invoice" type="xsd:anyType"/></message>
    <message name="BrokerServiceIntf_submitDocumentResponse">
        <part name="result" type="xsd:string"/></message>
    <message name="InvalidDocumentException"><part name=
            "InvalidDocumentException" element=
            "tns:InvalidDocumentException"/>
    </message>
    <portType name="BrokerServiceIntf">
        <operation name="submitDocument" parameterOrder="Invoice">
            <input message="tns:BrokerServiceIntf_submitDocument"/>
            <output message
                ="tns:BrokerServiceIntf_submitDocumentResponse"/>
            <fault name="InvalidDocumentException" message=
                    "tns:InvalidDocumentException"/>
```

```
        </operation>
    </portType>
    <binding name="BrokerServiceIntfBinding" type=
                        "tns:BrokerServiceIntf">
        ...
    </binding>
    <service name="WebServiceBroker">
        ...
    </service>
</definitions>
```

Code Example 6.2 WSDL for Receiving the Invoices

Although you can modify the EIS systems that participate in Web service interactions to export the Web service interfaces, a better approach uses a J2EE connector to plug the EIS system into the J2EE application server. The connector by its nature does not intrude on the EIS. This latter strategy takes advantage of the capabilities of the J2EE server. Among other advantages, using connectors allows the transactional and security contexts of a J2EE application server to carry forward to the EIS application. Plus, the EIS can use the thread pools of the application server. In conjunction with connectors, you use JAX-RPC from the J2EE application server to expose a Web service interface. See Figure 6.6.

❐ To expose a Web service interface for an EIS, use JAX-RPC in front of a connector.

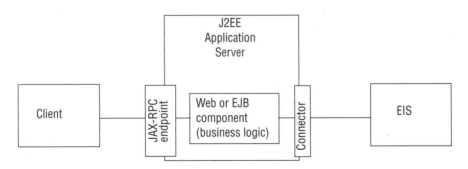

Figure 6.6 Using JAX-RPC and Connectors

For example, the adventure builder enterprise wants to use Web services to integrate its existing CRM system, which provides services to manage customer relations, to process orders. The department that owns the CRM module not only wants to maintain control of the software, it wants to use a generic interface that can handle user requests from multiple sources (Web site, telephone, OEM channels, and so forth). Web services are the best way to create such a generic interface, for these reasons:

- Web services establish clear, defined boundaries. Since Web services can provide an interface with clear, defined boundaries of responsibilities, the CRM department has the responsibility to only maintain the endpoint and publish a WSDL describing the endpoint.

- Web services provide controlled access. Outside requests to the CRM must come in through the service interface, and the CRM department can apply its access control parameters to limit access, plus it can log each access.

- Web services support multiple platforms. Because it does not control the hardware and software platforms other departments use, the CRM department can accommodate any platform by using Web services.

- The current generation of Web services is best suited for applications with a limited need for transactions and security. The main purpose of the CRM system is to allow status queries on existing orders. As such, it has little need for transactions. It also has limited need for security, since all access to the module happens within the corporate firewall.

Developers have a choice of endpoint types for implementing the Web service representing the EIS: either an EJB service endpoint or a Web-based JAX-RPC service endpoint. Solely from an integration point of view, either type of endpoint works well since Web and EJB components can both directly use JDBC and J2EE connectors. For example, the adventure builder enterprise receives invoices using an EJB service endpoint, as well as JAX-RPC service endpoints for other functions.

Returning to the CRM problem, the adventure builder enterprise could use a small J2EE application that uses a J2EE connector to connect to the CRM system. Such an application needs to have a JAX-RPC endpoint to expose the required Web service functionality.

Today, since many EIS vendors are providing built-in Web services support, developers can use connectors and leverage this support directly to avoid writing a

JAX-RPC wrapper. If you choose to follow this path, ensure that the EIS vendor provides a WS-I Basic Profile-compatible Web service. If the vendor does not, consider writing an adapter layer yourself to handle any differences. This approach may require upgrading your EIS system to a new software version, a risk you may not want to take. In such cases, consider using the recommended connectors and JAX-RPC approach.

❏   Consider using the built-in Web services support provided by the EIS vendors to avoid writing additional interfaces.

6.3.2   Enterprise Beans and JMS Approach

You can use enterprise beans and JMS layers, separately or combined, to develop an integration layer. With this approach, you use a J2EE application server to provide an enterprise bean layer for synchronous interactions. For asynchronous interactions, you place a message bus in the enterprise and require that applications use it.

The adventure builder enterprise uses this strategy for integrating applications within one department. For example, a single department owns the order processing module. Within that department, different groups handle various aspects of order processing, such as credit card payments, supply chain interactions, customer relations, and so on. In this workflow arrangement, interactions among these departmental groups are handled in a loosely coupled, asynchronous manner using JMS. When it needs to provide synchronous access, a group may use a remote enterprise bean interface. (See Figure 8.3 on page 345.)

Using enterprise beans and JMS does not preclude the use of XML, which is an additional benefit. For example, the adventure builder enterprise uses the same invoice document listed in Code Example 6.1 when sending a JMS message within its order processing center. The message-driven bean that receives the JMS message applies XML validation and translation logic just like any Web service endpoint.

6.3.3   The Connector Approach

When using connectors, the new EAI application is programmed directly against an interface provided by the EIS. For new applications that are also J2EE applications, you use a connector to access the EIS. You can either buy an off-the-shelf connector or write your own.

If you want to provide a simple isolation layer, you should consider writing a data access object, or DAO class, to hide the internal details of the EIS. A data access object encapsulates access to persistent data, such as that stored in a data management system. It decouples the user of the object from the programming mechanism for accessing the underlying data. It can also expose an easier-to-use API. Typically, you develop a data access class for a specific business function or set of functions, then client applications use these classes. Another common use is to layer data access objects on top of connectors, or resource adapters, thus isolating applications from the details of the connector interactions. Often, each resource adapter interaction has a corresponding data access object, whose methods pass input records to the adapter as parameters and return output records to the client application as return values.

Using a connector reduces the complexity of the integration layer. Note that when using the connector approach, the EAI application is tightly coupled with the EIS since the application directly uses the data model and functionality of the EIS. Since there is minimal layering, it also increases performance. However, it is an approach that works best when the integration problem is small in scope. Since it does not put into place a true integration architecture, this approach may limit the ability to scale the integration layer as the enterprise grows. Given these advantages and disadvantages, consider using this approach as a basic building block for other strategies.

6.3.4   Combining Approaches into an Integration Architecture

In many cases, architects combine these various integration layers into a single integration architecture. The end result—the mix of integration layer types—is in large measure driven by the requirements of each enterprise's situation. Architects need to consider the realities of the current state of the technologies and weigh that against future promises.

For example, Web services, as they exist today, have some shortcomings: They do not deliver the heavy-duty process integration, data transformation, and security capabilities required by many EAI scenarios. Similarly, services for transactional integrity and reliable messaging are not yet in place. Since security and transactional context propagation are critical business requirements, these are important factors to consider when using a Web services approach.

Data binding is another issue to consider. Web services are a good solution when data binding requirements are straightforward, such as mapping simple data types to Java data types. However, when it is necessary to manipulate complex relational or binary from an EIS, you may want to consider other solutions, such as using the J2EE Connector architecture, which provides a metadata facility to dynamically discover the data format in the EIS.

Table 6.1 compares these approaches for different integration problems and indicates the approaches best suited for these integration problems. The adventure builder enterprise uses Web services for partner and inter-department interactions, and the enterprise beans with JMS (EJB/JMS) approach for intra-department interactions.

Table 6.1 Comparing Different Integration Approaches

Operation	Connector Approach	EJB/JMS Approach	Web Services Approach
Coupling with EIS	Tight coupling. Uses EIS data model directly.	Can add a layer of abstraction in the EJB/JMS layer.	No hardware/software platform coupling. Can add multiple layers of abstractions and translations.
Transactional support	Available	Declarative, automatic context propagation	Global transaction propagation is not currently available. The endpoint implementation can use transactions for the business logic.
Supporting asynchronous operations	J2EE 1.4 platform adds asynchronous capabilities to connectors.	Message-driven beans provide an easy-to-use abstraction for receiving asynchronous events from EISs.	Currently no asynchronous support. WSDL provides a primitive mechanism for one-way calls, although the quality of service is low.
Performance	Highest	Overheads because of remote calls, and requirements of running a server.	Significant overheads because of remote calls, requirements of running a server, and of XML processing and validation.
Heterogeneous platform support	Requires that the client is programmed in Java.	Requires a J2EE application server (available on a broad range of hardware/software platforms).	Supported on a variety of hardware/software platforms.

Table 6.1   Comparing Different Integration Approaches (*continued*)

Operation	Connector Approach	EJB/JMS Approach	Web Services Approach
Security features	Can directly integrate with the EISs security model.	Provides application server security mechanisms.	Limited. HTTPS is supported.

6.4   Data Integration Guidelines

Recall that enterprise data may be kept in various types of data stores, including relational databases, non-relational databases, directory servers, and so forth. Some common strategies that help to integrate data from these different types of data stores are data mapping, data transformation, and data filtering.

6.4.1   Data Mapping in EAI Applications

Enterprises use various types of data stores to hold data, and each such data store persists the data according to its own layout and using its own data types. This is true even within a single enterprise. Thus, there are many varied external representations of data. Often, external data representations are relational in nature because most commonly data is stored in a relational database. EAI applications need to know how to access this data. It is important to map external data to the data structures used within an EAI application.

An important issue to consider when integrating data sources is to decide on a mapping layer. Generally, you have these options for relational data:

❐   Create a formal object-oriented data model.

❐   Create a generic data-holder layer.

The formal object-oriented data model relies on object-relational mapping technologies to map data from relational data sources to an object-oriented format. You may use such mapping technologies as Enterprise JavaBeans container-managed persistence, Java Data Objects, or even the data access object strategy. There are a number of advantages to this option. For one, you can reap the traditional advantages of an object-oriented approach, notably reusability, since you establish a mapping layer that can be reused by other applications.

When you use the EJB container-managed persistence technology, you also can rely on the EJB container's security features to control access to the data. You also leverage the performance benefits of the EJB container-managed persistence engine, which uses data caching to improve performance. Finally, by using these technologies, you can take advantage of the mapping tools that come with them.

The other option for representing relational data is to create a generic layer to hold the data. For this approach, you use JDBC APIs to handle data from relational data sources. The JDBC RowSet technology, in particular, makes it easy to access relational data in an efficient manner. (Keep in mind, however, that JDBC RowSet technology is not yet standard in the J2EE platform.) The RowSet technology, through the WebRowSet feature, gives you an XML view of the data source. Its CachedRowSet capabilities lets you access data in a disconnected fashion, while the FilteredRowSet functions give you the ability to manage data in a disconnected manner, without requiring heavyweight DBMS support. By using a generic layer to hold data, you have a simpler design, since there is no real layering, and you avoid the conceptual weight of a formal data model. This approach may have better performance, particularly when access is tabular in nature (such as when selecting several attributes from all rows that match a particular condition).

❐ To access data stored in non-relational data sources, it is best to use connectors.

Connectors let you plug in non-relational data sources to the J2EE environment. For non-relational systems that do not have ready-made connectors available, such as home-grown systems, you need to write your own connector. See "Integrating Custom Legacy Systems" on page 283.

6.4.2 Data Transformation

Data transformation—the ability to convert data to an acceptable application format—is a common requirement for newer applications that need to access legacy data. Such transformation functionality is necessary because most legacy systems were not designed to handle the requirements of these subsequent applications.

To illustrate, a legacy system may store dates using an eight-digit integer format; for example, storing the date September 23, 2003 as 20030923. Another application that accesses this legacy system needs the same date formatted as either MM/DD/YYYY or 09/23/2003. The application needs to access the eight-digit date from the legacy system and transform it to a usable format.

Another example of data transformation might involve customer data. Customer data spans a range of information, and might include identity and address information as well as credit and past ordering information. Different systems may be interested in different parts of this customer data, and hence each system may have a different notion of a customer.

Even schemas, including industry-standard schemas such as Electronic Data Interchange For Administration, Commerce, and Transport (EDIFact), Universal Business Language (UBL), and RosettaNet, must be transformed to each other. Often enterprises need to use these industry-standard formats for external communications while at the same time using proprietary formats for internal communications.

One way you might solve the data transformation problem is to require that all systems use the same standard data format. Unfortunately, this solution is unrealistic and impractical, as illustrated by the Y2K problem of converting the representation of a calendar year from two digits to four digits. Although going from two to four digits should be a minor change, the cost to fix this problem was enormous. System architects must live with the reality that data transformations are here to stay, since different systems will inevitably have different representations of the same information.

❏ A good strategy for data transformation is to use the canonical data model.

An enterprise might set up one canonical data model for the entire enterprise or separate models for different aspects of its business. Essentially, a canonical data model is a data model independent of any application. For example, a canonical model might use a standard format for dates, such as MM/DD/YYYY. Rather than transforming data from one application's format directly to another application's format, you transform the data from the various communicating applications to this common canonical model. You write new applications to use this common format and adapt legacy systems to the same format.

❏ Use XML to represent a canonical data model.

XML provides a good means to represent this canonical data model, for a number of reasons:

- XML, through a schema language, can rigorously represent types. By using XML to represent your canonical model, you can write various schemas that unambiguously define the data model. Before XML, many times canonical data models were established but never documented by their developers. If you were lucky, developers might have described the model in a text document. It was easy for such a document to get out of sync with the actual types used by the model.

- XML schemas are enforceable. You can validate an XML document to ensure that it conforms to the schema of the canonical data model. A text document cannot enforce use of the proper types.

- XML is easier to convert to an alternate form, by using declarative means such as style sheets.

- XML is both platform and programming-language neutral. Hence, you can have a variety of systems use the same canonical data model without requiring a specific programming language or platform.

This is not meant to imply that XML is perfect, since there are some disadvantages to using XML to represent a canonical model. For one, to use XML you need to either learn the XML schema language (XSL) or use a good tool. Often, transforming XML requires you to use XSL, which is not an easy language to learn, especially since XSL is different from traditional programming languages. There are also performance overheads with XML. However, for many enterprise settings (and especially for integration purposes) the benefits of using XML outweigh its disadvantages, and the benefits of XML become more significant when you factor in future maintenance costs.

Code Example 6.3 shows an XML document representing invoice information. This might be the canonical model of an invoice used by the adventure builder enterprise. Since this document is published internally, all new applications requiring this data type can make use of it.

```
<?xml version="1.0" encoding="UTF-8"?>
<bpi:Invoice
    xmlns:bpi="http://java.sun.com/blueprints/ns/invoice"
    xmlns:xsi="http://www.w3.org/2001/XMLSchema-instance"
    xsi:schemaLocation="http://java.sun.com/blueprints/ns/
        invoice   http://java.sun.com/blueprints/schemas/
        invoice.xsd">
    <bpi: InvoiceId>1234</bpi:InvoiceId>
    <bpi:OPCPoId>AB-j2ee-1069278832687</bpi: OPCPoId>
```

```
        <bpi:SupplierId>LODGING_INVOICE</bpi:SupplierId>
        <bpi: status>COMPLETED</bpi:status>
    </bpi:Invoice>
```

Code Example 6.3   XML Document With Invoice Information

It is usually a good idea to provide the schema for the canonical data model.
By having the schema available, you can validate the translated documents
against it and newer applications can use the schema to define their own models.
Code Example 6.4 shows the XSD schema file for this invoice information.

```
<?xml version="1.0" encoding="UTF-8"?>
<xsd:schema
    xmlns:xsd="http://www.w3.org/2001/XMLSchema"
    targetNamespace="http://java.sun.com/blueprints/ns/invoice"
    xmlns="http://java.sun.com/blueprints/ns/invoice"
    elementFormDefault="qualified">
  <xsd:element name="Invoice" type="InvoiceType"/>
  <xsd:complexType name="InvoiceType">
      <xsd:sequence>
          <xsd:element name="InvoiceId" type="xsd:string"/>
          <xsd:element name="OPCPoId" type="xsd:string"/>
          <xsd:element name="SupplierId" type="xsd:string"/>
          <xsd:element name="status" type="xsd:string"/>
      </xsd:sequence>
  </xsd:complexType>
</xsd:schema>
```

Code Example 6.4   XSD Schema for Invoice Information

In addition to the XML form, the canonical model representation may be
needed in the Java Object form. Often, the Java Object form is needed, for example, when a substantial amount of business logic is written in the J2EE application
server. To use the canonical form for new code, you convert the canonical data
types (from an XML schema to Java or vice versa) in Java objects. That is, you
use the XML documents or their Java object representations as the stable integration point. (See "Web Services Approach" on page 266.) For example, Code

Example 6.5 shows the equivalent Java classes for the canonical model of invoice information.

```
public class Invoice {
    public string getInvoiceId();
    public Address getOPCPoId();
    public string getSupplierId();
    public string getStatus();
    // class implementation ...
}
```

Code Example 6.5   Java Class Equivalents for Canonical Invoice Information

Once the XML is defined, you can also use tools such as JAXB to generate the Java classes. (See "Flexible Mapping" on page 148.)

After establishing a canonical data model, you must devise a strategy to convert any alternate data representations to this model. Because it plugs its enterprise systems—billing, order processing, and CRM—in via an application server, the adventure builder enterprise exposes the canonical data model only through the external interfaces exposed by the application server. That is, only those components with external interfaces—Web service applications, remote enterprise beans, and so forth—expose the canonical data model. Since the external world needs (and sees) only the canonical data model, the adventure builder enterprise must transform its internal data representations—which have their own data model devised by its various EISs—to this same canonical model.

The data translation between the internal and external representations can be done before the data goes from the EIS into the application server—that is, the application server internally uses the canonical data model, which is generally recommended. Or, the data translation can take place just prior to sending the data out to the external world—that is, the application server uses the various EISs' native data representations. Sometimes the business logic necessitates this latter approach because the logic needs to know the precise native format. The translation is accomplished in one of two ways:

1. Use XSL style sheets to transform these alternate data representations, either when data comes in or when data goes out. XSL style sheets work for XML-based interfaces. In this approach, the application server internally uses the EIS

native formats and the translation happens just before the data either goes out to the external world or comes in from the outside.

2. Use a façade approach and do programmatic object mapping in the DAO layer. That is, you set up a DAO to connect an EIS to the application server. Write the DAO so that it exposes only the canonical data model and have it map any incoming data to the appropriate internal data model. Since this approach converts incoming data to the canonical form when the data arrives at the application server, the business logic internally uses the canonical data representation.

To understand the XSL style sheet approach, let's consider how the adventure builder enterprise receives invoices from various suppliers. In adventure builder's case, various suppliers submit invoices, and each supplier may have a different representation (that is, a different format) of the invoice information. Furthermore, adventure builder's various EISs may each have a different representation of the same invoice information. Code Example 6.6 shows an example of a typical supplier's invoice.

```xml
<?xml version="1.0" encoding="UTF-8"?>
<Invoice xmlns="http://java.sun.com/blueprints/ns/invoice"
    xmlns:xsi="http://www.w3.org/2001/XMLSchema-instance"
    xsi:schemaLocation=
        "http://java.sun.com/blueprints/ns/invoice
            http://java.sun.com/blueprints/schemas/
            invoice-lodging.xsd">
<ID>1234</ID>
<OPCPoId>AB-j2ee-1069278832687</OPCPoId>
<SupplierId>LODGING_INVOICE</SupplierId>
<status>COMPLETED</status>
<HotelId>LODG-6</HotelId>
<HotelAddress>1234 Main Street, Sometown 12345, USA
</HotelAddress>
<CancelPolicy>No Cancellations 24 hours prior</CancelPolicy>
</Invoice>
```

Code Example 6.6   Example of Supplier Invoice Information

Compare this listing of invoice information with that of adventure builder's canonical model, shown in Code Example 6.3. adventure builder can convert an invoice from this supplier to its canonical data model by applying in the interaction layer of the Web service the style sheet shown in Code Example 6.7. The style sheet defines rules, such as those for matching templates (`<xsl:template match-...>`), that are applied to the supplier invoice and corresponding XML fragment when the canonical model is generated.

```
<xsl:stylesheet version='1.0'
    xmlns:xsl='http://www.w3.org/1999/XSL/Transform'
    xmlns:bpi='http://java.sun.com/blueprints/ns/invoice'>
     <xsl:template match="text()"/>
     <xsl:template match="@*"/>
     <xsl:template match="bpi:Invoice">
      <bpi:Invoice xmlns:xsi=
           "http://www.w3.org/2001/XMLSchema-instance"
       xsi:schemaLocation=
           "http://java.sun.com/blueprints/ns/invoice
           http://java.sun.com/blueprints/schemas/invoice.xsd">
       <xsl:apply-templates/>
      </bpi:Invoice>
     </xsl:template>
     <xsl:template match="bpi:InvoiceRef">
          <bpi:InvoiceId><xsl:value-of  select="text()"/>
    </bpi:InvoiceId>
     </xsl:template>
     <xsl:template match="bpi:OPCPoId">
         <bpi:OPCPoId><xsl:value-of select="text()"/></bpi:OPCPoId>
     </xsl:template>
     <xsl:template match="bpi:SupplierId">
          <bpi:SupplierId><xsl:value-of  select="text()"/>
          </bpi:SupplierId>
     </xsl:template>
     <xsl:template match="bpi:Status">
          <bpi:status><xsl:value-of select="text()"/></bpi:status>
     </xsl:template>
  </xsl:stylesheet>
```

Code Example 6.7   Style Sheet to Convert Supplier Invoice to Canonical Model

The adventure builder application applies the style sheet when an invoice is sent to a supplier. See "Reuse and Pool Parsers and Style Sheets" on page 188 for more information about pooling style sheets.

Transition façades, which can apply to any object representation of data, are a more general solution for transformations. You can use transition façades to hide extra information or to provide simple mappings. To use a façade, you write a Java class within which you do manual data transformation and mappings.

You should also consider using one of the many tools available for data transformations. These tools simplify the data transformation task and make it easier to maintain.

❏ When data is in an XML document, it is easier to write XSL style sheets that do the required transformations.

❏ When you access data using EJB container-managed persistence, you can either directly modify the container-managed persistent classes or write façades to do the required transformations.

6.4.3   Data Filtering

When you do not have access to an application's code, such as for off-the-shelf packaged applications or for applications that cannot be modified because they are critical to a working business system, you might consider using filtering. That is, you construct a filter that sits in front of the application and does all necessary data translations.

Generally, data filtering goes hand-in-hand with data transformations. The canonical data model, because it must support all use cases within an enterprise, is often a good candidate for filtering. Since many applications do not need access to all data fields, you can filter data and simplify application development and improve performance by reducing the amount of data that is exchanged.

There are two types of filtering, and each has its own use cases:

1. Filtering that hides information but saves it for later use

2. Filtering that outputs only needed information

For example, in the adventure builder enterprise, a workflow manager receives the invoices sent by the different suppliers. Since it needs only an identifier to identify the workflow associated with the invoice, the workflow manager can filter the document to retrieve only this information. However, since it may need to pass the entire invoice—all the data fields in the invoice—to the next step in the workflow, the workflow manager must preserve the entire document. The workflow manager can accomplish this using flexible mapping. (See "Flexible Mapping" on page 148.)

On the other hand, you may want to apply data filtering before sending information. For example, a credit card processing component of a workflow may need to send credit information. The component should send only information required for privacy protection and should use data filtering to remove information that need not be passed to another application.

Filtering can be applied at the database level, too. Using filtering, you can obtain a simplified view of the data tailored to a particular application. In addition, using EJB container-managed persistence for data transformation makes it easier to filter data. The container-managed persistence mapping tools let you select a subset of the database schema, and this is analogous to filtering. If you are using the JDBC RowSet approach, you need only select the columns for the data that you care about.

You can also write façades that appropriately filter the data. In this case, the client code accesses data only through these façades.

6.5   Guidelines for Integration

Now that we've examined integration design approaches and techniques, let's look at some guidelines for integrating enterprise applications with EIS systems.

We examine guidelines for integrating legacy systems, particularly home-grown systems, and guidelines for using command beans. Although not as common, we mention guidelines for achieving integration by using metadata, registries, and versioning and evolution.

6.5.1   Integrating Custom Legacy Systems

Most enterprises have home-grown or custom EISs, also referred to as one-off systems, and these systems need to be integrated. As we have already seen, connectors are the best solution for integrating EISs in a J2EE environment. However, because these are custom systems, there are no off-the-shelf or vendor-provided connectors available for them as there are for well-known EISs. As a result, you may have to write your own connector for a home-grown EIS. The recommended way to write a connector is to use a connector builder tool. A tool such as this not only generates a connector, but (with the help of other J2EE application server services) it may also create a Web services layer.

Generally, there are two scenarios involving the integration of custom systems. In one case, two EIS systems need to interact with each other. The connector approach works well with this type of scenario: You merely write Java classes implementing the business logic for one EIS and use a connector to communicate to the other EIS system. In the second scenario, you intend to have several applications use a custom EIS. For this case, it is better to plug the custom EIS into the application server and expose the EIS's reusable business logic through the application server. You can expose the logic either by using enterprise beans with JMS or by using a Web services approach. If the situation warrants it, you can use both enterprise beans with JMS and a Web services approach together.

6.5.2   Using Screen Scraping for Integration

There are times when you may want to integrate an EIS that has no programming interface. Often, this happens with legacy mainframe applications. In these cases, you can resort to screen scraping to create a programming interface. With screen scraping, you write an adapter layer that acts as an end user entering data into the mainframe application, and this adapter layer serves as the programming interface. You then write a connector that uses this programming interface to accomplish its integration actions.

When resorting to screen scraping, be sure to keep in mind the limitations of the legacy system. Although you can integrate a new application to a legacy system, the original system has limitations that may make it unable to handle the new functionality. For example, suppose you used screen scraping to integrate a front-end application with a mainframe application designed to be interactive. The front-end application, since it has no human constraints, can suddenly pump in a high volume of requests to the mainframe application, which may not have been designed to handle such a load. It is hard to detect a problem such as this until runtime, when the system is suddenly overwhelmed with a high volume of requests. By this point in the development cycle, it may be quite expensive to fix the application.

6.5.3 Metadata

Metadata is information that describes the characteristics of a data set. For an EIS system, metadata describes the content, quality, and condition (among other characteristics) of the EIS's data.

EISs provide a range of access to this metadata. Some EISs provide programmatic access to their metadata, while others provide the metadata information in text form only, as a form of documentation. Sometimes, the metadata information is available through database system support tools. For example, some databases allow queries to learn its table names and schemas. Similarly, an EIS may give you access to its various quality of service parameters.

Metadata is often relevant to integration. Metadata allows you to use tools to discover properties of enterprise systems, and from this discovery to create appropriate, easy-to-use façades to the systems. By having access to metadata, tools can generate more meaningful classes.

Web services are designed to support metadata. Web services rely on WSDL files, which essentially provide metadata describing the services, the operations offered by the services, parameters for these operations, and so forth. Since these WSDL files are XML documents, they are accessible to tools and other programs. (See "Web Services Description Language" on page 36.)

Using an integration layer helps make metadata more explicit. When metadata is implicitly associated with EIS data, tools may have a difficult time discovering the metadata. For example, a database table column may represent distances from a certain point, and these distances are implicitly measured in miles. A tool that accesses the data from this table column may not be able to determine whether the distance is measured in miles or kilometers. By creating an integration layer, you can make this information explicit. You can name the methods that access the data in such a way as to indicate the associated metadata. For example, rather than have a `getDistance` method, you can call the method `getDistanceInMiles`. For Web services, the standard document formats that describe the service are designed to make the metadata more explicit.

Another way to make metadata explicit and accessible, especially for medium to large enterprises, is to store the metadata in a central location, such as a traditional LDAP directory. (LDAP, which stands for Lightweight Directory Access Protocol, is an Internet protocol that programs can use to look up information from a server.) You can make your EIS's metadata available to others in several ways. You can enable metadata support in your enterprise systems. The WSDL file that accompanies a Web service already defines metadata for the service. You may also provide specific methods that retrieve metadata related to quality of services, parameter constraints, and so forth. Publishing a schema for a document that a service accepts is another way to provide metadata.

When deciding what information to store in a directory, try to store data that is useful to more than one application. Storing metadata in a directory also helps if you need to analyze the impact of any changes to the application.

Also, consider implementing directory-based data sharing, since this enables applications to operate collectively. Such data sharing reduces management costs and improves an enterprise's overall responsiveness to business change. If you use this approach, be sure to set up authorization policies to control access to the data.

It is also important when using a directory service to locate authoritative or reliable sources of the data. A major reason for not using a directory service is outdated or suspect data. Users quickly learn that they cannot rely on the service and hence stop using it. Keep in mind, however, that a single application or database is rarely authoritative for all required data, and this may cause a data integration problem of its own.

6.5.4   Using Registries for Integration

You may want to consider using registries to integrate an application with an existing EISs, especially when you want a loose binding between the application and the systems with which it is integrated. For example, in the Web services approach, you can store the URL and the WSDL for the Web service in a UDDI registry. However, using a registry comes with the additional overhead of running and maintaining a registry server and the added programming complexity to have your application use the registry. The registry server may also be a single point of failure for your system.

Generally, it is not worthwhile to use registries for a small enterprise whose applications integrate with just a few EISs. Registries make more sense for medium and large integration architectures. You want to maximize the use of the registry among as many applications as possible.

6.5.5   Versioning and Evolution

Applications integrated with EISs change over time, as do the EISs. As these systems and applications evolve over their lifetimes, new versions of them emerge. Integration of the applications and EISs must be able to handle this evolution and versioning process.

Many enterprise applications change because of changes to the underlying business requirements. EISs change for similar reasons, too, but they may also change because of hardware and software upgrades and bug fixes. New functionality may be added to applications and existing functionality retired. Sometimes policies change and, as a result, applications must access EISs in a different manner.

Generally, it is easier to evolve the various components—the enterprise applications and EISs—than it is to evolve the integration layer, since it is the point of stability. Let's first look at some strategies to evolve EISs, and then discuss how to evolve the different types of integration layers.

Sometimes as it evolves, the changes to an EIS are internal only. The external functionality—the functionality visible to other applications—remains the same. When this is the case, you should strive to keep unchanged the original external interface specified in the integration layer. To do this, make the sort of changes to the internal implementation of the EIS that do not impact the external interface; that is, the internal implementation should be changed so that it adapts to the original external interface.

It is different when the integration layer evolves. One way to handle this is to use a transformation layer, which is an additional layer added to enable older applications to continue to work. A transformation layer accepts messages in the older style used by these applications and transforms them to the current format. Often, because of their looser coupling, it is easier to evolve integration layers that are Web services than other types of integration layers.

When you control both ends of the integration point (the Web services endpoint and the client), it is often easier to upgrade them both at the same time. When just the internal implementation of the Web service changes—and these changes have no affect on the external interface—you merely plug in the new implementation.

Internal implementation changes to the Web service that cause changes to the external interface can be relatively easier to handle if these changes enhance the service but do not modify the original service contract. In these cases, you can provide two sets of WSDL files, one describing the original service and the other describing the new, enhanced service.

However, more complex scenarios exist, and you cannot expect clients to immediately migrate to a new service implementation. Some clients may never migrate to the new service. For more complex scenarios, a good strategy is to publish a separate Web service endpoint that provides the new service version. Clients can migrate to the new service when convenient for them. You can keep the old service interface but re-implement the existing endpoint to use the new implementation of the service. You may even be able to publish the new endpoint under the same URL without breaking the existing clients. For example, if you are just adding some additional ports to your WSDL, you should be able to update the old WSDL with the new WSDL description and then existing clients should continue to work with no problems.

6.5.6   Writing Applications for Integration

One area in which you have quite a bit of flexibility involves how you code your new EAI application. Since the application is new, you have the maximum amount of choice for implementing how the application will access the various resources that it requires. The J2EE platform, which is moving in this direction, provides some facilities to help with this task.

The Java Business Integration (JBI) Systems Programming Interface, based on JSR 208, extends the J2EE platform with a pluggable integration infrastructure using WSDL-based message exchange. JBI is of most interest to integration-independent software vendors (ISVs) rather than enterprise developers. JBI enables ISVs to write integration modules that support business protocols, such as Business Process Execution Language (BPEL), and plug them into a J2EE application server using JBI mechanisms. JBI also provides these integration modules with useful services such as threading, context management, security, lifecycle management, connection pooling, timers, and so forth. As a developer, you deal with the Web services for the various JBI-based integration services provided by these ISVs.

6.6   Conclusion

This chapter examined some of the key issues for enterprise application integration. It began by illustrating typical integration problems encountered by enterprises, and then described the various integration technologies available with the J2EE 1.4 platform. These J2EE technologies are not limited to Web services only, though Web services represent one valid integration approach most useful in certain situations. In addition to Web services, the J2EE platform has technologies for integrating with relational databases and other types of data stores, messaging technologies, and EIS access technologies.

The chapter described the major J2EE application integration approaches—including using Web services, enterprise beans and JMS, connectors, and data access objects—and detailed the situations when it was most appropriate to use these different approaches. It also showed how the various approaches could be combined.

The chapter concluded with a set of guidelines for achieving data, application, and business process integration. It also presented some guidelines for integrating home-grown systems, along with how to leverage the capabilities of registries for integration purposes.

Chapter 7 discusses the approaches for implementing secure Web services.

Security

VIRTUALLY every enterprise application exposed through a Web service has a need for security at some level. An enterprise's data is an important asset to every business, and a good security system is necessary to ensure its safety and integrity. Businesses need to safeguard their systems and their data resources from malicious use by unauthorized intruders, both internal and external to the business, and from inadvertent or unintended mischief. Businesses also must keep message exchanges with other entities secure.

Security for Web services is two-fold: It encompasses both the security requirements of a typical enterprise as well as the particular security needs of the Web services themselves. An enterprise's business security requirements are well known, and it is just as important to identify the security needs of a service. For example, the developer of a Web service, after assessing its business needs, might only want to let a certain set of users access particular resources.

Setting up security also involves some usability issues. In particular, because Web services have a high degree of interaction with varied clients, it is important to keep security measures from being overly intrusive and thus maintain the ease of use of a service. A service needs to promote its interoperability and make its security requirements and policy known to clients. Often, a service needs to keep a record of transactions or a log of access made to particular resources. The service must not only guarantee privacy, but it must also keep these records in case a claim is made at some later date about a transaction occurrence.

To address security needs, enterprise platforms use well-known mechanisms to provide for common protections, as follows:

- Identity, which enables a business or service to know who you are

- Authentication, which enables you to verify that a claimed identity is genuine

- Authorization, which lets you establish who has access to specific resources

- Data integrity, which lets you establish that data has not been tampered with

- Confidentiality, which restricts access to certain messages only to intended parties

- Nonrepudiation, which lets you prove a user performed a certain action such that the user cannot deny it

- Auditing, which helps you to keep a record of security events

These are just some of the concepts important to security, and there are others such as trust, single sign-on, federation, and so forth. The chapter describes mechanisms to address and handle the threats to security, including credentials for establishing identity, encryption to safeguard the confidentiality of messages, digital signatures to help verify identity, and secure communication channels (such as HTTPS) to safeguard messages and data.

Keep in mind that the J2EE 1.4 platform does not invent new security mechanisms. Rather, the platform provides a programming model that integrates existing security mechanisms, and makes it easier to design and implement secure applications.

This chapter begins with an examination of some typical Web service security scenarios. It then covers the security features available on the J2EE 1.4 platform. Once the technologies are described, the chapter shows how to design and implement secure Web services using these J2EE technologies. The chapter also covers the emerging technologies for Web service security, in particular message-level security.

7.1   Security Scenarios

Enterprise environments with Web site applications have a variety of security use case scenarios. Although the spread of Web services has given rise to additional security use cases, these Web services application use cases have similar security needs to those of Web-based enterprise applications (such as browser-based applications accessing Web sites). Typically, Web site and Web service application use cases involve access to services through the Internet or an intranet, allow users to access certain sets of resources but not others, and allow users to perform some set of actions. In addition, users might require access to other resources, such as a database, and they might need to interact with other applications.

Some of the security needs of Web site applications and Web services are very similar. For example, a Web site application must authenticate its users, and a Web service application must authenticate its clients. However, Web services applications have additional security needs, because their use cases are typically application to application rather than user to application and because their communication interaction uses new technologies. Later in this chapter we examine security issues specific to Web services, plus we look at the specific details for implementing Web services-specific security mechanisms.

Let's first look at some typical Web services scenarios and examine the secure interactions between clients and services. Not only do we look at security issues relevant to client and service interactions, we also examine how service endpoints interact in a secure manner with resources and components of an enterprise to process requests. Before doing so, however, we examine basic security requirements.

7.1.1   General Security Requirements

Although varying greatly in implementation and functionality, J2EE Web services scenarios have common security requirements. They require certain security constraints for message exchange interactions and data passing between a client and a service. In addition to securing service and client interactions, Web service endpoints must be able to securely access other J2EE components (such as entity beans) and external resources (such as databases and enterprise information systems) to process client requests. While processing a client request, service endpoints may also need to interact with other Web services, and this, too, must be done in a secure manner.

Figure 7.1 shows a Web service interaction in which a client request to the service causes the service endpoint to interact with other components, resources, and systems. It illustrates that a Web service request can take many paths and result in interactions with different containers, components, and resources, including other Web services. Requests to a Web service start with a client sending a message to a Web service endpoint running in a Web or EJB container.

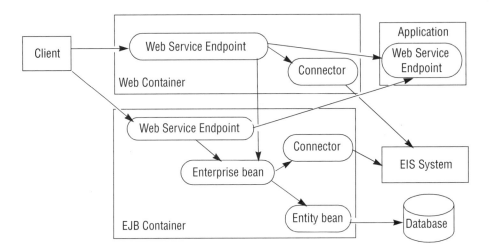

Figure 7.1   Anatomy of a Web Service Interaction

❏   However, designing a secure Web service involves more than just securing the
    initial interaction between the client and the service. For a truly secure service,
    you must also consider the security needs of the Web service endpoint's sub-
    sequent interactions with other J2EE components, resources, and so forth, that
    it undertakes to process the request.

Most client requests to a service require the service to access a series of components to fulfill the request and each call might have its own, unique security
requirement. This results in a chain of calls to various components, some of which
might be within the initiating component's security domain and others of which
are outside that security domain. With such a chain of component calls, each
cooperating component in the chain must be able to negotiate its security requirements. In addition, components along the chain might use different security protocols. In short, security needs to flow from a client to a called component, then to
other components and resources, while passing through different security policy
domains.

A J2EE application must be able to integrate its own security requirements
and mechanisms with those of different components and systems. For example, a
client might make a request to a Web service. The client call is to an endpoint,
which in turn might call other Web services, make IIOP calls, access resources,
and access local components. Each component—other Web services, local and

remote components, and resources—has its own security requirements. If it interacts with an EIS system, a Web service endpoint must be able to handle the security requirements and mechanisms that the EIS system requires for authentication and authorization.

Some of the common security requirements for a Web service are authentication, access control, establishing a secure channel for exchanging messages, message-level security, and securing the interaction with other components when processing requests. Let's examine how these security requirements express themselves with Web services.

7.1.1.1 Authentication

Authentication, or proving one's identity, is often required by both a Web service and a client for an interaction to occur. A Web service might require that clients provide some credentials—such as a username and password, or a digital certificate such as an X.509 certificate—to help in proving their identity. The client of a Web service might require that a service provide it with some evidence to help establish its identity, which typically is done using a digital certificate.

Furthermore, since a Web service might need to access other components and resources to process a client's request, there are authentication requirements between a service and resources that it uses. The service might need to provide identity information to authenticate itself to resources and components. The resources and components might also have to prove their identity to the service. The same authentication requirements hold true between Web services if the service endpoint needs to access other Web services.

Thus, authentication occurs across different layers and different types of systems and domains. Passing identity along the chain may also require that the identity change or be mapped to another principal.

7.1.1.2 Access Control

Controlling access to a service is as important as authentication. A service endpoint might want to let only certain authorized clients access its services. Or, an application might want to restrict different sets of its resources and functionality to different groups of clients. An endpoint might allow all clients to invoke its basic service, but it might grant some clients extra privileges and access to special functions. For example, you might want to limit access to only users who are classified as managers or to only users who work for a particular department. In short, all clients are not equal in terms of their permissions to access or use services or resources.

Because a service endpoint also needs to interact with other components and resources, the endpoint needs some way to control access to them. That is, the endpoint needs to be able to specify resources that have restricted access, to group clients into logical roles and map those roles to an established identity, and, while processing a service request, to decide whether clients with a particular identity can access a particular resource.

7.1.1.3   Secure Channel for Message Exchange

A client's utilization of a Web service entails numerous message exchanges, and such messages may contain documents, input parameters, return values, and so forth. Since not all messages require security, an application needs to identify those messages requiring security and ensure that they are properly protected.

Some message exchanges, such as passing credit card information, require confidentiality. For these messages, the interaction between a client and a Web service must be encrypted so that unintended parties, even if they manage to intercept the message, cannot read the data.

Interactions between a client and a Web service might require integrity constraints. That is, message exchanges between a client and a service might require a digital signature to verify that the message was not altered in transit. The message recipient, by validating a signature bound to a message, verifies the integrity of the message.

To handle interactions requiring integrity and confidentiality, it is important to establish secure channels for exchanging messages. Applications use HTTPS and digital certificates to establish such secure channels. HTTPS provides a secure message exchange for one hop between two parties.

7.1.1.4   Message-Level Security

Besides creating a secure communication channel between a client and a Web service, some Web service message exchanges might require that security information be embedded within the SOAP message itself. This is often the case when a message needs to be processed by several intermediary nodes before it reaches the target service or when a message must be passed among several services to be processed.

Message-level security can be useful in XML document-centric applications, since different sections of the XML document may have different security requirements or be intended for different users.

7.1.2 Security Implications of the Operational Environment

The operational environment within which Web services interactions occur is an important factor in your security design. Service interactions occurring entirely within an enterprise have very different security requirements than service interactions open to everyone on the Internet. Thus, the relationship among Web service participants—such as Internet, intranet, and extranet—is an important consideration. When participants are closely aligned, you have a greater ability to negotiate security requirements.

In essence, the more control you have over the environment in which the Web service participants run, the easier it is to solve your security design. For example, if the Web services limit communication to applications inside your enterprise, then the network's physical security might shield the Web service. The operational environment security might be sufficient to satisfy your security needs. Similarly, Web services in environments that require communication via a Virtual Private Network (VPN) might not need to worry about issues such as confidentiality, since the communication channel is already secure.

When all participants are trusted, such as within one enterprise, it is an easier matter to set up and exchange security keys. However, this is a difficult challenge for untrusted participants with an open Internet Web service.

7.2   J2EE Platform Security Model

The J2EE platform container provides a set of security-related system services to its applications and clients. These built-in container services simplify application development because they remove the need for the application developer to write the security portion of the application logic.

Security on the J2EE platform is primarily declarative and is specified externally from the application code. *Declarative security* mechanisms used in an application are expressed via a declarative syntax in a configuration document called a deployment descriptor. The declarative security model has the advantage of enabling you to easily change these declarative settings to match security policy.

Declarative references in the deployment descriptor, rather than program code, define much of the security for a J2EE application. The collection of security declarations forms the security policy for an application. When security is defined declaratively, the container is responsible for performing security and the application does not include code specifically for security operations. Since security references are in the deployment descriptor, developers can modify the security for an application by using tools or changing the deployment descriptor. At deployment, the container uses the application security policy declared in the deployment descriptor to set up the security environment for the J2EE application, just as it uses other references in the deployment descriptor to perform similar services for transactions, remote communication, and so forth. During runtime, the container interposes itself between the client calls and the application's components to perform security checks and otherwise manage the applications.

In addition to declarative security, the J2EE platform includes APIs to add security code into your components. *Programmatic security* refers to security decisions that are made by security-aware applications. Programmatic security, which allows an application to include code that explicitly uses a security mechanism, is useful when declarative security alone cannot sufficiently express the security model of an application. The J2EE programming model offers some programmatic services that help you to write security functionality into the application code.

As noted, rather than inventing new security mechanisms, the J2EE platform facilitates the incorporation of existing security mechanisms into an application server operational environment. That is, the J2EE security model integrates with existing authorization and authentication mechanisms, handling existing user identity information, digital certificates, and so forth. The model provides a unifying layer above other security services, and its coherent programming model hides the security implementation details from application developers. For example, the J2EE security model provides mechanisms to leverage existing Internet security standards such as Secure Sockets Layer (SSL).

In addition, the J2EE platform security model gives you the ability to provide security boundaries. Once you have established these security boundaries, you can map users to their organizational roles and combine users into logical groups according to these roles.

Let's look in more detail at the J2EE platform security services and mechanisms. This security model applies to Web services as well as to the entire J2EE platform. "Security for Web Service Interactions" on page 308 describes how a Web service application can leverage these J2EE security mechanisms.

7.2.1 Authentication

Authentication is the mechanism by which a client presents an identifier and the service provider verifies the client's claimed identity. When the proof occurs in two directions—the caller and service both prove their identity to the other party—it is referred to as mutual authentication.

Typically, a client interaction with a J2EE application accesses a set of components and resource, such as JSPs, enterprise beans, databases, and Web service endpoints. When these resources are protected, as is often the case, a client presents its identity and credentials, and the container determines whether the client meets the criteria for access specified by the authorization rules. The platform also allows lazy authentication, which allows unauthenticated clients to access unprotected resources but forces authentication when these clients try to access protected resources. The platform additionally permits authentication to occur at different points, such as on the Web or EJB tier. The J2EE container handles the authentication based on the requirements declared in the deployment descriptor.

Not only does the container enforce authentication and establish an identity when a client calls a component, but the container also handles authentication when the initially called component makes calls to other components and resources. Processing a client's request to a component might require the component to make a chain of calls to access other resources and components. Each subsequently called component might have its own authentication requirements, and these requirements might differ from those of the initially called component. The J2EE container handles this by establishing an identity with each call along the chain of calls. The J2EE platform allows the client identity established with the initial call's authentication to be associated with subsequent method calls and interactions. That is, the client's authenticated identity can be propagated along the chain of calls.

It is also possible to configure a component to establish a new identity when it acts as a client in a chain of calls. When so configured, a component can change the authenticated identity from the client's identity to its own identity. Regardless of how it is handled, the J2EE container establishes an identity for calls made by a component. Also, the J2EE container handles unauthenticated invocations that do not require a client to establish an identity. This mechanism can be useful for supporting use cases where a client does not have to authenticate.

7.2.1.1   Protection Domains

The J2EE platform makes it possible to group entities into special domains, called protection domains, so that they can communicate among themselves without having to authenticate themselves. A *protection domain* is a logical boundary around a set of entities that are assumed or known to trust each other. Entities in such a domain need not be authenticated to one another.

Figure 7.2 illustrates an environment using protection domains. It shows how authentication is required only for interactions that cross the boundary of a protection domain. Interactions that remain within the protection domain do not require authentication. Although authentication is not required within this realm of trust, there must be some means to ensure that unproven or unauthenticated identities do not cross the protection domain boundary. In the J2EE architecture, a container provides an authentication boundary between external callers and the components it hosts. Furthermore, the architecture does not require that the boundaries of protection domains be aligned with the boundaries of containers. The container's responsibility is to enforce the boundaries, but implementations are likely to support protection domains that span containers.

The container ensures that the identity of a call is authenticated before it enters the protection domain; this is usually done with a credential, such as an X.509 certificate or a Kerberos service ticket. A credential is analogous to a passport or driver's license. The container also ensures that outgoing calls are properly identified. Maintaining proper proof of component identity makes it easier for interacting components to trust each other. A J2EE developer can declaratively specify the authentication requirements of an application for calls to its components (such as enterprise beans or JSPs) and for outbound calls that its components make to access other components and resources.

The deployment descriptor holds declarations of the references made by each J2EE component to other components and to external resources. These declarations, which appear in the descriptor as `ejb-ref` elements, `resource-ref` elements, and `service-ref` elements, indicate where authentication may be necessary. The declarations are made in the scope of the calling component, and they serve to expose the application's inter-component or resource call tree. Deployers use J2EE platform tools to read these declarations, and they can then use these references to properly secure interactions between the calling and called components. The container uses this information at runtime to determine whether authentication is required and to provide the mechanisms for handling identities and credentials.

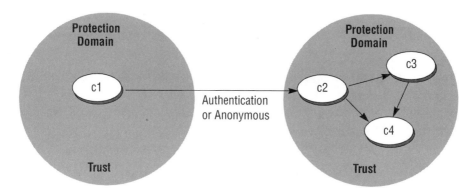

Figure 7.2   Protection Domain Established by Authentication Boundaries

7.2.1.2   Web Tier Authentication

Developers can specify that authentication be performed on the Web tier when certain components and resources are accessed, in which case the authentication is handled by the J2EE Web container. J2EE Web containers must support three different authentication mechanisms:

- HTTP basic authentication—The Web server authenticates a principal using the username and password obtained from the Web client. The username and password are included in the HTTP headers and are handled at the transport layer.

- Form-based authentication—A developer can customize a form for entering username and password information, and then use this form to pass the information to the J2EE Web container. This type of authentication, geared toward Web page presentation applications, is not used for Web services.

- HTTPS mutual authentication—Both the client and the server use digital certificates to establish their identity, and authentication occurs over a channel protected by Secure Sockets Layer.

Generally, for Web tier authentication, the developer specifies an authorization constraint to designate those Web resources—such as Web service endpoints, HTML documents, Web components, image files, archives, and so forth—that need to be protected. When a user tries to access a protected Web resource, the Web container applies the particular authentication mechanism (either basic, form-based, or mutual authentication) specified in the application's deployment descriptor.

It is important to note that J2EE Web containers provide single sign-on among applications within a security policy domain boundary. Clients often make multiple requests to an application within a session. At times, these requests may be among different applications. In a J2EE application server, when a client has authenticated in one application, it is also automatically authenticated for other applications for which that client identity is mapped. Web containers allow the login session to represent a user for all applications accessible to the user within a single application server without requiring the user to re-authenticate for each application. However, this mechanism is more appropriate for session-aware, browser-based Web applications; it is not as applicable to Web service interactions since Web services have no standard notion of session-oriented interactions. Other efforts provide similar security capabilities to Web services, such as the Liberty Alliance specifications (`http://www.projectliberty.org`).

7.2.1.3   EJB Tier Authentication

The EJB container has the ability to handle authentication. When a client directly interacts with a Web service endpoint implemented by an enterprise bean, the EJB container establishes the authentication with the client. Optionally, you can structure an application so that a Web container component may handle authentication for an EJB component. Several use case scenarios describe these situations.

One common scenario involves a Web tier component that receives a user request sent to it over HTTP. To handle the request, the Web component calls an enterprise bean component on the EJB tier, a typical scenario since many Web applications use enterprise beans. This is often done in browser-based Web applications and also with Web services applications that have a JAX-RPC Web endpoint. In these cases, the application developer places a Web component in front of the enterprise bean and lets the Web component handle the authentication. Thus, the Web container vouches for the identity of those clients who want to access enterprise beans, and these clients access the beans via protected Web components. Figure 7.3 illustrates how an application can be structured to use the Web container to enforce protection domain boundaries for Web components, and, by extension, for the enterprise beans called by the Web components.

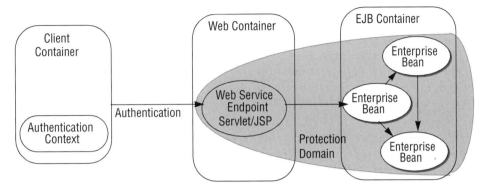

Figure 7.3   Using the Web Container to Establish an EJB Tier Protection Domain

Another use case scenario involves sending a SOAP request to an EJB service endpoint. Since the caller is making the SOAP request over HTTP, the Web service authentication model handles authentication using similar mechanisms— basic authentication and mutual SSL—to the Web tier component use case. However, rather than use a Web component in front of the EJB component, the EJB container directly handles the authentication. Note that in the J2EE platform, both Web and EJB tier endpoints support the same mechanisms for Web service authenication.

A third use case entails calls made directly to an enterprise bean using RMI-IIOP. This scenario is not common for Web services since they are not accessed with RMI-IIOP. However, some Web service endpoints, while processing a request, may need to access a remote enterprise bean component using RMI-IIOP. The Common Secure Interoperability (CSIv2) specification, which is an Object Management Group (OMG) standard supported by the J2EE platform, defines a protocol for secure RMI-IIOP invocations. Using the CSIv2-defined Security Attribute Service, client authentication is enforced just above the transport layer. The Security Attribute Service also permits identity assertion, which is an impersonation mechanism, so that an intermediate component can use an identity other than its own.

7.2.1.4   Enterprise Information System Tier Authentication

Many application components and Web service endpoints need to access enterprise information systems, such as databases or JMS resources. J2EE components get access to the connections of these resources through a resource manager connection factory. For example, the `javax.sql.DataSource` interface provides a resource manager factory interface to obtain a `javax.sql.Connection` for a database. JMS, JavaMail, and URL connection factories are also available for these common types of resources.

When integrating with enterprise information systems, J2EE components may use different security mechanisms and operate in different protection domains than the resources they access. In these cases, you can configure the calling container to manage for the calling component the authentication to the resource, a form of authentication called *container-managed resource manager sign-on*. The J2EE architecture also recognizes that some components need to directly manage the specification of caller identity and the production of a suitable authenticator. For these applications, the J2EE architecture provides a means for an application component to engage in what is called *application-managed resource manager sign-on*. Use application-managed resource manager sign-on when the ability to manipulate the authentication details is fundamental to the component's functionality.

The `resource-ref` elements of a component's deployment descriptor declare the resources used by the component. The value of the `res-auth` subelement declares whether sign-on to the resource is managed by the container or the application. With application-managed resource manager sign-on, it is possible for components that programmatically manage resource sign-on to use the `EJBContext.getCallerPrincipal` or `HttpServletRequest.getUserPrincipal` methods to obtain the identity of their caller. A component can map the identity of its caller to a new identity or authentication secret as required by the target enterprise information system. With container-managed resource manager sign-on, the container performs *principal mapping* on behalf of the component.

Care should be taken to ensure that access to any component with a capability to sign-on to another resource is secured by appropriate authorization rules. Otherwise, that component can be misused to gain unauthorized access to the resource.

The J2EE Connector architecture offers a standard API for application-managed resource manager sign-on. This API ensures portability of components that authenticate with enterprise information systems.

7.2.2   Authorization

Authorization mechanisms limit interactions with resources to collections of users or systems for the purpose of enforcing integrity, confidentiality, or availability constraints. Such mechanisms allow only authentic caller identities to access components. Since the J2EE application programming model focuses on permissions, which indicate who can do what function, authentication and identity establishment occur before authorization decisions are enforced.

After successful authentication, a credential is made available to the called component. The credential contains information describing the caller through its identity attributes. Anonymous callers are represented by a special credential. These attributes uniquely identify the caller in the context of the authority that issued the credential. Depending on the type of credential, it may contain other attributes that define shared authorization properties (such as group memberships), which distinguish collections of related credentials. The identity attributes and shared authorization attributes in the credential are collectively represented as *security attributes*. Comparing the security attributes of the credential associated with a component invocation with those required to access the called component determines access to the called component.

In the J2EE architecture, a container serves as an authorization boundary between the components it hosts and their callers. The authorization boundary exists inside the container's authentication boundary so that authorization is considered in the context of successful authentication. For inbound calls, the container compares security attributes from the credential associated with a component invocation to the access control rules for the target component. If the rules are satisfied, the container allows the call; otherwise, it rejects the call.

7.2.2.1   Declarative Authorization

Deployment establishes the container-enforced access control rules associated with a J2EE application. Generally, a deployment tool maps an application permission model, which is defined in the deployment descriptor, to policy and mechanisms specific to the operational environment.

The deployment descriptor defines logical privileges called *security roles* and associates them with components. Security roles are ultimately granted permission to access components. At deployment, the security roles are mapped to identities in the operational environment to establish the capabilities of users in the runtime environment. Callers authenticated by the container as one of these identities are assigned the privilege represented by the role.

The EJB container grants permission to access a method only to callers that have at least one of the privileges associated with the method. The Web container enforces authorization requirements similar to those for an EJB container. Security constraints with associated roles also protect Web resource collections, that is, a URL pattern and an associated HTTP method, such as GET or POST.

Although deployment descriptors define authorization constraints for an application, security mechanisms often require more refinement plus careful mapping to mechanisms in the operational environment in which the application is ultimately deployed. Both the EJB and Web tiers define access control policy at deployment, rather than during application development. The access control policy can be stated in the deployment descriptors, and the policy is often adjusted at deployment to suit the operational environment.

It is also possible during deployment to refine the privileges required to access components. At the same time, you can define the correspondence between the security attributes presented by callers and the container privileges. The mapping from security attributes to container privileges is kept to the scope of the application. Thus, the mapping applied to the components of one application may be different from that of another application.

A client interacts with resources hosted in a Web or EJB container. These resources may be protected or unprotected. Protected resources have authorization rules defined in deployment descriptors that restrict access to some subset of non-anonymous identities. To access protected resources, clients must present non-anonymous credentials to enable their identities to be evaluated against the resource authorization policy.

You control access to Web resources by properly defining their access elements in the deployment descriptor. For accessing enterprise beans, you define method permissions on individual bean methods. See "Handling Authorization" on page 320.

7.2.2.2 Programmatic Authorization

A J2EE container decides access control before dispatching method calls to a component. In addition to these container pre-dispatch access control decisions, a developer might need to include some additional application logic for access control decisions. This logic may be based on the state of the component, the parameters of the invocation, or some other information. A component can use two methods, `EJBContext.isCallerInRole` (for use by enterprise bean code) and `HttpServletRequest.isUserInRole` (for use by Web components), to perform additional access control within the component code.

To use these functions, a component must specify in the deployment descriptor the complete set of distinct `roleName` values used in all calls. These declarations appear in the deployment descriptor as `security-role-ref` elements. Each `security-role-ref` element links a privilege name embedded in the application as a `roleName` to a security role. Ultimately, deployment establishes the link between the privilege names embedded in the application and the security roles defined in the deployment descriptor. The link between privilege names and security roles may differ for components in the same application.

Additionally, a component might want to use the identity of the caller to make decisions about access control. As noted, a component can use the methods `EJBContext.getCallerPrincipal` and `HttpServletRequest.getUserPrincipal` to obtain the calling principle. Note that containers from different vendors may represent the returned principal differently. If portability is a priority, then care should be taken when code is embedded with a dependence on a principle.

7.2.3   Confidentiality and Integrity

Confidentiality mechanisms ensure private communication between entities by encrypting the message content so that a third party cannot read it. *Integrity mechanisms* ensure that another party cannot tamper with communication between entities; in particular, that a third party cannot intercept and modify communications. Integrity mechanisms can also ensure that messages are used only once. Attaching a *message signature* to a message ensures that a particular person is responsible for the content: In addition, the modification of the message by anyone other than the creator of the content is detectable by the receiver.

Configuring the containers to apply confidentiality and integrity mechanisms is done when an application is deployed into its operational environment. Components that need to be protected are noted as such. The corresponding containers can be configured to employ the required confidentiality and integrity mechanisms when interactions with these components occur over open or unprotected networks. Containers can also be configured to reject call requests or responses with message content that should be protected but is not.

The J2EE platform requires that containers support transport layer integrity and confidentiality mechanisms based on SSL so that security properties applied to communications are established as a side effect of creating a connection. SSL can be specified as requirements for Web components and EJB components, including Web service endpoints.

The deployment descriptor conveys information to identify those components with method calls whose parameters or return values should be protected. Details about interacting with a J2EE component using SSL are discussed in the next section. When a component's interactions with an external resource include sensitive information, these sensitivities should be described in the `description` subelement of the corresponding `resource-ref`. These elements make sensitive information available when security requirements are set at deployment.

7.3   Security for Web Service Interactions

Developers that rely on JAX-RPC to exchange messages between Web service endpoints and clients leverage the security services provided by the J2EE platform. The J2EE platform supports the WS-I Basic Profile 1.0 specifications for secure interoperable Web service interactions. WS-I security compliance requires HTTPS and single hop security for a request and reply between a client and service. The Basic Profile requires that the transport layer of HTTPS be combined with additional mechanisms for basic and mutual authentication.

The J2EE platform provides Web tier and EJB tier endpoints with similar security mechanisms for Web services. Most J2EE developers should already be familiar with its security mechanisms, since the platform already provides transport layer security and authentication support for non-Web service interactions involving browsers and Web pages.

With Web service interactions, both the request and the reply may have security requirements. In addition, Web service endpoints must interact securely with other components and resources when processing requests. Developers may also leverage other J2EE platform security mechanisms, such as authorization, to design and build secure Web services.

7.3.1   Endpoint Programming Model

Let's first look at the endpoint programming model and see how to design and implement a secure Web service interaction on the J2EE platform, that is, how to authenticate and establish a secure HTTPS channel. As with any J2EE component, you can use declarative mechanisms to define the security for a Web service endpoint. Similarly, you may include programmatic security mechanisms in your Web service endpoints, and your service endpoint can leverage the platform's declarative mechanisms.

The key requirements for a secure Web service interaction are authentication and establishing a secure SSL channel for the interaction. Let's first examine how to secure the transport layer, and then we'll look at the available authentication mechanisms.

7.3.1.1 Securing the Transport Layer

SSL and Transport Layer Security (TLS) are key technologies in Web service interactions, and it is important to understand how to establish an SSL/TLS-protected interaction and authenticate clients. Note that TLS is an enhanced specification based on SSL. References to SSL refer to both SSL and TLS.

SSL is a standard mechanism for Web services that is available on virtually all application servers. This widely used, mature technology, which secures the communication channel between client and server, can satisfy many use cases for secure Web service communications. Since it works at the transport layer, SSL covers all information passed in the channel as part of a message exchange between a client and a service, including attachments.

Authentication is an important aspect of establishing an HTTPS connection. The J2EE platform supports the following authentication mechanisms for Web services using HTTPS:

- The server authenticates itself to clients with SSL and makes its certificate available.

- The client uses basic authentication over an SSL channel.

- Mutual authentication with SSL, using the server certificate as well as the client certificate, so that both parties can authenticate to each other.

While browser-based Web applications rely on these same authentication mechanisms when accessing a Web site, Web services scenarios have some additional considerations. With Web services, the interaction use case is usually machine to machine; that is, it is an interaction between two application components with no human involvement. Machine-to-machine interactions have a different trust model from typical Web site interactions. In a machine-to-machine interaction, trust must be established proactively, since there can be no real-time interaction with a user about whether to trust a certificate. Ordinarily, when a user interacts with a Web site via a browser and the browser does not have the certificate for the site, the user is prompted about whether to trust the certificate. The user can accept or reject the certificate at that moment. With Web services, the individuals involved in the deployment of the Web service interaction must distribute and exchange the server certificate, and possibly the client certificate if mutual authentication is required, prior to the interaction occurrence. Since an interoperable standard for Web service certificate distribution and exchange does not exist, the J2EE platform does not require one. Certificates must be handled in a manner appropriate to the specific operational environment of the application.

A Web service can be implemented and deployed in either the Web tier or EJB tier. The security mechanisms are the same at the conceptual level but differ in the details. The endpoint type determines the mechanism for declaring that a Web service endpoint requires SSL. For a Web tier endpoint (a JAX-RPC service endpoint), you indicate you are using SSL by setting to CONFIDENTIAL the transport-guarantee subelement of a security-constraint element in the web.xml deployment descriptor. This setting enforces an SSL interaction with a Web service endpoint. (See Code Example 7.1.)

```
<web-app>
    <security-constraint>
        ...
        <web-resource-collection>
            <web-resource-name>orderService</web-resource-name>
            <url-pattern>/mywebservice</url-pattern>
            <http-method>POST</http-method>
            <http-method>GET</http-method>
        </web-resource-collection>
        <user-data-constraint>
            <transport-guarantee>CONFIDENTIAL</transport-guarantee>
        </user-data-constraint>
    </security-constraint>
</web-app>
```

Code Example 7.1   Requiring SSL for Web Tier Endpoints

Setting up SSL for EJB tier endpoints varies according to the particular application server. Generally, for EJB endpoints a developer uses a description subelement of the target EJB component to indicate that the component requires SSL when deployed. Although EJB endpoints are required to support SSL and mutual authentication, the specifications have not defined a standard, portable mechanism for enabling this. As a result, you must follow application server-specific mechanisms to indicate that an EJB endpoint requires SSL. Often, these are application server-specific deployment descriptor elements for EJB endpoints that are similar to the web.xml elements for Web tier endpoints.

7.3.1.2 Specifying Mutual Authentication

You can also specify HTTPS with mutual authentication for a Web service endpoint. For Web tier endpoints, you first specify a secure transport (see the previous section) and then, in the same deployment descriptor, set the `auth-method` element to `CLIENT-CERT`. (See Code Example 7.2.)

```
<login-config>
    <auth-method>CLIENT-CERT</auth-method>
</login-config>
```

Code Example 7.2   Requiring Mutual Authentication for Web Tier Endpoints

The combination of the two settings—`CONFIDENTIAL` for `transport-guarantee` (see Code Example 7.1) and `CLIENT-CERT` for `auth-method`—enables mutual authentication. When set to these values, the containers for the client and the target service both provide digital certificates sufficient to authenticate each other. (These digital certificates contain client-specific identifying information.)

Specifying mutual authentication for EJB service endpoints is specific to each application server. Usually it is done in a similar manner to specifying mutual authentication for Web tier endpoints.

7.3.1.3 Specifying Basic and Hybrid Authentication

With basic authentication, a Web service endpoint requires a client to authenticate itself with a username and password. The type of the Web service endpoint determines how to specify requiring basic authentication for the service. For a Web tier (JAX-RPC) service endpoint, set the `auth-method` element to `BASIC` for the login configuration (`login-config`) element in the `web.xml` deployment descriptor, as shown in Code Example 7.3:

```
<login-config>
        <auth-method>BASIC</auth-method>
        <realm-name>some_realm_name</realm-name>
</login-config>
```

Code Example 7.3   Requiring Basic Authentication for Web Tier Endpoints

For a Web service with an EJB endpoint, you use the application server-specific mechanisms to require basic authentication. Often, each application server's deployment descriptor includes an element for authentication for an EJB service endpoint that is analogous to the `web.xml auth-method` element.

A Web service may also require hybrid authentication, which is when a client authenticates with basic authentication and SSL is the transport. The client authenticates with a username and password, the server authenticates with its digital certificate, and all of this occurs over a HTTPS connection. Hybrid authentication compensates for HTTP basic authentication's inability to protect passwords for confidentiality. This vulnerability can be overcome by running the authentication protocols over an SSL-protected session, essentially creating a hybrid authentication mechanism. The SSL-protected session ensures confidentiality for all message content, including the client authenticators, such as username and password.

Enabling hybrid authentication for a Web service endpoint generally requires two operations (both previously discussed): setting the transport to use the confidentiality mechanism of HTTPS and setting the authentication of the client to use basic authentication. For EJB endpoints, you use application server-specific mechanisms. For Web endpoints, you set deployment descriptor elements. Code Example 7.4 demonstrates how to configure hybrid authentication by combining the deployment descriptor choices for basic authentication and confidential transport.

```
<web-app>
   <security-constraint>
      ...
      <user-data-constraint>
         <transport-guarantee>CONFIDENTIAL</transport-guarantee>
      </user-data-constraint>
   </security-constraint>
...
<login-config>
      <auth-method>BASIC</auth-method>
      <realm-name>some_realm_name</realm-name>
</login-config>
...
</web-app>
```

Code Example 7.4   Requiring SSL Hybrid Authentication for Web Tier Endpoints

When setting authentication requirements for a client, keep in mind that an endpoint can require a client to authenticate either by using basic authentication and supplying a username and password or by using mutual authentication with the client supplying a digital certificate. An endpoint cannot require a client to use both mechanisms.

When deploying an application that uses this type of hybrid authentication mechanism, it is important to properly set the security elements of the Web resource's deployment descriptor.

❐ Ensure that you set up an SSL transport for each endpoint that requires basic authentication. Otherwise, the client authenticator is not fully protected. For example, for Web endpoints, ensure that the `transport-guarantee` element of each protected Web endpoint is set to `CONFIDENTIAL` for an application using a hybrid authentication mechanism.

7.3.1.4 Publicizing Security Policy

Just as it needs to describe its methods and related information in a WSDL document, a Web service endpoint also needs to describe its security policy and make that information available to clients. If the WSDL document does not express the policy information, then the service must use other means to make its requirements known so that clients can be designed and implemented with those requirements in mind and be able to interact with the service.

At the present time, a WSDL description contains minimal information about the security characteristics of an endpoint—just the HTTPS location specified in the endpoint URL. The security functionality specified by the WS-I Basic Profile 1.0 only requires that Web services using HTTPS have `https` in the URI of the location attribute of the `address` element in its `wsdl:port` description. See Code Example 7.5.

```
<service name ="SomeService">
<port name="SomeServicePort" binding="tns:SomeServiceBinding">
<soap:address location="https://myhostname:7000/
    adventurebuilder/opc/getOrderDetails"/>
</port>
</service>
```

Code Example 7.5 WSDL Security Description

Since current WSDL documents have no standard mechanism to indicate whether an endpoint requires basic or mutual authentication, such information needs to be made available through service-level agreements between the client and endpoint. Future versions of the WSDL description may be extended to include descriptions of endpoint security requirements, perhaps by using metadata or annotations similar to CSIv2.

Since the present WSDL description for security is limited, you need to consider what other mechanisms you can use today to define security policies for endpoints. Generally, you should try to use the security mechanisms included with a particular vendor's application server. You have available options such as providing some metadata in another location, making some security assumptions among your partners, including security descriptions as a nonstandard part of JAXR entries, or even extending the WSDL description yourself. Not only that, your application and its endpoints may have built-in implicit assumptions, and you may need to provide a description of these unique security requirements. Clients need to be aware of all the requirements of a service so that they can be designed and implemented to interact properly with the service.

❒ It is recommended that you list security assumptions and requirements in the description elements that are part of a service component's deployment descriptor.

❒ In addition, have available for endpoint developers a separate document that describes the security policy for an endpoint. In this document, clearly describe the information needed by a client.

7.3.2 Client Programming Model

Client developers must handle some security requirements for their applications. The mechanisms for handling security vary according to the type of client. We focus on J2EE components, including enterprise bean and servlet components, acting as clients of Web services. J2EE clients can take advantage of the J2EE platform mechanisms when interacting with a Web service endpoint. You design and implement security for J2EE clients in the same way regardless of whether they interact with Java-based or non-Java-based Web services.

Other types of clients, such as non-Java or stand-alone J2SE clients, since they are not run within a J2EE container generally cannot use the services of the J2EE platform. Stand-alone J2SE clients can use the JAX-RPC technology outside of the J2EE platform if they include the JAX-RPC runtime in their stand-alone environment. If you develop a stand-alone J2SE client to be a Web service client, keep in mind that the J2SE platform provides its own set of services and tools to help you. You can use the Java Authentication and Authorization Service (JAAS), along with tools such as keytool, to manage certificates and other security artifacts. As just noted, you can also include the JAX-RPC runtime, then use its mechanisms to set up username and password properties in the appropriate stubs and make calls to the Web service. It is important to have your client follow the WS-I interoperability requirements, since doing so ensures that your client can communicate with any Web service endpoint that also satisfies the WS-I interoperability requirements.

The J2EE container provides support so that J2EE components, such as servlets and enterprise beans, can have secure interactions when they act as clients of Web service endpoints. The container provides this support regardless of whether or not the accessed Web service endpoint is based on Java. Let's look at how J2EE components use the JAX-RPC client APIs to invoke Web service endpoints in a secure manner.

As indicated in the section "Endpoint Programming Model" on page 308, a target endpoint defines some security constraints or requirements that a client must meet. For example, the client's interaction with the service endpoint might require basic authentication and HTTPS, or the client must provide certain information to access the endpoint.

The first step for a client is to discover the security policy of the target endpoint. Since the WSDL document may not describe all security requirements (see "Publicizing Security Policy" on page 313), discovering the target endpoint's security policy is specific to each situation. Once you know the client's security requirements for interacting with the service, you can set up the client component environment to make available the appropriate artifacts. For example, if the Web service endpoint requires basic authentication, the calling client container places the username and password identifying information in the HTTP headers. Let's take a closer look at what happens with both basic and mutual authentication.

For HTTP basic authentication, application server-specific mechanisms, such as additional deployment descriptor elements, are used to set the client username and password. These vendor-specific deployment descriptors may statically define at deployment the username and password needed for basic authentication. However, at runtime this username and identifier combination may have no relation to the principal associated with the calling component. When the JAX-RPC call is made, the container puts the username and password values into the HTTP header. Keep in mind that the J2EE specifications recommend *against* using programmatic JAX-RPC APIs to set the username and password properties on stubs for J2EE components. Thus, J2EE application servers are not required to support components programmatically setting these identifier values.

If the endpoint requires mutual authentication, the application server instance environment is set at deployment with the proper certificates such that they are available to the J2EE container. Since a client component's deployment descriptors have no portable, cross-platform mechanism for setting these security artifacts, they must be set using the particular application server's own mechanisms. In other words, an enterprise bean or servlet component that interacts with a Web service requiring mutual authentication must, at deployment, make the appropriate digital certificates available to the component's host container. The client's container can then use these certificates when the component actually places the call to the service.

Once the environment is set, a J2EE component can make a secure call on a service endpoint in the same way that it ordinarily calls a Web service—it looks up the service using JNDI, sets any necessary parameters, and makes the call. (See Chapter 5 for details.) The J2EE container not only manages the HTTPS transport, it handles the authentication for the call using the digital certificate or the values specified in the deployment descriptor.

7.3.3   Propagating Component Identity

Web service endpoints and other components can be clients of other Web services and J2EE components. Any given endpoint may be in a chain of calls between components and Web service endpoints. Also, non-Web service J2EE components can make calls to Web services. Each call between components and endpoints may have an identity associated with it, and this identity may need to be propagated.

There are two cases of identity propagation, differentiated by the target of the call. Both cases start with a caller that is a J2EE component—including a component that is a Web service endpoint. In the first case, the J2EE component or endpoint calls a J2EE component that is *not* a Web service. In the second case, the J2EE component or Web service makes JAX-RPC calls to a Web service.

7.3.3.1   Propagating Identity to Non-Web Service Components

All J2EE components have an invocation identity, established by the container, that identifies them when they call other J2EE components. The container establishes this invocation identity using either the `run-as(role-name)` or `use-caller-`

identity identity selection policy, both defined in the deployment descriptor. The container then uses either the calling component's identity (if the policy is to use the use-caller-identity) or, for run-as(role-name), a static identity previously designated at deployment from the principal identities mapped to the named security role.

Developers can define component identity selection policies for J2EE Web and EJB resources, including Web service endpoints. If you want to hold callers accountable for their actions, you should associate a use-caller-identity policy with component callers. Using the run-as(role-name) identity selection policy does not maintain the chain of traceability and may be used to afford the caller with the privileges of the component. Code Example 7.6 shows how to configure client identity selection policies in an enterprise bean deployment descriptor.

```
<enterprise-beans>
    <entity>
        <security-identity>
            <use-caller-identity/>
        </security-identity>
        ...
    </entity>

    <session>
        <security-identity>
            <run-as>
                <role-name> guest </role-name>
            </run-as>
        </security-identity>
        ...
    </session>
    ...
</enterprise-beans>
```

Code Example 7.6   Configuring Identity Selection Policies for Enterprise Beans

Code Example 7.7 shows how to configure client identity selection policies in Web component deployment descriptors. If run-as is not explicitly specified, the use-caller-identity policy is assumed.

```
<web-app>
    <servlet>
        <run-as>
            <role-name> guest </role-name>
        </run-as>
        ...
    </servlet>
    ...
</web-app>
```

Code Example 7.7   Configuring Identity Selection Policies for Web Components

7.3.3.2   Propagating Identity to a Web Service

Protection domains help to understand how clients set identity for Web service calls. (See "Protection Domains" on page 300.) Recall that a protection domain establishes an authentication boundary around a set of entities that are assumed to trust each other. Entities within this boundary can safely communicate with each other without authenticating themselves. Authentication is only required when the boundary is crossed. However, Web services are considered outside of any protection domain.

❐   When calling a Web service, be prepared to satisfy its security requirements. Web services are loosely coupled and it is more likely that a call to a service will cross protection domains.

Since Web service calls are likely to cross protection domains, identity propagation mechanisms (such as run-as and use_caller_identity) and security context are not useful and are not propagated to service endpoints. When a J2EE component acting as a Web service client specifies the run-as identity or the use-caller-identity, the container applies that identity only to the component's interactions with non-Web service components, such as enterprise beans. Some vendors may provide mechanisms to propagate identity across protection domains, but these mechanisms may not be portable.

This brings us to the question of how to establish identity for Web services. For the client making calls to a service that requires authentication, the client container provides the necessary artifacts, whether username and password for basic authentication or a digital certificate for mutual authentication. The container of the target Web service establishes the identity of calls to its service endpoint. The Web service bases this identity on the mapping principals designated by when the service was deployed, which may be based on either the client's username and password identity or the digital certificate attributes supplied by the client's container. However, since no standard mechanism exists for a target Web service to map an authenticated client to the identity of a component, each application server handles this mapping differently.

For example, Figure 7.4 illustrates how a caller identifier is propagated from clients to Web service endpoints and J2EE components. The initial client makes a request of Web service endpoint X. To fulfill the request, endpoint X makes a call on entity bean J, which in turn invokes a method on entity bean K. The client caller identifier A propagates from the endpoint through both entity beans. However, when entity bean K calls a method on service endpoint Y, since the Web service is not in the same protection domain, reauthentication must occur. Similarly, when endpoint X calls endpoint Z, the caller identifier cannot be propagated.

Applications can also use programmatic APIs to check client identity, and use that client identity to make identity decisions. For example, a Web tier endpoint, as well as other Web components, can use the `getUserPrincipal` method on the `HttpServletRequest` interface. An EJB endpoint, just like other enterprise bean components, can use the `EJBContext` method `getCallerPrincipal`. An application can use these methods to obtain information about the caller and then pass that information to business logic or use it to perform custom security checks.

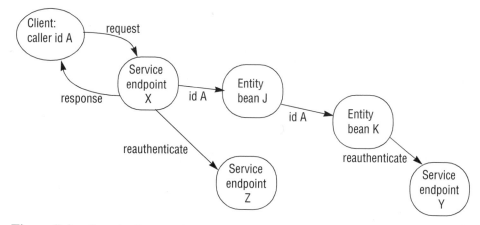

Figure 7.4 Security Propagation

7.3.4   Handling Authorization

Web service endpoints can restrict access to resources using the same declarative authorization mechanisms available to other J2EE components. From a security point of view, this capability facilitates integrating Web services with J2EE applications since the standard J2EE authorization mechanisms can be leveraged. When a Web service is called—and the calling client has been authenticated and its identity established—the container has the capability to check that the calling principal is authorized to access this service endpoint. A Web service is also free to leave its resources unprotected so that anyone can access its service.

Furthermore, components and resources accessed by the Web service endpoint may have their own access control policies, and these may differ from the endpoint's policies. The service endpoint's interaction with other components and resources is handled by the same mechanisms used by any J2EE component. That is, the authorization mechanisms for Web service endpoints are the same as for other components in the J2EE platform.

The tier on which your endpoint resides determines how you specify and configure access control. In general, to enable access control you specify a role and the resource you want protected. Components in both tiers specify a role in the same manner, using the `security-role` element as shown in Code Example 7.8. With Web tier endpoint components, access control entails specifying a URL pattern that determines the set of restricted resources. For EJB tier endpoints, you specify access control at the method level, and you can group together a set of method names that you want protected.

```
<security-role>
    <role-name>customer</role-name>
</security-role>
```

Code Example 7.8   Configuring a Role for an Authorization Constraint

What does this mean in terms of a Web service's access control considerations? Your Web service access control policy may influence whether you implement the service as a Web tier or an EJB tier endpoint. For Web tier components, the granularity of security is specific to the resource and based on the URL for the Web resource. For EJB tier components, security granularity is at the method level, which is typically a finer-grained level of control.

Let's consider a Web service with an interface containing multiple methods, such as the one shown in Code Example 7.9, where you want different access policies for each method. For a service endpoint interface such as this you might want to permit the following: Any client can browse the catalog of items available for sale, only authorized customers—for example, those clients who have set up accounts—can place orders, and only administrators can alter the catalog data. If you implement the service with a Web tier endpoint, then each method has the same protection because access control is the same for all methods that are bound to the port at the endpoint's URL. To handle a service with an interface containing multiple methods and different access policies, consider creating separate Web services where each service handles a different set of authorization requirements.

You have more flexibility if you implement the same Web service that has an interface containing multiple methods with an EJB endpoint. By using an EJB endpoint, you can set different authorization requirements for each method. See the next section, "Controlling Access to Web Tier Endpoints," and "Controlling Access to EJB Tier Endpoints" on page 323.

```
public interface OrderingService extends java.rmi.Remote {
    public Details getCatalogInfo(ItemType someItem)
            throws java.rmi.RemoteException;
    public Details submitOrder(purchaseOrder po)
            throws java.rmi.RemoteException;
    public void updateCatalog(ItemType someItem)
            throws java.rmi.RemoteException;
}
```

Code Example 7.9   Interface Methods Requiring Different Access Control

Keep in mind, however, that both Web and EJB tier endpoints can use programmatic APIs for finer-grained security. If you are willing to write code for access control, then both types of endpoints can be designed to handle the same security capabilities. However, it is generally discouraged to embed security code and use the programmatic security APIs in a component. A better approach keeps the security policy externalized form the application code and uses the declarative services with deployment descriptors.

❏ If you require finer-grained control for your access control policy, consider using an EJB endpoint, since it utilizes method-level control.

7.3.4.1   Controlling Access to Web Tier Endpoints

To control access to a Web component such as a Web service endpoint, the Web deployment descriptor specifies a `security-constraint` element with an `auth-constraint` subelement. Code Example 7.10 illustrates the definition of a protected resource in a Web component deployment descriptor. The descriptor specifies that only clients acting in the role of `customer` can access the URL `/mywebservice`. Note that this URL maps to all the methods in the service endpoint interface. Hence, all methods have the same access control.

```
<web-app>
....
<security-constraint>
    <web-resource-collection>
        <web-resource-name>orderService</web-resource-name>
        <url-pattern>/mywebservice</url-pattern>
        <http-method>POST</http-method>
        <http-method>GET</http-method>
    </web-resource-collection>
    <auth-constraint>
        <role-name>customer</role-name>
    </auth-constraint>
</security-constraint>
...
<login-config>
    ...choose either basic or client(for mutual authentication)
</login-config>
<security-role>
    <role-name>customer</role-name>
</security-role>

</web-app>
```

Code Example 7.10 Web Resource Authorization Configuration

In addition to controlling access to Web components, an application can provide unrestricted access to unprotected resources, such as a Web service endpoint, by omitting an authentication rule. Omitting authentication rules allows unauthenticated users to access Web components.

7.3.4.2   Controlling Access to EJB Tier Endpoints

The EJB deployment descriptors define security roles for an enterprise bean. These descriptors also specify, via the `method-permission` elements, the methods of a bean's home, component, and Web service endpoint interfaces that each security role is allowed to invoke.

Code Example 7.11 shows how to configure method-level access. The example specifies that the method `submitOrder`, which occurs on an interface of an enterprise bean Web service endpoint, requires that a caller belonging to the `customer` role must have authenticated to be granted access to the method. It is possible to further qualify method specifications so as to identify methods with overloaded names by parameter signature or to refer to methods of a specific interface of the enterprise bean. For example, you can specify that all methods of all interfaces (that is, remote, home, local, local home, and service) for a bean require authorization by using an asterisk (*) for the value in the `method-name` tag.

```
<method-permission>
    <role-name>customer</role-name>
    <method>
        <ejb-name>PurchaseOrder</ejb-name>
        <method-intf>ServiceEndpoint</method-intf>
        <method-name>submitOrder</method-name>
    </method>
</method-permission>
```

Code Example 7.11   Enterprise Bean Authorization Configuration

Some applications also feature unprotected EJB endpoints and allow anonymous, unauthenticated users to access certain EJB resources. Use the `unchecked` element in the `method-permission` element to indicate that no authorization check is required. Code Example 7.12 demonstrates the use of the `unchecked` element.

```
<method-permission>
    <unchecked/>
    <method>
        <ejb-name>PurchaseOrder</ejb-name>
        <method-name>getCatalogInfo</method-name>
    </method>
    <method>
```

```
    . . .
</method-permission>
```

Code Example 7.12 Enterprise Bean Unchecked method-permission

In addition to defining authorization policy in the method-permission elements, you may also add method specifications to the exclude-list. Doing so
denies access to these methods independent of caller identity and whether the
methods are the subject of a method-permission element. Code Example 7.13
demonstrates the use of the exclude-list.

```
<exclude-list>
    <method>
        <ejb-name>SpecialOrder</ejb-name>
        <method-name>*</method-name>
    </method>
    <method>
    . . .
</exclude-list>
```

Code Example 7.13 Enterprise Bean Excluded method-permission

7.3.5   JAX-RPC Security Guidelines

In addition to the guidelines noted previously, the following general guidelines sum
up the JAX-RPC authentication and authorization considerations.

❑   Apply the same access control rules to all access paths of a component. In ad-
     dition, partition an application as necessary to enforce this guideline, unless
     there is some specific need to architect an application in a different fashion.
     When designing the access control rules for protected resources, take care to
     ensure that the authorization policy is consistently enforced across all the paths
     by which the resource may be accessed. Be particularly careful that a less-
     protected access method does not undermine the policy enforced by a more rig-
     orously protected method.

❑   Declarative security is preferable to programmatic security. Try to use declar-
     ative access control mechanisms since these mechanisms keep the business

logic of the application separate from the security logic, thus making it easier for the deployer to understand and change the access policy without tampering with the application code. Generally, programmatic security is hard to maintain and enhance, plus it is not as portable as declarative security. Security programming is complex and difficult to write correctly, leading to a false sense of security. Use programmatic mechanisms for access control only when extra flexibility is required.

❒ If you have multiple Web tier endpoints with varying authentication requirements, consider bundling them in different .war files. An application (deployed within an .ear file) may use multiple Web service endpoints. It is possible that you may require different authentication for these endpoints—some endpoints may require basic authentication, others may require a client certificate. Since a web.xml file can have only one type of authentication associated with its login configuration, you cannot put endpoints that require different authentication in a single .war file. Instead, group endpoints into .war files based on the type of client authentication they require. Because the J2EE platform permits multiple .war files in a single .ear file, you can put these .war files into the application .ear file.

❒ Provide security policy descriptions in addition to those that the standard WSDL file provides. The WSDL file is required to publish only a Web service's HTTPS URL. It has no standard annotation describing whether the service endpoint requires basic or mutual authentication. Use the description elements of the deployment descriptor to make known the security requirements of your endpoints.

❒ Be careful with the username and password information, because these properties can create a vulnerability when configuring a client component to use HTTP basic authentication. Username and password are sensitive security data, and the security of your system is compromised if they become known to the wrong party. For example, do not store username and password values in the application code or the deployment descriptor, and if deployment descriptors do include a username and password, be sure to store the deployment descriptors in a secure manner.

❒ Consider using a "guarding" component between the interaction and processing layers. Set up an application accessor component with security attributes and place it in front of a set of components that require protection. Then, allow access to that set of components only through the guarding or front component.

A guarding component can make application security more manageable by centralizing security access to a set of components in a single component.

7.4   Message-Level Web Service Security

Message-level security, or securing Web services at the message level, addresses the same security requirements—identity, authentication, authorization, integrity, confidentiality, non-repudiation, and basic message exchange—as traditional Web security. Both traditional Web and message-level security share many of the same mechanisms for handling security, including digital certificates, encryption, and digital signatures. Today, new mechanisms and standards are emerging that make it not only possible but easier to implement message-level security.

Traditional Web security mechanisms, such as HTTPS, may be insufficient to manage the security requirements of all Web service scenarios. For example, when an application sends a document with JAX-RPC using HTTPS, the message is secured only for the HTTPS connection, that is, during the transport of the document between the service requester (the client) and the service. However, the application may require that the document data be secured beyond the HTTPS connection, or even beyond the transport layer. By securing Web services at the message level, message-level security is capable of meeting these expanded requirements.

7.4.1   Understanding Message-Level Security

Message-level security, which applies to XML documents sent as SOAP messages, makes security part of the message itself by embedding all required security information in a message's SOAP header. In addition, message-level security can apply security mechanisms, such as encryption and digital signature, to the data in the message itself.

With message-level security, the SOAP message itself either contains the information needed to secure the message or it contains information about where to get that information to handle security needs. The SOAP message also contains information relevant to the protocols and procedures for processing the specified message-level security. However, message-level security is not tied to any particular transport mechanism: Since they are part of the message, the security mechanisms are independent of a transport protocol such as HTTPS.

JAX-RPC hides the details of a SOAP message exchange, but, to understand message-level security, it's helpful to examine a SOAP message in more detail.

(See "Simple Object Access Protocol" on page 33 for more details about SOAP.) A SOAP message is composed of three parts:

- An envelope

- A header that contains meta information

- A body that contains the message contents

Figure 7.5 illustrates how security information can be embedded at the message level. The diagram expands a SOAP header to show the header's security information contents and artifacts related to the message. It also expands the body entry to show the particular set of elements being secured.

The client adds to the SOAP message header security information that applies to that particular message. When the message is received, the Web service endpoint, using the security information in the header, applies the appropriate security mechanisms to the message. For example, the service endpoint might verify the message signature and check that the message has not been tampered with. It is possible to add signature and encryption information to the SOAP message headers, as well as other information such as security tokens for identity—for example, an X.509 certificate—that are bound to the SOAP message content.

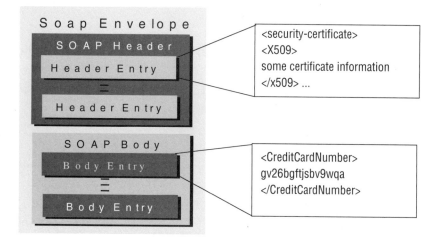

Figure 7.5   Embedding Security at the Message Level

In summary, message-level security technology lets you embed into the message itself a range of security mechanisms, such as identity and security tokens and certificates, and message encryption and signature mechanisms. The technology associates this security information with the message and can process and apply the specified security mechanisms. Message-level security uses encryption and it uses a digital signature to bind the claims—the identity attributes—from a security token to message content. It is possible to layer additional functionality on top of these basic mechanisms.

7.4.2   Comparing Security Mechanisms

The JAX-RPC over SSL (discussed in "Security for Web Service Interactions" on page 308) primarily concerns securing peer-to-peer communication. It relies on HTTP over SSL to create a secure channel between two peers.

Message-level security takes a different approach, since it embeds the security information within each message. Message-level security has different characteristics from SSL security. Let's compare these two approaches.

7.4.2.1   Transport Layer Security and SOAP Messages

HTTP over SSL protocol is a transport layer security mechanism that applies security protection to messages only when they are "on the wire," that is, during transport. A message is encrypted—and thus protected—while it is on the wire. However, the message data is decrypted at the transport layer boundary. At that point, the message is unprotected and vulnerable while it is passed to other system layers, whether operating system, application server, or J2EE application layers. Thus, the duration of protection using HTTP is the lifetime of the message on the wire at the transport layer.

Message-level security not only persists beyond the transport layer, it lasts for as long as the XML content is perceived as a SOAP message. Since the security is applied to the SOAP message, the protection remains and the security information is available to the application server container and to applications that have access to SOAP messages through mechanisms and APIs such as JAX-RPC handlers and SAAJ. The duration of protection for message-level security is the lifetime of the SOAP message, and this can span the transport boundary.

Message-level security has other advantages in addition to providing a longer duration of protection. Because security is part of the SOAP message, applications can support Web service interactions that require maintaining protection throughout the entire system or into the application layer. Having security as part of the message also makes it possible to persist both the message data and its security information. For example, perhaps to prove that a message was sent, an application may need to persist the message data and the digital signature bound to the message. Or, to protect against internal threats, an application may need to keep data in a SOAP message confidential, even to the application layer. HTTPS, since it only protects a message during transport, cannot give the application layer this encryption protection for the data.

7.4.2.2   Peer Entity and Data Origin Authentication

Two kinds of authentication in a network are: peer entity authentication and data origin authentication. With peer entity authentication, the security service verifies that the identity of a peer—in an association such as a session between a sender and receiver—is the identity claimed. Note that there must be an association between the two parties.

Data origin authentication verifies that the original source of a received message is as claimed, but, unlike peer entity authentication, no association between the sender and receiver is required. With data origin authentication, a target receiver can verify the identity of a message as belonging to the original message creator even if the message passes from its initial source through multiple participants before arriving at the target receiver.

A Web service interaction that uses HTTPS supports peer entity authentication, because the interaction covers just the connection between two peers. Message-level security supports data origin authentication, since its security is tied to the SOAP message itself rather than the transport mechanism.

Using HTTPS is disadvantageous in multi-hop scenarios where a message passes through numerous intermediate participants between the initial sender and target receiver, because each message exchange requires establishing a new association between the communicating participants. Furthermore, SSL requires that each participant decrypt each received message, then encrypt the same message before transmitting it to the next participant in the workflow. SSL, relying on peer entity authentication, does not support end-to-end multi-hop message exchange. (See Figure 7.6.)

Workflow participants using HTTPS

Figure 7.6   Authentication Between Point-to-Point Participants

Web service scenarios that pass messages to multiple participants lend themselves to using message-level security. Since message-level security is based on data origin authentication, an application that passes messages to numerous intermediary participants on the way to the target recipient can verify, at each intermediary point and at the final target recipient, that the initial message creator identity associated with the message is as claimed. In other words, the initial message content creator's identity moves with the message through the chain of recipients.

7.4.2.3   Levels of Granularity

In addition to handling end-to-end use cases, message-level security can provide security at a more granular level than HTTPS. The ability to apply security at different levels of granularity is important. Consider scenarios that handle XML documents, which are composed of a nested hierarchy of elements and subelements making them inherently granular. Message-level security, which is XML aware, can be more flexible in applying security mechanisms to a message than HTTPS.

For example, suppose you need to encrypt only certain elements or fragments of an XML document to be sent as a SOAP message. If you use HTTPS, you essentially encrypt the entire SOAP message since HTTPS encrypts everything passed on the wire. If you use message-level security, you can encrypt just a portion of the XML document, then send a SOAP message that is partially encrypted. Since encryption is computationally intensive, encrypting an entire document (particularly a large one) can impact performance.

Message-level security's finer-grained control in applying security protections is useful in common Web service interactions, such as end-to-end scenarios. You can apply different security to portions of a document so that participants in a workflow may only access those fragments applicable to their separate functions. For example, an application handling purchase orders may encrypt just credit card information. As the order passes among numerous workflow participants—customer relations, message brokers, supplier—only the appropriate participants, such as a financial department, can read the encrypted information. You could also apply different security mechanisms, such as different encryption algorithms, to various parts of a message, ensuring that only intended recipients can decrypt those parts of the message. Finer-grained control also supports intermediaries whose processing requires access to a small part of the message data, such as intermediaries that route messages to appropriate recipients.

7.4.2.4 Maturity of the Security Technologies

Message-level security is still an emerging technology, with relatively new specifications, some of which are not yet standardized. Moreover, these new specifications may not completely cover all security considerations.

HTTP over SSL is a mature, widely used and well understood standard technology. It is a technology that has been analyzed extensively and has held up against varied security threats. This technology supports both client and server authentication, data integrity, data confidentiality, and point-to-point secure sessions. The J2EE 1.4 platform relies on this technology to provide Web service interactions with standard portable and interoperable support.

Keep in mind that message-level security mechanisms are designed to integrate with existing security mechanisms, such as transport security, public key infrastructure (PKI), and X.509 certificates. You can also use both message-level security and transport layer security together to satisfy your security requirements. For example, you might use a message-level digital signature while at the same time exchanging the message using HTTP over SSL.

7.4.3 Emerging Message-Level Security Standards

Since it is a new technology, there are a number of emerging standards for message-level security. These new specifications, which are part of the Organization for the Advancement of Structured Information Standards (OASIS), the World Wide Web Consortium (W3C), the Internet Engineering Task Force (IETF), and other standards bodies, concentrate on message-level security for XML documents. New Java APIs are also emerging to support these industry Web service security standards. These APIS are developed as Java Specification Requests (JSRs) through the Java Community Process, and future versions of the Java platform may include them.

The emerging specifications address security issues—such as identity, security tokens and certificates, authentication, authorization, encryption, message signing, and so forth—as they apply at the message level. For those who want to explore these emerging standards on their own, here is a partial list of the more significant JSRs and specifications:

- JSR 105—XML Digital Signatures for signing an XML document. It also includes procedures for computing and verifying signatures.

- JSR 106—XML Digital Encryption for encrypting parts of an XML document.

- JSR 155—Web Services Security Assertions, which is based on Security and Assertions Markup Language (SAML), is used for exchanging authentication and authorization information for XML documents.

- JSR 183—Web Services Message Security Java APIs, which enable applications to construct secure SOAP message exchanges.

Let's look at how to apply message-level security mechanisms to build and send a SOAP message with some message-level security. For example, let's examine how message-level security APIs might put an XML digital signature on a purchase order document. A client first embeds the digital signature into the XML message, signing the message before sending it. The signature, which is an X.509 certificate, is embedded into the purchase order XML document along with other information. Code Example 7.14 shows the message header for this purchase order XML document with the embedded digital signature, per the XML Digital Signature specification. This code example is derived from the OASIS *Web Service Security: SOAP Message Security, Working Draft 17* document. See http:www.oasis-open.org/committees/documents.php.

```
<?xml version="1.0" encoding="utf-8"?>
<S:Envelope xmlns:S="http://www.w3.org/2001/12/soap-envelope"
    xmlns:ds="http://www.w3.org/2000/09/xmldsig#"
    xmlns:wsse="http://schemas.xmlsoap.org/ws/2003/06/secext"
xmlns:xenc="http://www.w3.org/2001/04/xmlenc#">

    <S:Header>
        <wsse:Security>
            <wsse:BinarySecurityToken
                ValueType="wsse:X509v3"
                EncodingType="wsse:Base64Binary" wsu:Id="X509Token">
                MIIEZzCCA9CgAwIBAgIQEmtJZc0rqrKh5i...
```

```
            </wsse:BinarySecurityToken>
            <ds:Signature>
                <ds:SignedInfo>
                    <ds:CanonicalizationMethod Algorithm=
                        "http://www.w3.org/2001/10/xml-exc-c14n#"/>
                    <ds:SignatureMethod Algorithm=
                    "http://www.w3.org/2000/09/xmldsig#rsa-sha1"/>
                    <ds:Reference URI="#myBody">
                        <ds:Transforms>
                            <ds:Transform Algorithm=
                            "http://www.w3.org/2001/10/xml-exc-c14n#"/>
                        </ds:Transforms>
                        <ds:DigestMethod Algorithm=
                            "http://www.w3.org/2000/09/xmldsig#sha1"/>
                        <ds:DigestValue>
                            EULddytSo1...
                        </ds:DigestValue>
                    </ds:Reference>
                </ds:SignedInfo>
                <ds:SignatureValue>
                    BL8jdfToEb1l/vXcMZNNjPOV...
                </ds:SignatureValue>
                <ds:KeyInfo>
                    <wsse:SecurityTokenReference>
                        <wsse:Reference URI="#X509Token"/>
                    </wsse:SecurityTokenReference>
                </ds:KeyInfo>
            </ds:Signature>
        </wsse:Security>
    </S:Header>

    <S:Body wsu:Id="myBody">
        <myPO:PurchaseDetails xmlns:myPO=
            "http://www.someURL.com/purchaseOrder">
            some message content here ...
        </myPO:PurchaseDetails>
```

```
        </S:Body>
    </S:Envelope>
```

Code Example 7.14 Embedding a Digital Signature in an SOAP Message

This XML document shows the SOAP envelope containing the message body for the purchase order details and the message header, with the digital signature for the message. The security portion of the header, which is part of the SOAP message itself, includes or references all the information necessary to describe and validate the signature details and artifacts, including:

- Information specifying the security token, which is an X.509 certificate associated with the message. This information is enclosed within the `wsse:BinarySecurityToken` element.

- A description of the signature algorithm and its details, enclosed within the `ds:Signature` element.

- References to the signed message body elements. This is shown in the `<ds:Reference URI="#myBody>` element and associated attribute, which references the body of this message.

- The signature value itself, which is inside the `ds:SignatureValue` element.

- Information about the key or keys used for signing, enclosed with the `ds:KeyInfo` element. In this case the keys are from the associated X.509 certificate.

Since the message-level security specifications are still evolving, the details in this example may change. Regardless, the example does highlight how to associate security information with a particular SOAP message and include the security information as part of the message itself. As message-level security JSRs and specifications finalize and are incorporated in the J2EE platform, the corresponding Java APIs and the J2EE containers will hide many of these details from the application developer.

7.4.3.1   Using Message-Level Security Mechanisms

How can you make use of these emerging technologies and Java API implementations as they become available? There are two ways to approach this problem:

1. You can make the security code and any supporting framework for message-level security part of your application by placing it in the application's `.ear` file. Although this is the portable approach, it may require more work. You should consider this approach if your situation necessitates it.

2. You can use application server-specific extensions that explicitly provide message-level security. This is the preferred approach. Since vendors try to make new features available before standards are finalized, some application servers may offer nonstandard extensions that integrate some message-level security capabilities. Eventually these specifications may become part of the standard J2EE platform, but they may differ from the implementations offered by these early adopters. Although it may not be portable, it is the easier approach and more likely to provide the intended security.

Some of these technologies are more mature than others. For example, the Java Web Services Developer Pack (Java WSDP) toolkit has already incorporated some of the digital signature standards. Java WSDP is an integrated toolkit from Sun Microsystems that allows Java developers to build and test XML applications, Web services, and Web applications using the latest Web service technologies and standards implementations. The Java WSDP toolkit is available at `http://java.sun.com/webservices/`. In addition, some Apache Foundation projects include implementations of emerging message-level security capabilities.

Let's look at how you might implement a portable strategy to incorporate message-level security into your J2EE application. Note that while this is possible, it is not a task for every application developer since it is usually quite difficult to write truly secure code. You should attempt this only if you feel comfortable handling security code, since it involves writing a framework for security. However, it may be a useful strategy if you need to use message-level security today and cannot wait for it to be incorporated into the J2EE platform.

Suppose you want to add a digital signature to a message involved in a single exchange between two participants. First, try to leverage existing J2EE technologies and mechanisms. For example, because JAX-RPC is the primary message exchange technology for Web service interactions, try to plug in your security code to the SOAP messages that JAX-RPC exchanges. This may enable your Web services with message-level security. You can then leverage the JAX-RPC built-in mechanisms to manipulate the XML messages being exchanged.

Recall from Chapter 2 that JAX-RPC has handlers that provide a mechanism to intercept a SOAP message at various points during processing of request and response messages. You can use the JAX-RPC handler to interpose on the message exchange at the points in the interaction where handlers are invoked. These points are:

- On the client side:
  - after parameters are marshalled into the request
  - before unmarshalling values returned in the response
- On the server side:
  - before unmarshalling parameters for dispatch
  - after marshalling return values into the response

Handlers intercept all requests and responses that pass through a Web service endpoint, providing access to the actual SOAP message exchanged as part of the Web service request and response. Handlers let you apply different logic for service requests, responses, and faults. To do so, you add the appropriate code to the handler methods `handleRequest`, `handleResponse`, and `handleFault`. You can use handlers to apply message-level security to messages exchanged as part of your service. Since they are configurable on both the client and the endpoint, you can customize handlers to apply security services at both the client and service sides.

You use the SAAJ API to inspect and manipulate raw SOAP messages. SAAJ also gives you a compound message view capability that lets you examine MIME-based attachments. With SAAJ, you can also embed the digital signature information into the XML document and add the necessary security information to the header and message. Also consider using existing implementations of message-level security functionality, such as the digital signature capability.

For portability, you must include the message-level security implementations in the application's `.ear` file. At this early stage, it is also recommended that you create a library of actions that wrap security tasks and the functionality of existing implementations of message-level security. This library of actions should provide a higher level interface to these security functions. When providing a security library around existing message-level security implementations, it is also a good idea to provide multiple defaults for common use cases, such as for obtaining X.509 certificates, handling verification faults, and so forth. Once the library is in place, you can use the SAAJ API from within the handler logic to access the SOAP message. Then, apply the message-level security with your security library. Figure 7.7 shows the main participants in this process.

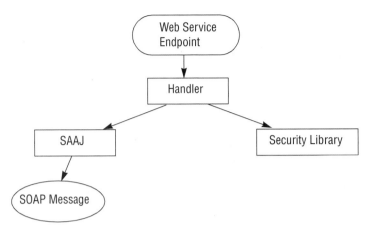

Figure 7.7   Implementing Message-Level Security

You may want to combine message-level security with other J2EE declarative and programmatic security mechanisms. For example, you may want to use HTTPS as the transport protocol even though the document is signed by a message-level mechanism. If you choose to use any of the J2EE declarative or programmatic security mechanisms along with JAX-RPC handlers, keep in mind the order in which the security constraints are enforced:

1. The container applies the declarative security mechanisms first.

2. The handlers run and apply their checks.

3. J2EE programmatic security mechanisms run after the handler checks.

You can also combine security mechanisms by adding some secure message-level functionality to an existing transport-level security solution. For example, if you have an existing Web service that uses SSL, you may want to add message-level integrity or confidentiality. Adding this security at the message level ensures that integrity or confidentiality persist beyond the transport layer.

7.5   Conclusion

This chapter explained the J2EE platform security model as it applies to Web service endpoints and showed how to use the platform security model in different security scenarios. In particular, it described the declarative security approach and mechanisms used in the platform and how the platform handles authentication, authorization, and transport layer security.

The chapter described how to implement a secure environment using the JAX-RPC technology. It discussed the JAX-RPC endpoint and client programming models, and how each model handles authentication, authorization, and transport layer security. The chapter also introduced the message-level Web service security model and provided guidelines for using this approach to security.

The next chapter, about the architecture of an actual Web service application, puts all the conceptual information covered so far into practice.

CHAPTER 8

Application Architecture and Design

PREVIOUS chapters in this book described different design considerations and motivations for Web services. They also described the various J2EE technologies used for implementing Web services and showed how developers might apply these technologies in an application. Where possible, the chapters offered guidelines for good design and highlighted the advantages and disadvantages among the technologies.

In this chapter, we illustrate how to apply these guidelines to the design and implementation of a real Web service application, the adventure builder enterprise. When architecting and designing Web service applications, you are faced with the significant challenge of constructing the various application modules so that they work together smoothly. We explain the motivational factors and issues that need to be considered, and make these issues concrete by showing how we came to the decisions we eventually made as we architected the adventure builder application. Through this examination, we hope to make it easier for you to determine how best to architect and design your own Web service applications.

8.1 Overview of Adventure Builder

We begin with an examination of the adventure builder application from a high-level, business perspective. Once we have outlined the application's functions, we shift to examining the architecture and design of the application itself.

Recall that the adventure builder enterprise provides customers with a catalog of adventure packages, accommodations, and transportation options. From a browser, customers select from these options to build a vacation, such as an Adventure on Mt Kilimanjaro. Building a vacation includes selecting accommodations, mode of transport, and adventure activities, such as mountaineering, mountain biking to a hidden waterfall, and hiking the mountain. After assembling the vacation package, the customer clicks the submit order option. The customer Web site builds a purchase order and sends it to the order processing center (OPC). The order processing center, which is responsible for fulfilling the order, interacts with its internal departments and the external partners and suppliers to complete the order.

In essence, the adventure builder enterprise consists of a front-end customer Web site, which provides a face to its customers, and a back-end order processing center, which handles the order fulfillment processing. See Figure 8.1.

As you can see from this diagram, there are four types of participants in adventure builder's business process:

1. **Customers**—Customers of the adventure builder Web site shop and place orders for vacation packages. They expect to have certain services available to them, such as the ability to track orders and receive e-mails about order status. Customers are expected to be browser based.

2. **Customer Web site**—The customer Web site provides the Web pages that let customers shop and place orders. The Web site communicates with the order processing center to submit and track purchase orders.

3. **Order processing center**—The order processing center (OPC) is at the heart of the adventure builder enterprise, responsible for coordinating all activities necessary to fulfil a customer order. It interacts with:

   - The customer Web site to handle order-related matters

   - Customers, sending them e-mail notifications regarding orders

   - A credit card service to collect payment

   - Suppliers to fulfill the items in an order

   - Internal adventure builder departments to support and manage the order fulfillment process

4. **External partners**—External partners, such as airlines, hotels, and activity providers, supply the services or components of a vacation. Other partners, such as a bank or credit card company, collect payments for the enterprise.

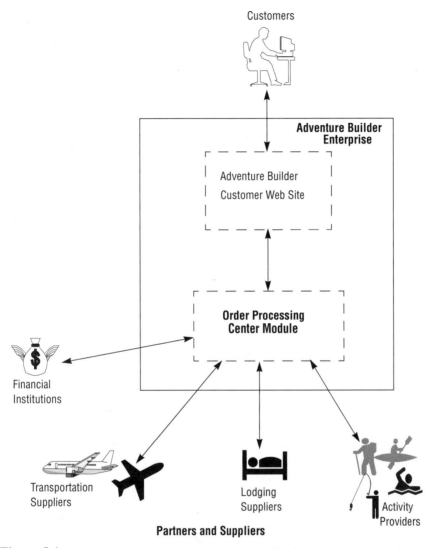

Figure 8.1   Adventure Builder Enterprise and Its Environment

The business problem for adventure builder is to ensure that these participants interact successfully so that it can sell and fulfill adventure packages. To solve this problem, the enterprise must architect, design, and build appropriate J2EE applications that provide the needed business functionality and tie the application modules together. Since the order processing center is the core module of the application, let's look at it in more detail, starting with its responsibilities for coordinating and communicating with other business units to fulfill orders. (Since this book is about Web services, we do not cover the design of the customer Web site in detail. Other books, particularly *Designing Enterprise Applications with the J2EE Platform, Second Edition*, address this area. See "References and Resources" on page xx.)

The order processing center module needs to perform the following functions:

- Receive customer orders from the customer Web site and process these orders

- Coordinate activities according to the business workflow rules

- Track an order's progress through the steps of the order fulfillment process

- Manage customer relations, including tracking customer preferences and updating customers on the status of an order. This includes sending formatted e-mails to customers about order status.

- Manage financial information, including verifying and obtaining approval for payment

- Interact with business partners—airlines, hotels, and adventure or activity providers—to fulfill a customer's adventure package.

- Provide and maintain a catalog of adventures and allow customers to place orders. The order processing center catalog manager needs to interact with external suppliers and also keep its customer offerings up to date.

8.1.1   Order Processing Center Sub-Modules and Interactions

First, let's examine the order processing center by decomposing it into its logical sub-modules. Figure 8.2 shows the main sub-modules of the order processing center and their relationships to the other participants.

- Order Receiver—Accepts purchase orders from the customer Web site. This sub-module starts the order fulfillment processing in the back end of the enterprise. Each order is identified by a unique ID.

- Workflow Manager—Enforces the process flow rules within the adventure builder application and tracks the state of each order during its processing. The workflow manager interacts with the internal departments and coordinates all the participants in the business process.

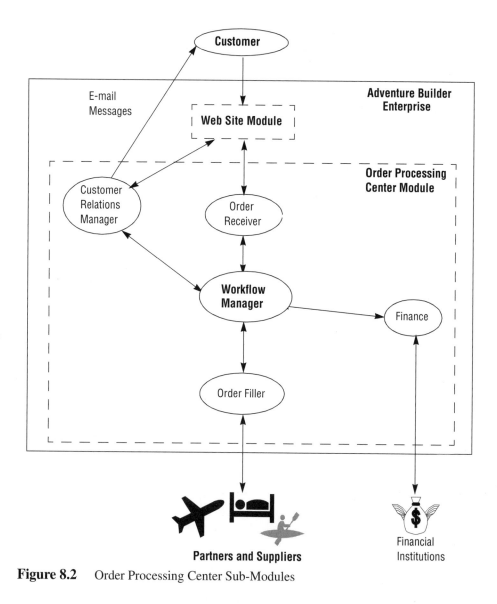

Figure 8.2 Order Processing Center Sub-Modules

- Finance—Interacts with external banks and credit card services that collect payments, and manages financial information.

- Customer Relations Manager (CRM)—Provides order tracking information to the customer Web site application. This sub-module also sends formatted e-mail notices about order status directly to clients.

- Order Filler—Exchanges messages with the various external suppliers to fulfill purchase orders. Messages include supplier purchase orders and invoices.

Keeping the picture of the various sub-modules in mind, let's map out the processing flow that occurs when a customer places an order. In particular, it is important to trace the messages and documents exchanged among participants.

- A purchase order flows from the customer Web site to the order processing center.

- The finance department and the credit card services exchange credit card payment requests and verifications.

- The order processing center order filler and the external suppliers exchange supplier purchase orders, invoices, and other documents.

- The workflow manager and other departments or sub-modules within the order processing center exchange internal messages.

Figure 8.3 shows the order fulfillment workflow. When it receives an order for an adventure package from a customer, the order processing center persists a purchase order. Before proceeding, it verifies that the customer has the available funds or credit for the purchase. If not, the order processing center cancels the order, notifies the customer, and updates the order status. Otherwise, it proceeds to fulfill the order, which entails breaking the entire adventure package order into sub-orders (such as a sub-order for a hotel room, another sub-order for airline reservations, and so forth). It sends the sub-orders to the appropriate suppliers, who fulfill these portions of the order and return invoices. The order processing center then joins these invoices for sub-orders so that the entire order is invoiced. The order processing center also updates the status of the order and notifies the customer.

8.2   Order Processing Center Architecture and Design

We start the examination of the order processing center architecture and design with the problem statement. We then look at the key design choices that were made to solve the problem.

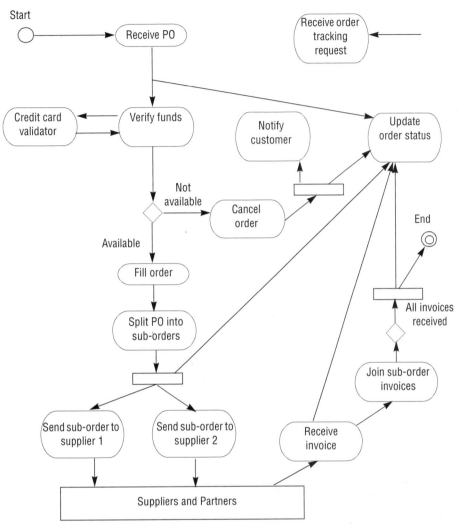

Figure 8.3   Order Fulfillment Workflow

8.2.1   Web Service Interaction and Message Exchange

The key architectural problem that the adventure builder enterprise must solve is the communication and interaction among different entities or applications, both internal and external entities. (Refer to Figure 8.2 on page 343, which shows the lines of communication between the application entities.) These entities and applications must communicate with each other, often exchanging messages such of documents of various types across numerous boundaries, and work together in a coordinated fashion to solve particular business problems.

Let's take a closer look at the message exchanges that occur during the order fulfillment process, starting with the communication between the customer and the customer Web site, and then from that Web site to the order processing center. Such communication is fairly typical of most Web services-based applications.

- Clients or customers communicate with the customer Web site via a Web browser.

- Once a customer places an order, the customer Web site communicates a purchase order to the order processing center.

- The customer Web site also follows up with the order processing center to ascertain the current status of an order.

- The order processing center sends credit card processing details for verification to the credit card service.

- The order processing center sends purchase orders to suppliers and receives invoices from these suppliers.

Within the order processing center module, different application entities handle such functions as receiving, tracking, and processing orders. These entities need to interact with each other to coordinate the processing of an order. Other application entities handle requests for order status.

Since you are building an application that enables different entities to communicate and interact to accomplish a set of tasks, you need to make design choices that foster this interaction. These choices center around communication technologies and message formats.

8.2.1.1   Communication Technologies

You must decide on the best communication technology for your application. Recall from "Communication" on page 23 that, when developing on the J2EE platform, you can use such communication technologies as JMS, RMI/IIOP, Web services, and so forth. Each technology is appropriate for different circumstances. For each interaction among the order processing center entities, we chose a particular communication technology.

For adventure builder, we chose to use Web services as the technology for communication between the order processing center and entities external to the order processing center, such as for the exchange of purchase orders and invoices with external partners and suppliers. We made this choice because we are primarily interested in achieving the greatest degree of interoperability among all modules and among all types of clients.

It is important for adventure builder to be able to integrate its functionality with that of its numerous partners, since they actually provide the services adventure builder offers to customers. Web services with its emphasis on interoperability gives these partners the greatest degree of flexibility in the technologies that they use. Web services also provide a good interface for separating and decoupling software systems. This is important for adventure builder since it is building on existing systems and modules developed and owned by different departments within the enterprise.

❏ For communication between the order processing center and entities external to the order processing center, we chose to use Web services.

Within the order processing center module, the communication among sub-modules primarily uses JMS. Since the order processing center controls the entire environment within the module, communication can be more tightly coupled. Most of the communication is between the order processing center workflow manager and the various department sub-modules, and all sub-modules are within this environment. Given the control over the environment and that most communication is asynchronous, using JMS is appropriate. Also, since there is additional overhead to using Web services, an application should use it only when it requires the benefits of Web services. For the communication among the entities within the order processing center, the overhead of Web services outweigh its benefits.

❏ We chose to use JMS for communications among entities within the order processing center.

Generally, Web services are a good choice for communication external to the enterprise, but they can also be applied to internal situations. The order processing center and customer Web sites are within the same enterprise, albeit different departments, and they use Web services rather than JMS. The order processing center module makes its services available as a Web service to the customer Web site—that is, the Web site uses the order processing center's Web service to fulfill an order. There are advantages to this implementation. For one, the Web site for the order processing center module may be hosted outside the firewall in a demilitarized zone (DMZ), even though the order processing center module itself is always inside the firewall. The Web site may conveniently use the HTTP port available on the firewall to communicate with the order processing center. Also, Web services allow both client and server to be on different hardware and software platforms. This makes Web services a natural choice, since the adventure builder Web site may be hosted on a different hardware platform (and software platform) from the order processing center module. Developers may want this platform flexibility since the Web site is on the Internet and may need to scale to handle very large loads. Furthermore, the Web site must be responsive to customers, whereas the order processing center module, since it works asynchronously, is concerned with achieving high throughput.

8.2.1.2   Message Format

The adventure builder business problem involves the exchange of many different types of messages, whose payloads contain documents such as purchase orders and invoices from different suppliers. Some of these message payloads adhere to an internal format and others follow standard formats. Since the system must handle multiple message types, we use XML as the message payload format.

While we can pass information either as XML documents or as Java objects, the choice of communication technology has implications for how information is passed through the system. Primarily, we use XML documents for communication on the edges on the enterprise, especially for messages exchanged with trading partners.

But since we also use JMS internally within the order processing center, we had to choose to either pass XML documents between sub-modules or to convert documents to Java objects. Since we are modelling a document-oriented system, and since the sub-modules represent different departments, we decided to pass XML documents among them. By passing information in this format, internally each department has control over binding to the particular Java objects they need within their module. Had we bound from XML documents to Java objects at the edges of the enterprise, then this sub-module independence would not be the case. Passing XML documents also plays well for our particular architecture, which has a centralized workflow coordinator or manager that keeps the individual sub-modules and departments from directly communicating. In short, this keeps our department sub-modules more loosely coupled.

❏ We chose XML to be the message format for communication with internal as well as external entities.

8.2.2 Communication Architecture

Figure 8.4 shows the architecture of the communication infrastructure for adventure builder.

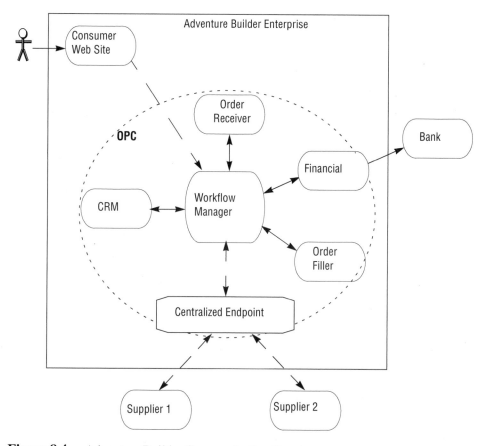

Figure 8.4 Adventure Builder Communication Structure

Note the following about the architecture:

- The order processing center uses a workflow manager, which contains all process rules and flow logic, to coordinate processing of the orders. The workflow manager also keeps track of the current state of each order while it is processed.

- Each participant knows its business functionality and how to execute its own step in the workflow; it does not need to know other steps in the process.

- Generally, each order processing center participant (such as the order filler) has a JMS resource and receives XML documents. The JMS resource is the integration point between the manager and each work module.

- A centralized endpoint manages the interactions between the suppliers and the order processing center. Rather than having a separate Web service endpoint for each message, all interactions between the order processing center and suppliers are grouped together and handled by a common endpoint and interaction layer.

- Other parts of the order processing center may act directly as clients to Web services without using the centralized endpoint. For example, the finance module uses the credit card service.

The order processing center internally uses a hub-and-spoke model where the workflow manager coordinates the participants in the order fulfillment process. Each participant receives an XML document from the workflow manager, processes the XML document by applying its portion of the business logic, and returns the result to the workflow manager. The workflow manager determines the next step to execute in the workflow and dispatches the appropriate request, by sending an XML document, to the proper participant. Each individual participant executes their part of the business functionality and has no need to know the overall process of the workflow.

The Web service endpoints, used on the edges of the order processing center for interactions between the order processing center and its external entities, have different considerations. You should consider each endpoint design individually, based on its particular interactions. Sometimes, to make communication more manageable, it's possible to group together sets of interactions into a simplified structure. See the next section for more details about endpoint considerations and choices. See "Web Service Communication Patterns" on page 358 for a discussion of more complex Web service interactions, as well as how to provide structure to Web service communications.

8.3   Endpoint Design Issues

The adventure builder developers considered a set of issues when designing a Web service. These issues encompassed such areas as the development approach for the Web service interface, the type of endpoint to use, the granularity of the service, the types of parameters to pass to the interface, the structure of the service's interaction and business processing layers, delegating to the business logic, the types of clients accessing the service endpoint, and deployment issues.

Earlier chapters addressed many of these issues. Here we try to show how such decisions are made in a real-world, comprehensive application. Note that this chapter bases its discussion using three of adventure builder's Web service interfaces:

1. The Web service interface between the order processing center and the customer Web site to receive customer orders

2. The order tracking Web service, which handles client requests for order status

3. The Web service interface between the order processing center and the external partners or suppliers

8.3.1   Web Service Interface Development Approach

When you implement a Web service, one of the first decisions you must make is the approach to use for developing the service interfaces. We followed the guidelines suggested in Chapter 3, particularly those in "Designing the Interface" on page 66. Let's look at the Web service interactions between the customer Web site and the order processing center, and also between the order processing center and the suppliers. Different issues pertain to the design of these service interfaces.

Because the same organization develops and controls the customer Web site and the order processing center, it is easy to propagate to the Web site module changes to the Web service interface that the order processing center provides to the Web site. Since we have control over all parties that have access to this Web service interface, the issue of stability of the interface is less important. Because it is easier, we opted to use the Java-to-WSDL approach to design and implement the Web service interfaces between the Web site and the order processing center.

The Web service interaction between the order processing center and the sup-pliers is a business-to-business interaction. Any order processing center changes to the interface affect many different suppliers. A stable interface also enables the participants to evolve in different ways. It is of paramount importance with such interactions that the interface between the communicating entities be stable. Since legal issues (see "Handling XML Documents in a Web Service" on page 105 for information about legal issues) may be important with business-to-business inter-actions, exchanged business documents should have an agreed-upon format and content, and for this it is best to use documents with existing standard schemas. For these reasons we used the WSDL-to-Java approach for the Web service inter-face between the order processing center and its suppliers.

- Although somewhat more complex, the WSDL-to-Java approach satisfies the overriding need for a stable Web service interface.

- To ensure that the WSDL-to-Java approach did not break interoperability, use various WSDL and schema editing tools to ensure that the WSDL and other artifacts comply with WS-I standards.

8.3.2   Endpoint Type Considerations

After you settle on the service interface development approach, you need to choose the type of endpoint for the interface. Recall from "Choice of the Interface End-point Type" on page 67 that you may implement a Web service endpoint either as a JAX-RPC service endpoint on a Web tier or as an EJB service endpoint on an EJB tier. The choice of endpoint type is primarily based on whether or not the business logic uses enterprise beans. If the business logic does use enterprise beans, it is often convenient to use an EJB service endpoint. If the application is primarily Web tier based, then it is best to use a JAX-RPC service endpoint.

The order processing center module exposes all of the Web services in the adventure builder application. Since the order processing center is implemented with a set of enterprise beans, it makes sense to implement these Web services as EJB service endpoints. Using a JAX-RPC service endpoint would introduce a Web layer that acts merely as a proxy, directing requests from the Web tier to the EJB tier and adding no value.

Using EJB service endpoints has some additional minor advantages as well. You can declare an EJB method to be transactional, resulting in the method body executing within a transaction. We found this useful since the order processing center requires transactional access to the database. An EJB service endpoint also allows method-based security controls, which is useful if you want certain methods to be publicly accessible but other methods to be restricted to authenticated users. You need to do additional work to get the equivalent capabilities in a JAX-RPC service endpoint.

8.3.3   Granularity of Service

It is important to design the service interface with the proper level of granularity. Because we want our application to perform well, we use coarse-grained interfaces for the Web services. When adding a Web service interface to existing applications, you want to identify the Web service interfaces that can be exposed. To do so, it is useful to look at the session bean-based application façades. Generally, it is not a good idea to convert each such application façade session bean into a Web service interface. You should design Web services to be more coarse grained than individual session beans. A good way to achieve a coarse-grained interface is to design the Web service around the documents it handles, since documents are naturally coarse grained. The adventure builder application applies these principles by exposing Web services that primarily exchange well-defined documents—purchase orders and invoices. These Web services may call multiple session bean methods to implement the services' business logic.

8.3.4   Passing Parameters as Documents or Java Objects

As already noted, a client invokes a service's functionality by calling the appropriate method on the service interface and passing the expected parameters. Developers must decide on the type of parameters passed to the Web service interfaces, and the parameter types determine the style of the interface. Parameters may be passed as either JAX-RPC value types or XML documents, which are represented as SOAPElement objects in the service interface. See "Parameter Types for Web Service Operations" on page 72 and "Exchanging XML Documents" on page 107 for detailed discussions on these choices. Note that since on the wire everything is in XML, the JAX-RPC value types are automatically mapped to their equivalent XML representations.

Passing XML documents raises different issues than passing Java objects. XML documents involve a certain amount of complexity, since the requestor must build the document containing the request and the receiver must validate and parse the document before processing the request. However, XML documents are better for addressing the business-to-business transaction considerations.

We used object parameters for the service interfaces between the customer Web site and the order processing center applications. Since both are contained within one enterprise, these services do not encompass business-to-business functionality. Moreover, the parameters map to specific document types that can be mapped easily to their equivalent JAX-RPC value types. Using these JAX-RPC value types eliminates the complexity of creating and manipulating XML documents.

Code Example 8.1 is an example of a Java interface for the order tracking service. It has one method, `getOrderDetails`, which expects a `String` argument and returns a Java `Object`, `OrderDetails`. A client submits an order identifier to retrieve information about an order, which is much simpler than having the client submit an XML document containing the same information.

```
public interface OrderTrackingIntf extends Remote {
    public OrderDetails getOrderDetails(String orderId)
                throws OrderNotFoundException, RemoteException;
}
```

Code Example 8.1   Interface Using Java Parameters

Choosing the return value type is not as straightforward. The `getOrderDetails` method returns specific order details, such as user name and shipping address, rather than the complete purchase order. It is possible to return this information as either a Java `Object` or in an XML document. We chose to return the order details in a `OrderDetails` Java `Object` since the details returned to the client—user identifier, addresses, and so forth—map to a specific schema. Hence, the service interface can create and use the equivalent JAX-RPC value types. The order fulfillment Web service interface, `PurchaseOrderIntf`, is designed similarly. (See Code Example 8.1.)

The order processing center service interface with suppliers exchanges XML documents rather than Java objects. Since suppliers are external to the enterprise, the service interface must be stable. Legal issues require exchanging business documents that conform to well-defined schemas. There are times when ensuring a stable interface is worth more than the simplicity of passing Java objects and the complexity of handling XML in the application code. The service interface may also need to support multiple document types in its methods.

Code Example 8.2 illustrates a JAX-RPC interface generated from the WSDL description where the order processing center acts as a client of a supplier and an XML document passes between them. To fulfill part of the customer's order, the order processing center module sends a purchase order to the supplier's Web service. For example, to fulfill a customer's travel request, the order processing center sends an order contained in an XML document to the airline supplier's Web service.

```
public interface AirlineReservationIntf extends Remote {
    public String submitDocument(SOAPElement reservationRequest)
                                        throws RemoteException;
}
```

Code Example 8.2 Interface Using XML Documents as Parameters

The service has a single method, `submitDocument`, which takes a reservation request document and returns a status. The service receives the request, does some preprocessing—such as validation of the document and security checks—then stores the request in a database for later processing.

Keep in mind that when a Web service method passes different types of XML documents, the WSDL description should use the generic type `anyType` to indicate the type of the method's parameters. Code Example 8.2 shows how `anyType` is mapped to `SOAPElement` in the generated JAX-RPC interface. Because the WSDL does not have the information to describe these documents, a separate schema holds the complete description of the documents. You need to publish the schemas for all documents that are exchanged. Publishing entails making the schemas available to clients at some known URL or registry.

On the Java platform, it is best to send an XML document as a `javax.xml.transform.Source` object. (See the discussion in "Java Objects as Parameters" on page 73 and "XML Documents as Parameters" on page 76.) However, we chose to send the XML document as a `SOAPElement` object because the WS-I Basic Profile does not yet support `Source` objects. (For more information, see "Interoperability" on page 86.)

8.3.5 Layering the Service

Normally, it's best when designing a service to separate the service's interaction layer from the business logic processing layer. This is especially true when an incoming request uses a different data model than the data model used by the business logic. Recall that a service may divide its processing into layers if it handles requests that require significant preprocessing or when there is extensive mapping between the internal data model and the incoming data.

The order fulfillment and order tracking Web service interfaces, since they use parameters that are objects, have no need for document validation or transformation. For both, there is minimal mapping from one data model to another, since the passed data mirrors for the most part the internal data model. Thus, both services do very minimal preprocessing of requests. As a result, we chose to merge the interaction and processing layers for these services.

Consider the order tracking Web service, which receives an order identifier as input and returns some order details. Since little preprocessing is required, the interaction and processing layers are merged into one layer. Although merged into one layer, the order tracker Web service interface does *not* expose the internal data model. It is important to keep the Web service interface from being tightly coupled to the internal data model, and not exposing the internal data model through the service interface accomplishes this. By avoiding tight coupling, we can change the internal data model without affecting the Web service interface and clients.

Instead, we created an `OrderDetails` Java object to hold the data in the service interface, thus removing the need to change the order tracker interface if the internal data model changes. The client's view of the `OrderDetails` object through the order tracker interface remains the same regardless of changes to the data model. See Figure 8.5.

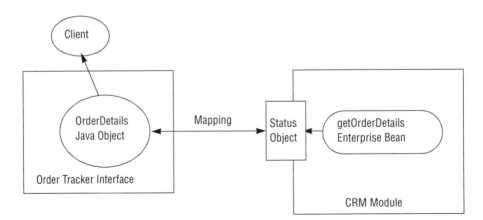

Figure 8.5   Separating CRM and Order Tracker Data Models

The Web service interfaces between the order processing center and the suppliers must validate and transform incoming XML documents to the internal data model before processing the document contents. We chose to do the validation and transformation in the interaction layer of the service before delegating the request to the processing layer.

8.3.6 Delegating to Business Logic

After receiving and preprocessing (if required) a request, the endpoint must next map the request to the appropriate business logic and delegate it for processing. Recall from "Delegating Web Service Requests to Processing Layer" on page 92 that much of this decision hinges on whether the request is processed synchronously or asynchronously.

The order tracking Web service interface uses a synchronous interaction for handling requests—processing is fast and a client waits for the response. Thus, the service interface maps a request to the appropriate business logic and immediately returns the results. adventure builder's Web services for processing the order workflow are asynchronous in nature since their business processing may be time consuming to complete and the client does not wait for the response. For these other Web service interactions—client submitting purchase order to the order processing center, order processing center placing orders with the suppliers, suppliers invoicing the order processing center—the service interfaces pre-process the requests and then delegate the request to the business logic. The interfaces use JMS messages to send the requests to a JMS queue associated with the business logic.

8.3.7 Client Considerations

For a client, the principal architectural consideration is choosing the best JAX-RPC service interface API to use to access the Web service. Clients can use a stub approach, dynamic proxies, or dynamic invocation interfaces (DII). When choosing a particular API, it is important to consider client requirements such as coupling, portability, the ability to dynamically locate and call services at runtime, and ease of development. Refer to Chapter 5 for more details.

Adventure builder's Web service clients use stubs, which is the simplest of the three modes. The stub mode requires the WSDL document along with the JAX-RPC mapping file to generate a set of proxies at development. A client at runtime uses these generated proxies to access a service. The stub mode of proxy generation provides the client with a tightly coupled view of the Web service, and it is a good choice when the service endpoint interface does not change.

With stubs, adventure builder uses the `javax.xml.rpc.Service` interface `getPort` method to access the Web service. Using this method removes port and protocol binding dependencies on the generated service implementation classes. As a result, it improves the portability of the client code since the client does not have to hard code a generated stub class. See "Locating and Accessing a Service" on page 219.

We also implemented exception handling from the client's perspective. To do this, we examined the interface generated from the WSDL file to see what possible exceptions the service might throw and then decided how to handle individual exceptions. See "Handling Exceptions" on page 230. The customer Web site, when it catches exceptions thrown by the order tracking service, maps the exceptions to client-specific exceptions. The client application detects these exceptions and redirects the user to an appropriate error page.

8.3.8   Publishing Web Service Details

A Web service endpoint is described by its WSDL file, and clients of the service need access to the WSDL to obtain basic information about the service. One way to disseminate this information to clients is to publish the WSDL files in a registry, if the service is open to the general public. Or, you can arrange a common location for the WSDL file that is known only to selected clients. You also must decide how to expose other details pertinent to the service, such as the business document schemas.

We decided to make the adventure builder Web services available in a well-known location, which clients can obtain from the deployment environment. These Web service interfaces are meant for specific business interactions between specific entities rather than for consumption by the general public. For this reason, we decided against publishing the services in a registry. Similarly, we decided to place the business document schemas at a well-known location, from which intended clients use these schemas.

8.4   Web Service Communication Patterns

Up to now we have concentrated on Web service interactions between two entities. Let's take a look at the bigger picture and see how Web service interactions operate within a larger business collaboration. Often Web service interactions are part of larger business collaborations that may involve multiple synchronous and asynchronous Web service interactions. Although Web service interactions within a single business collaboration may be related, current Web service technologies treat these interactions as stateless. As a result, a developer needs a way to associate messages that are part of a single business collaboration. This issue is made more difficult because collaboration sometimes requires that messages be split into multiple sub-messages, where each sub-message is processed by a different entity or partner. Not only does the developer need to relate these sub-messages to the original message, but the developer may also need to join together replies to the sub-messages.

As part of good Web service endpoint design, you need to consider the interactions in which the service is involved. Client-to-service endpoint communication is one such interaction. You may have other, more complex interaction patterns even involving multiple participants. For example, a particular request may take several Web service interactions to complete. This often happens when there are multiple steps in a workflow. Since different services process parts of a request, you need to correlate these interactions and identify individual requests that together make up a larger job.

The following sections present some strategies for handling these Web service communication problems. You can use these strategies separately or in combination, depending on an individual scenario.

8.4.1   Correlating Messages

Sometimes a business collaboration requires multiple Web service calls. In these cases, the developer needs a way to indicate that the messages passed in these Web service calls are related. A developer should use a correlation identifier to keep together messages for related Web service calls.

A correlation identifier is useful for Web services with interactions that are more complex than can be handled by a simple reply. When a Web service must invoke multiple processing steps to handle the request, the service often needs some means to identify the request at a later time. Correlation identifiers provide just such an identity for a request.

For example, a correlation identifier might be useful in these scenarios:

- A client submits an order and later wants to track the order status.

- A request is broken up into multiple subtasks that are asynchronously processed. The request manager aggregates subtasks as they complete, finally marking the entire job complete. Often, many jobs run at the same time, requiring the manager to correlate each job's multiple subtasks. Adventure builder's order processing module illustrates this scenario.

- A Web service interaction may require a higher level of service in terms of handling errors and recovery. If an error occurs, the service may have to track the state of the request.

- A client needs to make several request and reply interactions as part of a conversation, and it needs to identify those calls belonging to the conversation.

- A client may make duplicate submissions of a message, and the service needs to eliminate these duplications.

The correlation identifier must be unique in the participating systems. In addition, you must decide whether the client or the service generates the identifier, and where to generate it. For example, the calling client may generate an identifier, including it with calls to a service. Or, the service may generate the identifier and assign it to the incoming call, and perhaps return the identifier with the response.

The server can also embed useful information into an identifier that it generates, making processing easier. For example, a client often needs confirmation indicating that the server has received the client's message. An identifier generated at the server side can serve as a confirmation identifier. Server-side identifier generation also allows better control by providers, since they can employ their own policies.

The customer Web site collects information from a Web user and puts that information together into an order. The Web site then places the order into adventure builder's system via a Web service call to the order receiver module, passing the order information as a message. The order information includes the client-generated correlation identifier. The order receiver module receives the order message and uses the correlation identifier to eliminate duplicate order submissions.

A correlation identifier is a form of context information that needs to be communicated from the client to the server. For strategies on how to pass the correlation identifier from client to server, see "Passing Context Information on Web Service Calls" on page 366.

❑   Use correlation identifiers for associating groups of related messages.

8.4.2 Splitting and Joining Messages

Often, a service receives a request, which it fulfills as a series of subtasks run in parallel. When all tasks complete, the service gathers the results and checks if the criteria for completion is met. A service can split a message into subtasks, often including a correlation identifier with the individual pieces so that they can be rejoined successfully when they have all completed. Such identifiers may be needed since often subtasks complete out of sequence. A service can also independently use split and join operations.

For example, the order processing center receives a single purchase order from a customer. Figure 8.3 on page 345 shows the workflow for handling a message. The order processing center splits that order into a set of sub-orders: an order for an airline reservation, an order for a hotel room, and orders for all activities. It then sends each sub-order to the suppliers, and they process their tasks, invoicing the order processing center when completed. The order processing center aggregates these supplier invoices to fulfill the order.

How do you implement this split and join pattern? For guidelines on splitting an incoming document, see "Fragmenting Incoming XML Documents" on page 153. The order processing center splits a purchase order document into multiple XML documents by extracting the relevant information for each supplier, then sending that relevant information as a sub-order to the suppliers. It includes a correlation identifier with the sub-order to correlate all submessages generated from a single message.

For the join operation, the order processing center waits for all suppliers to fulfill the sub-orders, then it does some further processing to complete the order. Notification from suppliers may arrive in an arbitrary, nonsequential, order. The order processing center implements the join operation using message-driven beans. When it processes a sub-order, a supplier sends an invoice message to the order processing center through a Web service call. On receiving the invoice message, the order processing center workflow manager checks whether the join condition is met and updates its state accordingly. When all invoices are received, the workflow manager changes the order status to "COMPLETED" and directs the CRM system to notify the user.

Figure 8.6 shows split and join operations on an adventure builder customer purchase order. The customer orders an adventure package, plus hotel and airline reservations. All this information is contained with the purchase order. The order processing center logic splits the purchase order into sub-orders, and sends each sub-order to the appropriate supplier for processing. For example, the order processing center sends the activity sub-order to an activity supplier and the airline sub-order to the airline reservation processing. Each supplier, when it completes a sub-order, submits an invoice for its work. The order processing center receives the separate invoices at varying times. It checks to see if the join condition is met and updates the order status accordingly.

❏   When splitting messages, it is good to use correlation identifiers to later associate the responses during the join.

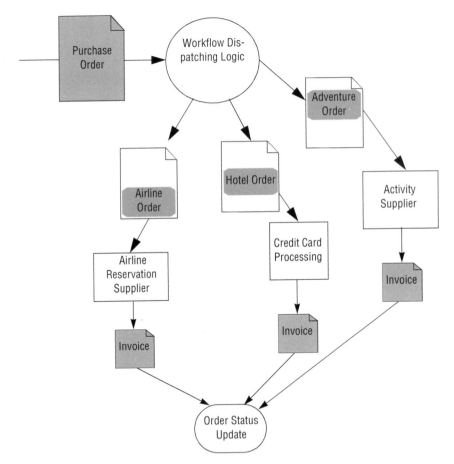

Figure 8.6   Split and Join Operations

8.4.3   Refactoring Synchronous to Asynchronous Interactions

Sometimes your application requires an asynchronous Web service interaction. Web services that use asynchronous interactions tend to be more responsive and scale better. However, Web services provide only a synchronous mode of operation, especially when using the HTTP protocol. In your application you can convert this synchronous interaction to an asynchronous request and reply. You may be able to refactor some of the synchronous interactions of a Web service application to asynchronous interactions.

Figure 8.7 illustrates a synchronous interaction. Notice how the client must suspend its processing until the service completes processing of the request and returns a response.

On the other hand, with the asynchronous interaction shown in Figure 8.8, the client continues its processing without waiting for the service. In both the synchronous and asynchronous communication figures, the vertical lines represent the passage of time, from top to bottom. The vertical rectangular boxes indicate when the entity (client or service) is busy processing the request or waiting for the other entity to complete processing. In Figure 8.8, the half-arrow indicates asynchronous communication and the dashed vertical line indicates that the entity is free to work on other things while a request is being processed.

When a component makes a synchronous call to another component, the calling component must wait for the receiving component to finish its processing. If the calling component instead makes the call asynchronously, the caller can proceed with its own work without waiting for the receiving component to do its job.

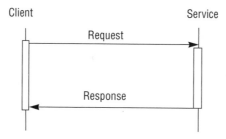

Figure 8.7   Synchronous Communication

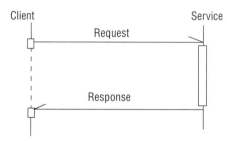

Figure 8.8   Asynchronous Communication

Let's look at what needs to be done to convert a synchronous endpoint to an asynchronous endpoint.

- Change a synchronous request/reply interaction into a request that returns void as the immediate reply.

- Change the client code to send the message request and immediately return.

- Have the client establish a reply address for receiving the response and include this reply address in the request. By including a reply address, the service knows where to send the response message.

- A correlation identifier needs to be established between the request message and the service response message. Both the client and the service use this identifier to associate the request and the reply.

- Refactor the server endpoint to accept the request, send it to a JMS queue for processing later, and immediately return an acknowledgement to the client. The service retains the correlation identifier.

- Have the service processing layer use a message-driven bean to process the received request. When a response is ready, the service sends the response to the reply address. In addition to the results, the response message contains the same correlation identifier so that the service requestor can identify the request to which this response relates.

- Have the client accept the response at a Web service that it establishes at the reply address.

Client   **Service**

Synchronous communication

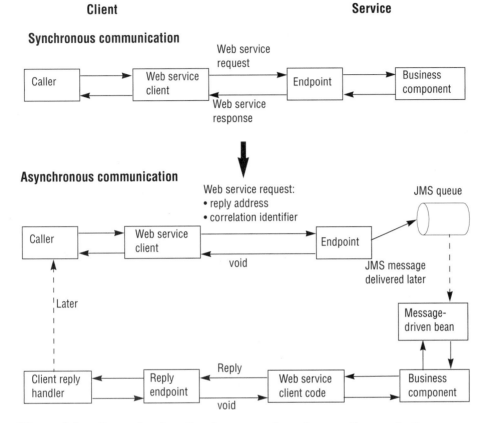

Figure 8.9 Converting from Synchronous to Asynchronous Communication

The JMS queue stores the messages until the message-driven beans are ready to process them, thereby controlling the rate of delivery. Thus, the component can process the messages without being overwhelmed, which helps the service to scale better. Figure 8.9 illustrates the process of converting an endpoint from synchronous to asynchronous communication.

Optionally, the client can further increase its responsiveness by employing some asynchronicity when making the Web service call itself. For example, a stand-alone client that uses a Swing GUI might spawn a thread to make the Web service call, allowing the client to continue its user interactions while the Web service handles the call. Or, a J2EE client component might use a JMS queue to make Web service calls—that is, rather than making the JAX-RPC call directly, the client places the request into a JMS queue and a message-driven bean makes the Web service call to deliver the request.

8.5   Managing Complex Web Service Interactions

An application may have multiple interactions with the same Web service, it may access different Web services, or it may expose many Web service endpoints. There may be different types of interactions. An application may be both a service and a client. A service endpoint may receive documents of multiple types and hence needs to handle them accordingly. All this makes for complexity in managing Web service interactions.

Message-level metadata and a canonical data model are common helper strategies that support complex interactions, and they are good building blocks for adding functionality to a Web service message exchange. By consolidating Web service endpoints, you can make an application's Web service interactions more manageable.

8.5.1   Passing Context Information on Web Service Calls

Web services may need to exchange context information when handling messages. This context data augments the message contents by providing some extra information about the contents and may include information on how to handle the message itself. For example, a purchase order consists of the message contents—items to purchase, customer and financial information—and you also may need to pass some extra information about the message, such as its processing priority. The Web service may also need additional context information indicating how to process the message, such as processing instructions or hints. This context information is often passed along with the message. The following are some use cases where such additional data may be needed.

- Security information needs to be embedded within the document. For example, you may want to include some message-level security or add a digital signature to an accounts payment document as part of a credit card transaction.

- A correlation identifier needs to be included with the message to indicate that the message is associated with a logical group of messages exchanged in a workflow.

- Transactional or reliability information may be included along with the message contents to indicate additional quality of service activities that should be applied before processing the message contents.

- A message needs to be processed on a priority basis.

Several strategies exist for including context information with a message exchange, as follows:

1. Context information can be passed as an extra parameter in the Web service method. You can define the Web service interface to accept not only the XML document message, but to also include a second parameter that encapsulates metadata.

2. Context information also can be passed as part of the document itself. You can embed the extra metadata within the XML document. When you parse the document, you extract the needed information.

3. Context information also can be passed in the SOAP message header. You can embed the metadata in the SOAP message header and write a handler to extract it and pass it to the endpoint.

The first strategy, including context information as part of the service interface by adding an extra field for the input parameters or return values, effectively makes the context information part of the WSDL. For example, Code Example 8.3 shows how the boolean parameter `priorityProcessing` is added to the `submitPurchaseOrder` method. The value of the parameter indicates whether the order should be processed before other orders. Besides complicating the service interface, you must remember to update the interface—and regenerate the WSDL—if you add to or change the context information. For these reasons, the strategy of including context information as part of the service interface results in code that is harder to maintain.

```
public interface MyWebService extends Remote {
// priorityProcessing is the data indicating that the purchase
// order needs to be processed on a priority basis
```

```
public String submitPurchaseOrder(PurchaseOrder poObject,
          boolean priorityProcessing) throws RemoteException;
}
```

Code Example 8.3   Context information in a Service Interface

The second strategy embeds the information directly in the message contents. (See Code Example 8.4.) You create additional elements within the XML document itself, making the context information part of the data model—either part of the request parameter message or the reply return data. Add the necessary elements to the message schema, then add the data elements to the XML document before sending the message. The receiving endpoint parses the document and extracts the information into its application code. There are disadvantages to this strategy. You must revise the document schema when you change the context information. To retrieve the context information, you must parse the document, which can be costly especially if the document passes through intermediaries. There is also no logical separation between the schema for the document request and the schema for the context information. For these reasons, embedding the context information in the message contents may also result in code that is harder to maintain.

```
<PurchaseOrder>
<Id>123456789 </Id>
...
<POContextInfo> <!-- This is where the context data begins -->
    <PriorityProcessing>True</PriorityProcessing>
    <!-- Other context data elements -->
</POContextInfo>
...
</PurchaseOrder>
```

Code Example 8.4   Context Information in a Document

The third strategy is to embed context information as a new subelement in a message's SOAP header. For this strategy, clients need to embed this information in a SOAP header and the service needs to extract it. The service can use a JAX-RPC handler to intercept the SOAP message and then extract the header while still keeping it associated with the document. The handler uses this context information to take appropriate actions before the business logic is invoked in the endpoint. This strategy is more elegant because it does not require you to modify the XML schema for the data model exported by the service. Instead, the handler unobtrusively determines the context information from the envelope's header, leaving the message body untouched and unaffected. See Code Example 8.5, which shows how to add context infromation to a SOAP header.

❐ This strategy is preferred to the others since it keeps the context information separate from the document contents and the service interface. This strategy also lets you encapsulate the context information processing in a handler, which keeps the handling logic for context information removed from the business logic.

There are some performance implications of this strategy, since each Web service endpoint invocation runs this handler to manipulate the SOAP message. The context information may be needed in only a few cases, but the handler runs with every invocation. This strategy may also be more difficult to implement.

```
<SOAP-ENV:Envelope xmlns:SOAP-ENV="SoapEnvelopeURI"
        SOAP-ENV:encodingStyle="SoapEncodingURI">
    <SOAP-ENV:Header>
        <ci:PriorityProcessing>True</ci:PriorityProcessing>
    </SOAP-ENV:Header>
<SOAP-ENV:Body>
        <opc:submitPurchaseOrder xmlns:opc="ServiceURI">
            <opc:PurchaseOrder>
                <!-- contents of PurchaseOrder document -->
            </opc:PurchaseOrder>
        </opc:submitPurchaseOrder>
    </SOAP-ENV:Body>
</SOAP-ENV:Envelope>
```

Code Example 8.5 Context Information in SOAP Headers

Sometimes, the handler needs to pass the context information (or the results of processing the context information) to the endpoint implementation. The way to do this is to use the JAX-RPC MessageContext interface, since this interface is available to both JAX-RPC and EJB service endpoints. If the handler sets the context information in the `MessageContext` interface, the service endpoint can access it. To illustrate, you first set up a handler class similar to the one shown in Code Example 8.6.

```
public class MyMessageHandler extends
            javax.xml.rpc.handler.GenericHandler {
    public boolean handleRequest(MessageContext mc) {
        SOAPMessage msg = ((SOAPMessageContext)mc).getMessage() ;
        SOAPPart sp = msg.getSOAPPart();
        SOAPEnvelope se = sp.getEnvelope();
        SOAPHeader header = se.getHeader();
        SOAPBody body = se.getBody();
        if (header == null) {
            // raise error
        }
        for (Iterator iter = header.getChildElements();
                    iter.hasNext();) {
            SOAPElement element = (SOAPElement) iter.next();
            if (element.getElementName().getLocalName()
                    .equals("PriorityProcessing")) {
                mc.setProperty("PriorityProcessing",
                    element.getValue());
            }
        }
    ...

    return true;
}
```

Code Example 8.6   Passing Context Information from Handler to Endpoint

Then, you can get access to `MessageContext` in the endpoint that receives the request. For an EJB service endpoint, `MessageContext` is available with the bean's `SessionContext`. Code Example 8.7 shows the enterprise bean code for the endpoint.

```
public class EndpointBean implements SessionBean {
    private SessionContext sc;
```

```
        public void businessMethod() {
            MessageContext msgc= sc.getMessageContext();
            String s = (String)msgc.getProperty("PriorityProcessing");
            Boolean priority = new Boolean(s);
            ...
    }
        public void setSessionContext(SessionContext sc) {
            this.sc = sc;
    }
        ...
}
```

Code Example 8.7   Endpoint Receiving Context Information from a Handler

8.5.2   Handling Multiple Document Types

A Web service, over time, invariably will need to expand its ability to accept documents of different types. Developers may add new functionality to the same service interface, and this functionality mandates new document types. Although you can accommodate these changes by adding new methods to the interface to accept alternate forms or types of documents, this approach may result in an explosion in the number of methods.

A better strategy for handling multiple document types is to design the service interface with this possibility in mind. You can do so by writing a generic method to represent a document-centric interaction. For example, instead of having multiple methods for each document type such as submitSupplierInvoice, submitSupplier2Invoice, and submitBillingInfo, the endpoint interface has a single method called submitDocument that receives all document types. To accept any type of document, you need to use xsd:anyType as the parameter type for the submitDocument method. The service interface does not have to change to accommodate new document types, just the service implementation changes. See Code Example 3.19 on page 110 for an example.

Since your interface changed to a single method, the implementation needs to change appropriately. The submitDocument method needs to map these documents to the processing logic that handles them. You can apply a Command pattern to this strategy to achieve flexibility in handling these documents. With a Command pattern, you place the commands to manage all schemas of the various document types in one place, identifying each command by schema type. To add a new schema, you simply add a new command that handles the new schema.

Figure 8.10 illustrates how you might apply this strategy. The Web service receives different types of documents from its clients. Each type of document maps to a schema. The service maintains a separate command for each document type represented by its schema. The command mapping happens in the interaction layer, separate from the processing layer and the business logic.

Using this strategy to handle multiple document types has an additional benefit: You can have the contents of the document, rather than the invoked method, determine the processing. To do so, you extend the logic of the command selection to include some of the document content. For example, if you wanted to apply business logic specific to a requestor, you might choose a command based on document type plus the identity of the requestor. For example, the adventure builder enterprise can apply additional business logic—such as verifying an invoice's authenticity—to invoices sent in by less trusted partners.

❏   Create an interface that has a single method to receive documents of different types. Use the Command pattern to map each document to its processing logic.

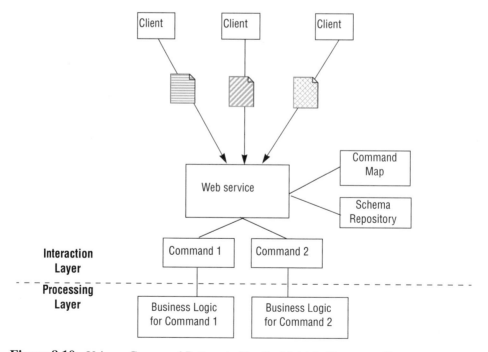

Figure 8.10 Using a Command Pattern to Handle Multiple Document Types

8.5.3   Consolidating Web Service Interactions

Consolidating Web service interactions is a good way to simplify the complexity of a Web service application. What starts as a straightforward Web service application with basic interactions between a client and a single service often grows into an application that exposes more endpoints and may itself act as a client to other services. The application communication becomes more complicated, and the business logic often becomes closely tied to a particular service. When the number of Web service interactions grows beyond a certain point, you may want to factor out common code for reuse.

For service interactions that rely on document passing, consider using a centralized manager that can broker the Web service interactions and consolidate the interaction layer of your Web services. This centralized manager can be responsible for both incoming and outgoing Web service interactions, and it can also consolidate all client access to a service. A centralized manager strategy applies only to interactions involving document passing, because such interactions can use an interface with a single method to handle all possible documents. Interfaces that pass objects as parameters do not have the flexibility to be this generic—a method passing or returning an object must declare the object type, which can only map to a single document type. The centralized manager needs to handle multiple document types by using the strategy described in "Handling Multiple Document Types" on page 371.

Take, for example, the order processing center interactions with its various suppliers. The order processing center is both a client of and a service to multiple suppliers. The order processing center and the suppliers engage in XML document exchange interactions, and often the interactions are asynchronous since they may span a fair amount of time. Without a centralized manager, your enterprise may have many point-to-point interactions among internal modules and external partners. This may result in the Web service code existing in many places throughout the enterprise. Each endpoint in these point-to-point interactions replicates the same work done by other endpoints, as do each of the clients. Keep in mind that as the number of services you expose grows, it becomes harder to manage this complexity.

Figure 8.11 illustrates how a centralized manager can simplify an enterprise's interactions with its external partners. The top part of the figure shows several entities of an enterprise each communicating with various external partners. The bottom part of the figure shows how much simpler it is to route the same interactions through a centralized manager.

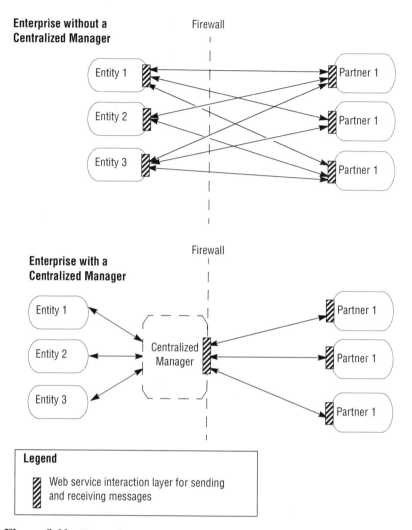

Figure 8.11   Enterprise Interactions with External Partners

To simplify things, the order processing center uses this centralized manager strategy to consolidate the Web service interaction layer code. The centralized manager handles all the Web service requests from the suppliers—it does any necessary preprocessing and interaction layer work, then dispatches requests to the appropriate processing layer business action component. To illustrate, we implemented this strategy between the order processing center Order Filler submodule and the supplier Web services. The centralized manager handles XML documents sent in by suppliers. The centralized manager extracts information from these incoming requests, and this information lets it know how to handle the request. It may reformat the message content or transform the content to the internal canonical form used by the enterprise. The centralized manager routes the reformatted message to the correct target system. It can also validate incoming documents and centralize the management of document schemas. For outgoing Web service calls, the centralized manager acts as the client on behalf of the internal modules.

Not only does it centralize interaction layer and client functionality so that it is easier to manage incoming and outgoing Web service messages, use of this strategy also decouples components that access a service from those that focus on business logic. Your enterprise ends up with a clean Web service layer that is decoupled from the processing layer.

For handling incoming requests, you can establish a single interface and endpoint that all clients use. You can add context information to each request to enable an easy identification of the type of the request, such as purchase order or invoice. When this single endpoint acts as the interaction layer for several Web services, it can perform a number of functions, depending on what is available to it. If it has access to schemas, the endpoint can perform validation and error checking. If it has access to style sheets, the endpoint can transform incoming requests to match the canonical data model.

The centralized manager may also handle security tasks appropriate for the interaction layer and can translate incoming documents to an internal, enterprise-wide canonical data model. The key point is that the centralized manager needs access to information that enables it to perform these services.

A centralized manager may also use a message router to route requests to the appropriate business component recipients in the processing layer. A message router is responsible for mapping requests to recipients.

❏ As the number of Web service interactions grow within your enterprise, consider consolidating them in a centralized manager.

8.5.4 Canonical Data Model

Establishing a canonical data model is a good strategy for exchanging messages that rely on different data models. (See "Data Transformation" on page 275 for more details on using a canonical data model.) The adventure builder enterprise receives messages from suppliers through the centralized manager, which provides a natural place to hold a canonical data model. The canonical data model we use is represented in XML. The order processing center provides the canonical data model used for its interaction with the Web site.

8.6   Building More Robust Web Services

The J2EE 1.4 platform and its Web service technologies conform to the WS-I Basic Profile standards. Conforming to these standards means that the platform uses HTTP as the underlying transport for Web service calls. Unfortunately, from a business communication point of view, the HTTP protocol provides only a low-level degree of robustness. To illustrate, HTTP has no automatic retries to reestablish a connection that disconnects. If the receiving end fails, the entire HTTP call fails and there is no attempt to connect later. This low-level degree of robustness is not necessarily bad, since it means that HTTP can accommodate the participation of all kinds of systems and networks in a distributed Internet environment. HTTP is also a fairly simple protocol that any system can implement with a reasonable amount of effort.

Despite using more reliable hardware and software systems and communication links, enterprises have no guarantee against failures. Failures may occur during a Web service request between a client and a Web service that may leave an application in an ambiguous state. For example, a problem may occur when either party (client or server) fails while in the midst of a JAX-RPC call. Other problems may occur due to lost messages, messages arriving out of order, messages mistakenly seen as duplicates when the same message arrives multiple times, or when the contents of messages are corrupted.

The WS-I Basic Profile does not specify a standard mechanism for handling Web service failures, and hence the J2EE platform standards do not yet include standard support for all such failures. Emerging standards specifications are beginning to enable robust Web service communications using standard interoperable mechanisms. In the meantime, you can achieve more robust Web service communication by adding this functionality to your own application code. It is worth the effort even though you may not be able to handle all types of catastrophic failures.

Writing your own code to make a service more robust may result in a reduction in interoperability. Loss of interoperability can be an unfortunate side effect when implementing solutions ahead of industry standards. In the following sections, we provide some strategies to add some robustness to your Web services. The solutions we propose here are limited to scenarios that involve a single request/reply message exchange between a J2EE client (a servlet or an enterprise bean) and a J2EE Web service endpoint using JAX-RPC as the communication technology.

8.6.1   Use Idempotent Endpoints

Duplication of messages can be a problem in a distributed environment. Different situations can cause duplicate messages, such as sender retries because of communication failures, maliciousness, or bugs in the code. Duplicate messages may also be due to user error, such as when an impatient user presses a submit button more than once. A message receiver must guard against unintended side effects (such as processing an order twice) because of these duplicate messages. Creating idempotent endpoints is one strategy a service can use to handle duplicate messages.

Idempotent refers to a situation where repeated executions of the same event have the same effect as a single execution of the event. Making your endpoints idempotent avoids the problem of a service processing duplicate instances of the same message or request. Even if a client mistakenly—or even maliciously— submits a request such as a purchase order (via a JAX-RPC call) more than once, the effect is the same as if the request was submitted just once.

Service endpoints that only perform read operations are naturally idempotent, since these operations do not have any side effects. For example, the adventure builder application's CRM order tracking Web service is naturally idempotent since it only invokes read operations. For Web services that perform updates or otherwise change state, you need to explicitly build idempotency. One way to do this is to leverage the semantics of the endpoint logic. If you know the effect of a single execution of an operation, you can change the program logic to ensure that multiple executions of the operation have the same result as a single execution.

Let's look at how to design an idempotent endpoint for services that perform updates or change state. First, to detect duplicate requests, you need to assign a correlation identifier to client interactions with a service. (See "Correlating Messages" on page 359.) This correlation identifier can be passed as context information and intercepted and processed by a JAX-RPC handler. (See "Passing Context Information on Web Service Calls" on page 366.) When the request is received, the endpoint should check to see if it is a duplicate request. For example, the order processing center's `submitPurchaseOrder` method can be made idempotent since we know its operation depends on an order identifier key value. Before executing the business logic, the `submitPurchaseOrder` method stores the order in the database with the order identifier as its primary key. If the same purchase order is sent again, the second attempt to store the same order identifier in the database results in a duplicate key exception, preventing the order from being processed a second time.

8.6.2   Use Client Retries with Idempotent Endpoints

Idempotent endpoints can help to set up a fault-tolerant Web service interaction. Because multiple service requests have the same effect as a single request, clients of a idempotent service can retry message requests until they are successful, without fear of causing duplicate actions. However, using idempotent endpoints for a fault-tolerant Web service adds to the application's complexity and may adversely affect performance. It is also not interoperable: Specifications for this area are still being designed, and it is doubtful that the standards that ultimately result will work with current custom-built schemes.

With a fault-tolerant design, a client needs to retry sending messages until successful. Typically the client retries only a fixed number of times and then fails. You also design the endpoint to be idempotent. You may also need an acknowledgment message, which can be part of the JAX-RPC reply message or a separate message (if using asynchronous processing).

Often before executing a retry, a client waits briefly so that transient conditions in the network or on the server may clear. When using synchronous Web service calls, the client—especially when it is a real person using the client—may find these waits unacceptable. In cases such as this, consider converting synchronous calls to asynchronous calls. See "Refactoring Synchronous to Asynchronous Interactions" on page 363.

While you design your logic, remember that a failure can occur at any point during a JAX-RPC interaction—when the client makes a call or the service receives it, while the service processes the call, when the service sends a reply or the client receives it, or when the client processes the reply. To recover from such failures, you may want the application code to log interaction state on the client as well as the endpoint. If a failure occurs, you can use the log to recover and finish the interaction, deleting the log when complete or otherwise marking it as finished.

How does a client effectively use a service with this type of robustness? You need to formulate a contract—a set of understood interaction rules—between the client and the service endpoint. These rules might specify that retries are allowed and how many, the overall protocol, and so forth. Generally, the client makes the call and can repeat the call if it is not notified of success within a certain time limit. The service is responsible for detecting duplicate calls.

8.6.3 Handling Asynchronous Interaction Error Conditions

Application design should include handling recoverable and irrecoverable exception conditions in a user-friendly manner. However, error handling is more complicated with distributed systems. Asynchronous interactions add further to application error handling complexity, principally because the interaction requestor is not available to receive an error report. In addition, human intervention may be needed to resolve the error condition.

Let's look at how the adventure builder application handles exception conditions. For its Web service interactions, the adventure builder application gives the interaction requestor a correlation identifier for the submitted request. The service endpoint implementation catches any exceptions that occur when the request is preprocessed. Exceptions might be an invalid XML document or XML parsing and translation errors. For asynchronous interactions, the service endpoint implementation uses JMS to send requests to the processing layer. In those cases, it may also encounter JMS exceptions. For these errors, the endpoint passes a service-specific exception to the requestor. For more information on designing this portion of the exception handling mechanism, see "Handling Exceptions" on page 80.

In adventure builder, exceptions may occur as follows:

1. **Case 1:** During any Web service interaction between the Web site and the order processing center or between the order processing center and the external suppliers. These Web service interaction exceptions are synchronous in nature and thus easier to handle than exceptions that arise in cases 2 and 3.

2. **Case 2:** Within the order processing center, while processing an order during any stage of the workflow management operation.

3. **Case 3**: During the order processing center interaction with partners, such as the suppliers and the credit card service.

Code Example 8.8, which illustrates Case 1, shows a portion of the code for the order processing center Web service interface that receives purchase orders from the Web module. The interface throws two kinds of service-specific exceptions: `InvalidPOException`, which it throws when the received purchase order is not in the expected format, and `ProcessingException`, which is throws when there is an error submitting the request to JMS. Note that the platform throws `RemoteException` when irrecoverable errors, such as network problems, occur.

```
public interface PurchaseOrderIntf extends Remote {
    public String submitPurchaseOrder(PurchaseOrder poObject)
            throws InvalidPOException, ProcessingException,
            RemoteException;
}
```

Code Example 8.8   Handling Exceptions in Web Service Calls

Exceptions that occur when processing an order either within the order processing center or during the interactions with partners (Cases 2 and 3) require a different handling approach. Since request processing is asynchronous, the client that placed the request is not waiting to receive any exceptions that you might throw. You also need to differentiate exceptions that require a client's intervention from those that may be temporary and possibly resolved on a retry. If an exception requires a client's intervention, you must inform the client in some way. For exceptions that may be temporary, you can designate a certain number of retries before giving up and informing the client.

For example, consider the order processing workflow of the order processing center. After the endpoint receives the purchase order from the client and successfully puts it in the workflow manager's queue, it returns a correlation identifier to the client. The client then goes about its own business. At this point, the workflow manager takes the order through the various workflow stages. Different exceptions can occur in each stage. These exceptions can be broadly categorized as those that require immediate client intervention and those that require an application retry.

Let's look first at exception conditions that require human intervention, such as notifying the customer or an administrator. Examples of such exceptions might be an incoming purchase order that needs to be persisted to the data store but the database table does not exist. Or, the credit card agency might not grant credit authorization for an order because of an invalid credit card number. When these exception conditions occur, it is impossible to continue purchase order processing without human intervention. The adventure builder application informs the customer via e-mail when such conditions happen.

Now let's look at handling exceptions that require the application to retry the operation. As an order progresses through the workflow stages, various exception conditions of a temporary nature may occur. There may be an error placing the order in a JMS queue, the database connection may be busy, a service may not be available, and so forth. For example, the workflow manager might try to invoke the supplier or bank Web service while that latter service is down. Or, the order processing center database may be temporarily unavailable due to a back-up operation. Since temporary error conditions often resolve themselves in a short while, asking the customer to intervene in these situations does not make for the best customer experience.

A strategy for handling temporary error conditions involves keeping a status indicator to signal retrying a failed step at a later time. The adventure builder application workflow manager, as it moves a purchase order through various stages, tracks the status of the order at each stage. If an error occurs, the workflow manager flags the order's status to indicate an error. By using the timer bean mechanism available in the J2EE 1.4 platform, the workflow manager can periodically examine orders with an error status and attempt to move these orders to their next logical stage in the flow. The timer bean activates after a specified period of time, initiating a check of orders flagged with errors and prompting the workflow manager to retry the order's previously failed operation. The order status, in addition to keeping an error flag, tracks the number of retry attempts. The workflow manager seeks human intervention when the number of retry attempts exceeds the fixed number of allowable retries.

8.7 Conclusion

In this chapter we examined the adventure builder enterprise application, in particular its Web service implementations. We discussed the rationale for our different Web service application design choices and illustrated how we went about implementing these various endpoints and communication patterns. Drawing on examples from the application, we tried to bring to life many of the Web service architectural and design issues.

The chapter covered the details of Web service design and implementation, including establishing a service's interaction and processing layers, selecting the appropriate endpoint type, determining the proper granularity, passing parameters between client and service, delegating to business logic, publishing and deploying the service, and client considerations. It also discussed how to extend a Web service's quality of service. It considered strategies such as using context information with messages, relying on a canonical data model, including a correlation identifier, and using registries, among other strategies for adding robustness to a service.

In this book, we have tried to cover the Web service standards as they currently exist and how you can develop Web services on the J2EE platform that conform to these standards. We have also tried to show how you can use the J2EE platform technologies to achieve additional robustness and quality of service beyond the current standards for your Web services.

Glossary

access control The methods by which interactions with resources are limited to collections of users or programs for the purpose of enforcing integrity, confidentiality, or availability constraints.

ACID The acronym for the four properties guaranteed by transactions: atomicity, consistency, isolation, and durability.

activation The process of transferring an enterprise bean from secondary storage to memory. See **passivation**.

applet A component that typically executes in a Web browser, but can execute in a variety of other applications or devices that support the applet programming model.

applet container A container that includes support for the applet programming model.

application assembler A person who combines components and modules into deployable application units.

application client A first-tier client component that executes in its own Java virtual machine. Application clients have access to some J2EE platform APIs (JNDI, JDBC, RMI-IIOP, JMS).

application client container A container that supports application client components.

application client module A software unit that consists of one or more classes and an application client deployment descriptor.

application component provider A vendor that provides the Java classes that implement components' methods, JSP page definitions, and any required deployment descriptors.

authentication The process by which an entity proves to another entity that it is acting on behalf of a specific identity. The J2EE platform requires three types of authentication: basic, form-based, and mutual, and it supports digest authentication.

authorization *See* **access control**.

authorization constraint An authorization rule that determines who is permitted to access a Web resource collection.

basic authentication An authentication mechanism in which a Web server authenticates an entity with a user name and password obtained using the Web client's built-in authentication mechanism.

bean-managed persistence Data transfer between an entity bean's variables and a resource manager managed by the entity bean.

bean-managed transaction A transaction whose boundaries are defined by an enterprise bean.

business logic The code that implements the functionality of an application. In the Enterprise JavaBeans model, this logic is implemented by the methods of an enterprise bean.

business method A method of an enterprise bean that implements the business logic or rules of an application.

callback methods Methods in a component called by the container to notify the component of important events in its life cycle.

caller Same as **caller principal**.

caller principal The principal that identifies the invoker of the enterprise bean method.

canonical data model A data model independent of any application that is used for EAI purposes.

client certificate authentication An authentication mechanism in which a client uses a X.509 certificate to establish its identity.

commit The point in a transaction when all updates to any resources involved in the transaction are made permanent.

component An application-level software unit supported by a container. Components are configurable at deployment time. The J2EE platform defines four types of components: enterprise beans, Web components, applets, and application clients.

component contract The contract between a component and its container. The contract includes life cycle management of the component, a context interface that the instance uses to obtain various information and services from its container, and a list of services that every container must provide for its components.

connection *See* **resource manager connection**.

connection factory *See* **resource manager connection factory**.

connector A standard extension mechanism for containers to provide connectivity to enterprise information systems. A connector is specific to an enterprise information system and consists of a resource adapter and application development tools for enterprise information system connectivity. The resource adapter is plugged into a container through its support for system-level contracts defined in the connector architecture.

connector architecture An architecture for integration of J2EE products with enterprise information systems. There are two parts to this architecture: a resource adapter provided by an enterprise information system vendor and the J2EE product that allows this resource adapter to plug in. This architecture defines a set of contracts that a resource adapter has to support to plug in to a J2EE product, for example, transactions, security, and resource management.

container An entity that provides life cycle management, security, deployment, and runtime services to components. Each type of container (EJB, Web, JSP, servlet, applet, and application client) also provides component-specific services.

container-managed persistence Data transfer between an entity bean's variables and a resource manager managed by the entity bean's container.

container-managed transaction A transaction whose boundaries are defined by an EJB container. An entity bean must use container-managed transactions.

context attribute An object bound into the context associated with a servlet.

conversational state The field values of a session bean plus the transitive closure of the objects reachable from the bean's fields. The transitive closure of a bean is defined in terms of the serialization protocol for the Java programming language, that is, the fields that would be stored by serializing the bean instance.

CORBA Common Object Request Broker Architecture. A language-independent, distributed object model specified by the Object Management Group.

create method A method defined in the home interface and invoked by a client to create an enterprise bean.

credentials The information describing the security attributes of a principal.

CTS Compatibility Test Suite. A suite of compatibility tests for verifying that a J2EE product complies with the J2EE platform specification.

data origin authentication A corroboration that the source of received data is as claimed.

data origin authentication service A security service that verifies that the identity of the original source of some data received by another participant is the identity as claimed. No association is required between the sender and receiver.

delegation An act whereby one principal authorizes another principal to use its identity or privileges with some restrictions.

demilitarized zone (DMZ) A small subnetwork that buffers the trusted internal network, such as a corporate private LAN, from an untrusted external network, such as the public Internet.

deployer A person who installs modules and J2EE applications into an operational environment.

deployment The process whereby software is installed into an operational environment.

deployment descriptor An XML file provided with each module and application that describes how they should be deployed. The deployment descriptor directs a deployment tool to deploy a module or application with specific container options and describes specific configuration requirements that a deployer must resolve.

digest authentication An authentication mechanism in which a Web client authenticates to a Web server by sending the server a message digest along its HTTP request message. The digest is computed by employing a one-way hash algorithm to a concatenation of the HTTP request message and the client's password. The digest is typically much smaller than the HTTP request and doesn't contain the password.

distributed application An application made up of distinct components running in separate runtime environments, usually on different platforms connected via a network. Typical distributed applications are two-tier (client-server), three-tier (client-middleware-server), and multi-tier (client-multiple, middleware-multiple servers).

DOM Document Object Model. A tree of objects with interfaces for traversing the tree and writing an XML version of it, as defined by the W3Cspecification.

DTD Document Type Definition. A description of the structure and properties of a class of XML files.

EAR file A JAR archive that contains a J2EE application.

EJB™ *See* **Enterprise JavaBeans**.

EJB container A container that implements the EJB component contract of the J2EE architecture. This contract specifies a runtime environment for enterprise beans that includes security, concurrency, life cycle management, transaction, deployment, naming, and other services. An EJB container is provided by an EJB or J2EE server.

EJB container provider A vendor that supplies an EJB container.

EJB context An object that allows an enterprise bean to invoke services provided by the container and to obtain the information about the caller of a client-invoked method.

EJB home object An object that provides the life cycle operations (create, remove, find) for an enterprise bean. The class for the EJB home object is generated by the container's deployment tools. The EJB home object implements the enterprise bean's home interface. The client references an EJB home object to perform life cycle operations on an EJB object. The client uses JNDI to locate an EJB home object.

EJB JAR file A JAR archive that contains an EJB module.

EJB module A software unit that consists of one or more enterprise beans and an EJB deployment descriptor.

EJB object An object whose class implements the enterprise bean's remote interface. A client never references an enterprise bean instance directly; a client always references an EJB object. The class of an EJB object is generated by the container's deployment tools.

EJB server Software provides services to an EJB container. For example, an EJB container typically relies on a transaction manager that is part of the EJB server to perform the two-phase commit across all the participating resource managers. The J2EE architecture assumes that an EJB container is hosted by an EJB server from the same vendor, so it does not specify the contract between these two entities. An EJB server may host one or more EJB containers.

EJB server provider A vendor that supplies an EJB server.

enterprise bean A component that implements a business task or business entity and resides in an EJB container; either an entity bean or a session bean.

enterprise information system The applications that comprise an enterprise's existing system for handling company-wide information. These applications provide an information infrastructure for an enterprise. An enterprise information system offers a well-defined set of services to its clients. These services are exposed to clients as local and/or remote interfaces. Examples of enterprise information systems include enterprise resource planning systems, mainframe transaction processing systems, and legacy database systems.

enterprise information system resource An entity that provides enterprise information system-specific functionality to its clients. Examples are a record or set of records in a database system, a business object in an enterprise resource planning system, and a transaction program in a transaction processing system.

enterprise bean provider An application programmer who produces enterprise bean classes, remote and home interfaces, and deployment descriptor files, and packages them in an EJB .jar file.

Enterprise JavaBeans™ (EJB™) A component architecture for the development and deployment of object-oriented, distributed, enterprise-level applications. Applications written using the Enterprise JavaBeans architecture are scalable, transactional, and secure.

entity bean An enterprise bean that represents persistent data maintained in a database. An entity bean can manage its own persistence or it can delegate this function to its container. An entity bean is identified by a primary key. If the container in which an entity bean is hosted crashes, the entity bean, its primary key, and any remote references survive the crash.

finder method A method defined in the home interface and invoked by a client to locate an entity bean.

form-based authentication An authentication mechanism in which a Web container provides an application-specific form for logging in.

group A collection of principals within a given security policy domain.

handle An object that identifies an enterprise bean. A client may serialize the handle and then later deserialize it to obtain a reference to the enterprise bean.

home interface One of two interfaces for an enterprise bean. The home interface defines zero or more methods for creating and removing an enterprise bean. For session beans, the home interface defines create and remove methods, while for entity beans, the home interface defines create, finder, and remove methods.

home handle An object that can be used to obtain a reference of the home interface. A home handle can be serialized and written to stable storage and deserialized to obtain the reference.

HTML HyperText Markup Language. A markup language for hypertext documents on the Internet. HTML enables the embedding of images, sounds, video streams, form fields, references to other objects with URLs, and basic text formatting.

HTTP HyperText Transfer Protocol. The Internet protocol used to fetch hypertext objects from remote hosts. HTTP messages consist of requests from client to server and responses from server to client.

HTTPS HTTP layered over the SSL protocol.

impersonation An act whereby one entity assumes the identity and privileges of another entity without restrictions and without any indication visible to the recipients of the impersonator's calls that delegation has taken place. Impersonation is a case of simple delegation.

integrity mechanisms Mechanisms that ensure that outside parties cannot tamper with communication between entities. Integrity mechanisms prevent outside parties from intercepting and modifying communication between entities, and they ensure that messages can be used only once.

IDL Interface Definition Language. A language used to define interfaces to remote CORBA objects. The interfaces are independent of operating systems and programming languages.

IIOP Internet Inter-ORB Protocol. A protocol used for communication between CORBA object request brokers.

initialization parameter A parameter that initializes the context associated with a servlet.

ISV Independent Software Vendor.

J2EE™ Java 2, Enterprise Edition.

J2ME™ Java 2, Micro Edition.

J2SE™ Java 2, Standard Edition.

J2EE application Any deployable unit of J2EE functionality. This can be a single module or a group of modules packaged into an .ear file with a J2EE application deployment descriptor. J2EE applications are typically engineered to be distributed across multiple computing tiers.

J2EE product An implementation that conforms to the J2EE platform specification.

J2EE product provider A vendor that supplies a J2EE product.

J2EE server The runtime portion of a J2EE product. A J2EE server provides Web and/or EJB containers.

JAR Java ARchive. A platform-independent file format that permits many files to be aggregated into one file.

Java™ 2 Platform, Standard Edition (J2SE platform) The core Java technology platform.

Java™ 2 Platform, Enterprise Edition (J2EE platform) An environment for developing and deploying enterprise applications. The J2EE platform consists of a set of services, application programming interfaces (APIs), and protocols that provide the functionality for developing multitiered, Web-based applications.

Java™ 2 SDK, Enterprise Edition (J2EE SDK) Sun's implementation of the J2EE platform. This implementation provides an operational definition of the J2EE platform.

Java IDL A technology that provides CORBA interoperability and connectivity capabilities for the J2EE platform. These capabilities enable J2EE applications to invoke operations on remote network services using the OMG IDL and IIOP.

JavaMail™ An API for sending and receiving e-mail.

Java™ Message Service (JMS) An API for using enterprise messaging systems such as IBM MQ Series, TIBCO Rendezvous, and so on.

Java Naming and Directory Interface™ (JNDI) An API that provides naming and directory functionality.

Java™ Transaction API (JTA) An API that allows applications and J2EE servers to access transactions.

Java™ Transaction Service (JTS) Specifies the implementation of a transaction manager that supports JTA and implements the Java mapping of the OMG Object Transaction Service (OTS) 1.1 specification at the level below the API.

JavaBeans™ component A Java class that can be manipulated in a visual builder tool and composed into applications. A JavaBeans component must adhere to certain property and event interface conventions.

JavaServer Pages™ (JSP) An extensible Web technology that uses template data, custom elements, scripting languages, and server-side Java objects to return dynamic content to a client. Typically the template data is HTML or XML elements, and in many cases the client is a Web browser.

JDBC™ An API for database-independent connectivity between the J2EE platform and a wide range of data sources.

JMS *See* **Java Message Service**.

JNDI *See* **Java Naming and Directory Interface**.

JSP *See* **JavaServer Pages**.

JSP action A JSP element that can act on implicit objects and other server-side objects or can define new scripting variables. Actions follow the XML syntax for elements with a start tag, a body, and an end tag; if the body is empty it can also use the empty tag syntax. The tag must use a prefix.

JSP action, custom An action described in a portable manner by a tag library descriptor and a collection of Java classes and imported into a JSP page by a taglib directive. A custom action is invoked when a JSP page uses a *custom tag*.

JSP action, standard An action that is defined in the JSP specification and is always available to a JSP file without being imported.

JSP application A stand-alone Web application, written using the JavaServer Pages technology, that can contain JSP pages, servlets, HTML files, images, applets, and JavaBeans components.

JSP container A container that provides the same services as a servlet container and an engine that interprets and processes JSP pages into a servlet.

JSP container, distributed A JSP container that can run a Web application that is tagged as distributable and is spread across multiple Java virtual machines that might be running on different hosts.

JSP declaration A JSP scripting element that declares methods, variables, or both in a JSP file.

JSP directive A JSP element that gives an instruction to the JSP container and is interpreted at translation time.

JSP element A portion of a JSP page that is recognized by a JSP translator. An element can be a directive, an action, or a scripting element.

JSP expression A scripting element that contains a valid scripting language expression that is evaluated, converted to a String, and placed into the implicit out object.

JSP file A file that contains a JSP page. In the Servlet 2.2 specification, a JSP file must have a .jsp extension.

JSP page A text-based document using fixed template data and JSP elements that describes how to process a request to create a response.

JSP scripting element A JSP declaration, scriptlet, or expression whose tag syntax is defined by the JSP specification and whose content is written according to the scripting language used in the JSP page. The JSP specification describes the syntax and semantics for the case where the language page attribute is "java."

JSP scriptlet A JSP scripting element containing any code fragment that is valid in the scripting language used in the JSP page. The JSP specification describes what is a valid scriptlet for the case where the language page attribute is "java."

JSP tag A piece of text between a left angle bracket and a right angle bracket that is used in a JSP file as part of a JSP element. The tag is distinguishable as markup, as opposed to data, because it is surrounded by angle brackets.

JSP tag library A collection of custom tags identifying custom actions described via a tag library descriptor and Java classes.

JTA *See* **Java Transaction API**.

JTS *See* **Java Transaction Service**.

message signature A means to ensure message integrity. A message signature, which is attached to a message, is a signed (that is, cryptographically enciphered using a public key mechanism) digest of the message contents calcuated using a one-way hash algorithm. A message signature ensures that the receiver can detect any unauthorized modification of the message by anyone other than the message sender.

method permission An authorization rule that determines who is permitted to execute one or more enterprise bean methods.

module A software unit that consists of one or more J2EE components of the same container type and one deployment descriptor of that type. There are three types of modules: EJB, Web, and application client. Modules can be deployed as stand-alone units or assembled into an application.

mutual authentication An authentication mechanism employed by two parties for the purpose of proving each other's identity to one another.

namespace A set of unique names defined for a particular context and which conform to rules specific for the namespace. XML schemas define namespaces.

naming context A set of associations between distinct, atomic, people-friendly identifiers and objects.

naming environment A mechanism that allows a component to be customized without the need to access or change the component's source code. A container implements the component's naming environment and provides it to the component as a JNDI naming context. Each component names and accesses its environment entries using the `java:comp/env` JNDI context. The environment entries are declaratively specified in the component's deployment descriptor.

ORB Object Request Broker. A library than enables CORBA objects to locate and communicate with one another.

OS principal A principal native to the operating system on which the J2EE platform is executing.

passivation The process of transferring an enterprise bean from memory to secondary storage. See **activation**.

peer entity authentication A corroboration that the peer entity in an association is as claimed.

peer entity authentication service A security service that verifies an identity claimed by or for a system entity in an association, thus preventing against a masquerade by the first entity. This service requires an association to exist between the two entities, and the corroboration is valid only at the time that the service is provided.

persistence The protocol for transferring the state of an entity bean between its instance variables and an underlying database.

POA Portable Object Adapter. A CORBA standard for building server-side applications that are portable across heterogeneous ORBs.

principal The identity assigned to a user as a result of authentication.

privilege A security attribute that does not have the property of uniqueness and that may be shared by many principals.

primary key An object that uniquely identifies an entity bean within a home.

QName A QName represents an XML qualified name consisting of a prefix and a local part.

realm *See* **security policy domain**. Also, a string, passed as part of an HTTP request during basic authentication, that defines a protection space. The protected resources on a server can be partitioned into a set of protection spaces, each with its own authentication scheme and/or authorization database.

Reference Implementation *See* **Java 2 SDK, Enterprise Edition**.

remote interface One of two interfaces for an enterprise bean. The remote interface defines the business methods callable by a client.

remove method Method defined in the home interface and invoked by a client to destroy an enterprise bean.

resource adapter A system-level software driver that is used by an EJB container or an application client to connect to an enterprise information system. A resource adapter is typically specific to an enterprise information system. It is available as a library and is used within the address space of the server or client using it. A resource adapter plugs into a container. The application components deployed on the container then use the client API (exposed by adapter) or tool-generated high-level abstractions to access the underlying enterprise information system. The resource adapter and EJB container collaborate to provide the underlying mechanisms—transactions, security, and connection pooling—for connectivity to the enterprise information system.

resource manager Provides access to a set of shared resources. A resource manager participates in transactions that are externally controlled and coordinated by a transaction manager. A resource manager is typically in a different address space or on a different machine from the clients that access it. **Note:** An enterprise information system is referred to as resource manager when it is mentioned in the context of resource and transaction management.

resource manager connection An object that represents a session with a resource manager.

resource manager connection factory An object used for creating a resource manager connection.

RMI Remote Method Invocation. A technology that allows an object running in one Java virtual machine to invoke methods on an object running in a different Java virtual machine.

RMI-IIOP A version of RMI implemented to use the CORBA IIOP protocol. RMI over IIOP provides interoperability with CORBA objects implemented in any language if all the remote interfaces are originally defined as RMI interfaces.

role (development) The function performed by a party in the development and deployment phases of an application developed using J2EE technology. The roles are: Application component provider, application assembler, deployer, J2EE product provider, EJB container provider, EJB server provider, Web container provider, Web server provider, tool provider, and system administrator.

role (security) An abstract logical grouping of users that is defined by the application assembler. When an application is deployed, the roles are mapped to security identities, such as principals or groups, in the operational environment.

role mapping The process of associating the groups and/or principals recognized by the container to security roles specified in the deployment descriptor. Security roles have to be mapped by the deployer before the component is installed in the server.

rollback The point in a transaction when all updates to any resources involved in the transaction are reversed.

SAX Simple API for XML. An event-driven, serial-access mechanism for accessing XML documents.

schema A set of tags and tag structure that may be allowed or are expected in an XML document.

screen scraping A technique for accessing a legacy information system by simulating user interaction with the legacy system's user interface.

security attributes A set of properties associated with a principal. Security attributes can be associated with a principal by an authentication protocol and/or by a J2EE product provider.

security constraint A declarative way to annotate the intended protection of Web content. A security constraint consists of a Web resource collection, an authorization constraint, and a user data constraint.

security context An object that encapsulates the shared-state information regarding security between two entities.

security domain An environment in which entities are presumed to trust one another.

security permission A mechanism, defined by J2SE, used by the J2EE platform to express the programming restrictions imposed on application component providers.

security permission set The minimum set of security permissions that a J2EE product provider must provide for the execution of each component type.

security policy domain A scope over which security policies are defined and enforced by a security administrator. A security policy domain has a collection of users (or principals), uses a well defined authentication protocol(s) for authenticating users (or principals), and may have groups to simplify the setting of security policies.

security role *See* **role (security)**.

security technology domain A scope over which the same security mechanism is used to enforce a security policy. Multiple security policy domains can exist within a single technology domain.

security view The set of security roles defined by the application assembler.

server principal The OS principal that the server is executing as.

service-oriented architecture A set of components that can be invoked and whose interface descriptions can be published and discovered.

servlet A Java program that extends the functionality of a Web server, generating dynamic content and interacting with Web clients using a request-response paradigm.

servlet container A container that provides the network services over which requests and responses are sent, decodes requests, and formats responses. All servlet containers must support HTTP as a protocol for requests and responses, but may also support additional request-response protocols, such as HTTPS.

servlet container, distributed A servlet container that can run a Web application that is tagged as distributable and that executes across multiple Java virtual machines running on the same host or on different hosts.

servlet context An object that contains a servlet's view of the Web application within which the servlet is running. Using the context, a servlet can log events, obtain URL references to resources, and set and store attributes that other servlets in the context can use.

servlet mapping Defines an association between a URL pattern and a servlet. The mapping is used to map requests to servlets.

session An object used by a servlet to track a user's interaction with a Web application across multiple HTTP requests.

session bean An enterprise bean that is created by a client and that usually exists only for the duration of a single client-server session. A session bean performs operations, such as calculations or accessing a database, for the client. While a session bean may be transactional, it is not recoverable should a system crash occur. Session bean objects either can be stateless or can maintain conversational state across methods and transactions. If a session bean maintains state, then the EJB container manages this state if the object must be removed from memory. However, the session bean object itself must manage its own persistent data.

Simple Object Access Protocol (SOAP). A text-based protocol that uses an XML-based data encoding format and HTTP/SMTP to transport messages.

SSL Secure Socket Layer. A security protocol that provides privacy over the Internet. The protocol allows client-server applications to communicate in a way that cannot be eavesdropped or tampered with. Servers are always authenticated and clients are optionally authenticated.

SQL Structured Query Language. The standardized relational database language for defining database objects and manipulating data.

SQL/J A set of standards that includes specifications for embedding SQL statements in methods in the Java programming language and specifications for calling Java static methods as SQL stored procedures and user-defined functions. An SQL checker can detect errors in static SQL statements at program development time, rather than at execution time as with a JDBC driver.

stateful session bean A session bean with a conversational state.

stateless session bean A session bean with no conversational state. All instances of a stateless session bean are identical.

system administrator The person responsible for configuring and administering the enterprise's computers, networks, and software systems.

transaction An atomic unit of work that modifies data. A transaction encloses one or more program statements, all of which either complete or roll back. Transactions enable multiple users to access the same data concurrently.

transaction attribute A value specified in an enterprise bean's deployment descriptor that is used by the EJB container to control the transaction scope when the enterprise bean's methods are invoked. A transaction attribute can have the following values: `Required`, `RequiresNew`, `Supports`, `NotSupported`, `Mandatory`, `Never`.

transaction isolation level The degree to which the intermediate state of the data being modified by a transaction is visible to other concurrent transactions and data being modified by other transactions is visible to it.

transaction manager Provides the services and management functions required to support transaction demarcation, transactional resource management, synchronization, and transaction context propagation.

tool provider An organization or software vendor that provides tools used for the development, packaging, and deployment of J2EE applications.

Universal Description, Discovery and Integration (UDDI) A standards-based specification for Web service registration, description, and discovery. Providers register their Web services in a UDDI registry and requestors use the registry to find services.

URI Uniform Resource Identifier. A compact string of characters for identifying an abstract or physical resource. A URI is either a URL or a URN. URLs and URNs are concrete entities that actually exist. A URI is an abstract superclass.

URL Uniform Resource Locator. A standard for writing a textual reference to an arbitrary piece of data in the World Wide Web. A URL looks like "protocol:// host/localinfo" where "protocol" specifies a protocol for fetching the object (such as HTTP or FTP), "host" specifies the Internet name of the targeted host, and "localinfo" is a string (often a file name) passed to the protocol handler on the remote host.

URL path The URL passed by a HTTP request to invoke a servlet. The URL consists of the Context Path + Servlet Path + PathInfo, where Context Path is the path prefix associated with a servlet context of which this servlet is a part. If this context is the default context rooted at the base of the Web server's URL namespace, the path prefix will be an empty string. Otherwise, the path prefix starts with a / character but does not end with a / character. Servlet Path is the path section that directly corresponds to the mapping that activated this request. This path starts with a / character. PathInfo is the part of the request path that follows the Servlet Path but precedes the query string.

URN Uniform Resource Name. A unique identifier that identifies an entity but doesn't tell where it is located. A system can use a URN to look up an entity locally before trying to find it on the Web. It also allows the Web location to change while still allowing the entity to be found.

user data constraint Indicates how data between a client and a Web container should be protected. The protection can be the prevention of tampering with the data or prevention of eavesdropping on the data.

WAR file A JAR archive that contains a Web module.

Web application An application written for the Internet, including those built with Java technologies such as JavaServer Pages and servlets, as well as those built with non-Java technologies such as CGI and Perl.

Web application, distributable A Web application that uses J2EE technology written so that it can be deployed in a Web container distributed across multiple Java virtual machines running on the same host or different hosts. The deployment descriptor for such an application uses the `distributable` element.

Web component A component that provides services in response to requests; either a servlet or a JSP page.

Web container An entity that implements the Web component contract of the J2EE architecture. This contract specifies a runtime environment for Web components that includes security, concurrency, life cycle management, transaction, deployment, and other services. A Web container provides the same services as a JSP container and a federated view of the J2EE platform APIs. A Web container is provided by a Web or J2EE server.

Web container, distributed A Web container that can run a Web application that is tagged as distributable and that executes across multiple Java virtual machines running on the same host or on different hosts.

Web container provider A vendor that supplies a Web container.

Web module A unit that consists of one or more Web components and a Web deployment descriptor.

Web resource collection A list of URL patterns and HTTP methods that describe a set of resources to be protected.

Web server Software that provides services to access the Internet, an intranet, or an extranet. A Web server hosts Web sites, provides support for HTTP and other protocols, and executes server-side programs (such as CGI scripts or servlets) that perform certain functions. In the J2EE architecture, a Web server provides services to a Web container. For example, a Web container typically relies on a Web server to provide HTTP message handling. The J2EE architecture assumes that a Web container is hosted by a Web server from the same vendor, so it does not specify the contract between these two entities. A Web server may host one or more Web containers.

Web server provider A vendor that supplies a Web server.

Web Services Description Language A general-purpose XML schema used to specify details of Web service interfaces, bindings, and other deployment details.

XML eXtensible Markup Language. A markup language that allows you to define the tags (markup) needed to identify the data and text in XML documents. J2EE deployment descriptors are expressed in XML.

XSD XML Schema Definition. An XML schema language standardized by W3C to describe XML documents.

Index

The Java™ Series

ISBN 0-201-63456-2   ISBN 0-201-70433-1   ISBN 0-201-31005-8   ISBN 0-321-24575-X   ISBN 0-201-70393-9   ISBN 0-201-48558-3

ISBN 0-201-74622-0   ISBN 0-201-75280-8   ISBN 0-201-76810-0   ISBN 0-201-31002-3   ISBN 0-201-31003-1   ISBN 0-201-48552-4

ISBN 0-201-71102-8   ISBN 0-201-70329-7   ISBN 0-201-30955-6   ISBN 0-201-31008-2   ISBN 0-201-78472-6   ISBN 0-201-78791-1

ISBN 0-201-31009-0   ISBN 0-201-70502-8   ISBN 0-201-32577-2   ISBN 0-201-43294-3   ISBN 0-201-91466-2

ISBN 0-321-19801-8   ISBN 0-201-74627-1   ISBN 0-201-70456-0   ISBN 0-201-77580-8   ISBN 0-201-78790-3

ISBN 0-201-77582-4   ISBN 0-201-91467-0   ISBN 0-201-70969-4   ISBN 0-321-17384-8

Visit www.awprofessional.com/javaseries for more information on these titles.

CD-ROM Warranty

Addison-Wesley and Sun Microsystems warrant the enclosed CD-ROM to be free of defects in materials and faulty workmanship under normal use for a period of ninety days after purchase (when purchased new). If a defect is discovered in the CD-ROM during this warranty period, a replacement CD-ROM can be obtained at no charge by sending the defective CD-ROM, postage prepaid, with proof of purchase to:

> Disc Exchange
> Addison-Wesley Professional
> Pearson Technology Group
> 75 Arlington Street, Suite 300
> Boston, MA 02116
> Email: AWPro@aw.com

Addison-Wesley and Sun Microsystems make no warranty or representation, either expressed or implied, with respect to this software, its quality, performance, merchantability, or fitness for a particular purpose. In no event will Addison-Wesley, Sun Microsystems, their distributors, or dealers be liable for direct, indirect, special, incidental, or consequential damages arising out of the use or inability to use the software. The exclusion of implied warranties is not permitted in some states. Therefore, the above exclusion may not apply to you. This warranty provides you with specific legal rights. There may be other rights that you may have that vary from state to state. The contents of this CD-ROM are intended for personal use only.

Java[TM] 2 Platform, Enterprise Edition 1.4 SDK
Binary Code License Agreement

READ THE TERMS OF THIS AGREEMENT AND ANY PROVIDED SUPPLEMEN-
TAL LICENSE TERMS (COLLECTIVELY "AGREEMENT") CAREFULLY BEFORE
OPENING THE SOFTWARE MEDIA PACKAGE. BY OPENING THE SOFTWARE
MEDIA PACKAGE, YOU AGREE TO THE TERMS OF THIS AGREEMENT. IF YOU
DO NOT AGREE TO ALL OF THE TERMS OF THE AGREEMENT, DO NOT
INSTALL, COPY OR OTHERWISE USE THE JAVA(TM) 2 PLATFORM, ENTER-
PRISE EDITION 1.4 SDK ("SOFTWARE"). IF YOU ARE ACCESSING THE SOFT-
WARE ELECTRONICALLY, INDICATE YOUR NON-ACCEPTANCE OF THE
AGREEMENT BY SELECTING THE "REJECT" BUTTON OR OTHERWISE PRO-
VIDING THE NEGATIVE RESPONSE REQUESTED. YOUR INSTALLATION,
COPYING OR USE OF THE SOFTWARE INDICATES THAT YOU AGREE TO BE
BOUND BY ALL THE TERMS OF THE AGREEMENT. If you are accepting the Agree-
ment on behalf of a corporation, partnership or other legal entity, the use of the terms
"you" and "your" in the Agreement will refer to such entity and the entity accepting the
Agreement represents and warrants to Sun that it has sufficient permissions, capacity, con-
sents and authority to enter into the Agreement. Sun Microsystems, Inc. Binary Code
License Agreement ("BCL") THE TERMS OF THIS AGREEMENT AND ANY PRO-
VIDED SUPPLEMENTAL LICENSE TERMS ARE COLLECTIVELY TERMED THE
"AGREEMENT".

1. LICENSE TO USE. Sun grants you a non-exclusive and non-transferable license for the
internal use only of the accompanying software and documentation and any error correc-
tions provided by Sun (collectively "Software"), by the number of users and the class of
computer hardware for which the corresponding fee has been paid.

2. RESTRICTIONS. Software is confidential and copyrighted. Title to Software and all
associated intellectual property rights is retained by Sun and/or its licensors. Except as
specifically authorized in any Supplemental License Terms, you may not make copies of
Software, other than a single copy of Software for archival purposes. Unless enforcement
is prohibited by applicable law, you may not modify, decompile, or reverse engineer Software. Licensee acknowledges that Licensed Software is not designed or intended for use
in the design, construction, operation or maintenance of any nuclear facility. Sun Microsystems, Inc. disclaims any express or implied warranty of fitness for such uses. No right,
title or interest in or to any trademark, service mark, logo or trade name of Sun or its licensors is granted under this Agreement.

3. LIMITED WARRANTY. Sun warrants to you that for a period of ninety (90) days from
the date of purchase, as evidenced by a copy of the receipt, the media on which Software
is furnished (if any) will be free of defects in materials and workmanship under normal
use. Except for the foregoing, Software is provided "AS IS". Your exclusive remedy and
Sun's entire liability under this limited warranty will be at Sun's option to replace Software
media or refund the fee paid for Software.

4. DISCLAIMER OF WARRANTY. UNLESS SPECIFIED IN THIS AGREEMENT, ALL EXPRESS OR IMPLIED CONDITIONS, REPRESENTATIONS AND WARRANTIES, INCLUDING ANY IMPLIED WARRANTY OF MERCHANTABILITY, FITNESS FOR A PARTICULAR PURPOSE OR NON-INFRINGEMENT ARE DISCLAIMED, EXCEPT TO THE EXTENT THAT THESE DISCLAIMERS ARE HELD TO BE LEGALLY INVALID.

5. LIMITATION OF LIABILITY. TO THE EXTENT NOT PROHIBITED BY LAW, IN NO EVENT WILL SUN OR ITS LICENSORS BE LIABLE FOR ANY LOST REVENUE, PROFIT OR DATA, OR FOR SPECIAL, INDIRECT, CONSEQUENTIAL, INCIDEN-TAL OR PUNITIVE DAMAGES, HOWEVER CAUSED REGARDLESS OF THE THEORY OF LIABILITY, ARISING OUT OF OR RELATED TO THE USE OF OR INABILITY TO USE SOFTWARE, EVEN IF SUN HAS BEEN ADVISED OF THE POSSIBILITY OF SUCH DAMAGES. In no event will Sun's liability to you, whether in contract, tort (including negligence), or otherwise, exceed the amount paid by you for Software under this Agreement. The foregoing limitations will apply even if the above stated warranty fails of its essential purpose.

6. Termination. This Agreement is effective until terminated. You may terminate this Agreement at any time by destroying all copies of Software. This Agreement will termi-nate immediately without notice from Sun if you fail to comply with any provision of this Agreement. Upon Termination, you must destroy all copies of Software.

7. Export Regulations. All Software and technical data delivered under this Agreement are subject to US export control laws and may be subject to export or import regulations in other countries. You agree to comply strictly with all such laws and regulations and acknowledge that you have the responsibility to obtain such licenses to export, re-export, or import as may be required after delivery to you.

8. U.S. Government Restricted Rights. If Software is being acquired by or on behalf of the U.S. Government or by a U.S. Government prime contractor or subcontractor (at any tier), then the Government's rights in Software and accompanying documentation will be only as set forth in this Agreement; this is in accordance with 48 CFR 227.7201 through 227.7202-4 (for Department of Defense (DOD) acquisitions) and with 48 CFR 2.101 and 12.212 (for non-DOD acquisitions).

9. Governing Law. Any action related to this Agreement will be governed by California law and controlling U.S. federal law. No choice of law rules of any jurisdiction will apply.

10. Severability. If any provision of this Agreement is held to be unenforceable, this Agreement will remain in effect with the provision omitted, unless omission would frus-trate the intent of the parties, in which case this Agreement will immediately terminate.

11. Integration. This Agreement is the entire agreement between you and Sun relating to its subject matter. It supersedes all prior or contemporaneous oral or written communica-tions, proposals, representations and warranties and prevails over any conflicting or addi-tional terms of any quote, order, acknowledgment, or other communication between the parties relating to its subject matter during the term of this Agreement. No modification of

this Agreement will be binding, unless in writing and signed by an authorized representative of each party. For inquiries please contact: Sun Microsystems, Inc., 4150 Network Circle, Santa Clara, California 95054

Supplemental Terms for Java 2 Platform, Enterprise Edition 1.4 SDK

These terms and conditions for Java 2 Platform, Enterprise Edition 1.4 SDK supplement the terms of the Binary Code License Agreement ("BCL"). Capitalized terms not defined herein shall have the meanings ascribed to them in the BCL. These terms shall supersede any inconsistent or conflicting terms in the BCL.

1.License Grant

A. Internal Use and Development License. Subject to the terms and conditions of this Agreement and your complete acceptance of this Agreement, Sun grants to you a non-exclusive, non-transferable, royalty-free and limited license to:

(i) internally reproduce and use the binary form of Software; and

(ii) host Software for third parties, provided that you: (a) only permit access to Software subject to an agreement that protects Sun's interests consistent with the terms contained in this Agreement; and (b) agree to defend and indemnify Sun and its licensors from and against any damages, costs, liabilities, settlement amounts and /or expenses (including attorneys' fees) incurred in connection with any claim, lawsuit or action by any third party that arises or results from the hosting of Software. For the purposes of this section, internal use includes deployment of Software in a production environment.

B. Redistribution. This Agreement does not grant you the right to redistribute Software. Please refer to the following URL for information regarding the redistribution of Software if you are interested in redistribution:

http://sun.com/software/products/appsrvr/appsrvr_oem.html

2.Additional Use Conditions

A. Whenever you are explicitly permitted to copy or reproduce all or any part of Software, you shall reproduce and not efface any and all titles, trademark symbols, copyright symbols and legends, and other proprietary markings on or accompanying Software. You acknowledge and agree as between you and Sun that Sun owns the SUN, SOLARIS, JAVA, J2EE, JINI, FORTE, STAROFFICE, STARPORTAL and IPLANET- related trademarks, service marks, logos and other brand designations ("Sun Marks"), and you agree to comply with the Sun Trademark and Logo Usage Requirements currently located at http://www.sun.com/policies/trademarks. Any use you make of the Sun Marks inures to Sun's benefit.

B. Software may contain source code that is provided solely for reference purposes pursuant to the terms of this Agreement. Source code may not be redistributed unless expressly provided for in this Agreement.

C. "Bundled Software" means any and all additional software bundled with or embedded in the Software (including without limitation the Java Development Kit), if any, and delivered to you as part of the Software. You may not use any Bundled Software on a stand-alone basis or use any portion of the Bundled Software to interoperate with any program other than the Software. Except for this restriction and those found below, the use of each such bundled or embedded product shall be governed by its license agreement. If you desire to use such Sun or third party products on a stand-alone basis, you must purchase a separate license permitting such use.

D. You may copy and use the header files and class libraries ("Redistributables") solely to create and distribute programs to interface with Software APIs ("Programs") only as explicitly provided in Software documentation provided that you (i) distribute the Redistributables complete and unmodified and only bundled as part of your Programs, (ii) do not distribute additional software intended to replace any component(s) of the Redistributables, (iii) do not remove or alter any proprietary legends or notices contained in the Redistributables, (iv) only distribute the Redistributables subject to a license agreement that protects Sun's interests consistent with the terms contained in this Agreement, and (v) agree to defend and indemnify Sun and its licensors from and against any damages, costs, liabilities, settlement amounts and/or expenses (including attorneys' fees) incurred in connection with any claim, lawsuit or action by any third party that arises or results from the use or distribution of any and all Redistributables and/or Programs.

E. You may not modify the Java Platform Interface ("JPI" identified as classes contained within the "java" Package or subpackages of the "java" package), by creating additional classes within the JPI or otherwise causing the addition to or modification of the classes in the JPI. In the event that you create an additional class and associated API(s) which (i) extends the functionality of the Java platform, and (ii) is exposed to third party software developers for the purpose of developing additional software which invokes such additional API, you must promptly publish broadly an accurate specification for such API for free use by all developers. You may not create, or authorize your licensees to create additional classes, interfaces, or sub- packages that are in any way identified as "java", "javax", "sun" or similar convention as specified by Sun in any naming convention designation.

F. You shall have the sole responsibility to protect adequately and backup your data and/or equipment used in connection with the Software. You shall not claim against Sun or its licensors for lost data, re-run time, inaccurate output, work delays or lost profits resulting from your use of the Software.

G. Software contains application Testing software components ("Verifier") for your convenience. However, you may not use the Sun tagline "J2EE(TM) Verified" or similar phrase designated by Sun to indicate your application's satisfaction of the J2EE Application Verification Criteria ("verification Tagline") based on the use of Software or Verifier under this Agreement. To obtain the right to use a Verification Tagline, you must license the J2EE Application Verification Kit from Sun, pay applicable fees, and execute a separate trademark license for the Verification Tagline.

H. Refer to the appropriate version of the Java Runtime Environment binary code license (currently located at http://www.java.sun.com/j2se) for the availability of runtime code which may be distributed with your applications.

I. Termination for Infringement. Either party may terminate this Agreement immediately should any Software become, or in either party's opinion be likely to become, the subject of a claim of infringement of any intellectual property right.

J. You acknowledge that at your request or consent optional features of the Software may download, install, and execute applets, applications, software extensions, and updated versions of the Software from Sun ("Software Updates"), which may require you to accept updated terms and conditions for installation. If additional terms and conditions are not presented on installation, the Software Updates will be considered part of the Software and subject to the terms and conditions of the Agreement.

K. You acknowledge that, by your use of optional features of the Software and/or by requesting services that require use of the optional features of the Software, the Software may automatically download, install, and execute software applications from sources other than Sun ("Other Software"). Sun makes no representations of a relationship of any kind to licensors of Other Software. TO THE EXTENT NOT PROHIBITED BY LAW, IN NO EVENT WILL SUN OR ITS LICENSORS BE LIABLE FOR ANY LOST REVENUE, PROFIT OR DATA, OR FOR SPECIAL, INDIRECT, CONSEQUENTIAL, INCIDENTAL OR PUNITIVE DAMAGES, HOWEVER CAUSED REGARDLESS OF THE THEORY OF LIABILITY, ARISING OUT OF OR RELATED TO THE USE OF OR INABILITY TO USE OTHER SOFTWARE, EVEN IF SUN HAS BEEN ADVISED OF THE POSSIBILITY OF SUCH DAMAGES. Some states do not allow the exclusion of incidental or consequential damages, so some of the terms above may not be applicable to you.

L. You may not publish or provide the results of any benchmark or comparison tests run on Software to any third party without the prior written consent of Sun.

M. Additional copyright notices and license terms applicable to portions of the Software are set forth in the THIRDPARTYLICENSEREADME file. In addition to any terms and conditions of any third party opensource/freeware license identified in the THIRDPARTYLICENSEREADME file, the Disclaimer of Warranty and Limitation of Liability provisions in paragraphs 4 and 5 of the Binary Code License Agreement shall apply to all Software in this distribution.

Java[TM] 2 Platform, Enterprise Edition 1.4 Tutorial
Binary Code License Agreement
Copyright 1994-2004 Sun Microsystems, Inc.

All Rights Reserved. Redistribution and use in source and binary forms, with or without modification, are permitted provided that the following conditions are met:

Redistribution of source code must retain the above copyright notice, this list of conditions and the following disclaimer.